JEAN SIBELIUS AND HIS WORLD

JEAN SIBELIUS
AND HIS WORLD

EDITED BY
DANIEL M. GRIMLEY

PRINCETON UNIVERSITY PRESS
PRINCETON AND OXFORD

Published by Princeton University Press, 41 William Street,
Princeton, New Jersey 08540
In the United Kingdom: Princeton University Press,
6 Oxford Street, Woodstock, Oxfordshire OX20 1TW
press.princeton.edu

For permissions information, see page xiii

Library of Congress Control Number: 2011926904

ISBN: 978-0-691-15280-6 (cloth)
ISBN: 978-0-691-15281-3 (paperback)

British Library Cataloging-in-Publication Data is available

This publication has been produced by the Bard College Publications Office:
Ginger Shore, Director
Anita van de Ven, Cover design
Natalie Kelly, Design
Text edited by Paul De Angelis and Erin Clermont
Music typeset by Don Giller

This publication has been underwritten in part by grants from
Furthermore: a program of the J. M. Kaplan Fund and
Helen and Roger Alcaly.

Printed on acid-free paper. ∞

Printed in the United States of America

1 3 5 7 9 10 8 6 4 2

Contents

Acknowledgments and Permissions

My first thanks are due to Leon Botstein, not only for his outstanding contribution to the current volume, but also for his leadership of the Bard Music Festival and for his creative vision, which continues to inspire audiences and scholars alike. I am indebted to the other contributors in this book, including the translators, for their stimulating engagement with Sibelius's life and work, and for responding to my editorial demands with unfailing patience, insight, and good humor. A very special debt of thanks is owed to Irene Zedlacher, Christopher H. Gibbs, and Paul De Angelis, who have held this project together throughout and who offered life support at critical moments of editorial crisis. It has been a privilege to work with the team assembled by the Bard Publications Office: copy editor Erin Clermont, Natalie Kelly, Ginger Shore, and Don Giller and Jack Parton, who offered expert assistance with the music examples. Any remaining errors or oversights are entirely my responsibility.

The Sibelius scholarly community is a remarkably supportive and generous one, and I am especially grateful to the following for their help and advice at various stages of the project: Glenda Dawn Goss, Gitta Henning, Tomi Mäkelä, and Timo Virtanen. I would also like to express thanks to the staff of the National Archives of Finland and the National Library of Finland (formerly Helsinki University Library), for their assistance with source materials and other related research questions; to the Central Art Archives at the Finnish National Gallery, Helsinki, for the images of paintings by Eero Järnefelt, Axel Gallen-Kallela, and Ilya Repin reproduced in Philip Ross Bullock's essay; to Lilo Skaarup at the Royal Theatre Archive in Copenhagen and Karsten Bundgaard, and Thomas Trane Petersen at the Danish Royal Library for the Kai Nielsen images reproduced in my own essay on the *Tempest* music; and to the Sibelius family for their gracious permission to print the previously unpublished material in my essay.

For most of the illustrations reproduced in Sarah Menin's essay I wish to acknowledge: the National Board of Antiquities, Finland, for the two photographs of the Paris Pavilion; the Museum of Finnish Architecture, Helsinki, for the interior view of the Viipuri Library; and the Alvar Aalto Museum, Jyväskylä, Finland, for the Aalto sketch of the New York World's Fair Finnish Pavilion.

For many of the photographs reproduced in Leon Botstein's essay I wish to acknowledge: photographer Anton Brandl and the Richard Strauss Institute, Garmisch, Germany, for the interior view of Strauss's villa; the Museum of Finnish Architecture, Helsinki, for the two photographs of the staircase in the Pohjola Insurance Company Building, the Saarinen design for the 1908 Parliament House competition, and Saarinen's 1921 rendering of Kalevala House; and S. C. Johnson Company, for the photograph of Johnson Wax Headquarters.

—Daniel M. Grimley

The following parties have also graciously granted permission to reprint or reproduce the following copyrighted material:

For permission to republish the musical examples from Symphony no. 1 (Example 1 on p. 26), Symphony no. 4 (Example 1 on p. 101), *Luonnotor* (Example 4 on p. 110), *Tapiola* (Examples 5 through 8 on pp. 115–18): © by Breitkopf & Härtel, Wiesbaden.

For permission to republish the musical examples from Symphony no. 3 (Example 1 on p. 62 and Examples 2a and 2b on pp. 63 and 64): © 1907 by Robert Lienau Musikverlag; and *Voces intimae* (Example 2b on p. 64 and Examples 2 and 3 on pp. 105–6): © 1909 by Robert Lienau Musikverlag. Frankfurt am Main (Germany). Reprinted by permission.

For permission to reproduce the facsimiles of sketches for *Cassazione* by Jean Sibelius (Figures 3a, 3b, and 3c on pp. 165–67): © 1994 Fazer Music, Helsinki. © Fennica Gehrman Oy, Helsinki. Published by permission.

For permission to republish four musical examples from Sibelius's *Tempest* music (Example 1 on pp. 200–207, Example 2 on p. 210, Example 3 on p. 213, and Example 4 on p. 217): © 1927 Edition Wilhelm Hansen AS, Copenhagen; and to publish the musical example from Symphony no. 7 (Example 1 on p. 249): © 1924 Edition Wilhelm Hansen AS, Copenhagen. International copyright secured. All rights reserved. Used by persmission.

For permission to reproduce these photographs—Figure 4 on p. 242 (interior of the Finnish Pavilion at the New York World's Fair 1939 in Queens, NY, designed by Alvar Aalto) and Figure 10 on p. 294 (traffic entrance to the Marin County Civic Center Administration Building, San Rafael, California, 1963): © Ezra Stoller/Esto.

For permission to reproduce the photograph, Figure 4 on p. 284, main entrance to Helsinki Railway Station, 1939: © Bettman/Corbis. For permission to reproduce the photograph, Figure 7 on p. 288, ceiling of the concert hall in Kleinhans Music Hall, Buffalo, New York: © Enid Bloch.

For permission to reproduce the photograph, Figure 8 on p. 292, ceiling detail in Unity Temple, Oak Park, Illinois: © Neil Levine.

For permission to publish the translation of the Erik Kruskopf–Simon Parmet exchange on pp. 341–53: Erik Kruskopf & *Hufvudstadsbladet* in Helsinki.

For permission to publish the translations of Theodor W. Adorno's "Gloss" and "Footnote" about Sibelius, found on pp. 333–37: © Suhrkamp Verlag, Frankfurt am Main, Germany.

For permission to reproduce the photograph, Figure 1 on p. 340, the Sibelius Monument by Eila Hiltunen: © Photographer Allan Baxter/ Getty Images.

Sibelius, Finland, and the Idea of Landscape

The music of Jean Sibelius seems richly evocative of a particular sense of time and place. Recently re-released footage of the composer directed by pioneering Finnish documentary filmmakers Heikki Aho and Björn Soldan offers a series of iconic images of the composer.[1] Spliced together from two independent reels of film, recorded in 1927 and 1945 at the composer's villa, Ainola, the visual images are accompanied by stirring performances of carefully chosen extracts from Sibelius's oeuvre—opening, of course, with the closing measures of *Finlandia*, conducted by Sibelius's son-in-law, Jussi Jalas. After the brief title sequence, Sibelius appears at the piano, characteristically with a large cigar, and then at his desk, annotating a score with an unsteady hand. He is then seen in evening conversation with his wife, Aino, after which the film shifts to Sibelius's daily constitutional walk through the villa's grounds, and to footage of Aino and their daughter, Margareta, in the orchard at Ainola. A more extended sequence, accompanied by the final pages of the Third Symphony, juxtaposes further footage of the composer at the piano with images of the Finnish landscape, redolent of the work of Sibelius's friend and contemporary, the photographer I. K. Inha—a surging river cascading over rapids, mist clearing from distant hills, and the pristine waters of a lake—underpinned by the Finnish/Swedish subtitle 'Sävelten maailmassa/I tonernas värld' (In the world of music).[2] The poignant final sequence returns to a profile shot of Sibelius's daughter, Margareta, playing the violin, with the nostalgic closing pages of the Romance in F, op. 78/2: music, nature, and the domestic family home all seem organically intertwined.

Such images of Sibelius as the symbolic father and progenitor of Finnish music maintain a strong hold in the popular imagination. In 1945, at the end of Finland's ordeal during the Second World War, they must have carried a particularly urgent significance.[3] For many listeners, Sibelius's Finland is still associated with a particular idea of northernness: an exotic realm of icy wastes, somnolent lakes, endless spruce forests, and untouched wilderness. This problematic vision of an idealized Nordic landscape has exerted a powerful influence on Sibelius reception, pointing toward what Peter Davidson (alluding to Glenn Gould, an enthusiastic fan of Sibelius's music) has called our "idea of north": the land beyond the northern horizon that is "always out of reach, receding towards the polar night, which is equally the midnight dawn in the summer sky."[4] Yet this is only a very partial representation of Finland

and the north itself, a poor reflection of the actual cultural contexts in which Sibelius's work was created and first heard.

A similarly reductive tendency can often be identified in biographical accounts of his music: Sibelius's creative career has frequently been read as a single narrative curve, the young late Romantic firebrand emerging from his modest lower-bourgeois upbringing in provincial Hämeenlinna 60 miles north of the capital, to lead his nation's cultural (and eventually political) emancipation, then swiftly turning aside from the vanguard of this dynamic folk nationalism toward an austere, linear classicism more appropriate for the modern age. It is a trajectory that apparently leads inexorably to the obsessive motivic unity of his final large-scale work, the tone poem *Tapiola*, and the thirty-year silence that followed until his death at the venerable age of 91 in 1957.

As the essays in this volume reveal, however, the true picture is more complex: Sibelius's world properly emerges as a richly diverse cultural community, a mini-continent of nations and musical traditions, of aesthetic ideas and vital artistic impulses. In Philip Ross Bullock's panoramic opening survey, Finland's Russian heritage is understood as a crucial but hitherto neglected part of Sibelius's creative constitution, both through the Tolstoy-inspired circle of his brothers-in-law, and in his own debt to Russian musical models. Timo Virtanen's essay similarly asks us to redirect our attention away from a view of Sibelius's music as obsessively goal-directed or crystalline, toward an improvisatory mode of musical composition in which themes and ideas can freely migrate from one musical context to another. Sibelius's debt to European symbolism is made vividly apparent in Jeffrey Kallberg's discussion of his music for Michael Lybeck's play *Ödlan* (The lizard): long upheld as a symphonist, Sibelius maintained an equally intensive interest in writing for the stage.

Sibelius's studies in Berlin and Vienna in the early 1890s had a formative influence on his musical development, and first brought him into direct contact with the Strindberg circle that scandalized the European literary scene. Sibelius's appearance at the Paris World Fair in 1900 established him as one of the leading composers of his generation, and seemingly defined the sound of Finland. Later it was the landscape of classical Italy that could capture his imagination—parts of the tone poem *Tapiola*, a musical representation of the Finnish forest world from the *Kalevala*, as Tomi Mäkelä observes in his account of Sibelius's ambivalent and poised attitude to modernism, were actually written on the island of Capri, in the distant Mediterranean. For Glenda Dawn Goss, the genuine high point of Sibelius's professional career was his visit to the 1914 Festival in Norfolk, Connecticut, where his idyllic-pastoral tone poem *The Oceanides* received its world premiere. During the 1920s and '30s

Sibelius was frequently lauded, both in the United States and Great Britain, as the true inheritor of the Beethovenian symphonic tradition, a role, as Byron Adams demonstrates, that rested upon deeply problematic assumptions regarding race and national character. Sibelius was used as a stick with which to beat the more overtly progressive modernism of a younger generation of continental European composers. Attempts to appropriate Sibelius's work by certain elements of the Third Reich in the late 1930s and early '40s were attacked by writers such as Theodor Wiesengrund Adorno, whose trenchant critique is the subject of Max Paddison's penetrating analysis. Such images of nature and landscape, promulgated so widely in Sibelius reception, remained problematic for a whole generation of modernists.

Understood in its own immediate cultural contexts, however, landscape can assume a different, if no less weighty significance in discussion of Sibelius's work. In the haunting incidental music for Shakespeare's final play *The Tempest*, as I point out in my own essay, Sibelius's creative attention is primarily occupied with the physical experience of being in the landscape, beaten and buffeted by the storm. Far removed from simplistic notions of organicism or purity, Sibelius's music, I argue, prompts a more critical and reflective sense of our relationship with the natural world, one that might be perceived as a nascent form of acoustic ecology.

This richer, more complex dialogue with natural forms and structures underpins Sibelius's shared concern with architectural notions of light and space, the subject of the two complementary final essays, by Sarah Menin and Leon Botstein. Through the contrasting work of Alvar Aalto, Eliel Saarinen, and the great American architect Frank Lloyd Wright, the natural world emerges as a source of inspiration for a group of creative artists grappling with common problems of community, environment, and individual subjectivity in the turbulent early years of the twentieth century.

Sibelius and His World concludes with a series of primary documents. The earliest source translated here is an extract from Adolf Paul's 1891 novella *Bok om en Människa* (A book about a human being), a lightly fictionalized account of Sibelius's student years in Berlin that shocked contemporary Finnish readers. Sibelius's own thoughts on the impact of folk music upon his work are expressed in characteristically elliptical fashion in a lecture that he read at Helsinki University in 1896. Never comfortable in formal academic surroundings, Sibelius's lecture is partly a schematic (and highly relativist) account of the origins of European folk music, and partly an aesthetic manifesto.

Landscape and nature are invoked as prominent metaphors in one of the earliest critical accounts of Sibelius's work, Erik Furuhjelm's 1917 biography, a short excerpt from which is presented here. For Furuhjelm,

Sibelius becomes "the sublimely realistic portrayer of nature." Yet it is the problematic nature of such claims that becomes the foundation for Adorno's landmark 1938 critique, the "Glosse über Sibelius." Discussions of nature and environment return a final time in the controversy outlined in an exchange of newspaper essays about the plans for a monument to memorialize the composer in Helsinki after his death. Inspired by the sights and sounds of the Finnish landscape, Eila Hiltunen's strikingly abstract design inspired considerable local opposition at the time of its unveiling in the late 1960s, yet it has now become one of the city's best-loved landmarks.

Sibelius's music thus serves as a threshold, rather than an endpoint: it can be understood as a window not purely on a particular vision of Finnishness, although such associations with his home country remain telling and evocative, but also as a portal to a much wider worldview, the intricately complex landscape of early twentieth-century musical politics. Listening to his works critically, almost a century later, we are perhaps better placed to gain a fuller sense of Sibelius's significance as one of the most powerful and persuasive voices in the repertoire, and a deeper understanding and appreciation of the "idea of north" that remained his continual inspiration and creative guide.

—Daniel M. Grimley

NOTES

1. The film is currently available at the Finnish Broadcasting Corporation's website (http://www.yle.fi/elavaarkisto/?s=s&g=8&ag=47&t=117&a=8909), and is discussed in *Jean Sibelius Kodissaan—i sitt hem—at Home*, edited by Jussi Brofeldt (Helsinki: Teos, 2010). I am grateful to Jussi Brofeldt for his assistance in accessing this footage.

2. Into Konrad Inha was part of Sibelius's circle of friends in the 1890s, and a keen member of the so-called Karelianists, who sought to recover evidence of Finnish folk traditions in the far east of the country. For a representative sample and discussion of Inha's work, see *I. K. Inha: Unelma maisemasta*, ed. Taneli Eskola (Helsinki: Musta Taide, 2006).

3. Accounts of the funeral ceremonies held following Sibelius's death suggest that he still held this privileged symbolic place in Finnish public life, even in 1957. For a brief description, see Erik Tawaststjerna, *Sibelius*, vol. 3, *1914–1957*, trans. Robert Layton (London: Faber and Faber, 1997), 331. Subsequent references to Tawaststjerna's biography in this volume refer either to Robert Layton's elegant but abridged English translation, or to Tawaststjerna's Swedish/Finnish original, as indicated in the appropriate citation.

4. Peter Davidson, *The Idea of North* (London: Reaktion Press, 2005), 8.

PART I
ESSAYS

Sibelius and the Russian Traditions

PHILIP ROSS BULLOCK

To discuss the music of Jean Sibelius in the context of Russian culture and history is to broach complex questions of national identity and musical influence. Although Finland's status between 1809 and 1917 as a Grand Duchy within the Russian Empire has been the subject of considerable recent work by revisionist historians, the policies of extreme Russification that were in place between 1899 and Finland's eventual independence eighteen years later have tended to cast the debate in terms of how a small nation bravely won self-determination despite the predations of a vast and arrogant imperial power.[1] This historiographical discourse has implications for our understanding of Sibelius's music and personality too, since, as Glenda Dawn Goss suggests, the composer has long served as an icon of Finnish national consciousness: "The real Sibelius has been obscured . . . by the tendency to see him solely through a nationalistic lens. This view received powerful impetus in connection with Finland's valiant and prolonged resistance to Russian domination, a resistance that Sibelius's music came to symbolize in the world."[2] The consequences of this tendency can be seen in a Finnish review of one of the major Soviet-era publications on Sibelius. Although little about the 1963 biography by Alexander Stupel seems immoderate or controversial today,[3] and indeed, many of its suggestions about Sibelius's connections to Russian music have since been independently corroborated and further developed, Dmitry Hintze's negative assessment of Sibelius's influence on Russian composers from Rimsky-Korsakov to Rachmaninoff is symptomatic of an era when political factors affected attitudes in the writing of national history.[4]

Notwithstanding such political considerations, many of the clichés that have come to be associated with Russian music as Europe's perpetual "Other"—Oriental exoticism, emotional intensity, technical insufficiency, even, as in the case of the reputation of Pyotr Tchaikovsky, sexual deviance and effeminacy[5]—have meant that commentators have tended to downplay comparisons between Sibelius and Russian composers, preferring instead to incorporate Sibelius into the European mainstream. The posture adopted in Walter Niemann's early writings—interpreted by James Hepokoski as "a priestlike gesture within the cultic institution intended to keep pure the sacred space of Germanic symphonism"—is a case in point.[6] Although dismissive of Sibelius's handling of the symphony, which he saw as nothing more than "an imitation of Tchaikovsky's *Pathétique* in a Finnish dialect,"[7] Niemann was nonetheless keen to emphasize Sibelius's status as a composer with organic, Western-oriented links to Scandinavia rather than Finland's occupying neighbor to the east. Crucially, for Niemann, Sibelius's works were free from the emotional and structural shortcomings that were supposedly so characteristic of Tchaikovsky:

> Sibelius's broad and expressive approach to melody frequently has an unmistakable affinity with that of Tchaikovsky, and as a symphonist, Sibelius has without question borrowed many ideas from the symphonies of the Russian master, above all the E-minor symphony and the *Pathétique*. Except that Sibelius is more reserved in his expression, less decorative, less contrived and sentimental, less differentiated than the Russian master, despite all of his striking intensity of emotion and Slavic fatalism. Against our will and as if hypnotized, we are at the mercy of the weak and sensual Russian. The stern and steely Finn appeals to heart and mind. You will search in vain in Sibelius for movements such as the half-barbarian finales of Tchaikovsky's symphonies.[8]

More unequivocal admirers of Sibelius's music continued this trend by pointing out how his symphonies departed from Russian models on both temperamental and structural grounds. Cecil Grey's argument that "the symphonies of Sibelius represent the highest point attained in this form since the death of Beethoven" rests on a concomitant dismissal of Russian music as "eastern rather than northern in geographical character and atmosphere."[9] Bengt de Törne, similarly keen to emphasize Sibelius's Teutonic credentials, ultimately dismissed the importance of Tchaikovsky's influence, seeing Sibelius as altogether more epic, virile, and self-possessed, and thus correspondingly free from the existential traits of the Russian soul: "Russian music is famous for its gloomy tints. Yet these magnificent sombre colours are essentially different from those of the North, being conditioned by the Slav atmosphere of submission, despair and death."[10] Any arguments in favor of Sibelius's exclusively and essentially Nordic identity are, whether consciously or not, indebted to a whole set of stereotypes about the national and emotional character of Russian music.

The situation has changed, of course, not least as a result of the publication of Erik Tawaststjerna's critical biography.[11] Not only did it paint a far more detailed picture of Sibelius's life than had previously been available, it also began to overturn widespread assumptions about his musical origins. As Tim Howell writes:

> Erik Tawaststjerna has revealed that far from being a nationalist figure separated from mainstream European developments by living in his native Finland, Sibelius travelled extensively, was fully aware of current trends in music, thought, discussed and came to terms with the complex nature of twentieth-century composition and from various stylistic influences gradually formed a personal and highly original style.[12]

Within this welcome development in Sibelius criticism, however, the influence of Russian music has been the subject of comparatively little detailed analysis, and figures such as Sibelius's Russian violin teacher, Mitrofan Wasilieff, have only recently been restored to the historical record. As Goss argues: "The idea of a *Russian's* helping to shape the national icon was more than most Finns could stand in the aftermath of the horrible events of the first half of the twentieth century."[13]

Thus the purpose of this essay is first to set out the broad political and historical context that shaped Russo-Finnish relations between 1809 and 1917, and second to consider the close personal, intellectual, and artistic ties that bound together cultural figures on both sides of the border, before then turning to an examination of the various ways in which Russian music played a profound role in Sibelius's evolution as a Finnish and European composer.

The Russian Empire and the Grand Duchy of Finland

In trying to disentangle some of the myths surrounding Sibelius's role in the development of Finnish national consciousness and the move to political self-determination, the best place to start is, ironically enough, one of his most obviously patriotic and overtly political works: *Finlandia*. Traditionally read as a protest against Russian domination, the work was subject to a highly politicized interpretation in which Sibelius himself was complicit:

> It was actually rather late that *Finlandia* was performed under its final title. At the farewell concert of the Philharmonic Orchestra before leaving for Paris, when the tone-poem was played for the first time in its revised form, it was called "Suomi." It was introduced by the same name in Scandinavia; in German towns it was called "Vaterland," and in Paris "La Patrie." In Finland its performance was forbidden during the years of unrest, and in other parts of the Empire it was not allowed

to be played under any name that in any way indicated its patriotic character. When I conducted in Reval and Riga by invitation in the summer of 1904, I had to call it "Impromptu."[14]

However, as Harold Johnson argues, this was a rather dramatic and even questionable interpretation of the situation, and one, moreover, that was written several decades after the events described:

> It is true that at the concert to which the composer alluded the tone poem was officially listed on the programme as *Suomi*, a title that had no meaning for the Russians. But in all the newspapers it was listed as *Finlandia*. Just how late is "rather late" we cannot say. It is a matter of record, however, that *Finlandia* was performed under that title in Helsinki during November 1901 and through the remaining years when Finland was still a part of the Russian Empire. Had Governor General Bobrikov been interested, he could have purchased a copy of *Finlandia* from a local music store.[15]

An investigation into the origins of *Finlandia* reveals a still more complicated story. The music that was to become *Finlandia* derives from the six *Tableaux from Ancient History* that were staged in Helsinki in November 1899. Ostensibly designed to raise money for the pensions of journalists, the tableaux offered, in Tawaststjerna's words, "both moral and material support to a free press that was battling to maintain its independence in the face of Czarist pressure."[16] In them were depicted significant stages of Finland's history, from the origins of the *Kalevala* and the baptism of the Finnish people by Bishop Henrik of Uppsala, to the sixteenth-century court of Duke John at Turku, and the events of the Thirty Years' War and the Great Northern War (during which Finland was ravaged by Russian forces between 1714 and 1721, a period referred to as "The Greater Wrath"). As Derek Fewster suggests, this particular historical scene may have been interpreted as an instance of anti-Russian sentiment around the turn of the century:

> The fifth tableau was intended as a striking allegory to modern Finland: Mother Finland with her children, sitting in the snow and surrounded by the genies of Death, Frost, Hunger and War, during the Great Northern War. Performing such an offensive tableau— intended as a "memory" of what Russia was all about—was a striking choice and a fascinating example of how the previously complaisant and loyal Finns now could be served anti-Russian sentiments without half the public leaving the theatre in outrage.[17]

In the sixth tableau, however, the depiction of Russia's involvement was subtly yet significantly transformed. Titled "Suomi Herää!" (Finland, awake!) it evoked the nineteenth century through a series of historical figures who had contributed to Finland's discovery of its own identity as a nation: "These included Czar Alexander II, the poet Johan Ludvig Runeberg, Johan Vilhelm Snellman inspiring his students to think of the possibility of Finnish independence, and Elias Lönnrot transcribing the runes of the epic, *Kalevala*."[18]

In order to understand the presence of such a seemingly unlikely figure as the Russian emperor Alexander II in the score that gave rise to a work as patriotic as *Finlandia*, it is necessary to look back at the circumstances of Finland's incorporation into the Russian Empire. Over the course of the eighteenth and early nineteenth centuries, Russia had been involved in a number of conflicts with Poland and Sweden centering on political and economic control over the Baltic region. With its recently founded capital, St. Petersburg, vulnerable to attack from the West, Russia sought to incorporate territory that would provide it with an adequate form of defense. To this end, Russia invaded Finland in February 1808, with Tsar Alexander I declaring his intention to annex the Finnish territories that had been part of the Swedish kingdom since the thirteenth century. By the end of the year, Finland was conquered, and in 1809 it was formally declared a Grand Duchy of the Russian Empire. Russia's imperial expansion did not, however, immediately lead to a period of Russification. Alexander was wary of Napoleon's ambitions (despite his support for Russia's attack on Sweden) and needed to guarantee Finland's loyalty in the event of any conflict with France. As Edward Thaden argues:

> Russia's position was not secure unless she could count on the cooperation of local native elites in newly annexed areas. To assure such cooperation, Russia allowed them to enjoy certain rights and privileges as long as they remained loyal to the tsar and with the implied understanding that they would maintain a well-regulated society arranged into traditional social orders.[19]

Russia itself was a multiethnic, multinational, multilinguistic empire, and its constituent elements enjoyed considerable de facto autonomy, not least because the empire's central administration was weak, and government across huge geographical distances was far from easy. It was also the case, as Janet Hartley has suggested, that "making Finland a Grand Duchy rather than directly incorporating the country into the Russian Empire would possibly also make Russia's gain more palatable to other European powers."[20] Within this context, Alexander's charter to the Finnish Diet at Porvoo (Borgå) in 1809 appeared to grant Finland considerable self-rule:

Having by the will of the Almighty entered into possession of the Grand Duchy of Finland, We have hereby seen fit once more to confirm and ratify the religion, basic laws, rights and privileges which each estate of the said Duchy in particular and all subjects therein resident, both high and low, have hitherto enjoyed according to its constitution, promising to maintain them inviolably in full force and effect.[21]

Even before convening a Diet (itself a striking gesture toward Finnish autonomy), Alexander had appeared to view Finland not just as an administrative province of Russia but as a nation in its own right. The manifesto proclaimed in June 1808 on the union of Finland with the Russian Empire contained the famous claim: "The inhabitants of conquered Finland are to be numbered from this time forth amongst the peoples under the scepter of Russia and with them shall make up the Empire."[22] Yet exactly what Alexander understood by such words as *constitution, basic laws,* and *rights* was open to considerable interpretation, as Hartley notes: "He was very careless in his use of potentially loaded words and concepts in his conversations and correspondence. . . . To some extent Alexander was simply using words and phrases which were fashionable at the time without much awareness of their potential significance."[23] Moreover, the practical implications of his words also went unelaborated: "Finland received no written constitution (nor any agreement about the form of government at all), no declaration of the rights of man, but simply a vague acknowledgment of the *status quo.*"[24]

Yet what mattered about Alexander's statements was not what particular form of constitution he had subscribed to, but the very fact that he appeared to have agreed to limit the exercise of autocracy at all. Within this semantic, legal, and institutional vacuum, Finland soon began to enjoy considerable practical autonomy, even if this remained the gift of the Russian autocrat rather than an inviolable constitutional right. Indeed, having established an autonomous administrative structure for the Grand Duchy, Alexander—perhaps unwillingly—established the conditions for its political development, both as a nation and as a state, in ways that would have been impossible under Swedish rule. Ironically, Russian autocracy may even have been advantageous to the development of Finnish autonomy, since the Governor-General—the tsar's personal representative in Finland and the only Russian official in the Grand Duchy—was the sole provincial governor not required to answer to the Governing Senate, the State Council, or the various ministries that exercised authority in Russia itself. Moreover, the constitutional position of Finland, and indeed of all the recently incorporated Baltic realms, was of direct interest to thinkers in Russia, too. Alexander had a reputation as something of a liberal reformer and, together with his adviser Mikhail Speransky, drew conclusions about the possible future of Russia from the social and political situation in the western provinces:

> Alexander . . . believed that Russia had much to learn from Finland, Poland, and the Baltic provinces. The free peasants from Finland, the emancipation of the peasants in the Duchy of Warsaw in 1807, the emancipation of the Estonian and Latvian peasants in the three Baltic provinces between 1816 and 1819, and the Polish Constitutional Charter of 1815 all seemed to offer examples that Russia herself might follow.[25]

Russian interest in Finland was not always so high-minded, however, and one of Russia's primary interests lay in isolating Finland from Swedish influence. Partly this was a question of securing Finland's loyalty, as Fewster observes: "The early Emperors were well aware of the importance of distancing the Finns from their previous Swedish identity and heritage: fostering or promoting an alternative Finnish nationalism was one way of combating possible revanchism and rebellious sentiments."[26] Respect for Finland's status may also have been a question of defending Russia's own autocratic makeup, with the Grand Duchy acting as a *cordon sanitaire* designed to protect Russia from European influence, as Michael Branch argues: "Russia isolated itself against the virus of Swedish constitutional structures and of the liberality of Swedish society by making Finland in 1809 virtually a self-governing country."[27]

Russian involvement in Finland was not simply based on benign absence or strategic self-interest. In a number of distinct ways, Russia actively supported the development of Finnish national consciousness and tolerated a degree of administrative autonomy. Many of the archetypal symbols of Finnish national consciousness were in fact dependent on Russian patronage and, at this early stage at least, were not indicative of any resistance or rebellion within the Grand Duchy itself. The establishment of institutions such as the University of Helsinki (moved to the capital after a fire at the Åbo/Turku Academy in 1827) and the Finnish Literature Society (Suomalaisen Kirjallisuuden Seura, founded 1831) was sponsored by the Russian authorities as a way of promoting a form of Finnish nationalism that would be both loyal and grateful to imperial rule.[28] The publication of Lönnrot's edition of the *Kalevala* by the Finnish Literature Society in 1835 was emblematic not just of the development of Finnish nationalism but, rather more subtly, of the shared intellectual interests of many Russian and Finnish scholars at the time. Branch points to the fact that "for much of the eighteenth and nineteenth centuries the largest and probably the most outstanding centre for academic research and learning in the North-East Baltic region was the Academy of Sciences in St. Petersburg."[29] In particular, the study of Finno-Ugric philology was a field that enjoyed considerable practical support in Russia:[30] "For almost 150 years, the Academy of Sciences together with bodies working under its aegis, provided a scientific apparatus for the planning and execution of fieldwork. Over the same period, the Academy assembled a library and an archive of Finno-Ugrian materials that was unsurpassed in Europe."[31] Typical of this project was the work of figures such as Matthias Castrén and Anders Johan Sjögren. Before becoming the first professor of Finnish language and literature at the University of Helsinki in 1850, Castrén, supported by the Academy of Sciences in St. Petersburg, carried out extensive ethnographic and philological fieldwork in northern Russia and Siberia. Likewise, the work of the linguist Sjögren, who traveled through Russia between the 1820s and the 1850s and did much to make St. Petersburg the leading center of Finno-Ugric studies, suggests that in the early phase of Finland's incorporation into the empire, Russo-Finnish relations were characterized by a degree of mutual interest.

The reign of Nicholas I from 1825 to 1855 continued the course set by Alexander I, and the Finns demonstrated little of the independent spirit of Congress Poland that led to the uprising of 1830–31; indeed, the Finnish Guard actively participated in the Russian suppression of the Polish uprising, and as Jussi Jalonen suggests, Finnish autonomy was, at least in part, a reward for its early loyalty to its new ruler.[32] Tuomo Polvinen argues that of all Russian provinces, Finland was the one that caused St. Petersburg the least anxiety:

> Through the bestowal and preservation of autonomy the regime successful secured the loyalty of the Finns. It was not in vain that Nicholas I had earlier advised: "Leave the Finns in peace. Theirs is the only province in my great realm which during my whole reign has not caused me even a minute of concern or dissatisfaction." As Osmo Jussila aptly points out, the Finns had acquired a "good conservative reputation" at the Imperial court in St. Petersburg; for a long time it was not considered necessary to question Finnish trustworthiness. On the contrary, during the reform era of the 1860s and 1870s the autonomous administration of the dependable Grand Duchy was decisively strengthened.[33]

If Nicholas I pursued Alexander's policy of benign coexistence, then the accession of Alexander II inaugurated a period of more explicit support for

Finnish autonomous administration and offered what David Kirby has called "an end to the period of 'frozen constitutionalism.'"[34] In part, Alexander II's approach to Finland was characteristic of the liberal tenor of the start of his reign, which saw a number of major reforms in Russia itself, including the abolition of serfdom in 1861. In 1863, he convened the Finnish Diet for the first time since 1809, and it was to meet regularly thereafter. His speech to the Diet struck what had become the traditional balance between respect for Finnish constitutionalism and Russian autocracy:

> Many of the provisions of the fundamental laws of the Grand Duchy are no longer applicable to the state of affairs existing since its union with the Empire; others lack clarity and precision. Desirous of remedying these imperfections it is My intension to have a draft law carefully prepared which will contain explanations and supplements to these provisions, and which will be submitted to the scrutiny of the Estates at the next Diet, which I contemplate convening in three years' time. Whilst maintaining the principle of constitutional monarchy inherent to the customs of the Finnish people, and of which principle all their laws and institutions bear the impress, I wish to include in this projected measure a more extended right than that which the Estates now possess in regard to the regulation of taxation and the right of initiating motions, which they formerly possessed; reserving for Myself however the initiative in all matters concerning the alterations of the fundamental laws.[35]

The tension here would play a major part in the conflicts that erupted around the turn of the century. On the one hand, Finns seized on Alexander's reference to the distinctly unautocratic "principle of constitutional monarchy inherent to the customs of the Finnish people," as well as on his intimation that any changes to Finnish legality would be subject to scrutiny by the Diet. On the other, the emperor arrogated to himself the explicitly autocratic right to alter the country's fundamental laws. For the time being, however, Russian interference was minimal, not least because after its defeat in the Crimean War Russia had little energy or authority to squander on the fruitless subjugation of an otherwise loyal province.

Finland in fact thrived as a nation within the Russian Empire far more than it would have done as a provincial backwater of Sweden, developing many of the symbols and institutions associated with nationhood that it had lacked under Swedish rule. A national bank had been established as early as 1812, and a separate currency—the mark—was issued from 1860. The language edict of August 1863 established Finnish as an equal language alongside Swedish. Not only were the Finnish people represented by a Diet and administered by a senate, but, from 1878, they were defended by an army commanded by its own officers.[36] Indeed, from the Russian point of view, there was considerable disparity between social and economic life on either side of the border. Partly this was a natural consequence of the different sizes of the two countries. Talented and ambitious Finns could readily take advantage of the career possibilities available to them through their much larger and comparatively underdeveloped neighbor, whether by serving in the Imperial army and the civil service (and not just in the State Secretariat for Finnish Affairs in St. Petersburg) or trading extensively and profitably with Russian partners. Conversely, institutional, social, and linguistic factors meant that Russians were often unable to achieve anything similar in Finland, which was governed primarily by local elites. Moreover, much of Finland's economic development was the direct result of not having to provide for many of the costs borne by the Russian Empire (Finns were not conscripted into the Russian army but could volunteer to serve). Thus when Nikolay Bobrikov arrived in Finland as Governor-General in 1898, his findings were typical of a strain in Russian nationalist thinking that was affronted by Finnish autonomy:

> He recognised that the country had achieved considerable prosperity, but claimed that it was based on the privileges so generously provided by the Russian monarchy throughout the decades. He cited above all the incomparably light share of the military burden borne by the Finns. This had freed labour for other tasks and saved funds, which were channelled, for example, into education, railways construction, and other projects. The Finnish treasury took no part at all in financing the Foreign Ministry of the Ministry for the Navy; nor did it provide a penny towards maintaining fortifications.[37]

This, then, was the context of Russo-Finnish political relations as it stood around the turn of the century. Finland's place in the loosely administered, multiethnic Russian Empire had provided the ideal conditions for its growth as a nation, and Finnish nationalists had made astute use of the opportunities available to them. Although tensions between Russia and Finland around the turn of the century ran high, it is important to recall that for a large part of the nineteenth century, the relationship had been cordial and productive.

By the 1890s, however, Russia had changed dramatically as well. Although still an empire in name, it had come to think of itself less as a diverse set of territories bound together by shared loyalty to the tsar, and more of a nation-state in the modern sense. It had begun to develop a far more efficient central administration, and formerly autonomous provinces came increasingly under the control of the government in St. Petersburg. In the case of the western borderlands, the discourse of Pan-Slavism meant that nations such as Poland or Ukraine were subject to Russification on ethnic grounds. In the Caucasus and Central Asia, Orientalist theories justified expansion because Russia saw itself as a European power bringing civilization to barbarian lands in the east. Finland, however, constituted a unique case: Russification could barely be defended on ethnic grounds, since Finland was not a Slavic nation; and its flourishing economy and progressive social makeup meant that it was not in need of Russian intervention to promote its further development and enlightenment. Yet geopolitical factors did play a significant role in shaping Russia's attitude to the Grand Duchy. Where Finland had once provided a barrier against Sweden, it had now come to resemble the weak link in Russia's defense against a newly united and increasingly confident Germany, to whom many Finns looked with considerable sympathy.

If Russian policy in Finland was in part a pragmatic response to such factors, it was also driven by ideology. By the 1890s, the tendency of many Finns to assert that their country was a constitutional monarchy in union with Russia offended Russian nationalist faith in the primacy of autocracy (not least because Finns referred to Alexander I as the instigator of their particular constitutional arrangement). Accordingly, the years referred to as the first and second periods of oppression (1899–1905 and 1908–17 respectively) can be seen, at least in part, as an attempt to resolve the ambiguities inherent in the statements made about the nature of Russian rule in Finland by Alexander I and reiterated by Alexander II. Patriotic Finnish senators argued that no changes could be made to national institutions without the express agreement of the Diet; yet the Russians preferred to treat both the Diet and the Senate as consultative bodies, whose purpose was to ratify and enact imperial legislation in what was no more than a province within the empire. Although the Finnish postal system had been placed under Russian control as early as 1890, the main attempts at curbing Finnish constitutionalism date from the period of Bobrikov's tenure as Governor-General (1898–1904). In February 1899, Nicholas II issued his so-called February Manifesto, which aimed to limit Finland's legislative power to specifically local issues, reserving imperial matters to the tsar and his government in St. Petersburg (although the nature of the difference between local and imperial issues was not clarified). In 1900, the Language Manifesto defined Russian as the official language of administration within the Grand Duchy. The Conscription Act of 1901 sought to bring military service in Finland into line with policy throughout the empire and force Finns to serve in the Russian army. Censorship was increased, and from 1903, Bobrikov was granted quasi-dictatorial powers to pursue the policies of Russification.

Russian attempts to limit Finnish constitutional freedom and stifle the expression of national consciousness were always going to provoke a sharp response on the part of Finns, whatever their political views, class background, or sense of national identity. Petitions were made directly to Nicholas II reminding him that, as tsar, he had sworn to uphold the oaths made by his predecessors. The most dramatic of these petitions was the Great Address of March 1900, containing more than half a million signatures collected without the knowledge of the Russian authorities. Nicholas's refusal to accept the delegation bearing the address only added to the impression that he had betrayed his constitutional vow. After Bobrikov's assassination by Eugen Schauman in 1904, Russification became the official policy in the Grand Duchy.[38] Yet it is important not to view Russian rule in Finland as a monolithic affair. While conservative newspapers wrote approvingly of Bobrikov's policies, politicians and members of the court expressed considerable reservations. Sergei Witte, Russian finance minister between 1892 and 1903, feared that Bobrikov's policies would provoke the resentment of otherwise loyal subjects. There was even support for Finland from within the imperial family. The widow of Alexander III, the Dowager Empress Maria Fyodorovna, wrote to her son, Nicholas II, to denounce Russian policy in Finland:

It is a perfect mystery to me how you, my dear good Nicky, whose sense of justice has always been so strong, can allow a liar like Bobrikov to lead and deceive you! . . . Everything there, where matters always ran smoothly and the people were always happy and content, is now shattered and changed and the seeds of discord and hate have been sowed—and all this in the name of so-called patriotism! What an excellent example of the meaning of that word!

Everything that has been, and is being, done in Finland is based on lies and betrayal, and is leading straight to revolution. . . .

The few Senators whom Bobrikov has allowed you to meet were his henchmen, who lied to you in saying that everything was fine and that only a small minority in Finland were protesting. Those who tell you that the crushing of that country is your history's noblest page are blackguards. Here and throughout Europe, indeed everywhere, enraged voices can be heard.

What causes me to suffer above all is that I love Finland just as I love all of Russia, and what causes me despair is that you, who are so dear to me, have been induced to do all these iniquities, which you would never have done on your own initiative.[39]

The Dowager Empress's views were certainly shaped by the fact that she was born Dagmar, Princess of Denmark, yet they are also testament to the diversity of views within elite circles in St. Petersburg. As Polvinen notes, "Bobrikov did not represent all of Russia."[40] And to see the history of Russo-Finnish affairs solely, or even predominantly, through the prism of his tenure as Governor-General is to neglect other significant aspects of the relationship between the two countries.

The complexity of Russian nationalism is mirrored as well by the intricacies of Finnish national identity around the turn of the century. Theories of nineteenth-century small-state nationalism tend to subsume Finland into a broad account of how homogenous ethnic and linguistic groups struggled to achieve self-determination within overarching multiethnic territories dominated by a particular ruling class (such as the Ottoman, Austro-Hungarian, Russian, and even British empires).[41] Yet Finland does not entirely fit this model, as Risto Alapuro argues: "It is not quite correct to picture Finland as a colonial territory on an Eastern European periphery struggling through nationalism to free itself from the dilemma of uneven development."[42] Alapuro then goes on to list the ways in which Finland constituted an exception to a widely accepted view of nationalism: Finland enjoyed its own autonomous administration within the empire; it was more economically advanced than the ruling power; and it was not governed by a foreign elite.[43] But the single factor that complicated nationalist responses to Russian rule in Finland was the complex composition of Finnish society. According to the received narrative of Finnish self-determination, a group of Finnish nationalists, freed from Swedish rule and unwilling to undergo Russification, developed a national language and culture that articulated its aspiration to statehood. Yet Finnish society in the nineteenth century was not always as homogenous or harmonious as this vision suggests. Divided into four estates (the nobility, the clergy, the burghers, and the peasants) and two major language groups (Finnish and Swedish), Finnish society was often subject to internal divisions—divisions that were further complicated by people who often had multiple allegiances to more than one social or linguistic faction. Thus, as Thaden notes, "when the long-dreaded full-scale attack of the Russifiers struck Finland the nation was in no condition to adopt a policy of united resistance. Although their dismay over the turn of the events was almost universal, the Finns' internal conflicts were so bitter that no agreement on a national policy could be achieved."[44]

Finnish responses to Russian policy in the Grand Duchy were, then, contingent on significant differences within Finnish society itself. The Finnish nationalist (or so-called Fennoman) movement was, initially at least, the greatest beneficiary of Russian rule; its cause was supported by the Russians in an attempt to weaken Swedish influence, and both politically and culturally its members were often sympathetic to Russian values, at least before the years of oppression. By contrast, members of the Swedish party (or Svecoman movement) "were on the whole more determined opponents of Russification than were Finnish speakers,"[45] and some even argued that "the 'ultra-Fennomans' were consciously or unconsciously serving the purposes of Russia."[46] Moreover, the Fennoman movement was internally divided along generational lines: "The established leaders of the Fennoman party were intellectually conservative, Lutheran-clerical, and anti-Semitic; they had little sympathy for liberal ideas."[47] Yet by 1880 or so, "some members of the party (particularly the younger ones), influenced in part by ideas from the West, considered it time to pay attention to problems of the modern world of wider relevance than Finnish-Swedish linguistic antagonism."[48] The causes that were of greatest interest to the Nuorsuomalainen Puolue (Young Finnish Party) were not those of language, culture, and nationality that had proved too divisive within Finnish society in the middle of the nineteenth century, but those of "liberalism, democracy, and constitutionalism."[49] Believing that these values were most ardently and effectively espoused by the Svecomans, the Young Finns put aside issues of language in order to defend the principles of Finland's constitutional freedoms, whereas the "Old Finns" (led by Yrjö Sakari Yrjö-Koskinen, who had Fennicized his Swedish name of Georg Zakarias Forsman) preferred a policy of compliance with what they saw as more moderate elements in the Russian administration.[50] Thus the question of whether Finland should pursue a policy of resistance to or accommodation with Russia revealed sharp fault lines within Finnish society itself.

Sibelius is often read in the context of his own age, and it is true he came to maturity as an artist at the height of Russification, becoming a symbol of Finnish resistance to imperial domination. Yet we should also look back to the earlier, more optimistic years in the Russo-Finnish relationship, years that did as much to form modern Finland as did the events of 1899 to 1917. When, during the years of oppression, Finns laid flowers at the statue of Alexander II in Helsinki's Senate Square, they were implicitly criticizing the current policies of Nicholas II by comparing him to his illustrious forebear. The monument to Alexander II depicts him surrounded by the symbols of "Law," "Light," "Labor," and "Peace," just as the nearby House of the Estates (1891) represents Alexander I confirming the basic laws of Finland at the Diet of Porvoo in 1809. And in 1900, in the wake of the February Manifesto, the Finnish pavilion at the Paris Universal Exposition included Ville Vallgren's stele for Alexander II as a positive symbol of Russia's role in Finnish history and society.[51] *Finlandia*, itself a product of the first wave of Russification, thus encapsulates a specific moment in a dynamic historical process and should be read against the evolving background of both Russian and Finnish societies. In its allusion to Alexander II as the spirit of history, *Finlandia* encodes the various competing ideas that Russia could signify to patriotic Finns in 1899, and embodies an interpretation of Finnish history in which Russia had played a constructive role quite distinct from the repressive policies of Nicholas II and his nationalist supporters.

Russian Culture and the Arts in Finland

Although some of Sibelius's works were clearly written with a patriotic intent (and perceived as such), his personality was by and large apolitical.[52] Ekman's biography quotes him as saying: "Politics have never interested me in themselves. That is to say—all empty talk of political questions, all amateurish politicising I have always hated. I have always tried to make my contribution in another way."[53] There were important personal considerations that led Sibelius to remain aloof from many of the most heated debates in Finnish society, not the least of which was his decidedly complex attitude to Finnish nationalism. Like many members of the Fennoman movement, he was a native speaker of Swedish. Despite the decisive influence of his marriage to Aino Järnefelt, a member of one of the most prominent Fennoman families, he was nonetheless capable of expressing considerable skepticism about key elements of the nationalist project. In 1910, for instance, he noted in his diary: "Looked at the *Kalevala* and it struck me—how I have grown away from this naïve poetry."[54] On the eve of the Great War, he likewise despaired about the quality of the Finnish leadership: "I would set greater store by the Swedish-speaking element of the population than I do by our Finns!"[55] Sibelius's silence on many of the key questions of turn-of-the-century Finnish politics (not least his explicit rejection of Robert Kajanus's interpretation of the Second Symphony as an anti-Russian narrative of Finnish self-realization) is persuasive evidence both of his acute sensitivity to being caught up in contentious topics and of the absolute primacy of artistic creativity in his emotional makeup.

The dominance of political factors in discussions of Russo-Finnish relations has tended to overshadow the profound cultural contacts that existed between the two countries. If Finnish politics were characterized by sharp debates about internal politics and external diplomacy, then the cultural sphere was more responsive to a broad range of cosmopolitan influences, of which Russia was but one.[56] Sibelius's exposure to Russia began early; his home town Hämeenlinna (Tavastehus in Swedish) hosted a Russian garrison. As Sibelius recalled:

> The Russian officers and their families brought a breath of another and larger world, which it was interesting to become acquainted

with, and provided the good citizens of Tavastehus with much material for wonder and observation. The Russian element played an important element in my childhood, for at that time the relationship between Finns and Russians was not what it became later: both sides tried to maintain a good understanding.[57]

Musically speaking, the many miniatures for violin and piano and for piano solo that Sibelius wrote from a young age clearly betray the influence of the Russian repertoire that would have been prevalent in the schools and salons of Hämeenlinna (and Helsinki, too). As Goss writes:

> Clearly, it was the violinists associated with Russia and especially with Saint Petersburg who were of first importance to him. With some awe he writes of meeting the violin "virtuoso" Trostchefsky, probably a music-loving lieutenant in the local garrison; of the nearly unbelievable performance of Gerhard Brassin, a Belgian violinist based in Saint Petersburg; of the fabulous violin that had been owned by Ferdinand Laub, professor of violin at Moscow Conservatory; of playing the works of Henry Vieuxtemps, another Belgian violinist who taught at the Saint Petersburg Conservatory; and of Jacques-Pierre Rode, who had been violinist to the czar. Sibelius's first violin teacher in Helsinki, Mitrofan Wasilieff, came to the Helsinki Music Institute from Saint Petersburg where he had played with the Imperial String Quartet; according to Sibelius, he bore the very best references from none other than Anton Rubinstein. Sibelius reports that he himself played Rubinstein's C minor quartet at a glittering evening held in one of Helsinki's elegant homes.[58]

A broader and more clearly articulated vision of Russian culture emerged in 1889, when Sibelius became acquainted with the group of young Fennoman artists associated with the Finnish-language newspaper *Päivälehti*. For all their nationalist credentials, figures such as Arvid and Eero Järnefelt nonetheless had strong connections with Russian artistic and social circles, as did their sister, Aino, who became Sibelius's wife in 1892. The Järnefelts' interest in the Russian arts stemmed largely from their family background; their mother, Elisabeth Järnefelt (née Clodt von Jürgensburg), was born into a prominent St. Petersburg aristocratic family in 1839. (By contrast, their father, Alexander Järnefelt, embodied the administrative and practical links between the two countries. After serving in the Russian army he returned to Finland as governor of Mikkeli, Kuopio, and Vaasa, as well as serving in the administration of the Finnish Senate.) Along with being a major author in his own right, Arvid Järnefelt was a prominent disciple of Lev Tolstoy, several of whose works he translated into Finnish and whose ideals he tried to embody in his daily life.[59] Tolstoyan principles of social equality, proximity to the people, passive resistance to evil, and the cultivation of the simple life ran deep in the Järnefelt family, and many of the copies of Tolstoy's works in Sibelius's library belonged in fact to his wife.[60] Sibelius himself was not immune from moments of Tolstoyan romanticism, here expressed in a letter to his wife: "In my new sheepskin coat I look like a veritable peasant. It feels so nice: it would be good if one did not have to pretend to be upper class in other circumstances as well."[61] Sibelius was generally more familiar with classical works of Russian literature, describing Fyodor Dostoyevsky's *Crime and Punishment* as "head and shoulders above Turgenev,"[62] and sending Aino a copy of Alexander Pushkin's *Eugene Onegin* from Vienna in March 1891.[63] But it was in the field of the visual arts that the Järnefelt family was most intimately connected with Russian culture. Elisabeth's family contained a large number of artists, including the sculptor Pyotr Clodt von Jürgensburg and the realist painter Mikhail Clodt. Appropriately enough, Eero Järnefelt trained at the Academy of Arts in St. Petersburg from 1883

Figure 1. Eero Järnefelt, *Summernight Moon*, 1889.

to 1886, and his paintings betray the profound influence of nineteenth-century Russian realism (see Figure 1).[64]

Eero was rather typical of Russo-Finnish relations in the visual arts.[65] Not only had previous generations of Finnish artists, such as Albert Edelfelt, also trained in St. Petersburg, but Russian patrons and critics generally looked to Finland for evidence of the vitality of the arts in the empire. Edelfelt himself was exhibited widely in Russia around the turn of the century and enjoyed the particular patronage of Nicholas II, painting a number of official and private portraits for the royal family.[66] And in the autumn of 1898, Sergei Diaghilev organized the inaugural exhibition of the Mir iskusstva (World of Art) group in St. Petersburg, in which paintings by both Russian and Finnish artists were displayed with equal prominence.[67] As the case of Edelfelt suggests, rising tensions between Russia and Finland did not necessarily impede cultural contacts between the two countries. Indeed, such contacts were indicative of a shared disdain for Russian autocracy, which frequently provided a common cause for Finnish and Russian artists. An important, if excessively mythologized, feature of the Russian arts was a critical attitude to authority. This attitude was typical of the liberal politics of the Russian intelligentsia, described by Richard Taruskin as "a noble tradition of artistic and social thought—one that abhorred injustice and political repression, but also one that valued social commitment, participation in one's community, and solidarity with people."[68] These were the politics of the Järnefelt family, as well as of many Finnish artists who adopted not just the artistic techniques but also the social commitment of their Russian colleagues. During periods of intense Russification, Russian artists lent their support to the Finnish cause, arguing that the autocracy did not represent Russia itself; similarly, Finnish artists could express anti-autocratic statements while maintaining their respect for what they saw as the positive aspects of Russian culture.

The convergence of such political and artistic agendas is perhaps clearest in the relationship between Akseli Gallen-Kallela and Maxim Gorky. In the wake of the first Russian Revolution of 1905, Gallen-Kallela organized a literary and musical evening that revealed the shared interests of Finnish nationalists and Russian radicals at the time:

> On 1 February 1906 . . . an unusual literary and musical evening took place in the Finnish National Theatre. Maxim Gorky and Eino Leino read excerpts from their works, and Kajanus conducted Tchaikovsky's Serenade for Strings and Sibelius's *Spring Song* and *The Ferryman's Bride* while the proceedings went to those who had suffered during the recent unrest in Russia, i.e., the revolutionaries. The thought of Tchaikovsky and Sibelius as symbols of the bond between Finnish in-

tellectuals and Russian radicals is not a little bizarre. After the general strike, many Russian revolutionaries took refuge in Finland where police vigilance was less strict, and where they could count on the support of both the bourgeois and the socialist elements in society. Gorky's journey had been organized on the Finnish side by Gallen-Kallela who was an active supporter of the resistance movement, even to the extent of hiding smuggled arms in his drawing-room sofa, and receiving Russian revolutionaries in his home. However, his ardour was somewhat cooled by the plans for a bank robbery that were mooted by some of the group, and he quietly withdrew to his country retreat![69]

Gallen-Kallela eventually helped to smuggle Gorky out of Finland and away from the attentions of the Russian authorities (Gorky would spend the next seven years in exile on Capri). Eero Järnefelt shared something of Gallen-Kallela's sympathy for the Russian radicals, although Sibelius— who attended a dinner hosted by his brother-in-law a few days later in honor of Gorky and Gallen-Kallela—does not appear to have recorded his reactions (more evidence, if any were needed, of his cautiously apolitical nature). Whatever the private feelings of Finns toward Russian revolutionaries, what is most striking about Gorky's stay in Finland in 1906 is the way in which Finnish artistic nationalism and Russian radical activism intersected and overlapped, at least for a time. Gallen-Kallela's 1906 portrait of Gorky is but one artistic trace of this particular moment, just as Ilya Repin's portrait of Gallen-Kallela in turn captures a later, more troubled episode in Finnish-Russian relations (Figures 2 and 3).

Yet the straightforward association between Finnish artistic nationalism and Russian liberal politics was not always so easily maintained, as the career of Robert Kajanus, Finland's leading orchestral conductor at the end of the nineteenth century and Sibelius's supporter (and sometime rival), suggests.[70] Kajanus enjoyed strong connections with Russia, traveling there regularly to conduct and performing Russian works back in Helsinki. When, in 1905, Nikolay Rimsky-Korsakov was dismissed from his position at the St. Petersburg Conservatory for supporting the right of students to engage in political protest,[71] Kajanus refused to conduct in Russia until Rimsky-Korsakov (as well as Alexander Glazunov and Anatoliy Lyadov) had been reinstated.[72] Yet Kajanus's behavior was not always so high-minded. In 1896, along with Sibelius and musicologist Ilmari Krohn, Kajanus applied for the position of director of music at the University of Helsinki. When Sibelius was nominated by the Finnish committee, Kajanus resorted to a number of strategies to have the decision overturned:

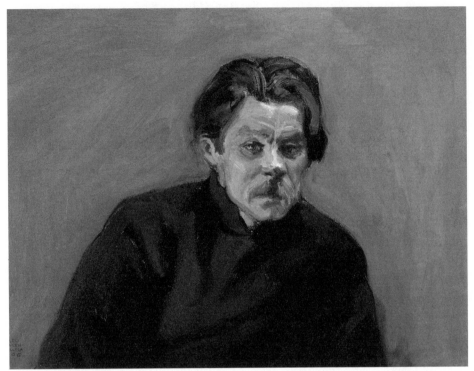

Figure 2. Axel Gallen-Kallela, *Portrait of Maxim Gorky*, 1906, Ateneum Art Museum, Helsinki.

A series of labyrinthine bureaucratic twists playing out over many months gradually revealed where the real power lay. It began with Kajanus's bitter objection to the decision and his demand for a new vote. He gained one supporter. Sibelius's name then went forward to Saint Petersburg, to the man with the final authority: Carl Woldemar von Daehn (1838–1900), Finland's minister-secretary of state. In a resourceful episode of shuttle diplomacy for which he later became notorious, Kajanus himself visited Saint Petersburg. . . . On July 29, 1897, von Daehn overruled the Finns' recommendation and appointed Robert Kajanus to the position.[73]

Although what actually happened remains unknown, Kajanus's direct appeal to the St. Petersburg establishment tainted his reputation for decades to come (Krohn was still repeating the story in the 1950s).[74] Even fifteen years later, in 1912, when Kajanus successfully urged the Russian authorities to support Finnish musical institutions threatened with major cuts to

Figure 3. Ilya Repin, *Portrait of Axel Gallen-Kallela,* 1920, Ateneum Art Museum, Helsinki.

the financial support provided by the Finnish senate, his astute intervention was greeted with hostility:

> Kajanus went to St. Petersburg to plead the orchestra's case with Glazunov and he obtained a meeting with Kokovstov, the President of the Council of Ministers who promised to take up the matter with

the Governor-General of Finland, Seyn. There is no doubt whatsoever that Kajanus acted in a spirit of complete altruism but his
intervention was much resented by certain nationalist elements and
aroused strong feelings, particularly among the Swedish-speaking
community, who saw him using his personal influence in the Imperial
capital to further his own ends. As a result he became the victim of
a highly vocal campaign and his concerts were boycotted.[75]

Even Sibelius was disturbed, noting in his diary that "Kajanus has again
appealed to St. Petersburg . . . and will bow and scrape to Kokovstov and
Seyn."[76] The various stories about Kajanus's involvement with Russian
artists and institutions illustrate the complex interaction of politics and
national identity that shaped not only how individuals acted but also how
they were perceived.

Sibelius and Russian Music

The potential influence of Russian music on Sibelius has been an important theme in critical discussion of his works from the very beginning of
his career as a composer.[77] Ironically enough, given the political situation
at the time, the impact of Russian works has been perceived most readily
in his compositions of the 1890s and early 1900s, from *Kullervo* (1891–92)
to the Violin Concerto (1903–4, revised version 1905). Although Sibelius's
letters and diaries contain few explicit or extended references to Russian
music, he was happy enough to affirm his admiration for Tchaikovsky in
particular, admitting to his wife that "there is much in that man that I recognize in myself."[78] The details of Sibelius's involvement with Russian music
are, however, largely tangential. As a young musician resident in what was
then part of the Russian Empire, Sibelius could well have pursued his
studies in the nearest city with an established and influential conservatory:
St. Petersburg. Yet despite the encouragement of his brother-in-law Eero
Järnefelt, Sibelius went instead to Berlin and Vienna.[79] (It would be a later
generation of Finnish composers who would orient themselves more explicitly toward Russia.)[80] In 1895, supported by Ferruccio Busoni, Glazunov,
and Rimsky-Korsakov, Sibelius approached Mitrofan Belyayev, whose influential publishing house dealt exclusively with Russian composers
around the turn of the century; again, the venture came to nothing.[81]
Sibelius's first trip to Russia—excluding passing through St. Petersburg
on his way to Italy in 1900—took place as late as December 1906, when
he conducted performances of *Pohjola's Daughter* and "Lemminkäinen's
Return" in St. Petersburg.[82] He returned the following November, con-

ducting the Third Symphony in both St. Petersburg and Moscow, where he also performed *Pohjola's Daughter* and a number of smaller pieces.[83] Initial reactions were promising. He had a firm advocate in the conductor Alexander Siloti, and even before his arrival, his name was mentioned in specialist music periodicals.[84] Years later, in an interview with *Svenska Dagbladet*, Sibelius recalled his reception in Russia with affection: "My most vivid recollection is of a concert in Moscow during the old times. There is an understanding of and an enthusiasm for music which has no counterpart elsewhere. For the Slavs, music lies in their blood."[85] The reviews of his first appearance in Russia were enthusiastic, with one explicitly linking him to the Russian tradition:

> Of contemporary artists, Sibelius, as a composer, stands closest of all, by virtue of his taste, inclinations and direction, to Rimsky-Korsakov. There is the same national feeling in music, natural, spontaneous and free, the same tendency to paint in sound, the same feeling for the world of fairy tales and ancient myth, and above all, the same sense of fantasy and boldness when it comes to orchestral color. . . . Having heard this piece ["Lemminkäinen's Return"], one can only regret that the late V. V. Stasov was unable to hear it performed. How this music would have enchanted him, with his hunger for talent and originality and his happy ability to relish things, which he retained in his old age.[86]

Yet reactions to performance of the Third Symphony in 1907 were more critical, and Sibelius's reputation was little helped by Siloti's careless premiere of *Nightride and Sunrise* at the end of 1908.[87] Ultimately, it would not be until after the Second World War that Sibelius's music became widely performed and appreciated in Russia, where his nationalist credentials, commitment to traditional forms, and moderate form of modernism could be readily accommodated within the framework of Socialist Realism, especially after the death of Stalin in 1953, when the Soviet Union once again began to open up to limited outside influences.[88]

If the story of Sibelius's encounter with Russia itself is largely one of misunderstanding and missed opportunities, then accounts of his openness to its music have been altogether more productive. Tawaststjerna's biography points repeatedly to Russian influences on works of the early period. The opening bars of the first movement of an early Suite for Violin and Piano (JS187, 1887–88) are held to "breathe an air of Slav melancholy" deriving ultimately from Tchaikovsky,[89] and the piano work "Au crépuscule" in F-sharp minor (JS47, 1887) is described as "a rather Tchaikovskian miniature."[90] Tawaststjerna also speculates that Sibelius's characteristic use of "long-sustained pedal points on the tonic in the major key which become mediant in the related minor" may be related to precedents in works by Mily Balakirev (*Islamey*) and Alexander Borodin (*The Polovstian Dances from Prince Igor*).[91] The work that evinces the most thorough-going engagement with Russian models is, though, the First Symphony (1899, revised 1900), whether in "the use of a motto theme that appears at the opening of the work," "many orchestral details," or "the chord of the dominant ninth . . . poised over a mediant pedal point,"[92] all of which are traced back to Tchaikovsky, particularly to his Sixth Symphony. By contrast, the alleged similarity between the main theme of the first movement and that of Borodin's First Symphony is, according to Tawaststjerna, "more readily discernable on paper than in performance."[93] (See Example 1.) Here, Tawaststjerna alludes to Cecil Gray's 1931 summary of Russian influences on the First Symphony:

> One notes in particular a strong Russian influence here and there, especially in the thematic material, which is unusual in his work. The first subject of the initial movement, for example, is strikingly akin to that in the first movement of Borodin's symphony in E-flat major, only sharpened and intensified; that of the second movement is distinctly reminiscent of Tchaikovsky, and the broad, sweeping theme of the *finale* is very much the kind of theme one finds in the last movements of Rachmaninoff or Glazounoff, only very much better.[94]

Gray's original observation was picked up and developed by Gerald Abraham, whose familiarity with Russian music meant that he was both more able and more inclined to discern such parallels:

> As Mr. Gray points out, the first subject proper is strikingly akin to that in the first movement of Borodin's Symphony in E-flat. . . . Admittedly, the relationship is merely one of melodic outline, not of rhythm, inflection, or general feeling. But, more curious still, there

Example 1. Comparative first movement themes in Sibelius and Borodin. Sibelius, Symphony no. 1, first movement (principal theme) and Borodin, Symphony no. 1, first movement (opening).

is a similar relationship between the latter part of the Borodin theme and Sibelius's *second* main subject. . . . Moreover, there are other Borodinesque traits in this first Sibelius Symphony: the throwing of the orchestral weight on to the second crotchet . . . , while only tuba and a drum mark the down-beat (cf. the scherzo of Borodin's Second Symphony), the overlapping descent of a figure through the orchestra coming off the climax just before the appearance of the second subject, the character of the scherzo with its quick repeated notes, the brassy scoring of the whole symphony.[95]

The novelty of Abraham's argument lay less in recognizing discrete and superficial motivic borrowings, and more in asserting the profound influence of Borodin's attitude to symphonic form on Sibelius's own practice. Gray had claimed that Sibelius achieved something entirely original in respect of symphonic form:

The nature of this revolution can be best described by saying that whereas in the symphony of Sibelius's predecessors the thematic material is generally introduced in an exposition, taken to pieces, dissected and analysed in a development section, and put together again in a recapitulation, Sibelius . . . inverts the process, introducing thematic fragments in the exposition, building them up into an organic whole in the development section, then dissolving and dispersing the material back into its primary constituents in a brief recapitulation.[96]

Abraham, keen to defend the status of Russian music by asserting its prior originality, argued that "Borodin had done this sort of thing more than thirty years earlier,"[97] before proceeding to give a summary both of Borodin's own method, and Sibelius's appropriation of the technique. Although both Gray's original observation and Abraham's subsequent development of it have since been questioned,[98] the notion that the Russian influence on Sibelius had as much to do with structure, argument, and development as with obvious thematic parallels remains a productive one.

Taking up the leads first suggested by Gray and Abraham (and subsequently developed by Tawaststjerna), other scholars have distinguished further Russian resonances. Joseph Kraus has considered similarities in voice leading, harmonic language, and tonal plan as evidence of Tchaikovsky's influence on the First Symphony.[99] Eero Tarasti has argued that "the endless repetition of short motifs or themes" in *En saga* (1892, revised 1902) is derived from "the techniques of Rimsky-Korsakov or Tchaikovsky."[100] Veijo Murtomäki situates *Skogsrået* (*The Wood Nymph*) in a genealogy of Russian musical ballads, including Balakirev's *Tamara*, Tchaikovsky's *Voyevoda*, and

Sergey Lyapunov's Ballade (a tradition subsequently continued by Glazunov and Sergey Taneyev),[101] and compares the work's "tragic slow finale" to "the Adagio lamentoso conclusion of Tchaikovsky's *Pathétique* Symphony."[102] Other works by Sibelius reflect the lighter and more lyrical aspects of Russian music. The Romance in C (1904) has been heard as an echo of Tchaikovsky (particularly his Serenade for Strings).[103] And it was the *Canzonetta* (1911) that prompted Igor Stravinsky—not otherwise sympathetic to Sibelius, whether as a romantic nationalist or a progressive modernist—to identify the musical links between Finland and Russia: "I like that Northern Italianate melodism—Tchaikovsky had it too—which was part, and an attractive part, of the St. Petersburg culture."[104] George Balanchine returned Sibelius's homage to this aspect of the St. Petersburg tradition by choreographing *Valse triste* as a ballet in Petrograd in 1922.[105]

Such arguments are particularly useful for challenging the still commonly held view of Sibelius that emphasizes his autonomous development and exclusively Finnish origins. Yet Sibelius himself denied such influences—as, for instance, in the case of Borodin's First Symphony[106]—and there is little conclusive evidence he was familiar with the works in question (his library contains few Russian scores and his letters and diary give few clues). Moreover, the comparisons adduced are often rather slight in the overall scheme of a given work.[107] In spite of Sibelius's denials, there is nevertheless a frequent tendency in criticism to assert that the characteristic features of Russian music were simply "in the air." Robert Layton, for instance, distances himself from Abraham's assertion that Sibelius's First Symphony was directly influenced by Borodin's First, yet defends his own sense of the importance of Russian works in indirect terms:

> The resemblances to which I alluded between "Lemminkäinen and the Maidens of the Island" and the First Symphony of Balakirev, and the slow movement of Sibelius's First Symphony and Tchaikovsky's *Souvenir de Florence* were intended to show a common cultural language. Sibelius obviously could not have known the Balakirev and probably did not know the *Souvenir de Florence* either.[108]

There were a number of ways in which Sibelius could have participated in the "common cultural language" that linked Helsinki with St. Petersburg and Moscow. As conductor of the Helsinki Philharmonic Orchestra, Kajanus regularly programmed Russian orchestral works.[109] Even if Sibelius was absent from such concerts, it seems likely that the two men discussed music that was of such particular interest to Kajanus. Busoni—who spent a considerable amount of time in Russia and Finland in the early 1890s—was a further possible channel of information. Sibelius would also have encountered a good deal of Russian music while conducting his own works in Russia or while visiting European capitols such as Berlin, Vienna, and Paris (his reactions to hearing works by Anton Arensky and Sergey Rachmaninoff in Berlin in October 1910 are noted in his letters and diary, for instance).[110]

Whether or not Sibelius's music derives certain structural and thematic features directly from Russian models, the audible parallels may also be related to the fact that both Russian and Finnish music share certain common sources. The first of these is Liszt's approach to the genre of the tone poem, the impact of which Sibelius readily admitted:

> I have found my old self again, musically speaking. Many things are now clear to me: really I am a tone painter and poet. Liszt's view of music is the one to which I am closest. Hence my interest in the symphonic poem. I'm working on a theme that I'm very pleased with. You'll hear it when I get home; that's if I have got so far with it and don't begin to have too many doubts.[111]

This statement—frequently cited in the secondary literature—has been interpreted in various ways. In part the result of Sibelius's self-perceived failure to write a Wagnerian music drama, it reveals his discovery of the music of the New German School, especially the tone poems of Richard Strauss, whose *Don Juan* had deeply impressed him in Berlin in 1890. Yet Liszt played a decisive role in Russia, too, where composers built on his legacy (as well as that of Hector Berlioz) in their search for a music that would fuse elements of the national, the programmatic, and the quasi-realistic. Indeed, as Pierre Vidal suggests, Sibelius's concept of the form drew more from Russian and Slavonic precursors than from Strauss:

> Inspired by his country and by ancestral myths, Sibelius did not draw upon the same sources as Strauss, for Sibelius avoided metaphysical, philosophical, and idealistic themes. Rather, we associate him instinctively with Smetana and the Russians, whose paradigms descend more from Balakirev's *Thamar* and Rimsky-Korsakov's *Sadko* than from Tchaikovsky's *Romeo and Juliet* or *Francesca da Rimini*, which are human dramas transposed onto the romantic-overture tradition. Sibelius was more captured than his forerunners by a sense of primeval beauty.[112]

At the same time, Russian composers were reinventing the symphony from the European periphery, with a work such as Tchaikovsky's *Pathétique* standing as much—if not more—for the very latest in musical modernity, as for any sense of national idiom (the very thing that Tchaikovsky so self-consciously repudiated). Murtomäki notes the prominent role played by

Russian composers in rejecting the conventional division between the competing genres of the symphony and the tone poem, and in using elements derived from one genre to revivify and extend the possibilities of the other: "Many Romantic composers after Liszt—for example, Borodin, Dvořák, Tchaikovsky, Mahler, Strauss, Rimsky-Korsakov, Scriabin—created works that narrowed the gap between symphony and symphonic poem."[113] More generally, he posits the influence of Russian music on Sibelius's explorations of symphonic form:

> There were also Russian sources for the musical fantasy. In the latter half of the nineteenth century subtitles like "orchestral fantasy" and "symphonic fantasy" were often used. Mussorgsky's *Night on Bare Mountain*, for instance, is a "symphonic fantasy," Tchaikovsky's *Francesca da Rimini* is a "fantasy," and his *Hamlet* and *Romeo et Juliette* are "overture-fantasies." . . . As there were close cultural contacts between Russia and Finland during the nineteenth century and as Tchaikovsky had been an important influence on Sibelius's music until his Second Symphony (1902), it is possible that the idea of the "symphonic fantasy" came to Sibelius from a Russian context.[114]

Once again, we are faced with speculation about a potential Russian influence on Sibelius that can be neither proven nor refuted. Instead, it is David Haas's analysis that more subtly links Sibelius to the Russian traditions in this respect:

> Although belonging to different generations, Sibelius and Tchaikovsky were chronologically situated to be heirs to the Beethoven symphony and the Liszt symphonic poem and unlike so many of their contemporaries declined to favor either genre, producing instead parallel series of numbered symphonies and programmatically entitled symphonic poems.[115]

If there are parallels here between Sibelius and Russian composers (particularly Tchaikovsky, but also symphonists from the "nationalist" school such as Balakirev, Borodin, and Rimsky-Korsakov), they relate primarily to their cognate reactions to a particular issue in European music more broadly, that is, the tension between the symphony and the tone poem.

Resemblances may also be explained by the recourse to shared material. As Tina K. Ramnarine observes, "Much of the folk material which inspired Finnish artists and scholars and which contributed to a national culture was paradoxically collected from a region which had been claimed, shared, and divided by both Finland and Russia."[116] The region in question is, of course, Karelia, whose culture played a decisive role in the formation of Finnish national identity. Yet Karelia extended well beyond the Finnish border into northern Russia; indeed, it was Russian Karelia—untouched by the Swedish influence that was predominant in southern and eastern Finland, and unaffected by the traditions and practices of the Lutheran Church—that was perceived by Finnish nationalists as preserving Karelian culture in its most pristine form. Lönnrot's first edition of the *Kalevala* was based on material collected in both Finland and Russian Karelia, and an influential travelogue—A. V. Ervasti's *Muistelmia matkalta Venäjän Karjalassa kesällä 1879* (Recollections from a trip to Russian Karelia during the summer of 1879)—further revealed the significance of the region across the border for the development of Finnish national consciousness.[117] In a letter to his wife in October 1891, Sibelius referred to the Finnish runic singer Larin Paraske as "a runo-singer from *Russian* Karelia" (my emphasis).[118] The impact of folk music from neighboring regions does much to explain apparent similarities between Sibelius and works by Russian composers. As Murtomäki speculates: "Could it be . . . that the 'Finnishness' in Sibelius's music consists of lifting certain traits from Karelian/Russian folk music and melodic traditions, a source shared by the extremely folk-music-conscious young Russian composers as well?"[119] In fact, this argument had already been made in the 1950s by Simon Parmet:

> The specific musical resemblance between Tchaikovsky and the young Sibelius, in particular, is to be found in certain easily recognizable turns of melodic phrase, in the long, sweeping lines, in the spontaneity of the music and its immediate, natural charm, and in its proximity to folk music. This last resemblance is particularly significant, as it supports the idea that Finnish folk music is more closely related to Russian folk music than we are generally inclined to believe.[120]

Indeed, Gray explicitly singled out Sibelius's Karelian works as those closest in spirit to the Russian national tradition:

> In writing music ostensibly Karelian in character and style Sibelius approaches as closely to that of Russia as Karelia itself does to Russian soil. The thematic material is sometimes strongly suggestive of various Slavonic masters, and the eightfold repetition in the trio of the "Alla Marcia" in the suite is as characteristic of Russian music as it is rare in that of Finland. "Karelia," indeed, is the sole work of Sibelius that one could easily believe to have been written by a Russian if one were to hear it without knowing who had composed it.[121]

Russian critics, too, have been particularly responsive to such arguments. Stupel suggests that a melody in the first of the *Lemminkäinen* Legends resembles a theme from Rimsky-Korsakov's tone poem *Sadko* (although he does not give details). The significance of his observation rests, however, less on the veracity of the resemblance than on the potential reason for its appearance: "This may be a question not just of direct influence, but also of the intonational proximity between the Karelian lyricism that nourished Sibelius's work, and that of northern Russia which inspired the author of *Sadko*."[122] A similar point is made by Vera Aleksandrova and Elena Bronfin: "Of particular interest is the question of the intonational relationship of certain of Sibelius's themes and melodies to Russian folk songs; it would seem that the reason for this is rooted in the proximity of ancient northern Russian folk melodies to early Karelo-Finnish musical folklore."[123]

The widely asserted influence of Karelian runic singing on Sibelius's musical language has been helpfully summarized by Robert Layton:

> Generally speaking the runic melodies that Sibelius took down from Paraske comprise two more or less rhythmically symmetrical four or five beat phrases that are within the compass of the first five notes of the major or minor scale. The notes, sometimes extended to embrace the flattened sixth or the flattened leading note, generally correspond with those of the five-stringed *kantele* and the main melodic protagonists in the *Kullervo* Symphony leave no doubt as to these runic influences. They persist throughout his career right up to *Tapiola*, whose basic idea falls within the compass of the *kantele*.[124]

These features are also characteristic of some nineteenth-century Russian music, especially that based on folk sources (see Example 2). In rhythmic terms, the key source here is the "Bridal Chorus" from Act 3 of Mikhail Glinka's *Life for the Tsar*, the prototype for subsequent 5/4 movements in similarly folkloric vein by Borodin, including the finale of his Second Symphony, the Scherzo of his Third Symphony (posthumously completed by Glazunov), or the maiden's chorus in Act 1, scene 2 of his *Prince Igor*. Stripped of its folkloric quality, this rhythmic trait is exploited in the second-movement waltz of Tchaikovsky's Sixth Symphony and Rachmaninoff's *Isle of the Dead*. Likewise, the limited melodic outline of runic song is cognate with aspects of Russian folksong, especially as used by nineteenth-century composers. The song on which the finale of Tchaikovsky's Fourth Symphony is based—"Vo pole beryoza stoyala" (In the field there stood a birch tree)—is constrained within the interval of a fifth, just as the first subject of the first movement of Vasily Kalinnikov's First Symphony traces that same interval before breaking out of it (it echoes, moreover, the opening theme of

"Karelian" model (Petri Shemeikka to Sibelius, 1892, cited in Murtomäki, "Sibelius and Finnish-Karelian Folk Music," 35)

Glinka, "Bridal Chorus," *Life for the Tsar*, Act 3

Borodin, Symphony no. 2, finale opening (from rehearsal number A)

Borodin, Symphony no. 3, Scherzo

Example 2. Nineteenth-century Russian music based on folk sources.

Borodin, "Maiden's Chorus," *Prince Igor*, Act 1, scene 2

Ti po - mi - luy nas, ne vo gnev te - be, ne vo -

bi - du bud', e - to on zhe vsyo, nash bla goy - to knaz' Vo - lo -

di - mir - to Ya - ro - sla - vich, nash knyaz' to Ga - lits - kiy!

Tchaikovsky, Symphony no. 6, second movement

Example 2 continued

Rachmaninoff, *Isle of the Dead*, opening

Tchaikovsky, Symphony no. 4, finale, second subject

Example 2 continued

Kalinnikov, Symphony no. 1, opening

Borodin, Symphony no. 3, opening

Borodin, Symphony no. 2, opening

Example 2 continued

the first movement of Borodin's Third Symphony). And to invert the argument, the shape of the opening motive of Borodin's Second Symphony even
recalls the very contours of runic song itself. Thus, if a work like *Kullervo*
appears to betray a number of distinctly Russian influences, this is not
necessarily because it is explicitly modeled on Russian sources (although Goss
has recently suggested that Sibelius may indeed have drawn on Russian folksong collections during the composition of the symphony).[125] Rather it is
because Sibelius's Karelian sources are similar to some of the folksongs that
fed, directly or otherwise, into the works of Russian composers.[126]

Apart from any purely musical parallels, there are certain thematic
associations in Sibelius's compositions inspired by the *Kalevala* and Russian
works based on *bïlinï* (epic poems), such as Rimsky-Korsakov's *Sadko* (performed in Helsinki in 1895), and later pieces such as Reynhold Glière's
Third Symphony (*Il'ya Muromets*, 1909–11). Although it has not been a
dominant theme in the study of the *Kalevala*, a number of folklorists have
argued that similarities between elements of the *Kalevala* and certain of

the Russian *bïlinï* attest either to the shared origins of or mutual influence between the Karelian and Russian traditions.[127] In the late nineteenth century, for instance, Vsevolod Miller pointed to a series of parallels between the figures of Sadko and Väinämöinen that were, he suggested, the result of the close links between the Finns and the citizens of the medieval city-state of Novgorod, to the northwest of the East Slavonic heartlands of medieval Kievan Rus.[128] Whether or not there are any direct connections between Finnish and Russian works inspired by the *Kalevala* and the *bïlinï*, they nonetheless attest to a shared interest in myth and origins that was characteristic of Russian and Finnish art around the turn of the century.[129]

If critics have been assiduous in positing connections between Sibelius and Russian music in his earlier, "romantic nationalist" works, they have also tended to assume that in the wake of his turn to classicism and modernism from the Third Symphony onward the Russian influence wanes, or simply vanishes. Where Russian works had been so generative when it came to the questions of nationalism, folklore, and myth central to Sibelius in the 1890s and early 1900s, they seemed less likely to inspire his turn to abstraction and the search for a pan-European, quasi-universal form of musical communication. Murtomäki summarizes Sibelius's change of style in the early twentieth century as an explicit rejection of the kind of nationalism he had learned from Russian models:

> With the revisions of *En saga* (1892/1902) and the Violin Concerto (1904/05), he was distancing himself from the nineteenth-century romantic style and trying to find a new, more classical way of composing. According to this explanation, Sibelius sought to reorient himself away from Wagnerism and the New German School; those composers who had espoused these ideals in Bohemia, Russia and Scandinavia tended to be associated with national Romantic schools and denigrated as folklorists.[130]

The work that seems best to encapsulate this process of evolution is the Third Symphony. Writing about a Russian review of a 1907 performance of the symphony in St. Petersburg, Johnson argues: "It is worth nothing that there were no references to Tchaikovsky. Indeed, the Third may be regarded as the beginning of Sibelius's attempt to break away from the style of the heavy-handed 'Romantic' symphony."[131] Yet even here, some observers have detected residual links with the Russian traditions. Edward Garden, for instance, suggests that Sibelius took "Balakirev's First Symphony in C major as a starting point for his Third Symphony in the same key."[132] While observing a superficial similarity between the opening figure of the Third Symphony and that of Borodin's Second,[133] Burnett James prefers to see the relationship between Sibelius and Borodin in terms of their sense of organic symphonic growth stemming from a process of "preliminary thematic fragmentation."[134] Tawaststjerna suggests a further Russian parallel: "The work can be most nearly compared with Glazunov's pastoral Eighth Symphony, also composed in 1907, although Glazunov's classicism seems far smoother and more traditional than that of Sibelius."[135] If there is some confusion in Tawaststjerna's description of the Eighth (it was in fact the Seventh Symphony of 1902 that was called "The Pastoral"), then his analogy reminds us that Russian music stands for far more than the nationalist legacy of the second half of the nineteenth century. When critics interpret the classicism of the Third Symphony as a move away from a nationalist dialect heavily influenced by Russian originals, they often fail to note that a similar move was under way in Russia itself (and if musical comparisons are made, they tend to be with Busoni's "junge Klassizität"). Goss alludes to early twentieth-century visual culture in this respect—"Graphic clarity and classical impulses were streaming in from many directions, and Saint Petersburg was one. A number of that city's artists, among them Valentin Serov, had begun to rethink their styles"— and cites Solomon Volkov's evocation of the classicism of such poets as Mikhail Kuzmin, Nikolay Gumilyov, and Osip Mandelstam.[136] Yet in the musical field, too, younger composers were rejecting what they perceived to be the nationalist prescriptions of Balakirev and Stasov in favor of greater academic discipline—something already presaged in Rimsky-Korsakov's works from the 1870s onward[137]—and a greater range of cosmopolitan influences from contemporary Western Europe. The dominance of Stravinsky's works of the 1920s onward in discussions of Russian musical neoclassicism has tended to eclipse this intervening generation. In St. Petersburg, it was Glazunov (Sibelius's exact contemporary) who was striving to fuse elements of the national with the supposedly "universal"; and in Moscow, the German classical tradition was enthusiastically promoted by Taneyev (who, incidentally, thought Sibelius's Third Symphony "an unusually poor composition.")[138]

The most complete account of the Russian aspects in the Third Symphony is, though, by Glenda Dawn Goss. Noting that Sibelius's personal and professional connections with Russia were particularly strong around the time of the work's composition (in particularly in the form of his relationship with Siloti), Goss argues that the "new symphony's features seemed gauged to suit the Saint Petersburg milieu."[139] Although her initial piece of evidence—"that theme in the first movement, undulating sensuously over bass drones sounding the perfect fifth in the strange key of B minor"[140]—is very much in the established tradition of citing isolated and superficial likenesses as evidence of Russian influence (here, as an instance of the work's Oriental coloring), Goss's argument rests principally on the symphony's innovative construction, and in particular the ambiguous form of the third-movement finale that has proved such a distinct challenge to analysts and commentators.[141] Taking issue with a widespread interpretation of the symphony, according to which it constitutes a self-conscious rapprochement with the mainstream, Austro-German school, she sees the symphony as embodying an ambivalence about Germanic forms of symphonic argument that was shared by earlier generations of Russian composers. Noting in passing that the symphony shares the key of Rimsky-Korsakov's Third Symphony, she ultimately posits Glinka's *Kamarinskaya*—and in particular its initial juxtaposition of two apparently dissimilar themes that are subsequently revealed to be related, as well as its structure as a series of ostinato variations—as a possible source for the constructional principle of Sibelius's work.[142] The sonata-form first movement develops the idea of "two sharply differing themes that, in the course of development, are revealed as springing from the same fundamental idea," and the finale explores the principle of Russian variation technique: "Rather than being 'developed' in any systematic, Germanic way, his theme revolves, its circular iterations driving the symphony to a close in a triumphal C major."[143] Most crucially, Goss posits significant Russian influences even where they do not necessarily strike the listener; the Third Symphony cannot sensibly be said to sound anything like *Kamarinskaya* or the later Russian works it inspired. As Howell suggests, for all Sibelius's potential debt to Russian works, his approach to symphonic structure was altogether more organic: "Simplistically, the Russian idea of 'transition,' particularly as evidenced in Tchaikovsky, concerns a passage which *separates* two surrounding blocks of material and this is completely at variance with Sibelius' technique of continuity."[144] From now on, the lessons of Russian music were to become more profoundly assimilated into Sibelius's own musical language and may indeed have become more productive, relating less to superficial motivic detail and orchestral color than to issues of symphonic structure and harmonic language. Moreover, the realization that Sibelius's later compositions draw part of their inspiration from Russian models allows us to perceive deep and underlying connections between works from all periods of his career, from *Kullervo* through to *Tapiola*.

The notion that Russian models may have inspired new thinking about symphonic structure accords well with James Hepokoski's various analyses of Sibelius in terms of rotational form. As Hepokoski explains, "rotational form" refers

> to the presence of an extended, patterned succession of musical events (often a collection of "themes"), which are then revisited one or more

times (recycled or "rotated through") with internal variations in intensity, motivic growth, interpolated or deleted material, and so on.[145]

Hepokoski's definition suggests numerous Russian precursors, beginning
with Glinka's double variations in *Kamarinskaya*, to the variations, sequences,
and repetitions that were so central to the symphonic practice of the nationalists and Tchaikovsky. Indeed, Hepokoski draws attention to the
Russian roots of Sibelius's technique:

> It was doubtless also from Russian symphonic composition, which at
> least from Glinka's *Kamarinskaya* onward had also explored circular
> stasis, that Sibelius learned of some of the most common generic slots
> within a "nationalistic" symphony or concerto for such repetitive
> "peasant" themes. These include the scherzo's trio and especially the
> first or (even more characteristically) the second theme of the finale—
> as a kind of "concluding" device or reductive "folk-goal" of the entire
> work: one thinks, for example of Tchaikovsky's Second and Fourth
> Symphonies or the Violin Concerto; and even Stravinsky's early
> Symphony in E-flat and, for that matter, the conclusion of *The Firebird*
> pay homage to the convention. In Sibelius the Second Symphony
> (three reiterations of the same theme in the finale's exposition, eight
> in its recapitulation) and the Violin Concerto have already been men-
> tioned in this respect, and to them we might add the earlier *En saga*
> and "Lemminkäinen's Return." (The Fourth Symphony is also exem-
> plary, but less obvious.) More remarkably, the entire finale of the Third
> Symphony is overtaken by the reiterative principle. And when the
> Fifth Symphony drives ultimately to the circular "Swan Hymn" of its
> finale, it is this convention that provides its most immediate ancestry.[146]

Furthermore, Hepokoski's arguments suggest that Sibelius's interest in
Russian models was not just a question of symphonic form in and of itself, but
was also profoundly linked to issues of national identity. In borrowing and
developing aspects of Russian practice, Sibelius was seeking to reposition his
own work in relation to the dominant traditions of symphonic form as represented by the Austro-German tradition: "Much of the most characteristic
language of the Fifth Symphony's first movement is one of stasis, circularity,
and neighbor-note activity. These procedures are fundamentally opposed to
'the principle of teleological progression' that had underpinned the traditional Germanic symphonic repertoire."[147] Citing once more the example of
the Third Symphony as a work of profound transition, Hepokoski usefully
illustrates how Sibelius's innovation was in part a product of a dialogue between national (and even nationalist) traditions in the era of early modernism:

From the last two movements of the Third Symphony (1907) onward, Sibelius seems to have embarked on one of the most remarkable (and least understood) formal projects of his age. As he proceeded into the last half of his career, he grew dissatisfied both with the received notions of musical form as identified in the reified schemata provided in the various *Formenlehre* textbooks (architectonically balanced sonatas, rondos, themes and variations, and so on) and with the various *de facto* families of formal deformation that had become common practice among the early modernist composers around the turn of the century.[148]

Turning briefly to Taruskin's analysis of Stravinsky's modernist style in terms of *drobnost'*, *nepodvizhnost'*, and *uproshcheniye* ("the quality of being a sum of parts," "immobility," and "simplification"), we can observe a parallel, if rather different response to the same Russian tradition that stimulated aspects of Sibelius's rotational technique.[149] In both cases, Russian models—Glinka, the New Russian School's nationalist works of the 1860s onward, explorations in symphonic form by Balakirev, Borodin, Rimsky-Korsakov, and Tchaikovsky—explicitly served both Sibelius and Stravinsky in their early and explicitly nationalist phases (Sibelius's *Kalevala* works of the 1890s through to the revised version of *En saga*, Stravinsky's ballets for Diaghilev). Yet they also stimulated the seemingly more abstract developments in form, structure, and argument that characterized both composers' postnationalist periods (Sibelius's four last symphonies and *Tapiola*, Stravinsky's neoclassicism).

Another approach to understanding the sources of Sibelius's musical language is that taken by Howell. Having surveyed potential Russian influences on Sibelius's early symphonic works,[150] Howell argues:

Much in the way of analysis of the music by Sibelius has concentrated, often exclusively so, on the thematic level. This tends simply to reveal the most obvious, easily detected and assimilated correspondences which, despite providing a satisfying network of germ-motive identity, prove unsatisfactory in the shallow and distorted musical viewpoint arising from such selectivity.[151]

Not only do such accounts fail to deal with the deeper structural organization of individual compositions; they fail to discern underlying principles that link works from different periods. Howell's particular interest is in tracing how Sibelius's melodies (derived, in part, from elements of runic song) affect structure and form across the entire chronological range of his output: "What is of interest melodically is the use of modality, its effect on the tonal organisation of early pieces and the repercussions this was to have in the extended tonal language of Sibelius the symphonist."[152] Many of the features he explores—cyclical and extended tonality, and forms of modality based on whole-tone scales and octatonic sets—are also to be found in the works of Claude Debussy. However, because Sibelius appears to have been unfamiliar with his music until 1905 at the earliest,[153] Howell attributes them to "their independent absorption of Wagnerian influence."[154] The influence of Richard Wagner on both composers is genuine enough, yet the harmonic characteristics singled out by Howell have analogies in the Russian tradition, too. Thus any similarities between the ways in which Sibelius and Debussy handle the relationship between modality, harmony, and long-range structure may well be related to the impact of Russian music, and when contemporary critics heard echoes of the French impressionists in Sibelius, they were most likely responding to a shared Russian influence, albeit at one remove. In both France and Finland, composers exploited the means revealed to them by Russian composers to establish new means of tonal organization and symphonic syntax quite unlike the schemes inherited from the Austo-German tradition. And in each case, the legacy of nationalism drove the search for new forms, establishing the Franco-Russian axis (taking in, of course, Helsinki) as the leading instance of modernity around the turn of the century.[155]

A prominent theme in the secondary literature on Sibelius has been his use of mediant relations both as a means of effecting modulations at the local level and as an approach to structuring symphonic form more profoundly. Of the third movement of *Kullervo*, Tawaststjerna notes that "the central key relationship, F–C-sharp–F, a major third, provides a strong form-building factor. In many later symphonies similar relationships play a decisive role."[156] In the First Symphony, Goss notes "the fluid interplay between keys a mere third apart: E minor and G major in the first movement; E-flat major and C minor in the second; and C major and A minor in the fourth."[157] In that same work's finale, Murtomäki similarly notices the importance of mediant modulation: "In the recapitulation the second theme wanders around in thirds and descends through the series A-flat major–F minor/F major–D-flat major/B-flat minor–G-flat major/E-flat minor–B major before settling on the dominant of the main key."[158] Layton traces "the considerable tonal freedom" in *En saga* to its use of mediant relations: "The work opens in A minor and ends in E-flat minor, its furthermost pole, while the most important key area of the work is C minor and its relative major, E-flat major."[159] Sibelius's own claim that the *Lemminkäinen* Suite was a symphony in all but name is corroborated by Howell's observation that, whatever the order in which the movements are played, the mediant relationships between them lends the suite an overall sense of formal unity:

The overall key-scheme, considering later concerns for a tonal cycle operating over an entire work, would support the symphonic view: E-flat major–A minor–F-sharp minor–(C minor)/E-flat major, displaying minor-third relationship which so often characterize internal key schemes of the component pieces. Ironically, it is the original order of the movements which would make this more schematic: E-flat–F-sharp–A–(C)/E-flat.[160]

Now, it cannot be claimed that the prominence of such key relationships in Sibelius derives solely from the Russian context. As Murtomäki observes, such canonical works of the Austro-German tradition as Brahms's Second Symphony and Beethoven's Ninth also employ aspects of mediant tonality.[161] In Sibelius's Second Symphony, Murtomäki suggests that "the tonal progression D major–F-sharp minor–A major . . . which resembles obviously the three-key exposition developed by Schubert,"[162] and also that "the influence of Liszt may have served as a starting point."[163] Liszt and especially Schubert were, of course, held in high regard by Russian composers, not least for their innovations in harmonic structure. As Richard Taruskin points out, Schubert became "the godfather of the New Russian School" by dint of "the mediant progressions that are the very essence of early Romantic harmony."[164] Russian composers displayed their indebtedness to such models with little sense of restraint, evincing "a notable tendency to make the symmetry of the third relations explicit in a literal way that composers to the west normally did not exploit."[165] The first movement of Rimsky-Korsakov's Third Symphony is structured around a series of rotations through major and minor thirds, and Tchaikovsky exploited the potential of this technique in the first movement of the Fourth Symphony, which "with its key relationships of rising minor thirds (F minor–A-flat minor–C-flat major/B major–D minor–F major/minor) is one of Tchaikovsky's great inventions."[166]

As well as structuring the relationships between movements and sections, this emphasis on the interval of a third had distinct implications for the role of harmony in a work as a whole. In the Second Symphony, as Tawaststjerna points out, "rising [major] thirds often give an impression of the whole-tone scale."[167] Murtomäki sees the Third Symphony as taking this blurring of the boundaries between diatonic and the whole-tone material a stage further: "The tonal scheme of the Third Symphony forms a logical pattern centered around the axis of major thirds C–E–G-sharp/A-flat, but it also contains progressions in minor thirds as well as the tension between diatonic and whole-tone material—all elements on which the later symphonies are based."[168] As well as the whole-tone scale, mediant relations (whether in the major or the minor) are likely to lead to the creation of so-called octatonic sets—that is, modes constructed out of alternating tones and semitones. The interplay between conventional di-atonic harmony and the modal world of whole tone and octatonic scales is pursued most rigorously in the Fourth Symphony, a work in which Sibelius achieves a particularly close integration of surface melodic ges-ture, intermediate harmonic progression, and profound symphonic syntax. The opening gesture of C–D–F♯–E ushers us into a world where whole-tone scales, octatonicism, and mediant relations predominate. Writing about the first movement exposition, Tawaststjerna illustrates how the key rela-tions are derived from the opening thematic material: "a Dorian A minor —leading to a Lydian C major—then F-sharp major. Thus we see that the augmented fourth of the germinal cell is reflected in the basic tonal lay-out."[169] This process is further played out at the level of the symphony as a whole, with the four movements unfolding in the order: A minor– F major–C-sharp minor–A major.

Tawaststjerna suggests that "this tension between tonality as a structural force and whole-tone textures was typical of the time, and part of the wider erosion of major-minor classical tonality."[170] He even alludes to po-tential parallels in the Russian musical world: the Coronation Scene from Modest Musorgsky's *Boris Godunov* and Alexander Scriabin's *Prometheus* chord.[171] Yet the notion that Sibelius's explorations in non-diatonic forms of harmonic procedure might have explicitly Russian roots seems barely to have been considered. Elliott Antokoletz, in one of the most detailed studies of such elements of the Fourth Symphony, suggests that the simi-larities are indicative of affinity rather than influence: "Sibelius's general use of semi-functional diatonic folk modes and their cyclic-interval (whole-tone and, as we shall also see, octatonic) transformations reveals an affinity more with the melodic-harmonic palette of his folk-inspired contempo-raries (e.g. Bartók and Stravinsky) than with the ultrachromaticism of nineteenth-century Romantic composers."[172] Joseph Kraus makes a passing comparison between the use of the octatonic set in the Fourth Symphony and "'magical' music from 19th-century Russian opera, particularly Glinka's *Ruslan and Lyudmila*." It is, he conjectures, "as if some distant musical memory from Sibelius's exposure to the St. Petersburg circle has now been refashioned by the composer into music so very much his own."[173] But Sibelius was alert to far more than the formal potential of Russian-inspired harmonic procedures, having also discerned what one might term the "semiotic" potential of octatonicism and whole-tone scales. Going back to Glinka, and the music for Chernomor in *Ruslan and Lyudmila*, these tech-niques had been used by Russian composers to evoke the otherworldly and the fantastic, reaching their apogee in Stravinsky's Russian ballets. In the case of Sibelius, the associative implications of this musical language are explored most resolutely in iconic works dealing with the Finnish landscape and mythology, such as *Luonnotar* or *Tapiola*. Having learned not only what Russian music sounded like, but also what it meant (to both composers and audiences), Sibelius was able to employ its techniques to evoke similar associations with the pagan and the primitive in Finnish culture.[174]

In the case of the Fourth Symphony, though, the suggestion of links to the fantastic realm of the Russian and Finnish folk imagination seems altogether more singular. After all, it is the uncompromising severity, austerity, and purity of this work that has long served as evidence of Sibelius's commitment to some form of musical modernism. Yet there is evidence that the work was not conceived as the ultimate expression of absolute symphonic form. In the wake of its first performance in April 1911, the critic Karl Fredrik Wasenius asserted that the Fourth Symphony depicted a journey to Mount Koli and Lake Pielinen.[175] Sibelius publicly denied this account, although it is possible that this was due to Wasenius having revealed the initial inspiration behind what was a very private composition. But even without the knowledge that Sibelius and his brother-in-law Eero Järnefelt had indeed visited Mount Koli and Lake Pielinen in September 1909, the Fourth Symphony betrays the influence of one of Sibelius's own explicitly programmatic and folkloric works. Tawaststjerna traces the symphony's use of modal elements and the interval of an augmented fourth/diminished fifth to similar instances in the much earlier *Kullervo*, as well as suggesting that "its opening bars give the . . . impression of entering Tuonela" (the realm of the dead in Finnish mythology).[176] But the decisive parallel is with *Pohjola's Daughter*, which, he argues, "anticipates the Fourth Symphony in its tonal layout":

> It has moved from G minor through B-flat to E major just as the exposition of the first movement of the Symphony moves from A minor to C major and then F-sharp. So we can see Sibelius replacing the classical tonic-dominant key relationship with a contrast based on the tritone. But the parallel between the tone poem and the Symphony goes even further. In the final group there appears a sequential motive into which the tritone is woven. These four notes anticipate the opening idea of the Fourth Symphony.[177]

The link back to *Pohjola's Daughter*, warmly received on the occasion of its premiere in St. Petersburg as a work with profound links to the Russian traditions, allows us to posit the Fourth Symphony as a work similarly related to those traditions. Sibelius's profound assimilation of Russian influences extends far beyond programmatic tone poems on a nationalist theme to symphonic structures that appear, initially at least, to have little in common with that school. The recognition that works as original as the

Fourth Symphony and *Tapiola* build on techniques inherited much earlier likewise suggests that works such as the Fifth Symphony, in which "all movements are based on axial tonality, and both minor and major third axis are exploited equally,"[178] and the Sixth Symphony, whose modal tonality is characterized by whole-tone and tritonal inflections,[179] also belong to this genealogy. What Sibelius learned from Russian music was not so much its ability to convey psychological narrative or evoke place through ethnographic detail (witness his horror at Wasenius's claim to know the supposed topographical inspiration for the Fourth Symphony), but rather its capacity for suggesting the hidden yet palpable forces at work in the natural world. Much as he was a composer shaped by modernity, he was also keenly aware of the lingering presence of the premodern, the primitive, and the pagan; the subjective and highly personal perception of this presence forms the subject matter of many of his works—even one as apparently abstract as the Fourth Symphony—and constitutes his most significant debt to Russian models.

Russia was more than just a productive influence on the formal and technical means available to Sibelius; it also served as a salutary warning about the potentials and perils of musical nationalism. From the outset, critics had discerned the influence of Tchaikovsky in many of Sibelius's works. In Finland, this could often be a sign of admiration, as in Karl Flodin's review of the *Lemminkäinen* Suite,[180] or both Flodin's and Kajanus's reaction to the Second Symphony.[181] If Sibelius was happy enough to concur with such assessments, then this was because, domestically at least, Russian music represented the search for national identity in music, as well as the latest in progress and modernity. Inspired by his friends and colleagues, he cultivated a deliberate interest in Russian music as a way of countering what he saw as Germanic conservatism and cultural superiority. His teacher at the Helsinki Music Institute, Martin Wegelius, had little time for Russian music, dismissing Tchaikovsky's *Sérénade mélancolique* as "violinistic drivel."[182] His teacher in Berlin, Albert Becker, was "the personification of musical conservatism,"[183] and writing to his fiancée from Vienna in January 1891, Sibelius offered the following summary of the views he encountered there:

> The Germans are far too conventional and do not respond in the least to new movements in either art or literature. They loathe both the French and the Russians, and one cannot talk about anything Scandinavian without trotting out the conventional nonsense about "barbarians." One cannot escape the conclusion that as far as art is concerned the Germans are finished. They could not produce an Ibsen, a Zola or a Tchaikovsky; they see everything through blinkers —and bad ones at that![184]

By signaling his belief that the German tradition had run its course, and aligning himself with the latest developments in European art in Scandinavia, France, and Russia (and note that Tchaikovsky is the only composer in his list), Sibelius was making an implicit point about the future direction of Finnish music, as well as espousing a deliberately cosmopolitan outlook. For Sibelius at this time, Russian music was to be valued not so much because it was national, but more profoundly because it was modern.

Outside of Finland, however, such comparisons took on a quite different set of connotations. If, on Sibelius's trips to Berlin and Vienna in the early 1890s, the example of Russian music had offered liberation from the Germanic conservatism and the validation of his vocation as a composer of Lisztean tone poems, then subsequent visits to Continental Europe revealed to him the perils of nationalism. As Hepokoski argues:

> From Sibelius's point of view, the most galling problem was one of reception. The European public that he had hoped to address (the public concerned with legitimating and institutionalizing "modernism" in the arts) had repeatedly refused to perceive his more recent symphonic works in categories commensurate with his musical thought. Listeners and critics—with the influential Walter Niemann perhaps first among them—had often collapsed him into a mere "nationalist," an epigone of Tchaikovsky and the Russians, the exotic composer of the cold North, and so on.[185]

Sibelius's perception of these anxieties was particularly acute during his trip to Paris in 1900. He was accompanying the Helsinki Philharmonic Orchestra on its European tour during a period of intense Russification in the wake of the February Manifesto, and nationalist rhetoric in the Finnish party ran high. Finland had gained its own pavilion at the Universal Exposition in Paris only after considerable effort and intrigue.[186] Aware that France and Russia were political allies (having signed an *entente* in 1894 against the triple alliance of Germany, Austro-Hungary, and Italy), Sibelius seems to have suspected Russian involvement everywhere:

> Would you believe it, but they have printed *Russie* on the concert tickets! That will now be crossed out and they will put *Finlande*. Kajus [i.e., Kajanus] was here this morning and said he was worried about this. One notices Russia's influence here in all sorts of ways, we've had difficulties in getting rehearsal time at the Trocadéro. They constantly make difficulties and keep on altering times. [Aino] Ackté has

been a tireless organizer. Well, we'll see what will happen to our concerts: I am very curious. The pro-Russian papers are bound to heap abuse on us, above all me as I am so nationalistic.[187]

In fact, French reaction to his music appears to have been largely positive, and sympathy for the Finnish cause was palpable.[188]

For all that Sibelius's patriotism was stirred by being in Paris, the tour may also have caused him to reflect on his reception as a nationalist composer, particularly as he tried to establish a reputation as a symphonist in Germany. As he strove to develop a more abstract and supposedly "universal" musical language from the early 1900s onward, recurrent references to other nationalist traditions—usually Russian, but also in the form of comparisons with Edvard Grieg—constituted both an affront to his Finnish patriotism, and a failure to understand his most recent development as an artist. As Hepokoski maintains:

> Under such categories, all of which had permitted those employing them to consign his music to the periphery, Sibelius's more recent music—puzzling in its acerbic character, markedly strained, and decidedly "difficult"—was subject not only to be radically misconstrued but also, in practice, to be casually dismissed.[189]

The very nationalism that had been so central to establishing Sibelius's reputation both at home and abroad, simultaneously threatened to confine him to a critical ghetto from which it would be all but impossible to escape. Such had been the fate of Russian music a decade or so before: the Universal Exposition of 1889 had done much to introduce French audiences to Russian composers, and in the intervening years, Russian music came to enjoy considerable prominence in concert programs throughout Western Europe.[190] Yet, as the case of Tchaikovsky demonstrates, even where Russian composers aspired to the techniques and standards of the European mainstream (as Sibelius himself did), they were frequently judged as exotic, barbaric, and quasi-Oriental. Whether his journeys through Continental Europe had alerted him to this phenomenon or not, Sibelius's reactions to composers from other nationalist traditions certainly suggest that he wished to learn from—and even distance himself from—their experiences. Traveling back to Finland from Italy in May 1901, Sibelius was introduced to Dvořák. The meeting, which he described in a letter to Axel Carpelan, seems to have provoked him to reflect on the nationalist cause: Verdi, he argued, had managed to be both national and European, yet Grieg spoke in little more than a local dialect.[191] The visit of Glazunov to Helsinki in November 1910 provoked yet more intense anxiety about his own reputation. Stirred by comments in both the Finnish and European press, he confided to his diary: "Am I nothing more than a 'nationalistic' curiosity, who must rank second to any 'international' mediocrity?"[192] His sensitivities were in part provoked by his suspicion that he had been supplanted by Glazunov in Kajanus's affections,[193] but they were also clearly related to his apprehension that the reputation of any nationalist composer would hinder the reception of any works conceived in a more abstract and universal vein (such as the Fourth Symphony, on which he was then at work). If the absence of any obvious Russian influences in works dating from after, say, the Violin Concerto, bespeaks an ambivalence about the specific value of the Russian traditions, then it also demonstrates Sibelius's profound sense of unease about the nationalist project itself.

By looking toward Russia, Sibelius learned a way of using folk motives, explored the parallel forms of the symphony and the symphonic poem, refined his harmonic language, and pursued a series of highly original explorations in symphonic syntax. Russian music offered a model of how to balance the lure of nationalism, the specific, and the self-consciously provincial on the one hand, and an interest in the abstract, the general, and the universal on the other. All of this may add substantially to our understanding of Sibelius as a composer—his sources, his borrowings, and his self-fashioning as a composer. Within the more general context of Finnish history, to look at Sibelius's interest in Russian music is to tell a more complicated story of a small nation's engagement with its bigger imperial neighbor not through the well-worn narrative of resistance and rebellion but through that of a creative and often ambiguous stimulus. It may also make us rethink the role played by Russian culture in Europe around the turn of the twentieth century, when Russian literature, music, and visual arts came to enjoy a new prominence in the early phase of European modernism. Most of all, though, to talk about Sibelius and the Russian traditions is to begin to refashion our view of Russia itself—not just as exotic, Eastern, untutored, mysterious, and barbarous, all of those myths that propelled the Ballets Russes and Stravinsky's early fame in Paris and London—but also as a modern, civilized, and advanced culture, one that was well connected to and profoundly integrated with Europe's other northern realms. If we have come to accept the complexity of Sibelius's place in Finnish history, culture, and society—a complexity itself indicative of Helsinki's exemplary status as a cultural crossroads between east and west, and even north and south, rather than as an isolated and even idealized outpost of Nordic national identity—then we also need to attend more carefully to the intricacy of Russia's musical meanings in the West.

NOTES

I am grateful to Liisa Byckling, Glenda Dawn Goss, Gitta Henning, and Timo Virtanen for their invaluable help and advice with my research and for their generous hospitality in Helsinki. Unless otherwise indicated, all translations are my own.

1. Major works in this field include Matti Klinge, *Finlands historia 3: Kejsartiden* (Espoo: Schildts, 1996), and his *Keisarin Suomi*, trans. Marketta Klinge (Espoo: Schildts, 1997); and Osmo Jussila, *Suomen suuriruhtinaskunta: 1809–1917* (Helsinki: WSOY, 2004). Accessible English-language versions of some of Klinge's arguments can be found in his *Let Us Be Finns—Essays on History*, trans. Martha Gaber Abrahamsen, Mary Lomas, Mirja Lavanne, and David Morris (Helsinki: Otava, 1990); and *The Finnish Tradition: Essays on Structures and Identities in the North of Europe* (Helsinki: SHS, 1993). Jussila's monograph is available in Russian as *Velikoye knyazhestvo Finlyandskoye*, ed. A. Yu. Rumyantsev, trans. V. M. Avtsinov et al. (Helsinki: Ruslania Books Oy, 2009). In terms of Sibelius scholarship, the impact of this revisionist school can best be seen in Glenda Dawn Goss, *Sibelius: A Composer's Life and the Awakening of Finland* (Chicago and London: University of Chicago Press, 2009).

2. Glenda Dawn Goss, Preface, *The Sibelius Companion*, ed. Glenda Dawn Goss (Westport, CT: Greenwood Press, 1996), xv–xvi.

3. Aleksandr Stupel', *Yan Sibelius, 1865–1957: Kratkiy ocherk zhizni i tvorchestva* (Leningrad: Gosudarstvennoye muzïkal'noye izdatel'stvo, 1963).

4. Dmitry Hintze, "Sibelius ja venäläiset klassikot," *Kirkko ja musiikki* 14 (1944): 9–11. The contents of Hintze's review are summarized in Glenda Dawn Goss, *Jean Sibelius: A Guide to Research* (New York and London: Garland Publishing, 1998), 179.

5. See, for instance, Richard Taruskin, "Pathetic Symphonist: Chaikovsky, Russia, Sexuality, and the Study of Music," *The New Republic*, 6 February 1995, 26–40, repr. in Taruskin, *On Russian Music* (Berkeley, Los Angeles, and London: University of California Press, 2009), 76–104.

6. James Hepokoski, *Sibelius: Symphony No. 5* (Cambridge: Cambridge University Press, 1993), 4.

7. Walter Niemann, *Jean Sibelius* (Leipzig: Breitkopf & Härtel, 1917), 49.

8. Ibid., 24–25.

9. Cecil Gray, *Sibelius* (London: Oxford University Press, 1931), 187 and 181 respectively.

10. Bengt de Törne, *Sibelius: A Close-Up* (London: Faber and Faber, 1937), 98.

11. All references in the present essay are to Robert Layton's English translation of Erik Tawaststjerna's *Jean Sibelius*, 3 vols. (London: Faber and Faber, 1976, 1986, 1997).

12. Tim Howell, *Jean Sibelius: Progressive Techniques in the Symphonies and Tone Poems* (New York and London: Garland Publishing, 1989), 268–69.

13. Goss, *Sibelius*, 69–70.

14. Karl Ekman, *Jean Sibelius: His Life and Personality*, trans. Edward Birse (London: Alan Wilmer, 1936), 140.

15. Harold E. Johnson, *Sibelius* (London: Faber and Faber, 1960), 88.

16. Tawaststjerna, *Sibelius*, vol. 1, *1865–1905*, 220.

17. Derek Fewster, *Visions of Past Glory: Nationalism and the Construction of Early Finnish History* (Helsinki: Finnish Literature Society, 2006), 260.

18. James Hepokoski, "*Finlandia* Awakens," in *The Cambridge Companion to Sibelius*, ed. Daniel M. Grimley (Cambridge: Cambridge University Press, 2004), 81–94. For descriptions of the tableaux, see Tawaststjerna, *Sibelius*, 1:220–22; and Goss, *Sibelius*, 254–72.

19. Edward C. Thaden, with the collaboration of Marianna Forster Thaden, *Russia's Western Borderlands, 1710–1870* (Princeton: Princeton University Press, 1984), 4.

20. Janet M. Hartley, "The 'Constitutions' of Finland and Poland in the Reign of Alexander I: Blueprints for Reform in Russia?" in *Finland and Poland in the Russian Empire: A Comparative Study*, ed. Michael Branch, Janet M. Hartley, and Antoni Mïczak (London: School of Slavonic and East European Studies, 1995), 41–59.

21. Quoted in D. G. Kirby, ed. and trans., *Finland and Russia, 1808–1920: From Autonomy to Independence: A Selection of Documents* (London and Basingstoke: Macmillan, 1975), 14–15.

22. Ibid., 13.

23. Hartley, "The 'Constitutions' of Finland and Poland in the Reign of Alexander I," 43.

24. Ibid., 48.

25. Thaden, *Russia's Western Borderlands*, 61. On general Russian attitudes toward Finnish autonomy, see Keijo Korhonen, *Autonomous Finland in the Political Thought of Nineteenth-Century Russia* (Turku: Turun Yliopisto, 1967).

26. Fewster, *Visions of Past Glory*, 92.

27. Michael Branch, "Introduction," in *National History and Identity: Approaches to the Writing of National History in the North–East Baltic Region, Nineteenth and Twentieth Centuries*, ed. Michael Branch (Helsinki: Finnish Literature Society, 1999), 11–16.

28. Many of these institutions were associated with the transfer of the capital to Helsinki. On this, see George C. Schoolfield, *Helsinki of the Czars: Finland's Capital: 1808–1918* (Drawer: Camden House, 1996).

29. Michael Branch, "The Academy of Sciences in St. Petersburg as a Centre for the Study of Nationalities in the North-East Baltic," in Branch, *National History and Identity*, 122–37.

30. "Finno-Ugric" refers to the supposed common origin of the Finnish and Hungarian languages—a source believed by early twentieth-century linguists to be independent from the Indo-European line of Western European languages or the Slavic languages of Russia and Eastern Europe.

31. Branch, "The Academy of Sciences in St. Petersburg," 122–23.

32. Jussi Jalonen, "On Behalf of the Emperor: The Finnish Guard's Campaign to Poland, 1831," *Slavonic and East European Review* 88/3 (2010): 468–94.

33. Tuomo Polvinen, *Imperial Borderland: Bobrikov and the Attempted Russification of Finland, 1898–1904*, trans. Steven Huxley (London: Hurst & Company, 1995), 21–22.

34. Kirby, *Finland and Russia*, 35.

35. Ibid., 52.

36. Edward C. Thaden, "The Russian Government," in *Russification in the Baltic Provinces and Finland, 1855–1914*, ed. Edward C. Thaden (Princeton: Princeton University Press, 1981), 13–108.

37. Polvinen, *Imperial Borderland*, 74.

38. See, for instance, Pertti Luntinen, *F. A. Seym: A Political Biography of a Tsarist Imperialist as Administrator of Finland* (Helsinki: SHS, 1985).

39. Polvinen, *Imperial Borderland*, 225.

40. Ibid., 279.

41. For a comparative study, see Dominic Lieven, *Empire: The Russian Empire and Its Rivals* (London: John Murray, 2000).

42. Risto Alapuro, *State and Revolution in Finland* (Berkeley, Los Angeles, and London: University of California Press, 1988), 90.

43. Ibid., 89–92.

44. C. Leonard Lundin, "Finland," in Thaden, *Russification*, 355–457.

45. Ibid., 399.

46. Ibid., 403.

47. Ibid., 401.

48. Ibid., 401–2.

49. Ibid., 406.

50. Ibid., 406–7 and 422–24.

51. Kerstin Smeds, "The Image of Finland at the World Exhibitions, 1900–1992," in Peter B. MacKeith and Kerstin Smeds, *The Finland Pavilions: Finland at the Universal Expositions, 1900–1992* (Helsinki: Kustannus Oy City, 1992), 12–105.

52. For a survey of Sibelius's patriotic works, see Veijo Murtomäki, "Sibelius: Composer and Patriot," in *Sibelius Forum II: Proceedings from the Third International Jean Sibelius Conference, Helsinki, 7–10 December 2000*, ed. Matti Huttunen, Kari Kilpeläinen, and Veijo Murtomäki (Helsinki: Sibelius Academy, 2003), 328–37.

53. Ekman, *Jean Sibelius*, 189.

54. Diary entry of 3 December 1910, quoted in Tawaststjerna, *Sibelius*, vol. 2, *1904–1914*, 161.

55. Diary entry of 30 July 1914, ibid., 282.

56. For a survey of mostly literary responses, see Ben Hellman, "The Reception of Russian Culture in Finland, 1809–1917," in Branch, *Finland and Poland in the Russian Empire*, 199–213.

57. Ekman, *Jean Sibelius*, 11. For more details of Sibelius's life at this time, see Glenda Dawn Goss, ed., *Jean Sibelius: The Hämeenlinna Letters: Scenes from a Musical Life, 1874–1895* (Esboo: Schildts, 1997).

58. Goss, *Jean Sibelius: The Hämeenlinna Letters*, 20. Tawaststjerna likewise notes the influence of Tchaikovsky on Sibelius's piano miniatures: "It never occurred to him that the pianistic layout of a Chopin could give way to a new kind of keyboard sonority such as that evoked by Debussy or that one could carry the pianistic difficulties of Balakirev's *Islamey* one stage further as did Ravel in *Gaspard de la nuit*. Accordingly his mistake was to use as a model of keyboard writing something that was already at the time of its composition pretty undistinguished: the keyboard miniatures of Tchaikovsky. Poetic feeling is powerfully distilled in the smaller pieces of Schumann, Chopin and Mendelssohn but in Tchaikovsky's waltzes, mazurkas, polkas, nocturnes and songs without words it is for the most part less deeply characteristic." Tawaststjerna, *Sibelius*, 1:177.

59. John I. Kolehmainen, "When Finland's Tolstoy Met His Russian Master," *American Slavic and East European Review* 16/4 (1957): 534–41. The influence of Tolstoy in Finland was the subject of an important exhibition titled *Children of Mother Earth: Tolstoyism in the Cultural History of Finland* at the Gallen–Kallela Museum in Espoo in the summer of 2010. The catalogue is available (in Finnish only) as *Maaemon lapset: Tolstoilaisuus kulttuurihistoriallisena ilmiönä Suomessa*, ed. Tuija Wahlroos and Minna Turtiainen (Helsinki: SKS, 2010).

60. *Catalogue of the Library of Jean Sibelius* (Helsinki: Helsinki University Library, 1973), 134–36.

61. Tawaststjerna, *Sibelius*, 1:104. Elsewhere, however, Sibelius was more skeptical: "Flirting with the workers worse than currying favour with the upper class. One has to crush so much of your own potentiality. Tolstoy's views on music are not wholly sound as he does not recognize that there are differences in musicality. He is on the right lines: but he takes his argument to unreasonable lengths" (undated note, 206).

62. Letter to Aino Sibelius, 1 January 1892, ibid., 101.

63. Letter to Aino Sibelius, 19 March 1891, ibid., 82.

64. Ilkka Karttunen, ed., *Eero Järnefelt ja venäläinen realismi/Eero Järnefelt and Russian Realism* (Punkaharju: Taidekeskus Retretti, 2007).

65. In addition to the artists discussed here, see also Ben Hellman, "'He had a Special Liking for our Country. . .' Vasili Vereshchagin and Finland," in *The Unlimited Gaze: Essays in Honour of Professor Natalia Baschmakoff*, ed. Elina Kahla (Helsinki: Aleksanteri Institute, 2009), 323–49.

66. Aimo Reitala, "The *World of Art* and Finnish Artists," in *The World of Art/Mir iskusstva: On the Centenary of the Exhibition of Russian and Finnish Artists 1898*, ed. Yevgenia Petrova, trans. Kenneth MacInnes and Philip Landon (St. Petersburg: Palace Editions, 1998), 215–37.

67. Many years later, in 1923, Diaghilev considered staging Sibelius's pantomime *Scaramouche* with the Ballets Russes, although nothing came of this plan. See Tawaststjerna, *Sibelius*, vol. 3, *1919–1957,* 221.

68. Richard Taruskin, *Defining Russia Musically: Historical and Hermeneutical Essays* (Princeton: Princeton University Press, 1997), 496.

69. Tawaststjerna, *Sibelius*, 2:46–47.

70. Kajanus conducted important performances of many of Sibelius's early works abroad, including the First Symphony in Paris. Yet his relationship with his younger colleague was sometimes fraught. In 1896, they both applied for the post of Professor of Music at Helsinki University; when Sibelius was awarded the post, however, Kajanus worked behind the scenes to have the position reopened and himself appointed. See Tawaststjerna, *Sibelius*, 1:190–93.

71. Lynn Sargeant, "*Kashchei the Immortal*: Liberal Politics, Cultural Memory, and the Rimsky-Korsakov Scandal of 1905," *Russian Review* 64/1 (2005): 22–43.

72. Helena Tyrväinen, "Robert Kajanus and the 'Rimsky–Korsakov Affair,'" *Finnish Musical Quarterly* 4 (2004): 18–25.

73. Goss, *Sibelius*, 228–29.

74. Johnson, *Sibelius*, 77–78.

75. Tawaststjerna, *Sibelius*, 2:212.

76. Diary entry for 13 January 1912, ibid, 212.

77. See, for example, Marc Vignal, *Jean Sibelius* (Paris: Fayard, 2004), 268–90.

78. Undated letter to Aino Sibelius from Kristiania/Oslo, July 1900, quoted in Tawaststjerna, *Sibelius*, 1:209. Sibelius's admiration for Tchaikovsky is also recorded in de Törne, *Sibelius: A Close-Up*, 80.

79. Tawaststjerna, *Sibelius*, 1:52–53.

80. Aarre Merikanto, for instance, spent the years 1914–16 studying with Sergey Vasilenko in Moscow, unable to travel to Germany because of the war. Tim Howell, "Aarre Merikanto (1893–1958): Modernism, Methods, and Madness," in *After Sibelius: Studies in Finnish Music* (Aldershot and Burlington, VT: Ashgate, 2006), 29–55.

81. Anthony Beaumont, "Sibelius and Busoni," in *Proceedings from the First International Jean Sibelius Conference, Helsinki, August 1990,* ed. Eero Tarasti (Helsinki: Sibelius Academy 1995), 14–20.

82. Tawaststjerna, *Sibelius*, 2:53–4.

83. Ibid., 79–82.

84. See, for instance, Iv. Lipayev, "Finskaya muzïka. Ocherk (Okonchaniye—IV)," *Russkaya muzïkal'naya gazeta*, 7–14 May 1906, columns 489–95.

85. Interview with *Svenska Dagbladet*, 27 February 1923, quoted in Tawaststjerna, *Sibelius*, 3:227–28.

86. 'Kontsertï i opera,' *Russkaya muzïkal'naya gazeta*, 7 January 1907, columns 31–39. Extracts from this review are also quoted in Tawaststjerna, *Sibelius*, 2:54.

87. Siloti made a number of unauthorized cuts in his St. Petersburg performance of *Nightride and Sunrise*, and the work may also have suffered from lack of adequate rehearsal (see Tawaststjerna, *Sibelius*, 2:97). For a general survey of Russian responses, see Maria Roditeleva, "Jean Sibelius—Seen by Russian Musicians," in *Sibelius Forum: Proceedings from the Second International Jean Sibelius Conference, Helsinki, 25–29 November 1995*, ed. Veijo Murtomäki, Kari Kilpeläinen, and Risto Väisänen (Helsinki: Sibelius Academy, 1998), 174–79.

88. For a survey of Soviet responses, see Vignal, *Jean Sibelius*, 1077–80.

89. Tawaststjerna, *Sibelius*, 1:23. The influence of Tchaikovsky, along with more "Slav melancholy," is discerned in "the main idea of the D minor Romance (1896)" (ibid., 178).

90. Ibid., 37.

91. Ibid., 50.

92. Ibid., 209–10.

93. Ibid., 212.

94. Gray, *Sibelius*, 132–3.

95. Gerald Abraham, "The Symphonies," in *Sibelius: A Symposium*, ed. Gerald Abraham (London: Lindsay Drummond Limited, 1947), 14–37 (15–16).

96. Gray, *Sibelius*, 135.

97. Abraham, "The Symphonies," 18.

98. "Gray's 'discovery,' according to which Sibelius would combine small fragments into themes as opposed to the reverse procedure of the classics, has turned out to be particularly debatable." Veijo Murtomäki, *Symphonic Unity: The Development of Formal Thinking in the Symphonies of Sibelius* (Helsinki: University of Helsinki, 1993), 3.

99. Joseph Kraus, "The 'Russian' Influence in the First Symphony of Jean Sibelius: Chance Intersection or Profound Integration," in Murtomäki, *Sibelius Forum*, 142–52.

100. Eero Tarasti, "Sibelius and Europe," in Murtomäki, *Sibelius Forum*, 43–51. Specifically, Tarasti discerns parallels between the opening of *En saga* and the "triple-metre dance at the end of Rimsky-Korsakov's *Sheherezade*."

101. Veijo Murtomäki, "Sibelius's Symphonic Ballad *Skogsrået*: Biographical and Programmatic Aspects of his Early Orchestral Music," in *Sibelius Studies*, ed. Timothy L. Jackson and Veijo Murtomäki (Cambridge: Cambridge University Press, 2001), 95–138, esp. 107n57.

102. Ibid., 108. See also Murtomäki's broad survey of Russian parallels in works by Sibelius: "Russian Influences on Sibelius," in Murtomäki, *Sibelius Forum*, 153–61.

103. Tawaststjerna *Sibelius*, 2:31; Johnson, *Sibelius*, 105.

104. Igor Stravinsky and Robert Craft, *Dialogues and a Diary* (Garden City, NY: Doubleday, 1963), 164, quoted in Tawaststjerna, *Sibelius*, 2:201–2. Stravinsky's comment was occasioned by the award of the Wihuri-Sibelius Prize in 1963, which prompted him to arrange Sibelius's *Canzonetta*, op. 62a, for two clarinets, four horns, harp, and double bass.

105. Goss, *Sibelius*, 237.

106. See translator Layton's note in Tawaststjerna, *Sibelius*, 1:212.

107. The most comprehensive attempt to disprove arguments in favor of any specific Russian influence is found in Malcolm Hamrick Brown, "Perspectives on the Early Symphonies: The Russian Connection Redux," in Tarasti, *Proceedings from the First International Jean Sibelius Conference*, 21–30.

108. Robert Layton, *Sibelius*, 4th ed. (London: J. M. Dent & Sons, 1992), 3. Layton's observations were initially made in the first edition of his monograph in 1965.

109. For a list of Russian works performed in Helsinki between 1885 and 1917, see Murtomäki, "Russian Influences on Sibelius," 160–61. Murtomäki's list is based on Nils-Eric Ringbom, *Helsingfors orkesterföretag 1882–1932* (Helsinki: Helsingfors orkesterförening, 1932), 91–126.

110. Tawaststjerna, *Sibelius*, 2:146.

111. Letter to Aino Sibelius, 19 August 1894, quoted in Tawaststjerna, *Sibelius*, 1:158.

112. Pierre Vidal, "The Symphonic Poems of Jean Sibelius and the European Tradition of the Form," in Tarasti, *Proceedings from the First International Jean Sibelius Conference*, 203–7 (203).

113. Veijo Murtomäki, "'Symphonic Fantasy': A Synthesis of Symphonic Thinking in Sibelius's Seventh Symphony and *Tapiola*," in Goss, *The Sibelius Companion*, 147–63.

114. Ibid., 151.

115. David Haas, "Sibelius's Second Symphony and the Legacy of Symphonic Lyricism," in Goss, *The Sibelius Companion*, 77–94.

116. Tina K. Ramnarine, "An Encounter with the Other: Sibelius, Folk Music and Nationalism," in Murtomäki, *Sibelius Forum*, 166–73.

117. William A. Wilson, "Sibelius, the *Kalevala*, and Karelianism," in Goss, *The Sibelius Companion*, 43–60, esp. 55–56.

118. Letter to Aino Sibelius, 31 October 1891, in *Sydämen aamu: Aino Järnefeltin ja Jean Sibeliuksen kihlausajan kirjeitä*, ed. Suvi Sirkku Talas, trans. Oili Suominen (Helsinki: Finnish Literature Society, 2001), 279–80.

119. Murtomäki, "Russian Influences on Sibelius," 158.

120. Simon Parmet, *The Symphonies of Sibelius: A Study in Musical Appreciation*, trans. Kingsley A. Hart (London: Cassell, 1959), 107. Parmet's book was first published in 1955 (in Swedish).

121. Gray, *Sibelius*, 76.

122. Stupel', *Yan Sibelius*, 48.

123. Vera Aleksandrova and Elena Bronfin, *Yan Sibelius: Ocherk zhizni i tvorchestva* (Moscow: Gosudarstvennoye muzïkal'noe izdatel'stvo, 1963), 141–42.

124. Robert Layton, "Sibelius—Twenty-Five Years On," in Tarasti, *Proceedings from the First International Jean Sibelius Conference*, 106–12. The melodies transcribed by Sibelius are reproduced in Veijo Murtomäki, "Sibelius and Finnish-Karelian Folk Music," *Finnish Musical Quarterly* 3 (2005): 32–36.

125. Goss, *Sibelius*, 130.

126. See also Murtomäki's description of the Third Symphony, which links the Finnish and Russian folkloric traditions, both directly and through their treatment in symphonic works: "The youthfully energetic main theme which opens the symphony is characterized by its narrow range and its rhythmical repetitiveness. The semiquaver rhythms in particular are related to Finnish and Estonian (also Russian) folk tunes, and can be compared, for example, with the Finnish folk song 'Tuku, tuku lampaitani' as well as with the theme of the Finale of Tchaikovsky's Fourth Symphony." Murtomäki, *Symphonic Unity*, 62.

127. V. Ya. Yevseyev, *Istoricheskiye osnovï karelo-finskogo eposa*, 2 vols. (Moscow and Leningrad: Izdatel'stvo Akademii nauk, 1957–60), 1:14–16. For a modern study of the relationship between the *Kalevala* and the *bïlinï*, see Z. K. Tarlanov, *Geroi i epicheskaya geografiya bïlinï "Kalevala"* (Petrozavodsk: Petrozavodskiy gosudarstvennïy universitet, 2002). Tarlanov's study is a typological study of names of characters and locations in the two traditions, with little attempt at detailed comparative analysis other than the observation that the *Kalevala* and certain of the *bïlinï* are epic works with origins in the same geographical area and dating from roughly the same period (the analogies are made on 225–31).

128. Vsevolod Miller, *Ocherki russkoy narodnoy slovesnosti*, 3 vols. (Moscow: Sïtina, 1897–1924), 1:289–99.

129. For a study that combines both historical and typological approaches to myth and makes a great many parallels between Sibelius and Slavonic music, see Eero Tarasti, *Myth and Music: A Semiotic Approach to the Aesthetics of Myth in Music, Especially that of Wagner, Sibelius, and Stravinsky* (Helsinki: Suomen Musiikkitieteellinen Seura, 1978).

130. Murtomäki, "Sibelius's Symphonic Ballad *Skogsrået*," 97.

131 Johnson, *Sibelius*, 116.

132. Edward Garden, "Sibelius and Balakirev," in *Slavonic and Western Music: Essays for Gerald Abraham*, ed. Malcolm Hamrick Brown and Roland John Wiley (Ann Arbor: UMI Research Press; Oxford: Oxford University Press, 1985), 215–18.

133. Burnett James, *The Music of Jean Sibelius* (Madison, NJ: Fairleigh Dickinson University Press; London: Association University Presses, 1983), 64.

134. Ibid., 52.

135. This statement is omitted in Layton's English translation, and is cited here from Erik Tawaststjerna, *Jean Sibelius*, 5 vols. (Helsinki: Otava, 1965–88), 3:95; and *Jean Sibelius*, 5 vols. (Helsinki: Söderström, 1991), 3:90.

136. Goss, *Sibelius*, 300.

137. Marina Frolova-Walker, *Russian Music and Nationalism from Glinka to Stalin* (New Haven and London: Yale University Press, 2007), 140–225.

138. S. Taneyev, *Dnevniki*, 3 vols. (Moscow: Muzïka, 1981–85), 3:360.

139. Goss, *Sibelius*, 336.

140. Ibid., 336.

141. For a survey of approaches, see Timo Virtanen, *Jean Sibelius, Symphony No. 3: Manuscript Study and Analysis* (Helsinki: Sibelius Academy, 2005), esp. 109–22.

142. Goss, *Sibelius*, 339–41.

143. Ibid., 339. On the role played by Glinka's *Kamarinskaya* in the development of Russian music, see Richard Taruskin, "How the Acorn Took Root: A Tale of Russia," *19th-Century Music* 6/3 (1983): 189–212, repr. in Taruskin, *Defining Russia Musically*, 113–51; and Marina Frolova-Walker, "Against Germanic Reasoning: The Search for a Russian Style of Musical Argumentation," *Musical Constructions of Nationalism: Essays on the History and Ideology of European Musical Culture 1800–1945*, ed. Harry White and Michael Murphy (Cork, Ire.: Cork University Press, 2001), 104–22.

144. Howell, *Jean Sibelius*, 9. Howell's comment relates primarily to the First Symphony, but can be justifiably extended to later works, such as the Third Symphony discussed here.

145. James Hepokoski, "The Essence of Sibelius: Creation Myths and Rotational Cycles in *Luonnotar*," in Goss, *The Sibelius Companion*, 121–46.

146. Hepokoski, *Sibelius: Symphony No. 5*, 24. Hepokoski also suggests that repetition "asks to be perceived as an identifier of a Finnish folk ethos" (23), and that it evokes "the characteristic melodic and metric configurations of Kalevalaic recitation." Moreover, Schubert and Bruckner provide cognates "within the Austro-Germanic tradition" (24).

147. Hepokoski, "Structural Tensions in Sibelius's Fifth Symphony: Circular Stasis, Linear Progression, and the Problem of 'Traditional' Form," in Murtomäki, *Sibelius Forum*, 213–36. The "principle of teleological progress" is borrowed from Carl Dahlhaus, *Nineteenth-Century Music*, trans. J. Bradford Robinson (Berkeley: University of California Press, 1989), 307.

148. Hepokoski, "The Essence of Sibelius," 128.

149. Richard Taruskin, *Stravinsky and the Russian Traditions: A Biography of the Works through "Mavra,"* 2 vols. (Oxford: Oxford University Press, 1996), 1:951–65.

150. Howell, *Jean Sibelius*, 7–10.

151. Ibid., 108.

152. Ibid., 194.

153. As Tawaststjerna notes: "Busoni had conducted *Nuages* and *Fêtes* the previous month, and it is reasonable to assume that he showed the scores to Sibelius, since we find the latter writing to Robert Kajanus recommending him to study and perform them. This was probably the first time he had encountered an important large-scale Debussy score, and Debussy's influence, along with that of Strauss, manifests itself already in *Pohjola's Daughter*" (Tawaststjerna, *Sibelius*, 2:21). A more decisive encounter took place in 1909, when both men met in London. Writing to Axel Carpelan, he includes Debussy's latest songs and the *Nocturnes* among those works that "have all confirmed my thoughts about the path I have taken, take and have to take." Letter to Axel Carpelan, 27 March 1909, quoted in ibid., 109.

154. Howell, *Jean Sibelius*, 219.

155. On the Russian influences on French music, see Steven Baur, "Ravel's 'Russian' Period: Octatonicism in His Early Works, 1893–1908," *Journal of the American Musicological Society* 52/3 (1999): 531–92.

156. Tawaststjerna, *Sibelius*, 1:114.

157. Goss, *Sibelius*, 277.

158. Murtomäki, *Symphonic Unity*, 37.

159. Layton, *Sibelius*, 96.

160. Howell, *Jean Sibelius*, 217. As originally performed, the movements were played in the following order: "Lemminkäinen and the Maidens of the Island," "Lemminkäinen in Tuonela," "The Swan of Tuonela," and "Lemminkäinen's Return." In Sibelius's 1947 revision of the suite, the order of the middle two movements is reversed.

161. Murtomäki, *Symphonic Unity*, 50 and 52, respectively. Elsewhere, Murtomäki considers the mediant relations structuring the movements of Brahms's First Symphony. See Veijo Murtomäki, "On the Symphonic Thought and Techniques of Sibelius," in Tarasti, *Proceedings from the First International Jean Sibelius Conference*, 113–17.

162. Murtomäki, *Symphonic Unity*, 50.

163. Ibid., 52.

164. Richard Taruskin, "Chernomor to Kashchey: Harmonic Sorcery; Or, Stravinsky's 'Angle,'" *Journal of the American Musicological Society* 38/1 (1985): 72–142 (quote at 79). Much of this material is repeated in *Stravinsky and the Russian Traditions*, 1:255–306.

165. Taruskin, "Chernomor to Kashchey," 86–87.

166. Murtomäki, *Symphonic Unity*, 19.

167. Tawaststjerna, *Sibelius*, 1:245–46.

168. Murtomäki, *Symphonic Unity*, 82.

169. Tawaststjerna, *Sibelius*, 2:181.

170. Ibid., 176.

171. Ibid., 180–81 and 184.

172. Elliott Antokoletz, "The Musical Language of the Fourth Symphony," in Jackson and Murtomäki, *Sibelius Studies*, 296–321.

173. Joseph C. Kraus, "'From Fragments into Themes' Revisited: Sibelius's Thematic Process," in Huttunen, *Sibelius Forum II*, 193–210.

174. For a related study of similar harmonic progressions as an embodiment of the "uncanny" in turn-of-the-century European music (with a particular emphasis on Wagner), see Richard Cohn, "Uncanny Resemblances: Tonal Signification in the Freudian Age," *Journal of the American Musicological Society* 57/2 (2004): 285–323.

175. Tawaststjerna, *Sibelius*, 2:170–71.

176. Ibid., 175.

177. Ibid., 57.

178. Murtomäki, *Symphonic Unity*, 143.

179. Ibid., 221.

180. "His thematic structures are more closely related to the Lisztian style while the influence both of Wagner and Tchaikovsky can be discerned." Quoted in Tawaststjerna, *Sibelius*, 1:166.

181. "Kajanus, for example, observed that with his Second Symphony, Sibelius demonstrated the flexibility of the allegedly old–fashioned symphonic form, just as Tchaikovsky has done with his *Pathétique*. . . . Other critics also made comparison to earlier composers: Flodin heard in the first movement the same rejoicing of nature . . . as he heard in Wagner's *Siegfried*, while the second movement could only be compared, he believed, with the finale of the *Pathétique*." See Kari Kilpeläinen, "Introduction," in *Jean Sibelius, Symphony No. 2 in D Major, Op. 43*, ed. Kari Kilpeläinen (Wiesbaden: Breitkopf & Härtel, 2000), viii–xi.

182. Tawaststjerna, *Sibelius*, 1:39.

183. Ekman, *Jean Sibelius*, 67.

184. Letter to Aino Sibelius, 8 January 1891, quoted in Tawaststjerna, *Sibelius*, 1:87.

185. Hepokoski, "Structural Tensions in Sibelius's Fifth Symphony," 215.

186. Smeds, "The Image of Finland at the World Exhibitions," 14–23.

187. Letter to Aino Sibelius, 27 July 1900, quoted in Tawaststjerna, *Sibelius*, 1:230.

188. Helena Tyrväinen, "Sibelius at the Paris Universal Exposition of 1900," in Murtomäki, *Sibelius Forum*, 114–28; and "Helsinki–Saint Petersburg–Paris: The Franco-Russian Alliance and Finnish-French Musical Relations," *Finnish Musical Quarterly* 1 (2003): 51–59.

189. Hepokoski, "Structural Tensions in Sibelius's Fifth Symphony," 215.

190. Elaine Brody, "The Russians in Paris (1889–1914)," in *Russian and Soviet Music: Essays for Boris Schwarz*, ed. Malcolm Hamrick Brown (Ann Arbor: UMI Research Press, 1996), 157–83.

191. Vignal, *Jean Sibelius*, 312.

192. Diary entry, 14 November 1910, quoted in Tawaststjerna, *Sibelius*, 2:160.

193. Sibelius's diary of 7 March 1912 records his reaction to Kajanus's visit to Russia in March 1911: "Strange to have him here in the house. He has now gone to St. Petersburg to listen to Glazunov who is his latest love." Quoted in Tawaststjerna, *Sibelius*, 2:213.

From Heaven's Floor to the Composer's Desk:

Sibelius's Musical Manuscripts and

Compositional Process

TIMO VIRTANEN

In the summer of 1943, while in conversation with his son-in-law conductor Jussi Jalas, the seventy-seven-year-old composer Jean Sibelius is reported to have declared: "Remember that after my death all my sketches must be burned. I don't want anybody to write 'Sibelius's *letzter Gedanke*,' or the like." And, he added: "Sketches are often finer than the original. Michelangelo, for instance."[1] Even a devoted admirer such as Jalas, who dutifully took notes from his discussions with Sibelius and often quoted the composer's statements in his own writings, knew that his master's words were to be taken with a certain reservation. And, fortunately, neither of Sibelius's rather puzzling demands came to pass: the composer's sketches were not thrown into the fire after his death, nor have scholars or musicians restrained themselves from occasionally attempting to discover, speculate upon, or write about his "final thoughts," or his authorial intentions, at least as far as his music is concerned. Today, we can study Sibelius's sketches and other musical manuscripts in an attempt to determine how his compositions evolved, how he wanted his music to sound, or how his musical sources should be interpreted and his works performed. Certainly, we would not know nearly as much about Sibelius's music—or his creative process—if his wishes had been followed and his sketches burned or left unattended for some other reason.

That is not to say, however, that all of the relevant primary documents have necessarily survived intact. Sibelius burned or destroyed some of his manuscripts himself—the fate of the Eighth Symphony, for example, has provoked the most spirited discussions and conjectures in the critical literature—and other sources are lost or otherwise unavailable.[2] In addition, there may be external factors that have determined the varying number of manuscript sources that have survived. For example, there are significantly fewer manuscripts preserved from works completed before 1904, when Sibelius moved to his villa, Ainola, than from the period following that date. Before 1904, Sibelius changed his address frequently (he had ten residences in Helsinki alone), and he evidently did not always transfer all of his papers from an old address to the new. We have, for instance, the following recollections of a Kerava girl who lived next door to the composer at one of the three residences (two in Helsinki, and one in nearby Kerava) where Sibelius stayed during the composition and revision of the First Symphony: "A laundry-basket full of music and writings was left" in Sibelius's apartment after his move back to Helsinki, which the housekeeper "Mrs. Jokela said would have made her rich, if she had saved them."[3] Despite such losses, the number of surviving Sibelius manuscripts is impressive. In 1982, the Sibelius heirs donated the entire manuscript collection from Ainola to the University of Helsinki Library (since 2006 known as the National Library of Finland), and in his annotated catalogue, Sibelius scholar Kari Kilpeläinen lists around 2,000 manuscript units of various sizes and type (though the total manuscript pages must reach well beyond that number). The primary materials offer both scholars and performers a rich and fruitful field for research.[4]

The largest number of manuscripts that have survived are most commonly those associated with Sibelius's large-scale—typically orchestral—works, dating especially from the Ainola years after 1904. He often worked on these projects over a lengthy period of time, or revised such works thoroughly so that they exist in two or more different versions. A typical example is the Violin Concerto, op. 47, with its two versions dating from 1904 and 1905, or the Fifth Symphony, op. 82, which Sibelius revised twice after the premiere of the original version in 1915 (the first revision is from 1916 and the final revision 1919). Other works that left behind an unusually extensive amount of sketch material include the symphonic fantasy *Pohjola's Daughter*, op. 49 (1906), the Third Symphony, op. 52 (1907), and the Seventh Symphony, op. 105 (1924). But, surprisingly perhaps, some of the works with substantial amounts of manuscript material were not very large-scale or "complicated" symphonic pieces; a good example of this latter category is *Cassazione*, op. 6 (1904), a work of about ten minutes' duration that exists in versions for full orchestra and smaller ensemble. The existence of two different versions does not really explain the astonishingly large number of sketches that have survived for this piece. It is more likely that material for the work was gathered and developed over several years, and that Sibelius was working on several different projects simultaneously at the beginning of the century.[5]

The fundamental problem in sketch studies is that we can never be sure whether the manuscript material for a certain work has survived in its entirety, or whether some of the sources—perhaps a large number, or even the majority of them—are lost. Drawing conclusions merely from the number of manuscripts available therefore always contains a seed of doubt and uncertainty. For instance, it may often be tempting to think that because a large number of sketches survive for a particular piece the work must have been especially troublesome or laborious for the composer. This is not necessarily the case: there may be other circumstantial reasons why an exceptional number of manuscripts survived. Among possible explanations, extensive sketch material could result from a lengthy compositional process with several interruptions caused, for instance, by traveling or work on other projects (meaning that the composer had to gather and collect his thoughts repeatedly by rewriting sketches when returning to the old material)—or possibly even from the relatively trivial concern that the composer was not always able to locate the right sketch pages when returning to his daily work and had to rewrite some passages before carrying on from where he had left off. More revealing than the number of (existing) manuscripts, therefore, are the characteristics of the sketches themselves. A single surviving sketch page for a certain work can sometimes be more revealing than tens of pages for another project. And this certainly appears to be the case for some of Sibelius's music.

Manuscript Types and Compositional Process

In his memoirs titled "The Master of Järvenpää," Sibelius's secretary, Santeri Levas, recalled that "Sibelius once mentioned that writing sketches increases a composer's productivity. . . . I remembered him saying sometimes that unused themes from his youth become grains of gold in a later age."[6] It is clear that Sibelius constantly noted down musical ideas—usually short thematic fragments—in a routine fashion, without necessarily having any particular work in mind. Sibelius's manuscripts include a large number of pages that might be described as thematic memos. Only later would he select usable themes from among these papers and begin to elaborate on the ideas and try to fit them into more extensive passages. Very often, Sibelius would mark especially noteworthy ideas with strong (color) pencil strokes or some other type of annotation, such as *Obs!*—abbreviated from the Swedish word *observera*, meaning "observe!"—in the margins of the manuscript pages. The ideas on a particular manuscript page could then develop in diverse ways, migrating through various compositional plans, and appear in final form across several works completed over a long period of time. Unused material might very well prove to be a grain of gold in a later stage of the composer's career.

The progress and characteristics of the compositional process sometimes depended upon the genre and the scale of the particular work concerned. Smaller-scale works, such as piano miniatures and songs, often evolved without the need for extensive sketching, whereas large-scale works quite understandably required more planning and elaboration, and hence resulted in more extensive sketch material. But other characteristics of the works, or single passages within an individual piece, might also have some bearing on the number of sketches involved. For example, it appears that more sketches and drafts have survived for transitions and developmental sections than for purely thematic passages, and more materials exist for expositions than for recapitulations—the first movement of the Third Symphony (1907) is exemplary here, as we shall see below. But even for some large-scale compositions, we may have only a few surviving manuscript sources, particularly where the music is based on repeated or recurring sections—the principle that James Hepokoski has appositely described as "rotational form." No sketches whatsoever survive for the tone poem *Luonnotar*, op. 70 (1913), for example, which is largely built from two extended rotations and features no extensive developmental passages, and the surviving manuscript materials for the second movement of the Third Symphony are similarly limited.

In other cases, even short thematic statements or brief passages required numerous sketch pages. The opening theme of the first movement of the Third Symphony, for instance, has survived as dozens of sketches and drafts revealing numerous slight alterations made incrementally. As can be seen from a draft for the opening page of the movement (see Figure 1), Sibelius initially planned to begin with an entirely different thematic idea from that which appears in the final version (see the third staff). The opening theme as we know it today is largely based on a series of scalar progressions, whereas the initial idea for the opening, with its ascending open fifths, was closer to the rugged opening theme of the slow movement of the Fourth Symphony.[7] Astonishingly, this "fifth motive"— notated in ink—was from the outset already followed by material familiar from the opening passage in its final form (see measure 3ff in Figure 1). In this draft it can also be seen how the opening's definitive thematic idea—notated in pencil above and partly over the "fifth motive"—eventually found its way into its final position in the score.

Sketches and drafts often contain evidence of Sibelius's intense self-criticism, including deleted or erased passages, comments or instructions, and other dos and don'ts, such as *meilleur, besser, bättre* (French, German, and Swedish words for "better") or *längre* (Swedish for "longer" or "more

Figure 1.

extended"). Other times the manuscript pages reveal moments of conviction or contentment, expressed, for example, with the words *soll* or *soll sein* (shall be). The same French and German phrases occur in Beethoven's sketchbooks, and it is interesting to speculate how consciously Sibelius may have emulated the working pattern of such a canonic figure, whose methods had attracted particular attention thanks to Gustav Nottebohm's studies, published shortly before Sibelius studied in Berlin and Vienna in the early 1890s.

Typically, Sibelius's thematic sketches and more extensive (continuity) drafts were notated on a pair of staves (as in Figure 1) and comprise a melodic line with occasional bass notes or chordal "accompaniments." Sibelius often outlined extensive passages, including entire sections of a sonata form movement, in such continuity drafts. At this stage, the composer's view of the composition as a whole and the materials belonging to that particular work could still be far from fixed, and materials occurring harmoniously together in a certain draft could still find their way into a different piece later. Among the manuscript materials for the first movement of the Third Symphony, there is a two-page draft that begins with the "fifth motive" described above (Figure 2a, staves 1–2). Then, after four measures, material familiar from the opening of the movement appears in its final form (staves 1–8, exclusive of the empty staves). This passage leads to one presenting an idea that later appeared in the tone poem *Pohjola's Daughter* (the crossed-out staves). After another intermediate passage featuring an entirely new thematic idea (Figure 2b, staves 1–2), a repetition of the aborted "fifth idea" from the opening page (staves 3–4, exclusive of empty staves), and *forte* material heard in the horns during the first movement's exposition (staves 9–10), the music leads to a passage that we now recognize from the second movement of the String Quartet in D Minor, *Voces intimae*, op. 56 (Figure 2b, final four staves).[8] To summarize, in addition to the Third Symphony, the materials included on the two pages of the folio refer to three other works completed during the years 1906 to 1911, namely:

Pohjola's Daughter, *Voces intimae*, and, more distantly, the Fourth Symphony. One of the other ideas contained in this draft does not appear in any work known today. This complex overlayered amalgam of ideas is hardly rare among Sibelius's manuscript pages and is an illustrative example of his general compositional working routine.

Figure 2a.

Figure 2b.

The Case of *Cassazione*

In his biography of the composer, Erik Tawaststjerna discusses the inter-connections between the sketch materials for the Fifth, Sixth, and Seventh symphonies in some detail.[9] The manuscript sources for the Third Symphony similarly reveal connections with at least six other pieces, finished either before the symphony or following its completion.[10] The situation with *Cassazione*, however, is even more complex: twelve pieces in total have some material connection with the work. These pieces were completed over the course of a decade, covering approximately the period between the First and Fourth symphonies respectively (c. 1899–1910).[11] Figure 3a shows a draft that begins with material from the closing Allegro moderato section of *Cassazione* (originally in A minor, but transposed to C minor in the final version of the work). Following the opening measures, a new folksong-like thematic idea appears on staves 3 and 4 that originates from the time of the composition of the First Symphony.[12] This idea did not anchor itself in *Cassazione*, but appears five years later in the piano piece "Air varié," op. 58, no. 3 (1909).[13] And even here, the material associated with *Cassazione* is unrelated to the first version of the work (for full orchestra), but belongs rather with the later version (for small orchestra).[14]

The fragments in a further source (manuscript HUL 1585 in the Finnish National Library) illustrate the complex network of ideas associated with different compositions—originally intended for a single work— in an even more compact form than the pages from the source materials for the Third Symphony discussed above. The sketch (Figure 3b) opens with an idea— helpfully labeled "a" by the composer himself—that later appears in the Funeral March of *In memoriam* from 1909: on one of Sibelius's manuscript pages, this idea has been subtitled *Memento mori*. This idea is followed by "b," a short passage appearing in *Pohjola's Daughter*, and still later a trill idea familiar from *Cassazione* itself, "c." The same materials appear in a different order further down the page (staves 6 and 7, crossed out).

Figure 3a.

Following an empty staff, and not directly connected with these fragments, Sibelius has notated a sketch for the scene "Trois soeurs aveugles" (Three blind sisters) from his incidental music to Maurice Maeterlinck's play *Pelléas et Mélisande*, op. 46 (1905).

If the origins of *Cassazione* are at least indirectly connected with the compositional genesis of the First Symphony, Fig 3b illustrates a much later stage of the compositional process related to the work.[15] The draft shown in Figure 3c (HUL 0272, p. 1) opens with a fanfare-like idea, and the following measures contain material that eventually appeared in the opening movement, "Die Jagd" (The hunt), of the orchestral suite *Scènes historiques II*, op. 66 (1912). Staves 3 and 4 subsequently present the Allegro moderato theme from *Cassazione* (see also Figure 3a).

Thus *Cassazione*, a relatively neglected work which is seldom performed today and which Sibelius himself left unpublished, appears to be a key stage in the developing network of his compositional plans over a period of nearly fifteen years.[16] If we consider the way in which the folksong-like

Figure 3b. Note "a," "b," and "c" at the top.

Figure 3c.

idea from the manuscripts for the First Symphony, the "fifth motive" from the manuscripts for the Third, and the *Cassazione* ideas migrated through several compositional drafts and finally appeared (in slightly modified form) in the piano work "Air varié," *In memoriam*, the slow movement of the Fourth Symphony, and the opening number from *Scènes historiques II*, some sense of the complex interrelationships between Sibelius's music from the final years of the nineteenth century and his modernist highwater mark in 1911–12 can be gained. *Cassazione* hence suggests the existence, at some level, of a meta-work, a schematic creative project that underpins many of the pieces from this period, much as the themes and ideas in his 1914–15 sketchbook do for the late works from the Fifth Symphony through *Tapiola*. Furthermore, the mobility of Sibelius's working process neatly explodes any idea of the autonomous artwork, regardless of the apparently "absolute" quality of his symphonic works.

Orchestral Drafts, Fair Copies, and Later Revisions

In the case of Sibelius's orchestral music, early drafts on two staves were frequently followed by more detailed instrumental drafts and score fragments. According to Levas:

> [Sibelius] heard his music already orchestrated. Most composers first make a piano draft of their work and then arrange it for the orchestra. Sibelius never did that. He wrote directly in full score bar-by-bar. Once, in the early days, I asked whether he ever had to consider which instrument he needed to use in a particular context. "Never," replied Sibelius without a moment's hesitation. "My music is already arranged. The actual work of instrumentation is therefore entirely foreign to me. I allow the musical thoughts to speak for themselves."[17]

This anecdote certainly does not tell the truth, at least in every case. Sibelius's drafts reveal that there were often moments of hesitation in his compositional work, including matters of instrumentation, and that he could indeed change his mind regarding the orchestration of a particular passage, sometimes even drastically.[18]

For Sibelius, the term *fair copy* rarely refers to a definitive, neatly written score. He very often made extensive revisions to his fair copies, and sometimes a manuscript that was clearly intended as a final version turned out to be only a complete draft and had to be written out once again. An early version of the entire second movement of the Third Symphony has survived in this form. Judging from markings in the manuscript, Sibelius sent the score to a copyist, who began to prepare orchestral parts from the score, but then decided to revise the movement. He added plans for the final version to the manuscript in pencil and then revised the score—while also changing the instrumentation considerably.[19]

Sibelius similarly made revisions to many of his works after their first performance. The most well-known cases are *En saga*, op. 9; "Lemminkäinen and the Maidens of the Island" and "Lemminkäinen in Tuonela" from the four *Lemminkäinen* Legends, op. 22; the Violin Concerto; and the First and Fifth symphonies. He also planned to revise other works, such as the orchestral ballade *Skogsrået* (*The Wood Nymph*) op. 15, and *Cassazione*, but never realized his intentions. Sibelius's eagerness in such cases to return to earlier compositions and revise them has strongly challenged the idea of a definitive version (or *Fassung letzter Hand*), and the author's copies of his own scores sometimes contain additions and changes made many years after publication.[20] In addition to the early version of the Third Symphony's second movement, the current critical edition, Jean Sibelius

Works (JSW) has already published more than twenty previously unpublished (early) versions of Sibelius's compositions, including the 1892 version of *En saga*.

Manuscripts and "Profound Logic"

In his discussion of Sibelius's working methods, Levas further recalled how the composer "emphasized that he only wrote music which he had already heard in advance in its final form."[21] There often appears to be an assumption that a composer's compositional work proceeds in a strictly linear fashion, beginning with an overall idea, or a mental "image" of the work as a whole, and then striving toward the faithful execution of that "image" through a logical, linear chain of events. The compositional process thus constructs larger formal units from smaller fragments or ideas, ideally by following the principles of "motivic development" (or "organic variation") to ensure the ultimate cohesion (or "unity") of the final composition. In Sibelius's case, however, there is no evidence to support this kind of procedure, at least if we consider the genesis of his large-scale orchestral works. On the contrary, sketch studies of Sibelius's larger pieces have revealed that he did not always have a clear picture of the work in its entirety at the outset of the compositional process, nor, in many cases, for an extended period of its genesis, and that he took final decisions concerning the form and thematic content of a work only after a series of unsuccessful attempts at completion. This also means that, typically, the compositional process was not a linear or goal-oriented evolutionary progression but a more seemingly unforeseeable or improvisatory process, in which one step forward could be followed by two—or sometimes even three—steps back. Sibelius did not, in fact, construct his works from small motives by propagating or developing them "organically." On this point alone, Sibelius's comments, as reported by Levas, seem to correspond with the evidence supplied by sketch studies of the sources themselves:

> Cecil Gray and many other writers after him have explained that Sibelius first presents his motives as small fragments, and then, as the work proceeds, arranges them into an actual theme. Once, in the autumn-winter of 1950, when this issue came up in discussion, Sibelius stated quite categorically: "It is not true at all. I do not build my themes from fragments."[22]

In the light of more recent scholarship, we can see that Sibelius was not a composer who cultivated his large-scale works systematically from a few small motivic cells into larger "symphonic" constructions. Rather, the compositional process seems to have been a question of selecting and then weaving together the right components from a rich tapestry or network of diverse threads. The issue was one of assembling a continuous large-scale form from thematic material that was compiled over many years, and was never initially intended to be used in a single, specific work. In his analytical study of the first movement of Sibelius's Fourth Symphony, Schenkerian theorist Edward Laufer refers to Levas's account above, and elegantly frames his conclusions about the work's structure in a way that supports the evidence supplied by sketch studies. "The themes are not built out of small fragments," Laufer explains. "Rather, different themes may be associated by their having fragments in common; that is, certain components recur in the various themes. This does not mean that all the themes are somehow the same. Like brothers and sisters in the same family, they have certain features in common—yet each theme is different and individual."[23] In his apocryphal discussion about the symphony with Gustav Mahler in 1907, Sibelius is famously reported to have declared his admiration for "the profound logic that creates an inner connection between all motives" in a symphonic work.[24] While notions of compositional logic and profundity might seem hard to sustain in our current critical environment, the phrase could perhaps be understood not in terms of creating large organisms from smaller motivic cells, but rather as the way in which such "profound logic" manifests itself in assembling a sense of continuity from a rich variety of ideas. One essence of Sibelius's mastery might thus lie in his diligence and patience in testing his ideas, and his skill in dovetailing such originally heterogenous materials through various compositional plans and processes in a way that sounds both seamless and determined.

From Composer's Desk to Scholar's Study

In a letter to the singer and pedagogue Anna Sarlin dated June 1905, Jalmari Finne wrote: "Sibelius spoke extremely beautifully about music. Among other things, he said: 'For me, music is a fascinating mosaic which God has assembled, he takes all the pieces in his hand, throws them down into the world, and we have to reconstruct the picture.'"[25] In light of the connections between different works revealed among the pages of his sketches, the study of Sibelius's manuscripts has raised what may seem like a paradoxical question: What is actually meant by a sketch for a particular work? Sibelius apparently did not always have a clear picture of the identity of the piece he was working on, and so how can we, in turn, construct such an image? How can we plausibly define the work to which a certain manuscript belongs, if the materials occurring in the manuscript refer to several different compositions from across a broad timeframe? The network of ideas and materials is often highly complex, and the picture that emerges is similarly complex and multidimensional.

The quotation about God's mosaic from Jalmari Finne's 1905 letter—better known from Sibelius's diary entry of ten years later, where it relates to the composition of the Fifth Symphony—may be understood as a poetic metaphor for the composer's work, a devout mission demanding daily effort, patience, and a humble mind.[26] In terms of sketch studies, however, it can be understood in a more technical sense as describing, in a clear and concise manner, the compositional genesis of many of Sibelius's large-scale works. During the creative process, Sibelius's task was to discover which fragments belonged together, and in what order, and subsequently what kind of picture—or multiple pictures—lay behind the puzzle of the mosaic pieces themselves. Sketch studies reveal that, in many cases, Sibelius's mosaic pictures could have taken a very different form from those we are familiar with today, and that many of his works represent only one possible realization from among a variety of potential combinations suggested by the ideas on the pages of his working manuscripts. Hypothetically, Sibelius could have contented himself with the first version of the Third Symphony's second movement, or with the first versions of *En saga*, the Violin Concerto, or the Fifth Symphony. Even here, it is possible that Sibelius may have remained open in certain respects to further revisions.

But Sibelius's mosaic metaphor can also be applied to sketch studies of his music as an entire subdiscipline. Just as Sibelius worked with individual mosaic tiles as a composer, so a source scholar works with the manuscript materials Sibelius left behind as his creative legacy. The composite impression of the genesis of his works created on the basis of the fragmentary sketches and drafts that survive in the Finnish archives and elsewhere inevitably remains open to differing perceptions, perspectives, and critical revisions. Comprehensive readings or definitive versions exist even less in the field of sketch studies than in a composer's oeuvre. However, while admitting that our mosaic image of a particular work will always necessarily remain incomplete, our understanding of that work should always be grounded in its compositional history, from some perspective of the ideas that the composer notated in their manuscript pages, and in the creative decisions that he or she made en route.

NOTES

1. Jussi Jalas's notes from conversations with Sibelius, dated 17 July and 27 August 1943, respectively. Sibelius Family Archive, Box 1, National Archives of Finland, Helsinki. We do not know the broader context for these statements, nor is their meaning entirely clear: by "original" Sibelius probably meant the completed, final score text, but his reference to a *letzter Gedanke* (final thought) remains open to interpretation.

2. For instance, Sibelius reported to his copyist that he had lost the autograph score of *Finlandia* in Berlin—possibly on a train—in November 1900. The copyist had to reconstruct a new score copy from the orchestral parts. This copy, which obviously served as the engraver's copy, is lost as well. See Fabian Dahlström, *Jean Sibelius: Thematisch–bibliographisches Verzeichnis seiner Werke* (Wiesbaden: Breitkopf & Härtel, 2003), 113–14. For the Eighth Symphony, see Erik Tawaststjerna, *Jean Sibelius*, vol. 5, *1919–1957* (Helsinki: Otava, 1988), 336–37.

3. Hilli Jokela, cited in Vesa Sirén, *Aina poltti sikaria: Jean Sibelius aikalaisten silmin* (Helsinki: Otava, 2000), 176.

4. Kari Kilpeläinen, *The Jean Sibelius Musical Manuscripts at Helsinki University Library* (Wiesbaden: Breitkopf & Härtel, 1991). The Sibelius manuscript collection in the National Library has expanded further since 1982, with several donations and acquisitions. In addition, manuscripts are preserved in other archives, such as the Sibelius Museum (Turku, Finland) and the Sibelius Academy (Helsinki), and in private collections.

5. For discussion of an interesting smaller-scale example, see Jukka Tiilikainen's study of the song "Dolce far niente," op. 61, no. 6, in "The Evolution of Jean Sibelius's Songs as Seen in His Musical Manuscripts," *Sibelius Forum II: Proceedings from the Third International Jean Sibelius Conference, Helsinki, 7–10 December 2000*, ed. Matti Huttunen, Kari Kilpeläinen, and Veijo Murtomäki (Helsinki: Sibelius Academy, 2003), 39–49.

6. Santeri Levas, *Järvenpään mestari* (Porvoo–Helsinki: Werner Söderström, 1960), 242. Levas (1899–1987) worked as Sibelius's secretary from 1938 until the composer's death in 1957.

7. See the fifths C–G and A♭–E♭ in mm. 1–2, as well as their continuation (the ascent E♭–F–G) in measure 2. The "fifth motive" also appears in connection with sketches for the funeral march *In memoriam*, op. 59 (1909).

8. At the bottom of the first page, on the two last staves, Sibelius has written an annotation in Swedish: "*Vidare med detta motiv*" (further with this motive) as a reminder or instruction to himself.

9. Erik Tawaststjerna, *Sibelius*, vol. 3, *1919–1957*, trans. Robert Layton (London: Faber and Faber, 1997), 15–31. See also Kari Kilpeläinen, "Sibelius's Seventh Symphony: An Introduction to the Manuscript and Printed Sources," in *The Sibelius Companion*, ed. Glenda Dawn Goss (Westport, CT: Greenwood Press, 1992).

10. Besides the pieces mentioned above, these works include *Valse triste*, op. 44a (1905) from Sibelius's incidental music to Arvid Järnefelt's play *Kuolema*, *Kyllikki;* Three Lyric Pieces for Piano, op. 41 (1906); and the first movement, "Die Jagd" (The hunt), from the orchestral suite *Scènes historiques II*, op. 66 (1912).

11. In addition to the two symphonies (nos. 1 and 4), the ten other compositions linked with the material for *Cassazione* are the Violin Concerto; *Cortège*, JS 54 (1905); *Pohjola's Daughter*; the song "Aus banger Brust," op. 50, no. 4 (1906); the "Dance Intermezzo" *Pan and Echo*, op. 53 (1906); the Third Symphony; the piano pieces "Air varié" and "Ständchen," op. 58, nos. 3 and 9 (completed in 1909); *In memoriam*; and "Die Jagd."

12. It is possible that Sibelius planned to open the First Symphony with the folksong-like theme. In one of the drafts for the symphony, the final slow introduction material for the solo clarinet is preceded by this thematic material (in G minor), with the tempo indication Allegro moderato.

13. This idea also occurs in sketches connected with the song "Aus banger Brust" and the piano piece "Ständchen."

14. According to previous assumptions (see, for instance, Jean Sibelius, *Dagbok 1909–1944*, ed. Fabian Dahlström [Helsinki: Atlantis, 2005], 20), Sibelius reworked the version for small orchestra in 1905. However, Sibelius's markings in the orchestral parts of that version alongside correspondence with his wife reveal that both versions of *Cassazione* were completed in 1904.

15. The connection with the Fourth Symphony is revealed in a sketch where *Cassazione* materials appear alongside the chorale-like idea heard for the first time in measure 159ff in the finale of the Symphony.

16. It should be added that Sibelius returned to the (unpublished) *Cassazione* materials as late in his compositional career as 1926, when he used the hymn-like passage from the work as the closing Epilogue of his incidental music to Shakespeare's play *The Tempest* (see Daniel M. Grimley's chapter in this volume).

17. Levas, *Järvenpään mestari*, 242.

18. According to a note by Jalas, dated 19 May 1940 (Box 1, Sibelius Family Archive, National Archive of Finland), Sibelius explained that "the tuba suddenly fell out of my imagination after the Second Symphony. I do not hear it anymore." The composer evidently failed to remember that he had in fact used the instrument in several works following the symphony, including *Pohjola's Daughter*, the tone poem *Night Ride and Sunrise*, op. 55 (1908), and *In memoriam*.

19. The early version of the movement has been published as an appendix in the critical edition of the symphony (Jean Sibelius Works, 1/4, ed. Timo Virtanen, 2009).

20. All of the available early versions, selected drafts, sketches, and other manuscripts for Sibelius's works will be published in volumes of the ongoing critical edition of his oeuvre.

21. Levas, *Järvenpään mestari*, 384.

22. Ibid., 243.

23. Edward Laufer, "On the First Movement of Sibelius's Fourth Symphony: A Schenkerian View," in *Schenker Studies* 2, ed. Carl Schachter and Hedi Siegel (Cambridge: Cambridge University Press, 1999), 127–59, quote at 141.

24. Sibelius's discussion with Mahler was first documented in Karl Ekman's biography, *Jean Sibelius: En konstnärs liv och personlighet* (Helsinki: Holger Schildts, 1935). There are no contemporary records of the details of their meeting.

25. Jalmari Finne to Anna Sarlin, 28 June 1905, PR 170, Finne Archive, National Archive of Finland.

26. For the diary entry, dated 10 April 1915, see *Dagbok*, 223.

Theatrical Sibelius:

The Melodramatic Lizard

JEFFREY KALLBERG

For nearly thirty years of his career starting around 1898, Sibelius regularly wrote music to accompany productions of staged drama. Paradoxically, his considerable engagement with the theater of his time remains obscure. On the one hand, thanks first to Sibelius's own concert suite arrangements of large portions of the music he composed for dramatic productions and, second, to the recent spate of recordings of both these concert suites and the majority of the original dramatic scores, we can listen with ease to nearly all of the remarkable music he wrote for the theater.[1] On the other hand, since the scores and recordings omit the verbal scripts, we fathom with difficulty the original function of this music.[2] The music is familiar; its theatrical contexts are not.

Modern critics most commonly index Sibelius's theatrical music against his symphonies and tone poems and mine the theatrical repertory for evidence of stylistic progress or thematic migration. And with generally wise results: one can scarcely imagine approaches to the music for *The Tempest*, say, that did not consider it as a grand and craggy culminating gesture of Sibelius's career, one to be measured against such works as the Seventh Symphony and *Tapiola* (see Daniel M. Grimley's essay in this volume). Or considering the music for *Ödlan* that will occupy us in more detail below, it is surely of crucial significance to grasp the role this dramatic music plays in the evolution of Sibelius's stylistic experiments in the "crisis" years 1908–12, and to perceive its consanguinities with *Voces intimae* and the Fourth Symphony.[3] Indeed, Sibelius's own compositional practices sometimes invite this sort of comparative reckoning: the Seventh Symphony entered into the compositional (and perhaps biographical) history of the incidental music to Arvid Järnefelt's *Kuolema* when Sibelius cited a characteristic harmonic progression from the *Tempo di valse lente* (what would become known in concert arrangement as the *Valse triste*) near the end of the symphony (mm. 518–22).

At the same time, Sibelius's choices of plays for which he agreed to compose music tell us something about his general aesthetic sympathies. That he gravitated strongly toward symbolist playwrights and plays shows the contemporary nature of his tastes. Although financial considerations and the demands of the playwrights and directors who commissioned him doubtless also factored into his decisions to write music for productions of plays by Maeterlinck, Strindberg, and Järnefelt (among others), these decisions likewise manifest his affinity with the modern—an affinity with which to reckon as we locate Sibelius and his music among the artistic trends of the early twentieth century.[4]

Sibelius provided an enormous variety of music for use in the theater. A piece like *Jedermann* (Everyman, or *Jokamies* in the Finnish translation of Hofmannsthal's play that Sibelius set in 1916) demonstrates some of this range, from brief dabs of instrumental color (the few seconds of brass and timpani playing a single chord for the entrance of a character) to the nine-minute Largo, sempre misterioso for strings and timpani that accompanies the dialogue between Good Works and Everyman. The music for *The Tempest* is replete with similar contrasts: on one side, the lengthy overture that opens the play, portraying the ship sinking beneath the waves; on the other side, the pithy orchestral outbursts that accompany Ariel's multiple entrances and exits.

Mirroring this variety in kinds of pieces that Sibelius composed for dramatic productions was a multiplicity of other kinds of compositions that should also be considered "theatrical." The majority of his efforts went toward music for multiple-act dramas staged in prominent theatres, but his melodramas, tableaux, historical "scenes," and opera (including various unrealized operatic plans) must also factor into a broader understanding of his approach to theatrical music.[5] Sibelius's repeated forays into these various kinds of theatrical works form part of a general European vogue in the early decades of the twentieth century for creative efforts that synthesized drama, music, and pictures.[6] Some of the most important repercussions of this fashion, and especially those concerned with melodrama, resonated in the nascent realm of cinema.[7]

The music Sibelius composed for use in two scenes of Mikael Lybeck's play *Ödlan* offers fascinating insight into his theatrical thinking. Having made his literary name as a novelist and poet, Lybeck started writing the play—his first—in 1907, and published it in 1908.[8] The story of *Ödlan* develops out of a triangular relationship among the main characters: Alban, the conflicted and sensitive head of the family estate; an older, sensual but viperous cousin Adla (whose name is a near homonym for the green lizard, *ödla*, found on the family crest and in the title of the play); and the innocent and virtuous Elisiv. Adla tempts Alban sexually; he initially resists, his more chaste love focusing on Elisiv and expressed largely through music (Alban is a violinist). Startled by a lizard on the porch of the estate, Elisiv falls, strikes her head, and falls into a deathly coma. Alban later briefly gives in to Adla's temptations, but when she triumphantly dons a costume that appears symbolically to represent a green lizard, he kills her and loses his mind. The dramatic burden of *Ödlan* lies largely in the play of symbols.[9] Pulled between the ethereal goodness of Elisiv (as represented through music) and the slithery cunning of Adla (signaled through lizards both real and costumed), Alban loses his grounding in reality.

Sibelius composed his music in 1909, and the play premiered at the Swedish Theatre in Helsinki on 6 April 1910.[10] Though initial reviews were favorable, the play closed after six performances, and was not revived thereafter.[11] *Ödlan* is one of the few works of Sibelius's theatrical music that does not come down to us in a rearranged concert suite: the extant manuscript score, housed in the Sibelius Museum in Åbo (Finnish: Turku), contains, as far as one can tell, what Sibelius conducted at the premiere of Lybeck's play. (The version of the score published by Fazer, and based on Sibelius's manuscript, unaccountably omits the cues that link the dialogue and stage directions with specific moments in the music.[12] Tables 1 and 2 provide the information necessary to restore these cues.) Because Sibelius never stripped the dramatic associations from the music, it remains bound to Lybeck's play and hence little known. But it is precisely these associations with Lybeck and his intellectual milieu that render the score particularly valuable historically.

And just what kind of score is it? Lybeck's printed stage directions refer a few times to the playing of "the orchestra" or "the whole orchestra," but Sibelius—perhaps exercising a sense of practical stagecraft and considering the expenses related to including music in a stage production—had other ideas, writing instead for a small string ensemble.[13] Quite small: Sibelius told Lybeck that though the ensemble should preferably contain nine players, it could be reduced to as few as six.[14] A penciled annotation in Sibelius's hand on the title page suggests seven performers—2 first violins, 1 second violin, 1 viola, 2 violoncelli, 1 contrabass—played in the premiere. Contrary opinions that Sibelius intended the piece for a string orchestra look at the instrument headings in the score, which use the plural forms "Alti" and "Celli," an article about the play published the day of the premiere that referred to music played by "a little string orchestra," and Lybeck's stage directions, which use the word *orchestra*.[15] But such conjecture seems erroneous. Indeed, as we will see, the chamber-sized accompaniment is important to its generic identity, at least as conceived by Sibelius.

Table 1. Sibelius's annotations to *Ödlan* score, Act 2, scene 1.

MEASURE NO.	SIBELIUS'S CUE SYMBOL	TEXTUAL INCIPIT FROM LYBECK	TRANSLATION	PAGE NO. IN LYBECK	COMMENT
Before 1		Elisiv: Älskade! Alban: Snart, snart, Elisiv! . . .	Elisiv: Darling! Alban: Soon, soon, Elisiv! . . .	87	
Before 1		(Bakom scen)	(Behind stage)		Sibelius's own direction, not in Lybeck
After 2		. . . Nu låter jag själen stiga!	. . . Now I let the soul rise!	87	
7		(En dansvisa springer fram)	(A dance tune starts up)	87	Crossed out in score
End of 11		(Ett litet barn gråter)	(A small child cries)	88	
13–16		(Fältet har ingen sol, etc.)	(The field has no sun, etc.)	88	
26–27		(Skymningen mörkare, Vålnader.)	(The twilight darker, Phantoms)	88	
29–31	⊕	(En vålnad, högre och rakare än de andra, glider in på den öppna platsen.)	(A phantom, higher and more erect than the others, glides into the open area)	88	Lybeck reads "planen" (open space) rather than "platsen."
32	⊕	Elisiv: Alban! . . . Alban! (Fullständigt mörker)	Elisiv: Alban! . . . Alban! (Complete darkness)	88	
End of 37		(Ridå)	(Curtain)	88	

Sibelius's acquaintance with Lybeck dated back to the 1890s, but more recently the two men interacted in the Euterpist circle, a group of Finnish (largely Finnish Swedish) poets, novelists, playwrights, visual artists, and composers who, starting around 1902, sought ways to translate (figuratively and literally) the modern and symbolist creative spirit of France into their own Nordic culture.[16] Among the manifestations of this interest in the aesthetic values of the French were creative efforts that sought, in single works, to unite symbolic resonances from different artistic media. Often this symbolic melding was anything but restrained: it cannot have escaped Sibelius's notice when he considered collaborating with Lybeck that *Ödlan* teems with musical imagery, both verbal and (potentially and eventually) sounding. But in other ways, the symbolic affinities could be quite subtle. George C. Schoolfield, in his epochal survey of Finland's literature, notes that Lybeck's

Table 2. Sibelius's annotations to *Ödlan* score, Act 2, scene 3.

MEAS. NO.	SIBELIUS'S CUE SYMBOL	TEXTUAL INCIPIT FROM LYBECK	TRANSLATION	PAGE NO. IN LYBECK	COMMENT
Before 1		Förspel.	Prelude.		
14		(Ridån höjer sig	(The curtain rises	132	
28–30	1	Elisabeth: Hon kommer hitåt. Alida: Hvem är hon? o.s.v.	Elisabeth: She is coming this way. Alida: Who is she? etc.	132	
46	2	Elisabeth: Ja, ja, hon närmar sig. Ottokar: o.s.v.	Elisabeth: Yes, yes, she is drawing nearer. Ottokar: etc.	133	
63 (last beat)	3	Elisabeth: Säg mig–hvem har lefvat? o.s.v.	Elisabeth: Tell me –who has lived? etc.	133	
63–68		(ton!)	(tone!)		Written above the entrance of each part, with the exception of Vc in 68
75–76	4	Ottokar: Äfven lifvet skall jag glömma. o.s.v.	Ottokar: Even life I will forget. etc.	134	
106	5	Alida: Om jag har lefvat?	Alida: If I have lived?	134	
140	6	(Alida: Nej, nej . . . Alban . . .)	(Alida: No, no . . . Alban . . .)	135	
149		(Elisiv synlig)	(Elisiv visible)	135	
151–53	7	(Elisiv: Alban! Är det du som spelar?)	(Elisiv: Alban! Is that you who is playing?)	135	
163–64	8	(Elisiv: Ack, nej, nej . . . jag vet . . .)	(Elisiv: Oh no, no . . . I know . . .)	135	
180	9	(Elisiv: Måste jag dö?)	(Elisiv: Must I die?)	136	
233–35		Alida: Ja—ja	Alida: Yes—yes	138	Sibelius appears to have aligned each "ja" with the individual chords in 234 and 235.
After 235		Elisiv: Hvem? (Musiken upphör för ett ögonblick)	Elisiv: Who? (The music ceases for a moment)	139	
236	10	(Alida: Men han vet det icke.)	(Alida: But he does not know it.)	139	
291–92		(Ridå)	(Curtain)	140	

characters commonly exhibit a sense of reserve, and seem to communicate symbolically through their silences, an observation that Schoolfield smartly uses to bolster his argument for the patent similarities to Maeterlinck that one perceives in *Ödlan*.[17] But Sibelius, too, rendered silence symbolic—we need only to think of the great resonating voids at the end of the Fifth Symphony to remember that he was one of the twentieth-century's great composers of silence—and his perception of this shared value with Lybeck must have served as a further incitement to contribute music to the play.

What kind of work does Sibelius's music do for *Ödlan*? The composer's manuscript preserves a theatrical document, replete with prompts that respond to the needs of practical stagecraft. Some of his decisions, though simple, were crucial: locating the ensemble behind the stage meant that the music would project invisibly across the action out to the audience, an effect that surely enhanced the otherworldly imagery that pervades the two scenes he set. He responded to the dialogue, of course (and more about this later), but he also necessarily paid close attention to Lybeck's stage directions, making sure to synchronize musical phrases with various events on stage (phantoms rising), ambient sounds (the cry of a small child), the extinguishing of lights, and the rising and falling of the curtain.

Despite the abundant musical imagery in Lybeck's play, *Ödlan* requires actual sounding music just twice. At the end of Act 2, scene 1, which only has three brief passages of dialogue, the music largely engages and supports Lybeck's extensive stage directions. By contrast Act 2, scene 3 is more intensively a traditional conversational drama, with speaking parts for four actors spread across eight full pages of Lybeck's printed text, all of which Lybeck wished to be accompanied by music. Working from the printed edition of Lybeck's play, Sibelius carefully crafted his music for the two scenes in ways that both shape and fit the flow of the drama.[18]

For Alban, music represents the sole realm in which tormented living souls could find release: "Music has never given the living any pain!"[19] Music allowed expression to soar, unlike burdensome words: "Words are too heavy, they impede, but tones, tones. . . ."[20] Confessing these sentiments to Elisiv in Act 2, scene 1, Alban sways the emotions of the chaste girl, who calls Alban her lord and master. Her declaration that "I am the violin" leads Alban to pick up his instrument and play, the only means by which he can express his love for her.[21] Thus it fell to Sibelius to provide the necessary diegetic music. Strikingly, though, Lybeck's stage directions call for Alban to disappear just before he starts playing; the visual focus of the audience shifts from Alban to the backlit Elisiv, and on the images (and the non-diegetic sounds) she experiences in reaction to Alban's performance. Initially these visions all convey a sense of warmth and well-being: the voices of children calling to one another; a broad, blooming, sunlit field with butterflies flitting about; a dance tune. But they transform themselves after sensing the distant cries of a small child (marked already by Alban as a ghostly sound associated with the memory of his dead mother, Alida),[22] and at the moment when Elisiv can no longer distinguish between the visions induced by the music and the reality of the summer night, the visions turn grim. The light in the field disappears, and the scene resembles instead an abandoned grave for the dead (en öfvergifven hvilostad för döda); the earth seems to tremble; and finally dark phantoms travel up and down the stairs. Sibelius's music bears a dual dramatic burden in this scene: it at once supports the visual images that Elisiv—and in turn the audience—sees, and it provides the sonic coherence that lets the chain of images seem like a logical sequence. Or, said another way, the muteness of the characters onstage requires the medium of sound to move the drama forward, to convey both Alban's love for Elisiv and the doom that this love will soon entail.[23]

Sibelius organized the three sections of this scene around the idea of gestural and timbral return: attention at the beginning and end of the movement falls on the solo violin (Alban's violin). That these outer sections differ thematically and tonally serves the dramatic trajectory: the move from the sweetly diatonic A-major tune of the opening to the darkly expressive, tritone- and semitone-besotted G-sharp-minor melody of the final section underscores (literally) the emotional transformation from Elisiv's visions of love to visions of phantoms. In the final segment, the static accompanying tremolo, the traditional stuff of otherworldly happenings in music, shades our impressions of Elisiv and Alban. Agency here is vague— do the tritones and tremolos stem from Alban's playing, do they reflect Elisiv's troubled psyche, or both?—but the music effectively conveys that the characters' connections with reality are tenuous.

Sibelius's use of stasis in this scene likewise seems particularly noteworthy. The second and third sections each cultivate repetition in their own way: the second with syncopated pitches in the second violin that emphasize the tonic A (these in turn accompany a slow rising and falling chromatic melodic motive), the third, as mentioned, through the tremolos on the new tonic of G-sharp minor. Prolonged repetitiveness of course gives rise to musical tension, an obviously effective strategy as the visions onstage grow more disturbing. But such passages also reflected a long personal history in Sibelius's works, and would have an equally long critical history in the ensuing years, with particular attention paid to their roles in conveying impressions of primitive, bleak landscapes. The spatial trope seems important in Ödlan, but the imagery now is roped inward, onto the delimited space of the stage and into the unlimited space of the imagination.

"All music, Elisiv, I mean all great music, aims out over the boundaries . . . the boundaries between life and death."[24] Alban's declaration in Act 2, scene 1 in effect describes one of the functional roles of Sibelius's music: it signals the threshold states between life/death, waking/sleep, consciousness/unconsciousness that the drama repeatedly asks us to contemplate. While Act 2, scene 1 offers the visions of a conscious Elisiv, Act 2, scene 3 presents her unconscious delirium. An unnatural light falls over the stage: the grounds of the Eyringe estate give the appearance of petrifaction, as if they were coated with volcanic ash. Below the stairs lies a huge lizard, its head on the ground and its eyes gleaming like fiery slits.[25] In the background, phantoms flit back and forth; in the foreground Ottokar, Elisabet, and Alida (Alban's mother), all departed spirits, converse slowly among themselves. Lybeck instructs the actors playing Ottokar and Elisabet to speak in a monotone, with each word articulated plainly and true to the letter. Only Alida is allowed to speak in warm, living accents. When the words of the characters finally become audible to the audience, the ensuing dialogue is heavily laden with symbolism. Ottokar, Elisabet, and Alida gaze on Elisiv, each noting (and some ruing) her inescapable march toward death. When Elisiv finally speaks, she first cries out for Alban, but then realizes he cannot hear her in this uncanny, ghastly place.[26] And if he cannot hear her, then she must be facing death: "Must I die"?[27] She begs Alida to tell her if Alban really loves her; Alida hesitantly admits only that Alban loves, but does not say who; Elisiv determines with a shudder that he loves the lizard.[28] Finally resigned to her fate, Elisiv lets go, of Alban and of life. At the moment she exclaims to Alban "you cannot follow me!" the lizard's blazing eyes are extinguished, and recalling Alban's pronouncement about the liminal powers of great music, Elisiv cries, "Let your tones carry my soul beyond life's boundaries!"[29]

Sibelius set this entire scene to music. Indeed, the prelude begins to shape the audience's impressions of Elisiv's delirious visions even before they see the set or hear an actor speak. Of course, Sibelius wrote this prelude on Lybeck's instructions (the stage directions call for music before the curtain rises, and even specify that the music of this scene should draw on motives from the earlier scene), but this does not lessen the impression of a composer choosing gestures for maximum dramatic impact. We will momentarily consider some of the musical evidence for this impression, but for now we should consider other signs of Sibelius's dramatic planning in this scene. Most important from the standpoint of grasping his theatrical savvy is the series of numbers, from 1 to 10, he marked successively in the score. These are not rehearsal numbers, at least in the conventional musical sense, for normal rehearsal letters appear elsewhere in the score. Rather, since the numbers coincide with the majority of the textual incipits that

Sibelius wrote in the score, it seems likely that these symbols served as cues for the entire ensemble: relayed somehow from backstage, where the musicians played, they would have helped the actors on stage to deliver their lines at the appropriate musical moments. Together with the frequent breaks in the dialogue (Lybeck wrote "Pause—the music continues," or some close variant thereof, eight times), Sibelius's numerical scheme allowed for the coordination of music and words.[30] Allowing for a normal conversational flow to the dialogue (and even granting a wide range of tempi both for the delivery of the lines and performing of the music), many of the dialogues that follow Sibelius's numerical cues feature significant passages where the actors remained silent, and where, consequently, the music stands at the forefront of the audience's attention.[31]

Sibelius's numerical cues reveal some interesting facts that impinge on the understanding of the music. First, the dramatic trigger for the recall of the lyrical solo violin theme from the first movement, in the measures before cue 6, is Alida's memory of Alban, her son. These first seem to be nondiegetic sounds, music that only Alida imagines, but somehow, in her delirium, Elisiv overhears it, too, for it eventually rouses her to utter her first words of the scene (at cue 7): "Alban! Is that you playing?"[32] Second, a cue signals the sole passage in these movements given over to pure dialogue without musical accompaniment, occurring near the end of the scene (just before cue 10). The musical silence shocks, so as to draw attention to Lybeck's dramatic stroke: Elisiv's realization that Alban loves the lizard ("Ödlan—ödlan!"). Alida devastatingly intones, "All his thoughts, all his words, the whole life's dream—it is only escape. But he does not know this," and the music resumes.[33]

In most sections of dialogue, the coordination of words and music between the cue symbols is not terribly difficult (and recall that Sibelius knew from the pauses marked in Lybeck's stage directions that when the actors finished speaking, the music was supposed to continue). The exception is the section of the scene that follows the final cue 10. Here the music must accommodate some fifteen sentences of dialogue, and—atypically within the sections bounded by cue numbers—the music shows considerable variety of style. It begins with a sinister *ppp* tremolo passage played *sul ponticello* that stops and starts several times, moves centrally to a final recollection of the melody from cue 9 (a recollection that eventually gains a syncopated repetitive accompaniment that itself reminds us of the middle section of the first movement), and finally shifts, suddenly and surprisingly, from G-sharp minor to G minor for the final *ppp* tremolo chords. Lacking specific instructions from the composer, it could be perplexing to ascertain how the music should fit with the words. But the review published by K. F. Wasenius on the day of the premiere (and thus presumably based on rehearsals) provides clues that help determine the pacing of the declamation in this final passage:

> Elisiv's grand sacrifice of herself when she says "Alone, alone, I must meet the transfiguration" and "let your tones carry my soul beyond life's boundaries" has inspired Sibelius to a formally transfigured music with a melodic structure that in exalted flight under sweet harmony soars upwards to ever higher glory, until, from its sublime culmination on Elisiv's words "I'm so tired" in wonderful motion, it sinks down, so that the words: "but you—you must be happy—my beloved" die away.[34]

From Wasenius's description, the passage "Ensam, ensam måste jag möta förklaringen" (Alone, alone, I must meet the transfiguration), which occurs roughly halfway through this exchange, must begin somewhere around the start of the recollection of the melody from cue 9, hence around measure 251. This is the only passage that fits his description as "formally transfigured music" (loosely allowing "transfigured" to mean a return to music heard earlier) and "sweet harmony that soars upwards to ever higher glory." "Låt dina toner bära min själ bortom livets gränser" (Let your tones carry my soul beyond life's borders) could follow around measure 264. As would fit the sense of the text, Wasenius must have meant that the sinking down begins with the words "Jag är så trött" (I am so tired), hence around measure 271. And the dying out around "men du—du, måste bli lycklig—min älskade" (but you—you must be happy—my beloved) would mesh well with the beginning of the syncopation, around measure 277.

Considering the whole movement once again, its formal shape is rather complex, with enigmatic motivic snippets, partial motivic returns, and thematic recollections from the music from Act 2, scene 1. Textual echoes spurred some of the motivic repetitions, thus for Elisabet's "Säg mig—hvem har lefvat?" and Alida's "Om jag har lefvat" (cue symbols 3 and 5; see Table 2) Sibelius used the same eerie descending-unison motive. Though this network of motivic interrelationships partially helps stitch the movement together, what more determines the experience of the first two-thirds of it is its pervasive chromaticism, expressed both harmonically and melodically. From the opening chords of the prelude, which effectively prolong the unstable sound of the augmented triad, to the semitonally inflected motives that dart in and out of the hazy harmonies, the opening minutes of this scene (apart from the C-major/minor return of Alban's amorous solo violin tune from the first movement) largely grant only fleeting senses of tonal grounding.

Sibelius called on more than floating tonality and chromatic melody to convey a sense of unmoored form. Most notable is the way the opening two-thirds of the movement calves off small chunks of musical material. Fragments of ideas interrupt other unrelated fragments; they end in sudden outbursts or in unmeasured silence. This lends an almost modular feeling to the opening minutes, a sensation only slightly mitigated by motivic repetition. To be sure, the modularity fits excellently with the needs of the drama, and especially with Lybeck's repeated insistence that the music should continue to fill pauses in the dialogue. But it also must be noted that this way of assembling larger units of musical sense out of the shuffling about of small, only partly interrelated shards of phrases had long been a feature of Sibelius's general musical style. (The exposition of the first movement of the Second Symphony provides an excellent point of comparison.) The ability to draw on this stylistic predilection in dramatic contexts helps explain Sibelius's affinity with writing music for the theater, and his continued successes in the medium.

This prolonged instability created by the constant breaks in continuity and pervasive chromaticism in the second movement of *Ödlan* lends it a clear expressive arc. Sibelius reserved true thematic identity and relative harmonic stability for the moment when Elisiv begins to realize she must die: "Måste jag dö?" Everything prior to that point serves as a kind of extended structural upbeat to the sense of emotional release that arrives with Elisiv's painful question. By itself, Lybeck's line is touching, but Sibelius's simple, foursquare theme guides the response toward true poignancy. Moreover, the presence of melody here represents a conceptual return: the only other significant melodic passages in the music to *Ödlan* are associated with Alban (the solo violin music in the first movement). The extended melody at the end of the second scene also conjures Alban, but now as an object of loss for both Alida and Elisiv. With this memory embedded within it, the melodic accompaniment transforms their dialogue from touching to heartbreaking.

In such moments, when the music pulls the viewer toward trenchant emotions, *Ödlan* reveals its relationship to the genre of melodrama, a musico-dramatic kind that, as we noted earlier, enjoyed great popularity around the turn of the twentieth century.[35] Sibelius composed a number of stand-alone melodramas, works that normally allowed the possibility of performance in smaller venues, a more delimited plot, the texts ordinarily deriving from poetry rather than from dramas (the notable exception here being the original melodramatic version of *Skogsrået* [*The Wood Nymph*], which sets an extended narrative poem by Viktor Rydberg), and the words delivered by a single speaker. Sibelius scored the majority of his melodramas for varieties of chamber ensembles: recitation, soprano, violin, cello, and piano (found in two early melodramas, *Näcken* and *Svartsjukans natter*), or recitation and piano (*Skogsrået* and *Ett ensamt skidspår*). Thus when Sibelius decided to score the music of *Ödlan* for just a handful of players, he drew on the more intimate (and intensified) sound world that he most commonly gravitated toward in melodrama.[36]

This generic affiliation was not lost on Sibelius's first listeners. Julius Hirn (known as Habitué) in his review in *Nya Pressen* described Sibelius's contribution as "the melodramatic tone poem."[37] And K. F. Wasenius summed up Sibelius's achievement in the second movement:

> In this entire big scene with its difficult musical statements one shall search in vain for a dead or stereotypically treated moment. It constitutes one big illustration, even celebration of the author's visions and words. The music nowhere remains still, instead undergoes psychological transformations to an extent that grants it a unique, leading place in the realm of melodrama.[38]

Wasenius's words are key, not only for situating the music to *Ödlan* but also for understanding Sibelius's creative purpose in much of his theatrical oeuvre. In speaking of the illustrative powers of the composer's music, its ability to set into relief both words and visual images, and in framing the idea of psychological transformation, Wasenius limns the music of the play as a "mode of excess" with respect to the script.[39] That Sibelius's music, accompanying spoken words and the artifacts of staging, fabricates the affective beyond perhaps explains the ease with which it also conveys the otherworldly: profound emotions and the spirit world, as so often in his work, represent two sides of the same expressive coin.

NOTES

1. An excellent compilation of much of this repertory is *The Sibelius Edition: Theatre Music*, vol. 5, BIS-CD 1912/14 (2008). This set does not, however, include the music to *Ödlan*; for this, see *The Sibelius Edition: Chamber Music*, vol. 9, BIS-CD 1924/26 (2009), as well as a 1995 recording on the Koch Schwann label (3-1786-2), with Tapio Tuomela conducting the Folkwang Kammerorchester Essen.

2. As interesting and finely performed as the recordings in the previous note are, both fundamentally misrepresent Sibelius's conception of *Ödlan* by omitting the spoken text. A recording of dramatic music can never completely capture the experience of actors onstage, sets, and costumes, but it is plain that Sibelius, apart from briefly entertaining the notion of crafting a set of symphonic variations based on the concluding theme from the second movement, never intended *Ödlan* to be heard without the spoken text the music

was meant to accompany. Later in life, he made the point directly: "Musiken till Ödlan är omöjlig för annat än teatern" (The music for Ödlan is impossible for anything other than the theater. This letter of 13 January 1936 is quoted in Fabian Dahlström, *Jean Sibelius: Thematisch-bibliographisches Verzeichnis seiner Werke* (Wiesbaden: Breitkopf & Härtel, 2003), 27. On the same page, Dahlström cites Sibelius's letter of 19 November 1909 to Breitkopf & Härtel, in which he mentions the idea of symphonic variations on the concluding theme.

3. Rabbe Forsman makes the case that *Ödlan* marked a fundamental step for Sibelius toward the sound world of the Fourth Symphony. See "Sagan om Satu: Jean Sibelius och ett finskt kulturkomplex. Sånger kan jag, som ej konungens maka, ej son av mänska kan. (Eddan)," *Ny tid*, 23 June 2006, http://www.nytid.fi/arkiv/artikelnt-684-1283.html. On the "crisis" years, see James Hepokoski, *Sibelius: Symphony No. 5* (Cambridge: Cambridge University Press, 1993), 10–18.

4. Andrew Barnett's claim that Sibelius "pandered to the taste of the dedicatee" in writing his music for the symbolist plays both downplays the importance of his artistic choices and interests—Barnett feels these choices relate more to the "dreamy, imaginative and spiritual side of [Sibelius's] personality that had been evident since his childhood"—and denigrates the composer's own artistic impulses, which would appear to have little to with "pandering." See Barnett, *Sibelius* (New Haven: Yale University Press, 2007), 156–57.

For a more sympathetic overview of Sibelius's musical engagements with symbolist drama, see Eija Kurki, "Sibelius and the Theatre: A Study of the Incidental Music for Symbolist Plays," in *Sibelius Studies,* ed. Timothy L. Jackson and Veijo Murtomäki (Cambridge: Cambridge University Press, 2001), 76–94. Kurki focuses mainly on the music for *Kuolema*, *Belsazars gästabud*, and *Svanevit*.

5. For an excellent examination of the continuities and conceptual relationships among the variety of theatrical works that Sibelius composed, see Tomi Mäkelä, *"Poesie in der Luft": Jean Sibelius, Studien zu Leben und Werk* (Wiesbaden: Breitkopf & Härtel, 2007), 216–32.

6. See Manuela Schwartz, "'Une union encore plus intime de la poésie et de la musique': Schauspielmusik am Ende des 19. Jahrhunderts in Frankreich," in *Stimmen—Klänge—Töne: Synergien im szenischen Spiel,* ed. Hans-Peter Bayerdörfer (Tübingen: Gunter Narr Verlag, 2002), 253–64.

7. Silent cinema did not make serious inroads into Finland until around 1919, so any awareness Sibelius might have had about cinematic appropriations of melodrama would have derived from his travels abroad. On Finnish silent cinema, see Antti Alanen, "Born Under the Sign of the Scarlet Flower: Pantheism in Finnish Silent Cinema," in *Nordic Explorations: Film Before 1930,* ed. John Fullerton and Jan Olsson (Sydney: John Libbey, 1999), 77–85; and, in the same collection, Peter von Bagh, "Silents for a Silent People," 86–90.

For studies of the relationships among cinema and various earlier dramatic forms that mixed media, see Manuela Schwartz, "Visualisierung der Musik—Musikalisierung der Bilder: Zur konzeptionellen Wende in Oper, Schauspielmusik und Film des Fin de siècle," in *Zeitenwenden—Wendezeiten: Von der Achsenzeit bis zum Fall der Mauer* (Dettelbach: Verlag J. H. Röll, 2000), 151–68; Ben Singer, *Melodrama and Modernity: Early Sensational Cinema and Its Contexts* (New York: Columbia University Press, 2001); and John Mercer and Martin Shingler, *Melodrama: Genre, Style, Sensibility* (London: Wallflower Press, 2004).

Finally, for a fascinating study that considers early twentieth-century musical style through the lens of the cinema of the time, see Rebecca Leydon, "Debussy's Late Style and the Devices of the Early Silent Cinema," *Music Theory Spectrum* 23 (2001): 217–41.

8. The most detailed exploration of the genesis and literary context of Lybeck's play, and the best close reading of it, remains Erik Kihlman, *Mikael Lybeck: Liv och Diktning* (Helsinki: Mercators Tryckeri Aktiebolag, 1932), 389–412.

9. As if this were not already plain in nearly every exchange of the play, Lybeck has Alban state the matter baldly: "Jag är skrämd från lifvet. Allt jordiskt är ondt. Allt jordbundet. Och ödlan är symbolen." (I am frightened of life. Everything earthly is pain.

Everything tied to the earth. And the lizard is the symbol.) Mikael Lybeck, *Ödlan: Ett Skådespel* (Stockholm: Albert Bonniers, 1908), 78.

10. The written sources tell us (and Sibelius's biographers endlessly repeat) that he tackled the commission from Lybeck with great enthusiasm, but that he grew irritated with it as he tried to finish it. Though revelatory from a biographical point of view (Sibelius grappled often with negative thoughts toward works he was composing), neither point ought to carry much weight in an informed exploration of the worth and meaning of the music that accompanies Lybeck's play.

Barnett's good discussion of the music from *Ödlan* includes Sibelius's glowing acceptance of the assignment from Lybeck (*Sibelius*, 199). Sibelius's negative remark came in a diary entry of 23 September 1909: "Mikaels 'ödla' pinar mig. Måste snabbast möjligast lemna den ifrån mig." (Mikael's "lizard" torments me. Must hand it over as fast as possible). See Jean Sibelius, *Dagbok 1909–1944*, ed. Fabian Dahlström (Helsinki: Svenska Litteratursällskapet i Finland; Stockholm: Atlantis, 2005), 36.

11. John Rosas, "Sibelius' musik till skådespelet ödlan," *Suomin musiikin vuosikirja* (1960–1961): 50.

12. Jean Sibelius, *Music for the Play "The Lizard" by Mikael Lybeck (Musik till skådespelet "Ödlan")*, Op. 8 (Helsinki: Edition Fazer, 1994).

13. For references to "the orchestra" in various forms, see Lybeck, *Ödlan*, 88 and 131

14. Erik Tawaststjerna, *Jean Sibelius: Åren 1904–1914* (Keuruu: Atlantis, 1991), 193.

15. For the reference to "en liten stråkorkester," see the article by K. F. Wasenius ("Bis") published in *Hufvudstadsbladet* on 6 April 1910, as cited in Rosas, "Sibelius' musik till skådespelet ödlan," 52.

16. For a good discussion of the Euterpist movement and its relationship to Sibelius's music for *Ödlan*, see Glenda Dawn Goss, *Sibelius: A Composer's Life and the Awakening of Finland* (Chicago: University of Chicago Press, 2009), 306–12.

17. George C. Schoolfield, "A Sense of Minority," in *A History of Finland's Literature*, ed. George C. Schoolfield, (Lincoln: University of Nebraska Press, 1998), 404.

18. On the headings for each scene, Sibelius noted the relevant page numbers of the printed edition of the play.

19. Lybeck, *Ödlan*, 75: "Musiken har aldrig gjort de lefvande något ondt!"

20. Ibid., 84: "Ordet är för tungt, det hindrar, men tonerna, tonerna . . ."

21. Ibid., 86: "Jag är violinen."

22. Ibid., 85.

23. The classic examination of muteness in dramatic melodrama is Peter Brooks, *The Melodramatic Imagination: Balzac, Henry James, Melodrama, and the Mode of Excess* (New Haven: Yale University Press, 1995), 56–80.

24. Lybeck, *Ödlan*, 80. "All musik, Elisiv, jag menar all stor musik, sträfver ut öfver gränserna . . . gränserna mellan lifvet och döden."

25. Ibid., 132: "Nedanför trappstegen en stor, stor ödla, med hufvudet på marken och ögonen glimmande som eldspringor."

26. Ibid., 136: "Hvad här är hemskt, hemskt!" (How ghastly, ghastly it is here—*hemskt* also means "uncanny").

27. Ibid.: "Måste jag dö? Hvarför får jag inte lefva?" (Must I die? Why can I not live?)

28. Ibid.,138–39. Amid this exchange, the motive of the crying baby returns. Alida responds to Elisiv's pleading to know if Alban loves her by saying she hears a small, abandoned child cry, and was that Elisiv?—"Jag hör ett barn gråta—ett ensamt öfvergiftet barn. Är det du, Elisiv?"

29. Ibid., 140: "Du får inte följa mig! Låt dina toner bära min själ bortom lifvets gränser!"

30. The first example of "Paus—musiken fortfar" appears in ibid., 132. Lybeck's favorite variant was "Paus—musiken starkare" (Pause—the music stronger), 133.

31. The other option—to radically slow down the delivery of lines so that dialogue and music concluded together—seems dramatically unlikely, even if the characters are articulating their monotonal words very carefully.

32. Lybeck, *Ödlan*, 135: "Alban! Är det du, som spelar?"

33. Ibid., 139: "Alla hans tankar, alla hans ord, hela lifvets dröm—det är flykt allenast. Men han vet det icke."

34. "Elisivs storslagna uppoffrande av sig själv då hon sager 'Ensam, ensam måste jag möta förklaringen' och 'låt dina toner bära min själ bortom livets gränser' har inspirerat Sibelius till en formligen förklarad musik med en melodik, som i exalterad flykt under ljuvlig harmonik svingar sig uppåt till allt högre glans, tills den från sin sublima kulmen, vid Elisivs ord 'Jag är så trött' i underbara gånger sjunker ned för att vid orden: 'men du—du, måste bli lycklig— min älskade' dö bort." I derive this quote of Wasenius's review from Otto Andersson, *Jean Sibelius och Svenska Teatern* (Åbo: Förlaget Bro, 1956), 36, but the date of publication has been corrected from that presented in Rosas, "Sibelius' musik till skådespelet ödlan," 52.

35. An excellent critical survey of the cultural and aesthetic evolution of the melodrama from the eighteenth century to the twentieth century is Jacqueline Waeber, *En musique dans le texte: Le Mélodrame, de Rousseau à Schoenberg* (Paris: Van Dieren, 2005).

36. Two important exceptions are *Grevinnans konterfej* (Countess's portrait), an exquisite melodrama for voice and orchestra from 1906, and the orchestral accompaniment to the dialogue between Good Works and Jedermann in the eponymous work from 1916.

37. Quoted in Andersson, *Jean Sibelius och Svenska Teatern*, 35, as "det melodramatiska tonpoemet," but incorrectly identifying the newspaper as *Hufvudstadsbladet*. Rosas, "Sibelius's musik till skådespelet ödlan," 52, gives the correct attribution.

38. "I hela denna stora scen med dess svåra musikaliska uppgifter skall man förgäves söka ett dödt eller chablonmässigt behandladt moment. Den utgör ett enda förklarande, ja förhärligande af författarens syner och ord. Musiken står ingenstädes stilla utan undergår städse pyskologiska omgestaltningar i en vidd som förlänar den en enastående rangplats inom melodramats område." From the review in *Hufvudstadbladet*, as quoted in Rosas, "Sibelius's musik till skådespelet ödlan," 52.

39. "Mode of excess" derives from the full title of Brooks, *The Melodramatic Imagination*. See also the admirable concluding chapter in Waeber, *En musique dans le texte*, 405–26.

The Wings of a Butterfly:
Sibelius and the Problems of Musical Modernity

TOMI MÄKELÄ

The closer I nestled, with all the fibers of my being, to the animal—the more enfolded my innermost soul became—the more this butterfly, in action and deed, assumed the color of human resolution; and finally, it was as if its capture was the price I had to pay to gain my humanity again.

—Walter Benjamin

And the highest enjoyment of timelessness—in a landscape selected at random—is when I stand among rare butterflies and their food plants. This is ecstasy, and behind the ecstasy is something else, which is hard to explain. It is like a momentary vacuum into which rushes all that I love. A sense of oneness with sun and stone.

—Vladimir Nabokov

At the beginning of his essay on music theory in secondary schools, Ernst Hofmann presents these beautiful lines as the translation of an authentic quotation from Jean Sibelius.: "I could, dear distinguished friend, introduce you to my work, but as a matter of principle I do not do so. Compositions to me are like butterflies. Once you have touched them, their magic is gone. They can still fly but they are not as pristine as before."[1] Sibelius's attitude, as presented here, is a provocative motto. In contrast, Hofmann courageously pleads for more music theory in the classroom: "It is not analytical methodology—applied sensitively and skillfully—that takes away young people's joy of music. Rather their lack of preparation denies them the understanding for analysis, which aims to unlock their understanding of the work."[2]

The editorial problem with Hofmann's Sibelius quotation is that no document with these words appears to exist.[3] Although the general attitude sounds like Sibelius, some of the details do not. As a matter of fact, Sibelius wrote to Axel Carpelan in a similar vein on 6 March 1901, but there are a few significant differences between his actual text and the quotation translated by Hofmann:

> I would surely like to introduce you, understanding man, to my work, but as a matter of principle I do not do so. To my mind, compositions are like butterflies: touch them once and the dust [stoftet] is gone— they may be able to fly but they are no longer so wonderful.[4]

In this case, the articulation of the idea is characteristically brilliant. And even more important, its details are typically Sibelian—stoftet, for example, suggests eternal dust, a phrase also used to refer to a person's ashes or mortal remains as well as a more domestic meaning. The composer was a master of aphorisms and metaphors, and had a refined vocabulary. This must be the letter Hofmann actually wanted to quote. The metaphor in Sibelius's original is significantly more plausible than in the text used by Hofmann. Sibelius was well acquainted with butterflies, and collected them as a schoolboy.[5] In his letter to Carpelan, he demonstrates his knowledge. He was not interested in "magic," whether in butterflies or music. But in the literature on Sibelius, magic and magicians are a favorite topic, not least in Bengt de Törne's 1937 volume, Sibelius: A Close-Up, a problematic book which for many years was regarded as one of the primary sources of information about the composer's life and his musical beliefs.[6]

The butterfly, a common metaphor for the passing moment and a creature with a terribly short life, is an interesting point of reference for a work of art. Music, of course, is the most transient art form of all. Looking for butterflies in Sibelius's writings and compositions, one finds love between a flower and a butterfly in "En blomma stod vid vägen" (A flower stood beside the road), a song based on Ernst Josephson's poem "Annas sagor" (Anna's Story) from his 1896 collection Gula rosor (Golden roses). The eight Josephson songs, op. 57, of early 1909, are among the most harmonically adventurous in Sibelius's whole output. In Josephson's poem, a girl destroys the "love," the beautiful and fragile balance in nature, as she places the butterfly in a box with a bird. Like the metaphor that Sibelius employed in his letter to Carpelan, a human being therefore destroys the sense of beauty, even if it is hard to see how her touch actually damages the delicate dust on the surface of the butterfly's wings.[7] Perhaps simply knowing the butterfly is no longer in its original natural state is sufficient to compromise its aesthetic appeal. The fascination for untouched beauty of any kind is popular in Western cultures and beyond.

In March 1901, Carpelan was closely interested in Sibelius's progress on his Second Symphony. Carpelan's concern was legitimate, since he had helped to finance the composer's trip to Berlin and Italy that winter. One of the reasons Sibelius, an enthusiastic high school entomologist, was thinking about butterflies may have been that some particularly beautiful species were already flying in Rapallo and Rome during his stay. But even in its authentic version, Sibelius's letter also expresses a lifelong antipathy toward musical analysis and scholarship in relation to the arts. He did not want to teach composition, develop a method, or write essays on music (as had been the fashion among progressive artists throughout the later decades of the long nineteenth century, the era of the avant-garde and self-reflection).[8] He was rarely willing to explain his art (except in 1896, as he was applying for a position at the University of Helsinki, where a presentation could not be avoided). He generally preferred short (but often brilliant) aphorisms to more detailed accounts of the secrets of creativity. This attitude contrasts with the idea of twentieth-century modernism as a praxis defined by rationality and explication, and places Sibelius on a radically different cultural path from that taken by a figure such as Arnold Schoenberg, who despite his music's expressivity and emotional power, searched intensively for a rational foundation, a system of beautiful but profound subliminal structures. For Sibelius, any rationalization of art and its creation was foreign; for him, works of art were not exemplars of a particular method: an attitude common to many modernists after Schoenberg, and even among Wagnerians who believed in leitmotifs as a system. Sibelius gives more the impression of a god-like creator than a head of school. And like a god, he preferred not to reveal his secrets to any external authority. Beyond that, he was afraid his creations would be destroyed by the scrutiny of others, like the butterfly that was fatally vulnerable to the simple touch of another being.

High standards of general education were a matter of course for the pre-1914 elite, not an object of desire as for earlier generations (or a rare luxury, as they arguably became later). Sibelius belonged to this elite. His relationship to academic learning and tradition was comparable to that of Friedrich Nietzsche a few decades earlier. For a while Nietzsche earned his living as a professor of ancient languages in Basel (in the 1890s, Sibelius was teaching in Helsinki), but in his later masterpieces, particularly Also sprach Zarathustra, his "Buch für Alle und Keinen" (A book for all and none), of 1883–85, Nietzsche created a more idiosyncratic synthesis of literature and academic philosophy. In this era, formal academic practices were criticized by sophisticated, well-trained individuals who had lost their respect for the title of "Professor." Sibelius himself hardly ever used the title except in a pejorative sense—his own accolade (from the University of Helsinki in 1916) was an "honores causae" only. Ironically, criticism of academic traditionalism soon opened the doors for the new academicism

of Schoenberg and his "School." Though Sibelius reacted mostly nega-
tively to academic practices and institutions, he was nevertheless interested
in Schoenberg. In a diary entry dated 9 February 1914, written in Berlin,
for example, Sibelius revealed that Schoenberg's string quartet, op. 10,
really gave him "a lot to think about," and that he developed a "terrific
interest in Schoenberg."[9]

Sibelius's butterfly metaphor fits the expressionist aesthetics of the
fragility of individual utterance better than it does academic logic. This was
combined with a readiness to deal with unlimited depths of sorrow and
pain, and a naturalistic directness, alongside a gothic textural complexity.
It is easy to find examples of the butterfly metaphor in the writings of
contemporaries. In Gottfried Keller's "Die Aufgeregten" (The excited
ones), which Schoenberg set in his Six Songs, op. 3 (1903), "ein holder
Schmetterling" (a proud butterfly) appears at a decisive moment:

Welche tiefbewegten Lebensläufchen,	What a deeply moved little résumé,
welche Leidenschaft, welch wilder Schmerz!	What passion, what wild pain!
Eine Bachwelle und ein Sandhäufchen	A brook's wave and a mound of sand
brachen gegenseitig sich das Herz!	Broke each other's heart!
Eine Biene summte hohl und stieß	A bee hummed vacantly and thrust
ihren Stachel in ein Rosendüftchen,	Its quill into a rose's fragrance,
und ein holder Schmetterling zerriß	And a proud butterfly tore
den azurnen Frack im Sturm der	Its azure coat in the storm of a May
Maienlüftchen!	breeze!
Und die Blume schloß ihr Heiligtümchen	And the flower closed its little shrine
sterbend über dem verspritzten Tau!	Dying upon the sprinkled dew!
Welche tiefbewegten Lebensläufchen,	What a deeply moved little résumé,
welche Leidenschaft, welch wilder Schmerz!	What passion, what wild pain!

The Six Songs might well be the work that Sibelius referred to in his
diary entry of 28 January 1914, describing a concert in Berlin when "a lied
of Schoenberg impressed me most deeply."[10] The song's sense of unlimited pain was indeed central to Viennese modernism. Theodor W. Adorno
writes a revealing anecdote about this in his *Philosophy of Modern Music*—
one of the moments when Adorno forgets his role as an academic writer
and turns instead to his rich store of firsthand knowledge as a contemporary of many distinguished modernists and their immediate predecessors.
Unfortunately, the last part of the common English version is a mistrans-
lation that makes it difficult to grasp Adorno's point: "The expression of
unmitigated suffering, bound by no convention whatsoever, seems ill-

mannered: it violates the taboo of the English governess who took Mahler along to a parade, and warned him: 'Don't get excited!'"[11] The last phrase in the German original, "der Mahler in die Parade fuhr, als die 'don't get excited' mahnte," uses the expression "ihr in die Parade fahren," which has nothing to do with a literal parade but simply means, metaphorically, "to protest against her." Little Gustav revolted against the governess (understandably so) when she told him not to "get excited"—as indubitably she often did, about anything. As far as we know, Mahler was never forced to watch a parade, imperial or otherwise, nor is it likely that he would have been excited by such an event. Any speculation on the early influence of incidental parade music in his later writing is out of place.

Sibelius the Progressive

Sibelius's most spectacular compositions provoke the question of the limits of aesthetic modernism and of musical modernity in general. Even his most "progressive" works are prototypes of what later became post-modernism or, in Milan Kundera's words, "antimodern modernism," a by no means systemic or methodological solution to the problems of artistic production.[12] The Fourth Symphony in A Minor, op. 63, composed between December 1909 and April 1911 in Helsinki and at Sibelius's villa Ainola, and the String Quartet in D Minor, op. 56, *Voces intimae*, written at Ainola and in Berlin and London in 1908–9, stand at the forefront of this debate in regard to both terminology and the history of style. In addition to these works, we could also add the eight expressionistic Josephson songs, op. 57, of 1909, and three airy Sonatinas for Piano, op. 67, of 1912. A much later wave of progressivism is introduced by *Tapiola*, op. 112, composed during spring/summer 1926 at home in Ainola and on the Italian island of Capri. Often ignored but instructive is the orchestral song *Luonnotar*, op. 70, of 1913.

Even in these essentially progressive works, Sibelius's musical architecture was situated within a classicist framework. His cosmopolitanism was rooted in the modernity of the fin de siècle rather than in twentieth-century modernism. The closest he got to the latter was his interest in the avant-garde of the early twentieth century, and even this association was never made public. Very few knew that he was buying and reading Schoenberg's scores. Sibelius did not confront the young modernist movements with the self-confidence of an established elderly professional, having tradition firmly behind his back, but rather from a position of anxiety. He realized the gap between his art and what he detected as the voice of the future in modernist scores. As a great modern but essentially traditional symphonist, he was mostly discussed by both biographers and his compositional apostles (such as Ronald Stevenson)[13] as an alternative to more youthfully aggressive forms of modernism. As a matter of fact, Sibelius was one of very few late-Romantic composers who were able to bring the old values into the new century in a slightly different shape.

Even today, most academics are trained within a modernist paradigm. As a result, isolated progressive elements with a modernist appearance have often been overemphasized in Sibelius's scores. It may be that such interpretations are influenced by our desire to resist the many critics who regarded Sibelius, pejoratively, as a reactionary and even anti-modernist figure. Indeed, the presence of either short or extended passages that were untypical of their time but common later does not make Sibelius a modernist or even a progressive, nor does the influence of established modernists' writing upon his work. The compositions that are the closest to the modernism of the early twentieth century (above all the Fourth Symphony and *Tapiola*) may be more accessible to a particular mode of theoretical inquiry than others. However, most of the modernist categories that we are trained to use are not entirely satisfactory if we consider the compositions *in toto*. It is too early perhaps to evaluate the relevance of modernist analysis on Sibelius, but it seems likely that analytic approaches still need to be developed that fit both his modernist and his earlier, more traditional pieces: approaches that make sense of both the seemingly modernist and the old-fashioned passages in individual works. The biggest challenge, however, will be to focus on the synthesis of the modern and postmodern, or to quote Wolfgang Welsch's famous phrase, the "postmodern modernism."[14] To be emphatically modern (that is, to question tradition and ask old questions in a new way) was natural to a composer born in 1865. But Sibelius deeply sensed the gap between the younger generation (including Schoenberg) and himself—the gulf that separated his post-Romantic and proto-postmodern modernity of the 1890s from the avant-garde modernism of the 1910s and later.

Modernism is a conscious, highly self-reflective avant-garde behavior, an attitude, sometimes even an ideology, rather than a collection of aims, intentions, or techniques generated by tradition. But even modernity is, as Adorno wrote, "a qualitative category, not a chronological one."[15] This makes it difficult to speak about an epoch of modernity in anything other than the most open, common sense of the "Modern Age." Clearly, Sibelius did not hold to the modernist attitude. Nor was he an anti-modernist. Both in private and professional life he was, rather, a conservative with a utopian, sometimes even revolutionary imagination. This mentality can be found among the monarchist founders of such utopian movements of the era as the Pan-European Union. It remained traditionalist even in its most daring moments. Though one finds passages in Sibelius's music that could readily have been composed by distinguished post–World War II masters (György Ligeti, John Adams, Wolfgang Rihm, Richard Rijnvos, and many others), they do not appear in a similar discourse. Equally, one finds bits and pieces of Chopin and Wieniawsky in his scores. This does not make him old-fashioned, either. Sibelius can be regarded as a contemporary model today (as he is indeed by many innovative and individualist composers, well beyond the borders of Finland). But even the most progressive moments in Sibelius's music remain essentially post-Lisztian. In the context of the 1910s and 1920s, this may seem conservative or even reactionary. Even if he was not conscious of it, Lisztian logic and texture influenced him till the end of his life.[16] He was not the only composer to penetrate beyond the surface of Liszt's music. But unlike Schoenberg, who wrote one of his best essays, "Franz Liszts Werk und Wesen," in 1911, Sibelius never explained this (or any other) great influence upon his work.[17] We know how impressed he was by Liszt in his formative years (the early 1890s), but we have been led to believe by later biographers that he soon got rid of this "Germanic" influence and swiftly became the living embodiment of the mythical Finnish seer Väinämöinen, a supposedly autonomous creative magus dwelling in the backwoods of a northern wilderness.

In order to appreciate Sibelius we have to leave behind the chronology of styles and tendencies. Sibelius's work transcends modernist teleology as well as the remains of Chronos and Prometheus. His lyrical strength is individual and expressive. Even in his most progressive moments it locates him in the domain of Kundera's anti-modernism rather than within the mainstream modernism of his day.[18] His profile is both extraterritorial and extrachronological.[19] Sibelius frees Liszt of his mid-nineteenth-century patina and makes his "New German" innovations seem timeless. This is why Sibelius's modernity, even his modernist elements, cannot be limited to a clear-cut period of production. He is one of the best musical examples of the composed "simultaneity of the non-simultaneous"—to employ Ernst Bloch's concept without his pejorative implications.[20] Superficially, at least, this makes Sibelius look (anachronistically) truly postmodern— a later trend and ideology recently summarized by Max Paddison as "a state of non-contradictory but dynamic plurality."[21] According to Paddison, modernisms are actually "defined by the conflict between the process of societal modernization and the claims of tradition."[22] The coexistence of such impulses (modernism vs. tradition) is a historical fact, but each fundamentally questions the other in both theoretical terms and structural manifestation. Postmodernism, on the other hand, is defined by its variety. The simultaneity of the non-simultaneous is its richness. A contrasting contemporaneous approach to modernism was traditionalist modernity, which Paddison, in reference to Thomas Kuhn's *The Structure of Scientific Revolutions* (1962), calls "a reflection upon established paradigms in order to continue to test them."[23] Unlike modernism, this version of modernity was able to absorb cultural contradictions, but they *remained* contradictions. Paddison insists on the parallel existence of cultures during the era of modernism, arguing powerfully against (postmodern) models of cultural permeability and transculturation.[24]

Sibelius's reaction to Schoenberg's music was both inspired and irritated. It is one of many possible reasons for the unusually progressive modernity of pieces like the Fourth Symphony. The depth of Sibelius's interest in Schoenberg has been treated extensively elsewhere.[25] Indeed, if we were to try to place Sibelius on the continuum of the era's central dichotomy of tonal vs. atonal musical languages, as personified by Richard Strauss and Schoenberg, Sibelius would need a position somewhere in between or beyond these two poles. In any case, the key parameter is harmony. His treatment of cadential (tonal) harmony developed in his earliest years, predating *Kullervo*, op. 7 (1891–92). He was already fascinated by the simultaneity of minor and major chords based on a single fundamental bass tone. In October 1888, he wrote to his uncle Pehr from Helsinki and described his ideas of an "experimental music": a music example he sketched shows C major and D-flat major simultaneously.[26] This is not quite a twelve-tone chord but—considering the year 1888—it suggests a tendency toward atonality and complete chromatic collections. Even though none of his compositions from these years include such pitch configurations, such youthful "experimental music" may once have existed. It is possible Sibelius destroyed such pieces in a later act of self-criticism. The letter of 1888 demonstrates his early bi-tonal sensitivity, an approach that even decades later remained an important part of his musical style, although it never became dogmatic. More important, Sibelius never attempted to systematize. Tonality in its broadest sense never fully disappears from Sibelius's scores, not even *Tapiola*. In the later works, specific keys are still marked. In the texture, however, such keys are at least attenuated or questioned. This questioning of tonality starts with the - bi-tonal "experiments" of the 1880s and develops as part of Sibelius's style over the years.

Sibelius was interested in the theoretical aspects of Schoenberg's *Harmonielehre*. In a diary entry dated 8 May 1912 he called it "ensidig" (one-sided), but he never wrote anything comparable himself. He would have had a lot to say about harmony, and he had promising ideas about "epic instrumentation" (diary entry, 9 June 1910)—a fascinating concept that seems neither to have a prehistory nor a future—but he never wrote more than a few words on either. His opportunistic ideas on the fruitful influence of folk music (1896, translated in the Documents section of this volume) begin with some conventional remarks about the development of Western music (Ars antiqua and Ars nova) and end up in chaos.[27] The impulse he gave to a new theory or aesthetics of music was so minimal that even his most ardent admirers were unable to articulate Sibelianism in music. The Sixth Symphony, op. 104, of 1923, one of the most "modal" (Dorian) in his oeuvre,[28] is called "Symphony in D Minor" in Fabian Dahlström's new catalogue of works[29]— but not, however, in the printed score. The Fifth Symphony, op. 82, of 1915–19, though clearly in E-flat major, is given no key in the score. Was Sibelius's omission of key signatures simply an attempt to make the Fifth and Sixth symphonies look more modern? By contrast the Fourth Symphony, one of his most dissonant works, is marked as being in A minor. Perhaps here the key signature can be read as an attempt to make the piece appear less atonal than it is in the interests of greater popularity?

Often, Sibelius seems to have more easily "finished" his most modernist and progressive works (in terms of harmony and texture) than his other pieces. Normally, he made many changes after the first performance. Even during the printing process, before an international premiere, Sibelius often continued to work on his scores. But *Tapiola* was printed before the first performance in New York, and it seems that Sibelius was satisfied with the result. Sibelius also seems to have made few revisions in the Fourth Symphony after the first performance. On 2 April 1911 he wrote: "The symphony is 'finished.' Iacta alea est! Necessary! It takes much manliness to look life in the eyes. Alas!"[30] The first performance took place the following day, and in a later context Sibelius mentioned the Fourth Symphony as a piece in which he would not change a single note, unlike the multiple revisions to which he subjected the more seemingly conservative or accessible Fifth.

When Sibelius was confronted with younger composers' music, even when he was fascinated by their work, he never considered taking on their project as his own. And not just because of his healthy skepticism toward systematization in the arts, or from a negative attitude toward new music. Rather, he saw his own limitations in regard to particular skills. A fairly complex reflection about his solitary position can be found in a letter dated 1 January 1911, in German to Rosa Newmarch, his British friend and advocate. Sibelius is certainly exaggerating his negativism, but if we ignore the anti-modernist opportunism (and subliminal anti-Germanism, in general less typical of Sibelius than of Newmarch), we find some valuable ideas:

> I had just returned from Berlin where I stayed for two months. As usual, I was overwhelmed by disgust for the "modern direction."

Out of that the feeling of loneliness arose. . . . To my astonishment I
can see that my compositions are frequently played on the continent,
even though they do not have anything of "Modernity" in them.[31]

This is the deepest level we reach in Sibelius's own thoughts on professional matters. Interacting with Newmarch, he wanted to display his
strongly individual position. It was not unimportant to Sibelius that his
work be truly progressive, even if modernism—"the modern direction"—
could not be his path. On 2 May 1911 he famously wrote to Newmarch
that his new symphony op. 63 was intended as a "protest against the compositions of today." Strangely enough, generations of sensitive critics ever
since have seen this composition as an integration of older Sibelianism
with the most recent musical developments. The Fourth Symphony is no
doubt a progressive composition for 1911. But then Sibelius was writing
to Newmarch and not to Busoni, and he was famous for adjusting himself
to any person he interacted with (including politicians and journalists).
As we read Sibelius's letters we must therefore be aware of audience and
expectations. To a certain degree, this was perhaps also the case with his
musical output.

As late as 1910, Sibelius planned to study counterpoint. On 18 June
1910 he wrote in his diary: "All true talents have made their way 'ad astra'
through their own studies." Obviously he felt that the knowledge he
gained from his various respectable teachers in Hämeenlinna, Helsinki,
Berlin, and Vienna was insufficient to enable him to cope with the artistic
and stylistic demands of the day. He needed to take care of progressive
techniques, and particularly post-Romantic voice leading, himself. Earlier
he had focused his attention principally on harmonic processes. That
could indeed mean limitation, since the goal of most modern composers
(Reger and Schoenberg among others, and even Busoni, but less successfully) was to combine horizontal and linear elements in a way similar to
Bach but within a wholly different stylistic framework. In Sibelius's diary
entry for 6 November 1910, we read: "I forced myself under colossal pressure to do half an hour's counterpoint." Admittedly, thirty minutes is not
very much, but it shows that Sibelius's desire to learn a different technique
was pressing. His aim was to remove the vertical paradigm of eighteenth-
and nineteenth-century musical syntax. On 16 June 1913 he wrote:
"Meditating on linear counterpoint!!" and on 9 March 1913, without any
hesitation, "My 'style' is far too homophonic." We do not have to agree
with Sibelius's self-criticism, but it certainly deserves to be pursued in future research.

Reger may indeed have been an important inspiration for Sibelius in
the years around 1910. He was both critical and enthusiastic about Reger

(diary, 15 October 1919): "National, German, complicated, also boring, but good just on account of its German kind." Beyond Reger and the idea of "German" style, one might expect Sibelius to focus on Bach, too, but Bach's name rarely appears in his writings (and never as a model). Less sensitive than Sibelius in many respects, not least as far as "German" style is concerned, was Sibelius's close friend and confidant Axel Carpelan, who frequently wrote down his personal thoughts about music and its prospects as though he were quoting Sibelius. Carpelan had a political mind. Even if he was practically penniless, he was able to raise money for Sibelius. On 26 April 1911 he wrote in an article on the composer: "In Germany above all, the home of the symphony, instrumental music is merely technique, a kind of science or engineering. It tries to conceal its inner emptiness with a huge technical apparatus."[32] James Hepokoski regards this as Sibelius's authentic opinion,[33] but rather than believing what contemporary commentators, friends, and the press wrote on his behalf, we should, as a matter of principle, be skeptical about anything written down outside Sibelius's diary and the original drafts of his letters. (The final versions of Sibelius's letters often tend to be more diplomatic and moderate in expression than the first drafts, which adopt positions that Sibelius was afraid of making public.) Even if Carpelan's (typically Scandinavian) polemics against all that was, or might be, perceived as "German" were not shared by Sibelius himself, he certainly was critical of inner emptiness wherever he sensed it. Nevertheless, he realized that he needed to learn a little more modernist "engineering" in music in order to be able to work more easily and manage more effectively his output and the "claims of tradition," as Max Paddison might say.[34] Certainly, one could argue that it is precisely because Sibelius recognized the limitations of such musical engineering that his music is as original and "Life-giving" as it is.[35]

The principal result of this self-critical reflection upon inner emptiness and counterpoint was the Fourth Symphony. It was supposed to have nothing of the "circus" in it.[36] On 20 July 1909 Sibelius criticized the "circus presentations of some conductors" as composers. He maintained that, by contrast, a "heavenly logic" was audible in his music.[37] James Hepokoski suggests that "the diffuse expansionism of Mahler and the technological sensationalism of Strauss and the younger Straussians" were the focus of Sibelius's criticism.[38] Theoretically, Mahler's Fifth Symphony (1904–5) might have irritated Sibelius and given him some reason to talk about a musical "circus," and Hepokoski is justified in pointing out that Sibelius disliked "younger Straussians." It is more likely, however, that Sibelius was thinking of popular orchestral compositions by colleagues such as Felix Weingartner and Siegmund von Hausegger, whose work was particularly prominent in contemporary German concert halls. In a diary note of

1 August 1912 Sibelius compared modern musical tendencies to a river under human control, with an artificial catchment and a strictly controlled flow, like a channel rather than a natural stream. This is a typical metaphor (and, in terms of water management, even a wise approach). According to Sibelius, however, a "natural" symphony should be more like a river that gets its water from smaller brooks. The motives should gain their shape organically and be able to find their own way. The metaphor is similar to the famous vision of Edgard Varèse: "There will no longer be the old conception of melody or interplay of melodies. The entire work will be a melodic totality. The entire work will flow as a river flows."[39] Both Sibelius and Varèse fell under the loose influence of Busoni. And both had old-fashioned counterpoint teachers in their formative years: Varèse learned with Vincent d'Indy and Charles-Marie Widor, Sibelius with Albert Becker and Robert Fuchs (whose nickname was "Fugenfuchs"). Sibelius and Varèse reacted independently but similarly to the academic practices of the previous generation of teachers. For them, the future of their music lay in natural processes and organic evolution, not man-made constructivism.

Between Influence and Irritation

Even though one cannot detect the shadow of a younger composer in any of Sibelius's works (his stylistic allusions and quotations include Wagner, Bruckner, Beethoven, Chopin, and other earlier composers), he was continuously aware of their music. As late as 29 April 1926 he wrote to Aino from Berlin: "In the music shops I study modern German and French music." At that time he was working on *Tapiola*, a composition that in many respects (above all texturally) would have been considerably more advanced than anything he might have purchased from a commercial music shop in Berlin even as late as 1926. So far no one has been able to demonstrate the influence of any contemporary artist on late Sibelius, either in general or on *Tapiola* in particular (interestingly, visits to other composers' homes are also not documented). Instead *Tapiola* has been compared rather with Ligeti and post-1945 minimalist music.[40] Even the expected quotations from Wagner or other similar sources are absent here—though the work's subject might suggest similar textures to those used in the Fourth Symphony, which refer to *Parsifal* and the music associated with Klingsor's castle. This, of course, does not make *Tapiola* better than the Fourth. Only critics strictly beholden to modernist premises see intertextuality in a negative way. Sibelius's obvious desire to construct his works in a complex manner (the key words in both works are logic and architecture) was ultimately classicist rather than up-to-date modernist.

According to the Wolfgang Rihm scholar Joachim Brügge, the reason for many of his colleagues' fascination with the Fourth Symphony is the "radical modernity of the musical language and the uncompromising consequence of the form."[41] (According to a comment in conversation with Reinhold Brinkmann, it is Rihm's favorite and "the most dissonant symphony.")[42] The central intervallic role of the tritone is one of the reasons for the "dissonant" character of the composition. But the work's peculiarities begin with the treatment of the keys. The main key, written on the front page of the score, is A minor. The second movement is in F major, the third in C-sharp minor, and the finale in A major, closing in A minor. Surprisingly enough for a symphony with such a formidable reputation, this is well within the tonal "norms" of late Viennese classicism. More interesting is Sibelius's loose manner of presenting the keys within the movements: the clarity of tonal processes is obscured by the "forward-leading melodic energetics" (*vorantreibende melodische Energetik*) of the work's opening gesture, its shapeless gestalt connoting "early expressionist aesthetics," as Brügge points out. Even more progressive here are Sibelius's soundscapes. From measure 4 onward, he divides the double bass line as it oscillates between F♯ and E, enriching the cellos acoustically. This creates what we would today call a stereophonic effect. The rhythm of the first measures is a written out *ritardando*. This is an example of the precise notation of texture in Sibelius's scores, and is typical also of the Schoenberg school, above all Alban Berg. It was already common in Vienna before the modernist era, and can therefore be attributed to Sibelius's study in Vienna under Karl Goldmark and Robert Fuchs. The meter is 4/4 throughout, but Sibelius notates the subliminal slowing of the pulse in eighth-note stages:

Example 1. Sibelius, Symphony no. 4, opening.

Another important Sibelian detail is that the tones C, D, E, and F♯ have motivic value as a collection rather than simply outlining the characteristic interval of a tritone. There is no melody or motive in the traditional sense. Instead, a magnificent kaleidoscope of colors emerges from the opening measures, as though Sibelius is indicating a blended, decidedly unmodernist wash of sound. The melodic profile of these tones is limited initially by the lower register, but becomes somewhat sharper following the entrance of the solo cello in measure 6. Gradually, some new tones are introduced: G♯, A, and G♮, and slowly the opening collection is transformed into a melodic line with a specific rhythmic identity. In measure 55 a counter-melody appears, followed by further contrapuntal voices, and the tritone dynamics of the beginning are replaced by a strong A-minor frame. The totality of six tones: C, D, E, F♯, G♯ and A form almost a complete A-minor scale. Yet the key of A minor remains weak due to the overlapping and alternating bass tones F♯ and E. F♯ indicates the direction of the following modulation, leading toward F-sharp major after rehearsal letter B (Adagio). The point where the tones A, C, and E sound for the first time over a bass F♯ (measure 7) creates a diminished seventh. However, the broader process whereby a small number of tones first become a scale, then a chord, then a melody, and finally a melody with counterpoints and a fully polyphonic texture, is like the demonstration of a modernist (Weberian)[43] introduction to the history of Western music in twenty measures. First we hear, symbolically, the tone C, both as a harmonic ground in the upper cellos and double basses, as well as the beginning of the pseudo-melodic line in the first bassoon and first violoncello. Equally important, all the instruments are divided and contribute to the multidimensional sound space.

More postmodern than modern is the easily recognizable quotation from Wagner's *Parsifal* in measure 40. It is preceded by no significant preparation. Hardly any other allusion in Sibelius's music is as obvious as this. The motive appears in the exposition in B minor, in the recapitulation in D minor. Despite its isolation, it functions as a syntactic bridge, with little if any contextualization in the detail of the surrounding measures. Yet in the very opening of the symphony Sibelius evokes an atmosphere similar to Klingsor's magic castle from the opera's second act. The music similarly passes through several tritones—"heftig, doch nicht übereilt"— with frequent leading tones. So in this broad sense, the *Parsifal* quotation in measure 40 is at least semantically prepared.

In measure 57 begin what Brügge calls "shadowy melodies, typical for Sibelius, . . . that disappear into nothing."[44] As Brügge suggests, "This passage is among the most exiting and modern in the history of symphony in the nineteenth and twentieth centuries."[45] Here, if anywhere, Sibelius shows how well he has understood Schoenberg's freely phrased and asymmetrical melodies, composed with Wagner's melodic innovations in mind. It is clearly risky to describe one of the most progressive passages in the modern symphony as essentially Wagnerian, but this label emphasizes the conservative yet simultaneously utopian character of Sibelius's work.

Another section that has often been compared with Wagner's *Parsifal* is the rhapsodic but monumental third movement, Il tempo largo.[46] Little can be achieved by applying the categories of traditional formal analysis, and more is perhaps revealed by invoking derivations of the narrative techniques of the 1910s: the programmatic background of the symphony lends particular direction to a narrative interpretation ("thoughts of a Wanderer," the Koli Mountain, etc., with the Wanderer perhaps even meaning Wotan).[47] With its wealth of Wagnerian solos and brass effects, Il tempo largo tends toward French impressionism—in some passages more directly than others. But ultimately we have a movement that is pluralist in style and thus truly Sibelian, with a broad spectrum of musical characters from mysterious chromatic lines to hymn-like tutti passages within the space of a single measure. One of the highlights of this remarkably rich movement occurs five measures after rehearsal letter F. Sibelius suggests a chorale-like apotheosis in the manner he would later adopt in his Fifth and Seventh symphonies. But in the Fourth the anticipated flight ends earlier than expected, and the promising musical material is suddenly cut short. Sibelius allows a few rather vague motives to appear, and reduces the stability of the meter and the melody. The texture tends toward the pitch C♯. Two upward-oriented figures remain of the principal motive in the final measures. Functionally they are based around dominant harmony: first D, E, F♯, A, G♯, and then G, A, B, D, C♯. Both figures are built over a pedal point on the low C♯. (To translate this into a more Debussyan context, the D♮ should be raised by a half-step to complete a whole tone collection G, A, B, C♯, and D♯.) Whether calling this passage C-sharp Locrian does justice to Sibelius's compositional logic must be left open to debate. That the interval of a tritone plays such a marked role in this work certainly supports an analysis of the whole composition based on Locrian processes, since this mode lacks a perfect fifth scale degree (the strategic fifth is substituted by a tritone, or diminished fifth). Generally speaking, modality is the third important element of pitch organization in Sibelius's music (besides diatonic tonality and post-Wagnerian chromatics). But the particular presence of the Locrian mode is symptomatic. This mode is hardly used elsewhere in Western music history or traditional European music. It can also be heard as a tonal scale with strong emphasis on the leading tone. Indeed, whether it is possible to identify individual modes in modern, post-tonal music with the same ease as tonality and chromaticism might one day become one of the most important questions in music theoretical work on Sibelius.

On Linear Intimacy

A brilliant example of Sibelius's use of chromatic tonality can be found in his String Quartet in D Minor, op. 56, *Voces intimae*, of 1909. It follows similar lines to Schoenberg in his early works; Sibelius was confronted with Schoenberg's chamber music soon after this project, if he had not encountered it earlier. Sibelius would never publish anything like *Voces intimae* again—neither for string quartet nor for comparable ensembles, even though the string quartet had been an early working medium and the format for four complete compositions. At least two of Sibelius's quartets can be considered of national value and one, *Voces intimae*, of international rank. Chamber music in general was by no means foreign to Sibelius, and he had plenty of practical expertise himself as a violinist in a string quartet. In Spring 1912, Sibelius did start to compose a new quartet (diary entry of 22 April), but it was never finished or elaborated. The project is almost irrelevant as it was often unclear to Sibelius in the early stage of composing a new work what would happen to the material he was currently modeling on piano or on paper—or during a walk around his grounds at Ainola or in a foreign city (see Timo Virtanen's essay in this volume).

Voces intimae, his fourth and hence final quartet, richly deserves its subtitle. Sibelius wrote the Latin inscription in his copy of the printed score above a set of chords in the slow movement. In measure 21 and following the Adagio di molto (in a section called Piú adagio), the phrase refers to a series of isolated triads played at a low dynamic level. It would be interesting to know at least whose voices Sibelius intended to capture here. The same idea occurs in another note for the publisher in the fair copy of the score, written on 12 June 1909.[48] Beyond the work's shared key, D minor, the quartet reveals a number of similarities with Schoenberg's string sextet *Verklärte Nacht*, op. 4, of 1899. Unfortunately, we do not know if Sibelius knew it when he composed op. 56 ten years later. Schoenberg's composition has five movements like *Voces intimae*, but three of them are in a fast meter. Certainly, *Verklärte Nacht*'s program, after a poem by Richard Dehmel, is an intimate text. But Sibelius's title, *Voces intimae*, also reflects his fluent (and unsentimental) use of Latin. It might have something to do with the fear of death. At the same time, it reflects the often sinister but suddenly optimistic mood documented on the opening pages of his diary, which he also began to maintain in 1909. The quartet was composed largely in London, Paris, and Berlin. In February 1909 Sibelius was undertaking corrections in the central third movement with the intimate chords, despite distressing pains from a small tumor in his throat. On 1 April 1909, he suddenly wrote in the diary: "Why do I flee from my quartet?" On 15 April, he continued on the same topic: "Quartet ready! I—my heart is bleeding—why this tragedy of life. Woe! Woe! Woe! That one exists! My God—!"[49] The existential "Woes" most likely have more to do with financial problems than difficulties in fulfilling the task of composing a string quartet. On the same day he wrote to Aino about the composition: "(It has been ready for ages already. But I have not given it away.) Lienau received it today. It has become beautiful. Of a kind that brings a smile to your lips even in the moment of death. I won't say more."[50] These sentences to his wife are more informative and less sinister than the cryptic lines in the diary. But the idea of a smile upon one's lips at the hour of death is appropriate, as the quartet easily sounds like an elegy. Sibelius smiles in *Voces intimae* rather like Schubert in his D-minor quartet *Der Tod und das Mädchen* (1824; D 810).

Sibelius's intimate voices can be heard from the very beginning of the first movement, Andante—Allegro molto moderato (Example 2). The eight-measure introduction starts as a dialogue between just two instruments: violin and cello. The tonal disposition is untypically clear. Sibelius begins in D minor, the functional dominant (A major) is present via the leading tone C♯—all this evoked without chords, using purely linear means. Even the unison at the start of the Allegro molto moderato (measure 9) is fundamentally linear: every voice gains a high degree of linear individuality. In general—even though the polyphony in *Voces intimae* and the Fourth Symphony is refined—Sibelius's voice leading is hardly a strength. Compared with his colleagues abroad, Sibelius's artistry lies more in his sense of harmony and orchestration than in counterpoint.

Example 2. *Voces intimae*, Andante, mm. 1–11.

The movement ends on the pitch A (in two registers). The transition to the second movement is therefore emphasized, rather than the individuality of each movement. The Vivace is a light scherzo in the Mendelssohn tradition. Here, too, the tonal foundation (A major) remains constant throughout. In the third movement, Adagio di molto, linearity is combined with progressive chromatic movement. The three chords, marked post factum as "*voces intimae*," are played *pianississimo*. After the preceding F-minor passage, they sound almost unreal, if not radically remote. Three times in succession we hear simple E-minor triads (Example 3). They are unprepared, and appear to have no consequences for the music's subsequent harmonic progression. Twenty-three measures before the end, the chords return on C♯ minor, before the original tonal foundation, D minor, is reestablished. In the first movement (Andante), static chords already disrupt the linear chromatic flow but to a less marked degree: for instance, in measure 38 (E major after C-sharp minor) or measure 42 (C-major chord after A major). The interruption of the polyphonic texture by a chord twenty-two measures before the end (A major after F-sharp minor) and then five measures later (F major after D minor) is peculiar. There are unexpected holes in the polyphonic texture of the second movement as well—a capricious effect within the scherzo topic that is repeated in a varied fashion toward the end of the movement. Though they are unspectacular harmonically, such moments prepare the intimacy of this central third movement.

Example 3. Sibelius, *Voces intimae*, più Adagio, mm. 22–27.

Brahms is the preeminent model in the fourth movement, an Allegretto (ma pesante) in D minor (in a heavy triple meter). The final movement initially returns to the Sibelian elegy of the beginning. Simple motives in a fundamentally tonal but modally and chromatically inflected context are confronted by each other. The remainder of the finale is not so much a rondo alla zingaresca (despite the Brahmsian fourth movement) but rather a Scandinavian *spelmans*-dance that brings the quartet to rushing conclusion in happy ecstasy.

In his orchestral music, Sibelius repeatedly extended the formal frame of the larger genres. *Voces intimae* is an isolated experiment in intimacy, and may be Sibelius's most important composition without orchestra. In comparison to other chamber music experiments of the era, *Voces intimae* demonstrates a clear sense of ambition. Mahler's piano quartet was never finished, and Richard Strauss's large oeuvre includes only a very few chamber music works and fragments, namely the string quartets op. 2 (1880) and op. 13 (1885). The originality of Sibelius's op. 56 lies in its unusual and effective post-Romantic characteristics and motivic-thematic processes. *Voces intimae* was completed shortly before the mature string quartets of Ravel, Schoenberg, and Hindemith. Like those composers, Sibelius distances himself from Brahms (despite the affinity in the fourth movement), the leading chamber music composer of the previous generation. Sibelius creates a texture that, despite the four-part polyphonic voice leading, moves more like orchestral music. Sibelius himself was critical of the work's orchestral timbre. In his diary on 24 April 1910 he wrote: "The melodic material is good but the sound could be 'lighter' and why not more a 'quartet—'. This 'cum grano salis'!"[51] But he never attempted to re-compose *Voces intimae* with this lightness in mind. He knew that the composition was difficult to improve, and, in his diary three days later he wrote with a certain sense of pride: "I believe I have passed the apprentice's exam. Look after your way on the open sea! You can already achieve 'something'!"[52] And, on 26 May 1910 Sibelius drafted a letter following the work's first performance in Helsinki: "Some weeks ago they performed 'Voces intimae' here with the local string quartet. . . . The work, by the way, was a great success. They all say it is my best work. I do not quite think so, but it belongs among the best."[53]

Sibelius's qualification is plausible. By 1910 he could already look back on three original symphonies, *Kullervo*, and the violin concerto, as well as many solo songs and choral works. His publisher wrote from Berlin on 14 January 1911, after the first German performance: "A few days ago I heard your string quartet for the first time, in the Tonkünstlerverein with the Ševčik Quartet. The performance was outstanding. . . . But indeed, rather different from the usual string quartets."[54] Among the more remarkable contemporary interpretations of *Voces intimae* must have belonged that of the Amar Quartet, with Paul Hindemith on the viola, at the Nordic Music Festival (Nordisches Musikfest) in 1924 in Heidelberg.[55]

Erik Tawaststjerna mentions Beethoven's string quartet, op. 59, no. 1, as a possible model for Sibelius's op. 56.[56] Interesting parallels can also be drawn between *Voces intimae* and other more contemporary string quartets. Sibelius certainly heard Claude Debussy's Quartet (1893) in London on 21 October 1910, and described the work in his diary as "refined but small." However, the work had previously been played in Helsinki in February 1907 by the legendary Brussels String Quartet,[57] and it is likely that Sibelius was in attendance since he was not abroad. Sibelius could hardly have heard Ravel's 1903 quartet, modeled on Debussy's work, in 1909, and even Reger's wonderful Quartet in E-flat Major, op. 109, was written almost parallel to *Voces intimae*. The first Schoenberg quartet, op. 7 (also in D minor), was written in 1905 but not performed until 1907. Again, we do not know how well informed Sibelius was as far as such points of concurrence were concerned—particularly in the case of chamber music. *Voces intimae*'s originality lies in effects that—like the works of Janáček and Stravinsky later—break the common sense of musical syntax. The textual flow is far from classical, and such effects mark unexpected changes of character. Reger's op.109 quartet is related to Sibelius's op. 56 at least in this respect. In both works the meter frequently loses its formal and syntactic power as a means of coherence. The harmonic rift created by the "intimate" chords in the third movement, for instance, represents extended tonality at the border of functionality. This device is typical of Reger, too, and a good example of Liszt's progressive maxim, as Reger acknowledged: "I follow the Lisztian sentence: 'Any chord can follow any chord,' and act, indeed, accordingly."[58] Similarly, Sibelius employed his "intimate" chords without functional consequences. This is one of the ways he was able to create unusual harmonic transitions in many of his works. To compare Sibelius and Reger in this way is to point out the stylistic position of these artists in the fluid situation between the legacies of Brahms the progressive and Wagner the revolutionary. In that sense, Eugen d'Albert was an alternative synthetic model for Reger,[59] as Karl Goldmark was more or less for Sibelius. Schoenberg—aware of Reger's efforts—elaborated it in a modernist style. But many more senior colleagues, including Sibelius, did not follow him.

Decomposing *Kalevala*

Among Sibelius's symphonic poems, two works stand out above the others: the tone poem for soprano and orchestra *Luonnotar,* op. 70, of 1913 (relatively neglected in the musicological literature),[60] and *Tapiola,* op. 112, of 1926. *Luonnotar* begins with a vibrating F-sharp-minor chord and ends in a vague F-sharp major plus the non-functional tones: D, F, and B. The harmonic language as well as the orchestration is free from convention. Sibelius includes a bass clarinet and two harps in the orchestra, mainly to illustrate the storm evoked by the work's text (drawn from canto 20 of the Finnish national epic, the *Kalevala*). The absence of a functional dominant in the opening measures means the tonality is weak. In *Finlandia,* op. 26, and the First Symphony, op. 39, Sibelius first questions but then affirms the work's final tonality. The functional dominant is prolonged and then elaborated in a manner also found in Brahms's compositions. The search for the tonality is an auxiliary cadence. In contrast, *Luonnotar* experiments with the contrast between a strong tonic and other weakened functions. The radical quality of this gesture culminates in mm. 21–22, where Sibelius presents a C-major chord as a substitute for the proper dominant of the following F-sharp-minor tonic triad. Despite this peculiar gesture, the pitch C does not get any special position at this point. The chord is a curious harmonic idea, only weakening the cadential harmony. Octatonic scales can also be identified in *Luonnotar*, but it is hard to verify whether they are used systematically. One reason to believe that Sibelius might have been consciously aware of them is that they are increasingly used toward the end of the piece; for instance, at the Tranquillo assai, eleven measures after rehearsal letter B at "Voi poloinen" (oh the poor one); after rehearsal letter K at "pesänsä; alkoi hautoa" (her nest; started to brood); thereafter at "Järkytti jäsenehensä" (trembled her body); and finally thirteen measures before the end, at "kuuksi kumottamahan" (to shine like the moon). This mixture of chromatic, modal, and tonal practices helps to locate *Luonnotar* between the Fourth and Sixth symphonies.

The absence of a functional dominant is particularly manifest in the closing measures. Even the final chord is not approached by means of a tonal cadence. The tonic emerges audibly as the foreign tones C♮, D, and A, vanish one measure before the end. Two measures before the close we hear the six tones C, F♯, C♯, D, A, and A♯ in several registers, creating an atonal collection (half a complete chromatic set). The transformation of this chord is remarkable. The atonal chord slowly emerges fourteen measures before the end and gradually disappears, leaving the tonic F-sharp-major triad alone. Five measures before the end the foreign tones are still heard in several registers, but later they appear in only a single register each. The soprano intonates each of the orchestra's chromatic tones with a single exception: instead of the melodic leading tone E♯, the soprano sings E♮. This lower variant might be a modal detail, but it may also simply be a chromatic variant (Example 4).

The soloist at *Luonnotar*'s first performance in 1913 was the Finnish soprano Aino Ackté, who had sung the title role in Richard Strauss's *Salome* in Leipzig in 1907 and London in 1910. Nonetheless, *Luonnotar* must have been a special challenge, particularly at the end of her vocal career. The melodic range stretches from middle C up to a high C♭. With *Luonnotar,* Ackté said adieu to her audience and simultaneously marked the zenith of her carrier as a performer of modern music.

Works like *Luonnotar* and *Tapiola* reveal that Sibelius was not a composer of simple nature impressions but of highly sophisticated soundscapes that

Example 4. Sibelius, *Luonnotar*, conclusion.

are difficult to place in familiar accounts of musical modernism. Their melodic development, continual search for formal innovation, and intensive reflection upon the possibilities of extending tonality make both compositions unique. Astonishingly, Sibelius's most progressive works are not symphonies but these tone poems. Tone poems—a Lisztian genre—also include Sibelius's most conventional, romantic compositions. But the borderline between programmatic and abstract art is highly porous. The presence or absence of a program, particularly in Sibelius's oeuvre, is no reason to call a composition exclusively either a symphony or a tone poem.

Sibelius's tone poems and symphonies form one of the strongest links between Liszt's *Les préludes* and Ligeti's *Atmosphères*. Like Liszt and Ligeti's compositions, *Tapiola* is not merely a naturalistic representation of "Nordic" woods and shadows, but rather a significant autobiographical document. With some hermeneutic effort, one can hear in *Tapiola* a synthesis of everything that Sibelius had to say about nature, its elements and mysteries. Simultaneously, it is the true farewell of a great architect, modernist, symbolist, and poet. The composition was commissioned by the Breslau-born American conductor Walter Damrosch (1862–1950), son of Liszt disciple Leopold Damrosch.[61] Damrosch Senior was founder of the New York Symphony Society. Sibelius had known Walter Damrosch since he visited the Norfolk Festival in Connecticut in 1914. No other commissioned work of Sibelius reaches such a high artistic level. The other American commission, *The Oceanides*, op. 73, of 1914, for example, pales by comparison. In a letter of 4 January 1926, Damrosch had asked for a symphonic poem of 15 to 20 minutes, and Sibelius delivered one without any doubt or hesitation. He finished the score on 27 September 1926. By 5 November Breitkopf & Härtel had already sent the orchestral material and score to New York. The first performance in New York took place on 16 December 1926, though sadly Sibelius was not present at this grand occasion.

Tapiola's program indicates a mixture of nature and mythology. The word "Tapiola" in the *Kalevala* refers to the domain of the Forest God, Tapio, and to the Nordic forest as a mythical landscape, also known as "Metsola." Despite the neo-impressionistic techniques in *Tapiola*, it is questionable whether the composition is truly about nature or landscape. Certainly, many listeners associate the music with natural spaces or atmospheric landscapes. But the composition's possible associations range much further to include a symbolic narrative interpretation drawn either from Finnish mythology or the composer's own rich imagination.

Generally speaking, Sibelius's landscapes should be regarded as landscapes of the mind or "phantasy landscapes." *En saga*, op. 9 (1892; rev. 1902), is a prime example. Realist musical landscape painting or impressionism are rare in Sibelius's output. In his miniatures and incidental music, for example, in the overture to Shakespeare's *The Tempest* (see Daniel M. Grimley's discussion in this volume), decorative or illustrative moments can be found with an intensity that is often expected (in vain) from his larger orchestral works. Sibelius's major works do not simply analyze or illustrate nature. They are documents of the effect of nature upon the mind of the artist, similar to the synesthesia promoted by such visual artists as Akseli Gallen-Kallela, Sibelius's most prominent Finnish contemporary. In some cases, nature was used as a semantic substitute for human matters, an individual's encounter with birth, death, the originary states of human life, and other favorite topics in late Romanticism.

The *Kalevala* is *Tapiola*'s main literary context. A narrative interpretation that accords with the *Kalevala*'s epic model may therefore seem likely. However, major parts of *Tapiola* were composed in Rome, Berlin, and on the "isola magica" of Capri.[62] Sibelius is not documented to have read the *Kalevala* during the voyage—facts that suggest the title needs further analysis. Sibelius seldom (if ever) took as a given Liszt's classical definition of programmatic music—that the program not only has an effect on a work's structure, but that its listeners must also know it in detail. Instead, Sibelius often deceived the audience with his titles. This possibility also has to be taken into account when listening to *Tapiola*. On the island of Capri, where Tiberius had once ruled over the Roman Empire and the mythical landscape remained omnipresent (the rocks of Scoglio del Monacone inspiring Arnold Böcklin's *Isle of the Dead* series), the impressions and ideas Sibelius had collected in Finland over the years while reading the *Kalevala* were amplified and elaborated. Sibelius may have been similarly inspired by Capri's woods, where he would not have seen a single Nordic *Picea abies*, the mythical tree of the Finns, but rather an overwhelming mixture of *Pinus halepensis*, *Laurus nobilis*, *Melaleuca armillaris*, and *Cupressus sempervirens*— a sight that from afar might have superficially resembled a Finnish forest with rocks. More important, Sibelius's mind was always open to ancient history and mythology, and Latin and Greek belonged among his favored subjects at the Finnish high school in Hämeenlinna. This does not mean that *Tapiola* is a mere "caprice," or an exercise in Nordic *Italianitá*. The intention is rather to open up discussion beyond the supposedly Finnish roots of the composition, thereby broadening its modernist validity.

Tapiola is less tightly connected (if at all) to the text of the *Kalevala* than *Kullervo*, op. 7, the four *Lemminkäinen* Legends, op. 22, or *Luonnotar*. There is no single passage in the epic that would fit with the tone poem as a program. The name of the mythical region Tapiola is briefly mentioned only a few times. In the 1849 edition that Sibelius normally used, Tapio and his court enter in Canto 14 (the legend of Lemminkäinen), and briefly reappear in Cantos 15, 32, and 46. We can summarize by suggesting that Tapiola is omnipresent as a mythical space in the *Kalevala*, but this hardly seems sufficient as the program for a single composition. The only evidence of a program, in fact, is the poem that is printed in the score, where it was published in English, German, and French. The original is obviously the German: the others are more or less opportune translations. Sibelius must have been asked to write or approve a programmatic text, just as Liszt would have done. He presumably gave some hints, but the poem is not by the composer himself—Sibelius did not write poetry—but probably by a member of the publishing house.

Da dehnen sich des Nordlands düstre Wälder	Widespread they stand, the Northland's dusky forests,
Uralt-geheimnisvoll in wilden Träumen;	Ancient, mysterious, brooding
In ihnen wohnt der Wälder großer Gott,	savage dreams;
Waldgeister weben heimlich in dem Dunkel.	Within them dwells the Forest's mighty God,
	And wood sprites in the gloom weave magic secrets.

The matter is best documented in Sibelius's correspondence with his publishers and Walter Damrosch before the first performance. Sibelius did not play a central role in discussion of the work's title and program, but he accepted all proposals. On 26 September 1926, Sibelius wrote to Breitkopf & Härtel in his customary diplomatic manner (particularly evident when the topic did not really interest him): "I find the poem at the beginning very beautiful. From my heart I thank you."[63] If Sibelius was ever concerned about a matter, he generally used more refined terminology. But the problem of a title associated with the woods first appeared as early as April 1926, when Sibelius wanted to explain what he was composing. Reading the letters between Sibelius and Aino during the weeks before the title was finalized might even open up the possibility that it was Aino's idea to call the work *Tapiola*, even if it is impossible to prove such a hypothesis definitively.[64] In June 1926, Sibelius wrote to Damrosch about the subject, but the final elaborated version of the title with fixed programmatic associations seems to have been Damrosch's idea, who wrote: "Tapiola, a wild Nordic desert where the God of the Woods and his nymphs are staying."[65] We might well be surprised to find Damrosch so well informed on Finnish culture. But before Damrosch receives full credit for the program, we need to know more about his assistants and his social milieu, and we should not underestimate the international popularity of the *Kalevala* at that time.

Several important people at Breitkopf & Härtel in Leipzig could have written a poetic text suitable for use as a program, including the firm's proprietor, Honorary Finnish Consul Hellmuth von Hase (1891–1979), who prepared the German translation of V. A. Koskenniemi's lyrics for *Finlandia*'s 1953 edition. Sibelius himself later stressed that he was inspired to write *Tapiola* by nature in its entirety "and nothing else," or "nothing that you might be able to express in words."[66] This is a symbolist position, and is no less limiting than something that can be found only in the

Kalevala. Sibelius had used the title "Forest Symphony" (also "The Woods" and "The Forest") in his early correspondence on the project with his wife, but ultimately this must have been too vague for the publisher and/or conductor. No doubt they felt that almost anyone could compose "The Woods," but only Sibelius could write a symphony on the great forests of the *Kalevala* itself, hence *Tapiola*.

Irrespective of the title's origins, the idea of writing a forest symphony in the first place was originally Axel Carpelan's. He wrote a number of prophetic letters to Sibelius, providing the first (albeit vague) ideas for *Finlandia*, op. 26 (1900), the Violin Concerto, op. 47 (1903–5), and even *Voces intimae*, op. 56.[67] However, it is unlikely that Sibelius had Carpelan's early suggestion solely in mind when he started on his *Tapiola* project. He had already composed nature-related compositions such as *Luonnotar*, *The Oceanides*, or even the early *Skogsrået* (*The Wood Nymph*), op. 15, without Carpelan's help.[68]

Despite its progressive or modernist passages, *Tapiola* really owes its origins to Liszt. His influence on modern music remains a relatively neglected topic, in spite of Schoenberg's important essay of 1911 on Franz Liszt.[69] Both James Hepokoski and Tim Howell, for example, have compared *Tapiola* with passages from Ligeti or other minimalist tendencies en gros.[70] The latter association, however, is based on a metaphoric rather than empirical (historical) use of the term "minimalist." Ligeti's "micropolyphony" and his techniques of space and texture (particularly the so-called *Feldtechniken*, or field techniques)[71] are in some ways close to what Sibelius is doing,[72] but other concepts are required if the work as a whole is to be discussed analytically. Erkki Salmenhaara, in contrast, emphasizes *Tapiola*'s principle of "organic variation,"[73] linking the piece rather with Schoenberg's notion of "total variation" and later ideas such as those of Karlheinz Stockhausen.[74] In all of these cases, *Tapiola* is not discussed as a melodic composition—a tendency in late Sibelius that begins with the Fifth Symphony, op. 82.[75] The most prominent passage that has inspired such talk of minimalism and micropolyphony is the Coda (mm. 513–634). The sheer length of this section is not out of proportion. If one interprets the work as a kind of sonata form, in the tradition of Liszt's great B-Minor Piano Sonata (as Ernst Tanzberger did in the 1940s),[76] the two-part exposition lasts 205 measures, the development a further 250, and the recapitulation (omitting the principal subject) only 50 measures. The Coda is remarkable not so much for its motivic content as for its use of texture. In mm. 513–68 a gradual accumulation of sound occurs, based on a tremolo figure from the second subject area. Then a rhythmic element emerges, quoting a figure from measure 356, whose melodic profile is drawn from the principal subject (Example 5).

Example 5. Sibelius, *Tapiola*, mm. 513–31.

The length and the homomorphous nature of this passage, a slow, completely anti-melodic and atonal accumulation over more than fifty measures, is remarkable in the stylistic context of the 1920s. The passage is prepared by shorter earlier sections with a tendency toward micropolyphony. The first of these is prepared from a chromatic motive in parallel thirds in measure 1 (*Largamente*). In measure 21 (*Allegro moderato*), this pattern becomes faster. Within five measures a steep accumulation of sound (starting *piano* and reaching *fortissimo crescendo*) follows, announced by a fortepiano attack in the wind instruments. This gesture returns in the Coda. The coherent melodic statements in measure 26 and following also evoke an effect that is typical of minimalism and its penetrative repetition of small, relatively redundant musical blocks. The same goes for mm. 157–81 in the second section of the exposition. But the purpose of such passages (for example, the texture of mm. 161–67, Example 6) is very different from minimalism as it later developed.

Such textural issues receive hardly any attention in the analyses by Salmenhaara (1970) or Ernst Tanzberger (1943, 1962). In the minimalism debate, however, they receive more attention than they properly deserve. They do not dominate the composition, but are rather merely elemental and explosive areas of rupture (comparable with what Reinhold Brinkmann describes as *"Ausbruchszonen"* in Schoenberg's piano works).[77] In *En saga* a preliminary version of these textural fields can be found on pp. 47–48 of the printed score: a similar tremolo texture lasts eighteen measures.

Example 6. Sibelius, *Tapiola*, mm. 161–67.

Normally such textures would function as an accompaniment, but in *Tapiola* they have been emancipated. No less modernist, as Cecil Gray noted in his 1931 study of Sibelius only a few years after *Tapiola*'s premiere, is the work's motivic concentration.[78] According to the brilliant American Sibelius scholar Harold E. Johnson, *Tapiola* was an experiment in composing a lot "out of nothing."[79] This does not suggest minimalism, but rather "maximalism" or "maximal music" in the sense that Ligeti used the term.[80]

But what about autobiography, rather than landscape or mythology, as a hidden program? Nothing speaks against the idea. Programmatic readings based on the printed anonymous poem, or on the *Kalevala*, contradict Sibelius's assertion that the work was inspired by "nature alone" and cannot be described in words. The theory that *Tapiola* is about confronting life and ultimately death fits this symbolist frame well. Such symbolist readings of *Tapiola* also suggest that landscape can gain a new interpretative context. According to Hans H. Hofstätter, "Landscape painting creates symbols for the loneliness of man, for his inferiority to the elemental power and to the mysterious almighty God, pictured in infinite space and effects of a cosmic power." This infinite space is the "Ur-symbol of the Faustian soul in contrast to the sensitive presence of the individual body."[81] As early as 1891 Sibelius, a sensitive twenty-six-year-old with a strong tendency toward hypochondria, asked a doctor to estimate how old he would be at the end of his life. The doctor replied, "certainly sixty"—without considering how time passes and how keenly some people remember such notions.[82] Sibelius reached that age in 1925 and respectful as he was, being the son of another doctor, for such medical advice, he became concerned. After all, he had no reason to believe the doctor would be wrong: his father had died at the age of forty-seven, his mother, Maria, at fifty-six, and brother Christian at fifty-three. Based on this genetic inheritance, Sibelius could not have expected to survive and become one of the oldest composers in the history of Western music. He had also lost important friends—such as Busoni when he died in 1923, aged only fifty-eight, and Martin Wegelius, the man who founded the music school that later became the Sibelius Academy in Helsinki, in 1906, at the age of sixty. To Sibelius in the 1920s, it must have seemed as though he had already outlived his generation.

Melancholy and tragic elements are easy to find in *Tapiola*'s score. The principal motive, omnipresent throughout the composition, begins with

Example 7. Sibelius, *Tapiola*, mm. 1–9.

the tones B and A♯ (suggesting a G-sharp minor context, but with E and D in the bass), a melodic gesture that readily implies a sense of sorrow:

Tapiola's final chord is B major, emphasizing the feeling of full closure within a tonal framework. The opening motive still appears in measure 610 in bright instrumentation (piccolo, clarinets in unison), transformed into major seconds. This diatonic variation of the motive, first heard in measure 246, becomes the answer to a B-minor version of the same idea in measure 593. The descending chromatic line, beginning in measure 588 and leading to the tone B♮ in measure 606, perhaps marks the transfiguration within the lyric ego from sorrow to eternal happiness. Out of the E-major sonority in measure 615 emerges an E-major seventh (the same chord with which the piece had opened but very differently contextualized), leading to the final B major after nine measures. The progression is

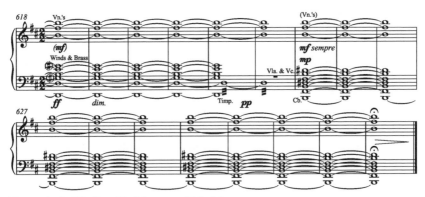

Example 8. Sibelius, *Tapiola*, mm. 618–34.

so slow that there is little sense of tonal consequence, and the final cadence becomes a simple "Amen" or benediction:

In the final section of the work, this transformation from simple pictorialism into a landscape of the mind, remote from any descriptive narrative, is made obvious by the sense of free pulsation and the meditative brightness of the closing B-major triad. Here the *Kalevala*-style epic becomes the interiority of a melancholy imagination. Sibelius's brother-in-law, the painter Eero Järnefelt, once traveled to Koli in eastern Finland with the composer, the location that became the inspiration for the Fourth Symphony, and wrote: "We can illustrate human thoughts and humor, seriousness, joy, angst, hatred, by means of landscape painting."[83] In *Tapiola* Sibelius also does this, perhaps inviting us to walk through a deep forest where life (and death) are visible in all their stages. Such a walk inspires all kinds of thoughts concerning human misery. But our fear may also vanish as we enjoy the presence of nature in the luminosity of the final B-major chord. Like Böcklin's painting *The Isle of the Dead* (1880–83) and Strauss's *Death and Transfiguration,* op. 24 (1888–90), in *Tapiola* the artist helps us to understand the flow of life and accept even the presence of the Swan of Death.

That Sibelius's art refers to the elemental in nature, not the figurative landscape, is documented by many aphorisms, metaphors, and small, poetic notes in his diary and other documents. On 4 June 1911, he wrote in his typically symbolist manner: "Wonderful day. Poetry in the air. Nature speaks." And on 18 February 1925, one year before *Tapiola*: "A nature poetry that drives one mad! But I mustn't succumb. This miraculously rich life is unendurable."[84] With such sentences in mind, and considering that *Tapiola* is Sibelius's final major composition, the work becomes one of the greatest farewell compositions in the history of music, alongside Mozart's *Requiem* fragment (KV 626), the *Adagio* from Bruckner's Ninth Symphony, and Richard Strauss's *Metamorphosen* of 1946.

Epilogue: The "Pastness of the Modernist Present"

According to the doctrines of modernism, old-fashioned music is supposed to have been composed earlier.[85] No doubt we can assess whether a composition is progressive, anachronistic, or simply a product of its day by keeping the history of compositional techniques in mind. But Sibelius belongs among those composers whose style makes such assessment difficult. The reasons are many. Even in his youth he had a loose personal attachment to traditionalism. He did not pass through any domineering school of composition where he might have mastered a particular technique too early. This is itself sufficient to explain why we can find old-fashioned and progressive moments within a single Sibelius work. Having said this, we need to say as well that in his case the idea of a singular modernism is absurd. The lack of a single compositional system explains his richness of invention, but also makes it difficult to use his music as the model for something new. Consequently, Sibelius taught very few composers (among them Uuno Klami, Leevi Madetoja, and Bengt de Törne). But many others began to imitate him—not least in England and the United States—just as their teachers had imitated Wagner or Brahms earlier. Both Brahms and Wagner, however, possessed a strong sense of compositional technique. Brahms believed in passive inspiration, the Romantic version of André Breton's *écriture automatique* of the *Manifeste du surréalisme* (1924), or, in Mahler's words: "One does not compose, one is composed."[86] Brahms described the compositional processes (somewhat ironically) during his extended walks in nature: "I consider it very adroit that I allow melodies to fall into my mind when I am out for a walk."[87] Yet perhaps such accounts of creative process should not be taken too seriously. The mixture of the conscious and subconscious, active and passive, conscious and supernatural forms of innovation and inspiration is typically human, and individual differences in disposition can certainly be studied but not to the exclusion of other forms of evidence.

Modernism is an attitude rather than an aesthetic quality. To evaluate modernism as an attitude means to evaluate its creative processes and artistic motives. This does not mean that modernism's manifestations cannot also be analyzed, but it may explain the ambiguity we are confronted with by modernist configurations in the oeuvre of composers whose own modernist attitude was ambivalent. We know that Sibelius was interested in the form and "logic" of his works (whether dictated by "God" or his own inner impulse), but we also know that he was motivated by isolated ideas and moments of inspiration as well as various musical traditions—and that he himself was deeply critical about this. Here again we find a mixture of modernist and other attitudes. We face a composer who sought tighter, more conscious control of his material, but whose greatness in the eyes of later generations lies in his unique ideas and innovations, whether inspired by Nordic nature or other cultures. Who can tell how often they should be regarded as the products of a brilliant creative mind with the rare privilege of having been born in Finland?

NOTES

The Walter Benjamin epigraph opening this essay is translated from "Schmetterlingsjagd" (1938), in *Berliner Kindheit um Neunzehnhundert* (Frankfurt am Main: Suhrkamp, 1987), 20–21; the Nabokov epigraph comes from Vladimir Nabokov, *Speak, Memory* (London: Penguin, 1967; repr. 2000), 103.

1. Ernst Hofmann, "Analyse aus der Sicht der pädagogischen Praxis," *Musik und Bildung* 3 (1979): 175–77. "Ich könnte Sie, hochverehrter Freund, in mein Werk einweihen, aber ich tue es aus Prinzip nicht. Mit den Kompositionen ist es wie mit den Schmetterlingen. Wenn man sie einmal berührt hat, ist ihr Zauber weg. Sie können zwar noch fliegen, aber sie sind nicht mehr so hübsch wie früher" (175).

2. Ibid. "Nicht die analytischen Methoden—falls einfühlsam und gekönnt durchgeführt—verleiden dem jungen Menschen die Freude an der Musik. Seine mangelnde Vorbildung verwehrt ihm das Verständnis für die Analyse, die ihm Schlüssel zum Werk sein will."

3. Walter Legge, in "Conversations with Sibelius" (*The Musical Times* 76/1105 [March 1935]: 218–20) quotes Sibelius using a similar metaphor concerning unfinished works: "You know how the wing of a butterfly crumbles at the touch? So it is with my composi-

tions; the very mention of them is fatal" (219). Sibelius obviously used the metaphor frequently over the years.

4. "Jag skulla nog gerna inviga Dig, förstående människa, i mitt arbete, men gör det af princip ej. Enligt min tanke är det med kompositioner som med fjärilar: tag i dem en gång, då är stoftet borta—de kunna nog flyga, men äro ej mera lika skära." Sibelius Collection, National Archives of Finland, Helsinki (henceforth NA). See also Fabian Dahlström, ed., *Högtärade Maestro! Högtärade Herr Baron! Korrespondensen mellan Axel Carpelan och Jean Sibelius 1900–1919* (Helsinki: Svenska litteratursällskapet i Finland, 2010), 75.

5. Erik Tawaststjerna, *Jean Sibelius: Åren 1865–1893*, ed. Gitta Henning (Helsinki: Söderström, 1992), 57.

6. Bengt de Törne, *Sibelius: A Close-Up* (London: Faber & Faber, 1937) 51, 59. For an analysis of this problematic book and its negative effect on Adorno, see Tomi Mäkelä, *"Poesie in der Luft": Jean Sibelius, Studien zu Leben und Werk* (Wiesbaden: Breitkopf & Härtel, 2007), 360–67.

7. On the structure of butterfly wings, see Satoshi Kishimoto, Qinghua Wang, Huimin Xie, and Yapu Zhao, "Study of the surface structure of butterfly wings using the scanning electron microscopic moiré method," *Applied Optics* 46/28 (2007): 7026–34.

8. See Eric Hobsbawm, *The Age of Revolution* (London: Abacus 1962; repr. 1996), 270. For a recent analysis of musical modernism in relation to this development see Max Paddison, "Centres and Margins: Shifting Grounds in the Conceptualization of Modernism," in *Rethinking Musical Modernism*, vol. 122, book 6, ed. Dejan Despíc and Melita Milin (Belgrade: Serbian Academy of Sciences and Arts, 2008), 65–81, quote at 74. See also Paddison's essay in the present volume.

9. See "Arnold Schönberg" in Mäkelä, *"Poesie in der Luft,"* 265–69.

10. Jean Sibelius, *Dagbok 1909–1944*, ed. Fabian Dahlström (Helsinki: Svenska litteratursällskapet i Finland, 2005), 183.

11. The entire original German reads: "Der von keiner Konvention gebändigte Ausdruck ungemilderten Leidens scheint unmanierlich: er vergeht sich gegen das Tabu der englischen Gouvernante, der Mahler in die Parade fuhr, als die 'don't get excited' mahnte." Theodor W. Adorno, *Philosophy of Modern Music*, trans. Anne G. Mitchell and Wesley V. Bloomster (New York: Seabury Press, 1973; repr. 1987), 41.

12. Lois Oppenheim, "Clarifications, Elucidations: An Interview with Milan Kundera," *Review of Contemporary Fiction* 9/2 (1989): 9.

13. Ronald Stevenson, letter to Sibelius, 25 October 1948, National Library of Finland, Collection 206, box 37. On Sibelius and Stevenson, see Mäkelä, *"Poesie in der Luft,"* 59–63, including a manuscript Stevenson dedicated to Sibelius.

14. Wolfgang Welsch, *Unsere postmoderne Moderne* (Weinheim: VCH Acta humaniora, 1987).

15. Theodor W. Adorno, *Minima moralia: Reflections on a Damaged Life*, trans. Dennis Redmond, http://www.efn.org/~dredmond/MinimaMoralia.html (2005), aphorism 140 ('Consecutio temporum').

16. Tomi Mäkelä, "Die 'poetische Dissonanz' in der Symphonik von Jean Sibelius: Kompositionstechnische Metamorphosen des Neudeutschen in der nordischen Moderne," *Liszt und Europa*, ed. Detlef Altenburg and Harriet Oelers (Laaber: Laaber, 2008), 343–63.

17. First published in *Allgemeine Musikzeitung* 38/42 (20 October 1911): 1088–90; later published in Arnold Schoenberg, *Stil und Gedanke: Aufsätze zur Musik. Gesammelte Schriften* 1, ed. Ivan Vojtěch. (Frankfurt am Main: Suhrkamp, 1976), 169–73.

18. Mäkelä, "Arnold Schönberg," 265–69.

19. On extraterritoriality, see Mäkelä, *"Poesie in der Luft,"* 351.

20. The phrase "Gleichzeitigkeit des Ungleichzeitigen" was elaborated by Ernst Bloch in *Tübinger Einleitung in die Philosophie* (Frankfurt am Main: Suhrkamp, 1963). For further discussion, see Carl Dahlhaus, "Gleichzeitigkeit des Ungleichzeitigen," *Musica* 41 (1987): 307–10.

21. Paddison, "Centres and Margins," 66.

22. Ibid., 68.

23. Ibid., 78.

24. Ibid., 69.

25. Mäkelä, "Poesie in der Luft," 265.

26. Jean Sibelius, The Hämeenlinna Letters: Scenes from a Musical Life 1874–1895, ed. Glenda Dawn Goss (Esbo: Schildts, 1997), 176.

27. Sibelius's translated manuscript appears in the Documents section of this volume.

28. Lionel Pike, "Tonality and Modality in Sibelius's Sixth Symphony," Tempo 216 (April 2001): 6–16. On modality in Sibelius's works, see the special Sibelius issue of the French magazine Musurgia 15/1–3 (2008).

29. Fabian Dahlström, Jean Sibelius: Thematisch-bibliographisches Verzeichnis seiner Werke (Wiesbaden: Breitkopf & Härtel, 2003), 435.

30. "Sinfonin är 'färdig'. Iacta alea est! Måste! Det fordras mycken mänlighet att se lifvet i hvitögat. Alltså." Sibelius, Dagbok, 74.

31. "Ich war gerade zurückgekommen aus Berlin, wo ich zwei Monate verweilte. Wie gewöhnlich, bekam ich einen unüberwindlichen Ekel für die 'moderne Richtung.' Und daraus wuchs 'alleingefühl'. . . . Zu meinem Erstaunen sehe ich dass man sehr viele meiner Compositionen aufführt auf dem Continent, obwohl die doch nichts von 'Modernität' in sich haben." See also Rosa Newmarch, Jean Sibelius: A Short Story of a Long Friendship (Boston: Birchard, 1939), 24; the original can be found in the Sibelius Family Archive in the NA.

32. Erik Tawaststjerna, Jean Sibelius: Åren 1904–14 (Stockholm: Atlantis, 1991), 220–21, quotes Carpelan's article in Helsingin Sanomat.

33. James Hepokoski, Sibelius: Symphony No. 5 (Cambridge: Cambridge University Press, 1993), 15.

34. Paddison, "Centres and Margins," 68.

35. On the concept of "Life-givingness" in music, see Marjorie Stoddard in a letter to the composer on 1 January 1938, National Library of Finland, Coll. 206, 37. See also Mäkelä, "Poesie in der Luft," 6–70.

36. Sibelius, letter to Newmarch, 2 May 1911, quoted in Tawaststjerna, Sibelius: 1904–1914, 221.

37. Sibelius, letter to Carpelan, 20 July 1909, quoted in Dahlström, Högärade Maestro! 246.

38. Hepokoski, Sibelius: Symphony No. 5, 15.

39. Edgard Varèse, "The Liberation of Sound" (1936), in Perspectives on American Composers, ed. Benjamin Boretz and Edward T. Cone (New York: W. W. Norton, 1971), 25–33, quote at 25.

40. Most recently, in Brigitte Pinder, Form und Inhalt der symphonischen Tondichtung von Sibelius (Berlin: Wissenschaftlicher Verlag Berlin, 2005), 422–32.

41. Joachim Brügge, Jean Sibelius: Symphonien und symphonische Dichtungen: Ein musikalischer Werkführer (Munich: Fink, 2009), 62.

42. Reinhold Brinkmann and Wolfgang Rihm, Musik Nachdenken (Regensburg: ConBrio, 2001), 141.

43. For an analysis of musical modernism as an evolution of scale, see Max Weber, Die rationalen und soziologischen Grundlagen der Musik (Munich: Drei Masken, 1921).

44. The German original reads: "Für Sibelius bezeichnende, schattenhaft-versponnene Melodiebögen . . . die sich wie im Nichts zu verlieren scheinen."

45. Brügge, Sibelius, 66.

46. Ibid., 72.

47. Carpelan's letter to Sibelius, 27 December 1909, in Dahlström, Högärade Maestro! 261–62. See also the context in Mäkelä, "Poesie in der Luft," 142.

48. Erik Tawaststjerna Archive, National Archives of Finland.

49. Sibelius, *Dagbok*, 35.

50. Quoted in Tawaststjerna, *Sibelius 1904–14*, 148.

51. Sibelius, *Dagbok*, 43.

52. Ibid.

53. Sibelius Family Archive, NA, Box 46.

54. Ibid.

55. Ruth-Maria Gleißner, *Der unpolitische Komponist als Politikum: Die Rezeption von Jean Sibelius im NS-Staat* (Frankfurt am Main: Peter Lang, 2002), 71.

56. Tawaststjerna, *Sibelius 1904–1914*, 153.

57. Erkki Salmenhaara, *Uuden musiikin kynnyksellä 1907–1958*. Suomen musiikin historia 3 (Porvoo: Werner Söderström, 1996), 54.

58. "Ich verfolge den Lisztschen Satz: 'Auf jeden Akkord kann jeder Akkord folgen' eben konsequent." Reger letter to Constantin Sander, 17 July 1902, quoted in Else von Hase-Koehler, *Max Reger: Briefe eines deutschen Meisters: Ein Lebensbild* (Leipzig: Koehler und Amelang, 1928), 94.

59. See Mäkelä, "Verunglückt auf der Reise: Das 'Erste Concert' (Fragment) von Max Reger mit Blick auf sein Klavierkonzert opus 114," in *Musikalische Moderne und Tradition*, Reger-Studien 6, ed. Alexander Becker, Gabriele Gefäller, and Susanne Popp (Wiesbaden: Breitkopf & Härtel, 2000), 37–54, quote at 39–40.

60. In his pioneering article on the genre, "Der Orchestergesang des Fin de siècle: Eine historische und ästhetische Skizze," *Die Musikforschung* 30 (1977): 425–52, Hermann Danuser does not discuss it at all; and Annegret Fauser in her *Der Orchestergesang in Frankreich zwischen 1870 und 1920* (Laaber: Laaber, 1994), only mentions it in passing (173). The most extended discussion to date is Hepokoski, "The Essence of Sibelius: Creation Myths and Rotational Cycles in *Luonnotar*," in *The Sibelius Companion*, ed. Glenda Dawn Goss, (Westport, CT: Greenwood Press, 1992), 121–46.

61. Breslau, formerly in Germany, is today Wrocław, in Poland.

62. Werner Helwig, *Capri: Magische Insel* (Frankfurt am Main: Insel, 1962).

63. "Das Gedicht im Anfang finde ich sehr schön. Vom Herzen danke ich Ihnen."

64. Suvi Sirkku Talas, *Syysilta: Aino ja Jean Sibeliuksen kirjeenvaihtoa 1905–1931* (Helsinki: Finnish Literature Society, 2007), 346–52.

65. "'Tapiola,' eine wilde nordische Einöde, wo Waldgott und seine Waldnymphen verweilen." Tawaststjerna, *Jean Sibelius: 1920–1957*, 240.

66. Santeri Levas, *Järvenpään mestari* (Porvoo: Werner Söderström, 1960), 129; Erkki Salmenhaara, *Tapiola* (Helsinki: Suomen musiikkitieteellinen seura, 1970), 23.

67. Carpelan to Sibelius, 28 March 1901, and Sibelius's diary entry, 1 May 1912, Sibelius Family Archive, NA.

68. The latter work is, of course, connected with the literary traditions of the saga, ballade, and legend, but elements of composed landscapes and nature spaces can be isolated in many other compositions, not least the symphonies. Mäkelä, "Poesie in der Luft," 289.

69. See Schoenberg, *Stil und Gedanke*, 169–73. For a more recent discussion of Liszt's influence, see Leon Botstein, "A Mirror to the Nineteenth-Century: Reflections on Franz Liszt," in *Franz Lizst and His World*, ed. Christopher H. Gibbs and Dana Gooley (Princeton: Princeton University Press, 2006), 516–65, especially Section VII, "Modernity and Meaning," 547–57.

70. Timothy Howell, "Sibelius's *Tapiola*: Issues of Tonality and Timescale," in *Sibelius Forum, Proceedings from the Second International Jean Sibelius Conference in Helsinki, 25–29 November, 1995*, ed. Veijo Murtomäki, Kari Kilpeläinen, and Risto Väisänen (Helsinki: Sibelius Academy, 1998), 237–46, quote at 245–46; Hepokoski, *Sibelius: Symphony No. 5*, 28. The authors introduced the concept of minimalism in *Tapiola* as a heuristic vehicle. Hepokoski mentions "proto-minimalist sound sheets," and in his article on Sibelius in the

New Grove Dictionary of Music and Musicians (ed. Stanley Sadie and John Tyrrell [London: Macmillan, 2001], 23:319–47) he writes "quasi-minimalist in effect" (338).

71. Salmenhaara, *Tapiola*, 35.

72. Friedemann Sallis, "Reading György Ligeti's *Lux aeterna:* An Exercise in Musicological Border-Crossing," *Muualla, täällä: Kirjoituksia elämästä, kulttuurista, musiikista,* ed. Helena Tyrväinen, Seija Lappaialinen, Tomi Mäkelä, and Irma Vierimaa (Jyväskylä: Atena, 2001), 137–52.

73. Salmenhaara, *Tapiola*, 56.

74. Karl Heinrich Wörner, *Karlheinz Stockhausen: Werk und Wollen 1950–1962* (Rodenkirchen am Rhein: Tonger, 1963), 56–72.

75. Lorenz Luyken, ". . . *aus dem Nichtigen eine Welt schaffen* . . .": *Studien zur Dramaturgie im symphonischen Spätwerk von Jean Sibelius* (Kassel: Bärenreiter, 1995), 249.

76. Ernst Tanzberger, *Die symphonischen Dichtungen von Jean Sibelius: Eine inhalts- und formanalytische Studie* (Wurzburg: Triltsch, 1943), 59. See also Mäkelä, "Sibelius and Germany— *Wahrhaftigkeit* Beyond *Allnatur,*" in *The Cambridge Companion to Sibelius,* ed. Daniel M. Grimley (Cambridge: Cambridge University Press, 2004), 169–81.

77. Reinhold Brinkmann, *Arnold Schönberg: 3 Klavierstücke op. 11: Studien zur frühen Atonalität Schönbergs* (Tutzing: Schneider, 1969).

78. Cecil Gray, *Sibelius* (London: Oxford University Press, 1931), 89.

79. Harold E. Johnson, *Jean Sibelius* (New York: Alfred A. Knopf, 1959), 201.

80. See the interview with Ligeti in "György Ligeti und Manfred Stahnke: Gespräch am 29. Mai 1993," in *Musik—nicht ohne Worte: Beiträge zu aktuellen Fragen aus Komposition, Musiktheorie und Musikwissenschaft,* ed. Manfred Stahnke (Hamburg: von Bockel, 2000), 121–52.

81. "Die Landschaftsmalerei schafft Symbole für die Einsamkeit des Menschen, für seine Unterlegenheit gegenüber den elementaren Kräften und für die rätselhafte Allmacht Gottes, die sie im unendlichen Raum und im Wirken kosmischer Kräfte zu versinnbildlichen sucht . . . , 'Ursymbol der faustischen Seele im Gegensatz zum apollinischen Symbol des sinnlich gegenwärtigen Einzelkörpers.'" Hans H. Hofstätter, *Symbolismus und die Kunst der Jahrhundertwende: Voraussetzungen, Erscheinungsformen, Bedeutungen* (Cologne: Du Mont, 1965), 162.

82. Sibelius to Aino Järnefelt, 29 October 1891, Box 95, Sibelius Family Archive, NA.

83. Quoted in Riitta Konttinen, *Sammon takojat: Nuoren Suomen taiteilijat ja suomalaisuuden kuvat* (Helsinki: Suomalaisen Kirjallisuuden Seura, 2001), 219.

84. Sibelius, *Dagbok*, 78 and 324.

85. The term "the pastness of the present" is Richard Taruskin's, from his *Text and Act* (New York: Oxford University Press, 1995).

86. "Man komponiert nicht, man wird komponiert." Quoted in Hermann Danuser, *Gustav Mahler und seine Zeit* (Laaber: Laaber, 1991), 54.

87. "Ich halte es übrigens besonders pfiffig von mir, dass ich mir beim Spazierengehen Melodien einfallen lasse." Letter to Elisabeth von Herzogenberg, quoted in *Johannes Brahms im Briefwechsel mit Heinrich und Elisabeth von Herzogenberg,* ed. Max Kalbeck (Berlin: Deutsche Brahms-Gesellschaft, 1908; repr. Tutzing 1974), 2:149.

"Thor's Hammer":
Sibelius and British Music Critics, 1905–1957

BYRON ADAMS

"The Spirit of the Age" is in reality an exceedingly loose expression; indeed, it would be truer to say that each generation is inspired, not so much by one great spirit or *Zeitgeist*, as by the antithesis, and sometimes conflict, of several contrasted attitudes towards life.
—David Cherniavsky, "Special Characteristics of Sibelius's Style"

Yielding to an ill-advised impulse for self-revelation, the German philosopher Theodor W. Adorno (1903–1969) retailed the following anecdote in print: "More than thirty years ago I once asked Ernest Newman, the initiator of Sibelius's fame, about the qualities of the Finnish composer. After all, I said, he had adopted none of the advances in compositional techniques that had been made throughout Europe; his symphonies combined meaningless and trivial elements with illogical and profoundly unintelligible ones; he mistook esthetic formlessness for the voice of nature. Newman, from whose urbane all-round skepticism someone bred in the German tradition had much to learn, replied with a smile that the qualities I had just criticized—and which he was not denying—were just what appealed to the British."[1] Certainly Adorno seems to have understood nothing about the British art of pulling an interlocutor's leg. He must have understood even less about this particular music critic, a pugnacious man who felt no compunction whatsoever about engaging publically in verbal fisticuffs, but who in this instance decided to have a bit of fun. Newman himself never appears to have alluded to this colloquy, but it is easy to conjure up a picture of the relish with which he must have told the story of this Teutonic bore to his fellow critics at the Wigmore Hall bar. How Newman must have enjoyed imitating Adorno's obtuseness while the philosopher's dismissal of Sibelius—a composer whose music Newman had long championed— was being rebuked in such a sly fashion. That Adorno, blinkered by his own perceived superiority, failed to see that the joke was on him must have provided Newman with a final, delicious twist of the knife.[2]

Whatever one might think of Adorno's opinion of Sibelius or his smugness as a self-appointed arbiter of modernism, his grasp of Newman's role in the growth of the Finnish composer's reputation in Great Britain was wanting.[3] The prime instigator of Sibelius's English reputation was not Newman, although he played a pivotal role later, but Sir Granville Bantock (1868–1946). Bantock was a distinguished composer, conductor, and pedagogue; in 1908 he was Elgar's successor to the Peyton Chair of Music at the University of Birmingham. Bantock enjoyed presenting new music to his students and his audiences: he was always on the alert for the appearance of exciting new composers on the horizon. Of Sibelius's four trips to Great Britain, made in 1905, 1909, 1912, and 1921, Bantock served as impresario for the first three. (Bantock recalled the Finnish composer's quiet satisfaction when the first music he heard in London upon arriving in 1909 was his own *Valse triste*.)[4] As a gesture of thanks, Sibelius dedicated his Third Symphony to Bantock. During an interview with Walter Legge published in 1934, Sibelius paid tribute to his British colleague: "To Bantock I owe more than I can say; as a young man he did more than a dozen men could do to get a hearing for my works, and best of all he induced orchestras to let me conduct them."[5]

Bantock did Sibelius an enormous favor by introducing him to Rosa Newmarch (1857–1940), a gifted linguist and author who proved a loyal champion. A rare woman among professional music critics, Newmarch provided the program notes for the Promenade Concerts conducted by Sir Henry Wood (1869–1944) from 1908 to 1926. She studied art history in Saint Petersburg with Vladimir Stasov and was an authority on Russian and Czech music. Her abridged translation of Modest Tchaikovsky's biography of his brother (1905) discreetly revealed the composer's homosexuality to the British. She was also a prolific and expert translator. With Sibelius's assistance, she translated many of his songs into English, thus insuring their dissemination beyond Scandinavia. Newmarch could be trying at times—in 1910, she arrived for a visit at Sibelius's home in Järvenpää and, to the dismay of the composer and his family, blithely stayed for several weeks. However, her advocacy spread the news of this gifted Finnish composer in a particularly effective fashion.[6]

In 1912, Bantock was responsible for persuading the Birmingham Festival to program Sibelius's Fourth Symphony, op. 63 (1909–11). By the premiere, Newman and other discerning musicians had already heard of the Finnish composer. From this point, until the rise of the avant-garde in the late 1950s and '60s, Sibelius held a place at the very center of British concert life. English conductors such as Wood and Sir Thomas Beecham

(1879–1961) were fervent advocates for his music. Wood in particular proved an indefatigable champion; he introduced Sibelius's work to Proms audiences when he conducted the composer's incidental music for Adolf Paul's play *King Christian II*, op. 27 (1898) on 26 October 1901. The trickle of Sibelius's scores programmed at the Proms widened into a stream—especially performances of *Finlandia*, which Wood conducted twice during the 1906 Proms season and often thereafter—that broadened into a river. In 1937, for example, the Proms season included a comprehensive orchestral cycle that included all of Sibelius's symphonies.[7]

As unlikely as it may seem, it was the 1912 premiere of the Fourth, this less than ideal Birmingham performance of Sibelius's most overtly modernist symphony, that marked the crucial turning point for his reception in England. The astonishment that greeted the symphony gave way to a new sort of appreciation, as Sibelius was transformed in the eyes of the British from a piquant nationalist of exotic origin into a modernist master.

Given the strenuous nature of the marathon concerts then favored by the organizers of British music festivals, the auguries for the positive reception of a complex new symphony were not propitious, especially for a score that even its composer described to Newmarch as having "nothing, *absolutely nothing*, of the circus about it."[8] Among the works originally scheduled to be presented at this festival were the premiere of Elgar's *The Music Makers* (1912), the first British performance of Scriabin's *Prometheus: Poem of Fire*, as well as Delius's *Sea-Drift* for baritone, chorus, and orchestra (1904). Delius was appalled that his work was to be performed under such conditions and wrote a letter of protest to Bantock: "Wood wrote to me that he is doing 'Sea-drift' at the Birmingham festival—On the Programme I see they have put it on the 4th day morning at the very end of a 4 hours Concert – Who is responsible for this friendly act? Sea-drift is unknown in Birmingham & requires some mental effort, & ought to be at the end of the first part or at the beginning of the 2nd Part – after the interval."[9] (Delius's complaint was effective, by the way, as *Sea-Drift* appeared on the opening concert of the four-day festival alongside the new works by Elgar and Sibelius.)

With his experience of British music festivals, Delius knew what Sibelius did not: that rehearsal time would be severely limited, especially on a concert that also included Beethoven's *Coriolan* Overture, Bach's Third "Brandenburg" Concerto, and Liszt's First Piano Concerto.[10] Conducting the rehearsals for the Fourth Symphony may have been a trying experience for Sibelius, with Bantock translating the composer's directions to the orchestra, and Wood, the official conductor of the festival, shouting directions to the players from offstage.[11] At the dress rehearsal,

Newmarch sat next to Delius, who "drawled at intervals in his soft, rather nasal voice" the equivocal observation, "Damn it, this is not conventional music."[12] Even Newmarch admitted, "One can hardly say that the Fourth Symphony was received with public enthusiasm at its first performance."[13]

To many musicians in the audience, however, including the young Philip Heseltine, who had not yet assumed the nom de plume Peter Warlock, the Fourth Symphony came as a decided contrast to Elgar's *The Music Makers* and as a revelation. As Heseltine wrote on 2 October 1912:

> Elgar's new choral work . . . I did not like at all: it seemed to me "sound and fury signifying nothing." . . . Elgar himself looked ill and care-worn, and conducted in a very listless manner, though at times a sort of nervous energy seemed to come over him for a minute or two. . . . Sibelius' new symphony was by far the best event of the evening: it is *absolutely original*—quite in a class by itself and uninfluenced by anything, save Nature! . . . it is very strange and mysterious, but at the same time, a work of great beauty, which one would appreciate more and more on repeated hearings.[14]

In this letter dashed off to a friend the day after the concert, Heseltine anticipated the vocabulary that British critics would use to describe both the Fourth Symphony and Sibelius's music in general: "absolutely original," "uninfluenced by anything," "nature," and "great beauty." Heseltine's judgment was hardly infallible—he dismissed Gustav Holst in favor of the ephemeral Bernard van Dieren. However, in the case of Sibelius, just as with his later championship of Bartók, he was prescient. Whatever else happened during the Birmingham Festival of 1912, the premiere of the Fourth Symphony marked the point at which many forward-looking British musicians began to turn away from Elgar, a brooding Englishman, and seek inspiration from a brooding Finn.

This change in Sibelius's status was not immediately apparent in press comments on the Fourth Symphony. Critical opinion was mixed, with the anonymous critic of the *Times* hedging his bets by praising the orchestration: "Sibelius brings a wealth of contrasted material; each instrument has a personality of its own; and that is why, although he uses an orchestra no bigger than that of Brahms's First Symphony, the orchestration is almost disconcertingly new. He scarcely ever makes instruments of different colours do the same thing." As Erik Tawaststjerna reported, "Other press comment was either guarded and respectful, as was, for example, the *Musical Times,* or directly uncomprehending, as was the *Standard:* 'Mr. Sibelius's music could be described as written in cypher and unfortunately he has omitted to provide us with the code.'"[15]

One critic fully grasped the score's import, however. As Tawaststjerna averred, "Ernest Newman saw that greater severity and concentration of the symphony as part and parcel of a more widespread stylistic trend: Schoenberg, he argued, was trying to do much the same thing but without the same success. Perhaps without realizing it, Newman was sowing the seeds of one of the most bitter polemics of the post-war years."[16] Whatever else he was doing without realizing it, Newman sowed the seeds of his ironic riposte to Adorno years later: Newman's approbation set the seal for acceptance of the Fourth Symphony into the British canon in a way that transcended applause of the hour.

Before delving into the deeper reasons for Sibelius's British popularity, a crucial factor, perhaps obvious but rarely remarked on, must be acknowledged. For reasons that will be discussed over the course of this essay, Sibelius appeared in Britain at a most opportune historical moment. His special positioning cannot be gainsaid: after all, he was hardly the only major composer promoted by Rosa Newmarch. In 1926, for example, she arranged for the greatest living Czech composer, Leoš Janáček, to travel to Britain. But despite her enthusiasm and expertise in public relations, Janáček enjoyed only a fraction of Sibelius's success with the British public.[17] Like Sibelius before his first visit to England, Janáček was known among the cognoscenti: *Příhody Lišky Bystroušky* (*Cunning Little Vixen*), which he had heard in Prague during the 1924 ISCM Festival.[18] Janáček's posthumous reputation in Britain was secured decades later, but until very recently, his influence has been modest compared with that of Sibelius. The Czech was the right man but, unlike the Finn, for him it was the wrong time.

Questions of historical caprice aside, Newman's high claims for the Fourth Symphony, which were echoed by younger writers such as Cecil Gray (1895–1951), Constant Lambert (1905–1951), and David Cherniavsky (1922–1954), indicate how much of a sea change had taken place. As Peter Franklin has observed, "Sibelius left England on 30 October 1912 almost as an honorary member of its musical avant-garde."[19] In any case, there were few if any dissenters from the general approbation of the Finnish composer during this era. Sibelius's music subsequently has influenced British composers from Ralph Vaughan Williams to Peter Maxwell Davies and has been performed often by conductors from Malcolm Sargent to Colin Davis. This investigation, however, focuses on the writings of a set of representative British critics in order to illuminate the several reasons that the Finnish composer became so important to English musical life during the interwar period.

Indeed, due to Newman, Gray, and Lambert, the Fourth Symphony became the most exalted part of a critically anointed trinity of Sibelian masterworks including the Seventh Symphony, op. 105 (1924) and the tone poem *Tapiola*, op. 112 (1926). British audiences, by contrast, were hard pressed to emulate Newman's enthusiasm for the Fourth Symphony. Unlike *Finlandia* or the refulgent Second Symphony, op. 43 (1902), the Fourth never became a popular favorite: most concertgoers admired rather than loved this challenging work; it continues to be the least performed of Sibelius's seven symphonies in England. In a review dated 28 March 1920, Newman bemoaned, "Sir Henry Wood and I seemed to be a minority of two in voting upon the Fourth Symphony. It appears to have bored everyone else with whom I have discussed it." Newman continued defensively, "But if other people are merely bored by the gloom of dense sunless forests I cannot say them nay. I would ask them, however, to take a little interest in Sibelius' Fourth Symphony on other grounds."[20] In a later essay published in 1937 titled "Sibelius no. 4: Its English History," Newman claimed, "There can be no doubt that the cause of the temporary setback in the Sibelius vogue was the coming of the war fast upon the heels of the production of the fourth symphony . . . in 1912 the No. 4 was rather a tough nut for the English to crack."[21]

Paradoxically, the lack of affection demonstrated by Newman's "general music-lover" toward the symphony proved one of the reasons for its critical esteem. In the 1920s, nothing bestowed modernist credentials upon a work of art like public incomprehension. Gray viewed British middle-class audiences with undisguised contempt: "As for the musical public in general, the less said the better. On the rare occasions when one of Sibelius's major works has been performed the reception has invariably been sullen and listless . . . the 'plain man' . . . simply will not listen to Sibelius at all—that is, to his best and most characteristic work."[22] But certain passages in the writings of both Gray and Newman provide a key to the reasons why the Finnish composer, unlike his less appreciated Czech contemporary, proved to be the right man at the right time for the British from 1912 until well after the Second World War.

A Man from the North

When Sibelius stepped ashore at Dover in 1905, he was welcomed, after a spot of unpleasantness in customs over some undeclared cigars, by a musical establishment that was in the throes of transition from an outmoded Wagnerian notion of modernity to a nationalistic brand of British modernism based upon folksong, Tudor music, and self-conscious vitality. The trials of Oscar Wilde in 1895 were a recent memory, and most British artists, who labored under strict social prejudices concerning those who engaged in the arts, had reacted decisively. (Although Wildean decadence never quite died out in Great Britain—as evinced by the careers of Lord Berners and Ronald Firbank, to cite only two examples—it went underground, often concealed in plain sight as what was knowingly called "eccentricity.") For most artists, however, especially those heterosexuals who suffered from fits of "homosexual panic"—the fear of being taken for a homosexual—a wholesale retrenchment was in order, one that mandated Norfolk tweeds instead of velvet jackets; cakes and plain ale rather than oysters and scented wine; bracing tramps over the Malvern hills rather than languid games of dominoes at the Café Royale; and, in music, modally-inflected diatonicism rather than the Wagnerian chiaroscuro of chromaticism.[23] Even Elgar, as indebted to Wagner as he was, encouraged younger British composers to create music that would be "something that shall grow out of our own soil, something broad, noble, chivalrous, healthy and above all, an out-of-door sort of spirit."[24] Note that in this exhortation, made during the course of the first public lecture in 1905 as Peyton Professor of Music at Birmingham University, Elgar uses the word *healthy*, a word that, like *clean*, possessed a distinct implication of controlled, sublimated, masculine heterosexuality. For Elgar and many of his contemporaries, achieving a "healthy" aesthetic for British music meant cultivating an "out-of-door sort of spirit": the musical salvation of the younger generation could only be achieved if they eschewed the hothouse morbidity of decadence for the health promised by nature.[25] Such concerns were part of a wider social anxiety concerning masculinity at a time when, as historian Dan Stone has observed, "the Edwardian period saw the emergence of fears of British decline, especially after the military shock of the Boer War and rapid German economic growth."[26]

Ironically, Elgar's friend Bantock, a purveyor of post-Wagnerian musical exoticism, was the person who invited Sibelius into British musical life, thus insuring the eclipse of Bantock's own perfumed style. Rosa Newmarch, however, immediately grasped Sibelius's potent appeal: "My fellow-guest proved to be a striking and characteristic example of a man from the North—a Viking type." In her memories of this first encounter, Newmarch recalled that Sibelius's hair was "the colour of oats in sunshine." If this was not enough to signal his attractiveness, Newmarch continued rhapsodically by apostrophizing his "ice-blue eyes" and his "well set-up figure, neat and admirably tailored."[27] Indeed, Newmarch may even have felt a bit crestfallen that Sibelius "had nothing of the *naiveté* or rusticity of a man brought up in a small country."[28] Although mildly disappointed that the Finnish composer was not wearing hand-sewn boots made from reindeer pelts, Newmarch discerned quickly the quality in Sibelius that thrilled his British admirers: his evident, unforced masculinity.

Less inhibited than her male colleagues, Newmarch gets right to the point in delineating Sibelius's masculine charisma. She does not hesitate to locate it in his music as well as his person, but the enthralled men reporting on the Finnish composer took refuge in metaphor. For Newman, Lambert, Gray and others, this musical Viking stood resolutely at the nexus of a whole series of British cultural tensions that they expressed through their writings by invoking a recurrent series of paradoxical binary oppositions. Sibelius was perceived as being at once a mystical pantheist and a rigorous, coldly calculating logician; as both a modernist and a classicist; as primitive as a rock and as modern as a machine; as utterly individual while being the voice of a race; and as being simultaneously without precedent and the rightful heir to the Beethovenian tradition. This inconsistency is striking now, but disturbed absolutely no one at the time. The vocabulary that Newman and other British critics employed is revelatory of both their attitudes and of the culture in which they flourished.

In his 1920 review of the Fourth Symphony, Newman's use of metaphors drawn from nature to illustrate the Finnish composer's aesthetic virility reaches a high point as he draws on the phallic symbolism inherent in prehistoric rocks. Newman's use of such language marked a new approach to the composer's music that emerged just after the First World War. Recall that Tawaststjerna's citation of Newman's 1912 account of the Fourth Symphony makes an invidious comparison between Sibelius's brand of modernism and that of Schoenberg. By 1920, however, it appears that Newman was interested as much in geology as he was in modernity:

> The new method has never been so successfully followed as in this Fourth Symphony. He disdains transition for transition's sake: he lays theme endways to theme as the builders of some prehistoric walls or buildings may have laid stone upon stone, without mortar between them . . . Music like this seems to have no softening atmosphere about it, no aerial perspective; every theme springs abruptly out of the earth and challenges the ear to take it in at once and adjust it to its fellows . . . For my part I like the stark strength and prehistoric roughness of the style; but it will evidently take some time for the general music-lover to feel at home in it.[29]

Newman was not alone in alluding to natural phenomena such as the "stark strength and prehistoric roughness" of granitic themes springing "abruptly out of the earth" to describe the masculine quality that he felt characterized Sibelius's music. In his biography of the composer, Gray expands to cosmic imagery when he contrasts the Fourth Symphony, which he likens to a dense "White Dwarf" star, with the Fifth, which he characterizes as a "Red Giant, a Betelgeuse of Music."[30] In *Music Ho!* Constant Lambert declared, "the climaxes of *Tapiola* and *The Oceanides* are a rising flood that carries all before it."[31] In a 1947 essay, Cherniavsky saw nature as the basis and source of Sibelius's achievement: "His style tends to conform to the ways of Nature. I have already mentioned his almost pantheistic love of the natural world and the force with which its elemental power and beauty have stimulated his mood and inspiration; yet in truth this influence has delved far deeper, right down to the very roots of his expression . . . A trend which is far deeper and more essential to his style . . . is his basic insistence on *organic* form, on *natural* growth, on uninterrupted continuity of expression, on the attainment of balance; of unity within diversity, and on complete freedom of his own ideas to achieve their own development and seemingly *inevitable* fulfillment with the whole."[32]

Gray is the most self-consciously iconoclastic of these critics; examples of absurd exaggerations and perplexing inconsistencies abound in his prose. In the adulatory pages on Sibelius found in his 1924 volume *A Survey of Contemporary Music*, Gray writes, "The key to both the strength and the weakness of Sibelius is to be found in his essentially primitive mentality—using the word primitive in its truest and best sense." Gray opines that Debussy, Stravinsky, and Matisse are also primitives, but of the wrong sort: "They are 'primitives' from being hyper-civilized, super-cultured, over-refined. With them primitivism is simply a form of romanticism, like the cult of orientalism a hundred years ago." He proceeds to contrast these "aesthetic primitives," easily identifiable as "decadent" by their culture and refinement, with "the true primitives, such as Mussorgsky, Borodin, and Sibelius in music, or Van Gogh and Henri Rousseau in painting." (Had Sibelius, a consummate professional, ever read Gray's volume, one wonders how he would have reacted to being lumped together with two amateurs who rarely managed to finish a score unaided by Rimsky-Korsakov.) Gray asserts that these artists "are primitive not from any theoretic or sentimental yearnings, but simply because their minds are simple, direct, unsophisticated." Gray goes on to further qualify Sibelius's primitivism with a series of caveats:

> The true primitive artist is irresistibly attracted to the great traditions and procedures from which the modern decadent endeavours constantly to escape . . . . If I call Sibelius a primitive, I do not intend to suggest that his work is necessarily crude, unfinished, or technically incompetent. All I mean to imply by this misused adjective is a type of mind which works instinctively rather than consciously and intellectually; and, as the instincts of a primitive race are keener and surer than those of civilized races, so the resultant art has

nothing of the clumsiness and uncertainty which we habitually associate with their workings.

Having twisted his prose into epistemological knots in an attempt to clarify his initial muddled assertion, Gray entangles himself further by adding: "Finally, it would be a mistake to imagine that I call Sibelius primitive because he happens to come from a country which stands somewhat off the beaten track."[33] Gray pays a convoluted tribute to Sibelius's aesthetic virility—making him safe for manly British ears—by certifying that he is "simple, direct" and, the supreme accolade, "unsophisticated." It comes as no surprise that Gray's highest praise is reserved for the Fourth Symphony, which he describes as "effortless, natural, and inevitable." The subtext is that, unlike Stravinsky, fatally compromised by his association with the decadence of Diaghilev's Ballets Russes, or Debussy, an epicene Frenchman, Sibelius is a paragon of virility who has escaped the taint of European decadence. The Finnish composer is "clean," untouched by the compromised, confused present: "Sibelius seems to belong to a different race, a different age even; whether to the past or to the unborn future it would be difficult to say."[34]

The Great Race

As flimsy and illogical as such assertions read today, Gray's rhetorical stammering and equivocation unwittingly exposed a pervasive unease over a perceived loss of masculinity. With the popular conflation between effeminacy and homosexuality that came in the wake of the Wilde trials, being "hyper-civilized, super-cultured, over-refined" were conditions that would lead ineluctably to enervation, loss of virility, a propensity toward masturbation, and, finally, homosexuality. "Civilization" was commonly presumed to sap both an individual man and an entire nation. According to such authors as Max Nordau, the accelerating pace of modern life, and especially the sophistication of modern cities, contributed to the degeneration of masculinity.[35] American sociologist George L. Mosse writes, "From the nineteenth century on, the guardians of nationalism and respectability felt menaced by the big city, the apparent center of an artificial and restless age. Such cities were thought to destroy man's rootedness." Cities were considered haunts of unnatural vice, for "it was further said that the extremes of luxury and poverty to be found in cities favored the practice of sexual deviance . . . When court cases concerning homosexuality were reported in the London press, the analogy to the biblical cities of Sodom and Gomorrah was almost always drawn."[36]

To combat the emasculating, rootless environment of the modern city, a patently ideological construction of "nature" was exalted to the status of a cult. Writing of the conflation of nationalism and nature-worship that arose during the fin-de-siècle, Mosse observes that becoming part "of nature . . . gave both sanction to the established order and meaning to individual lives . . . The healing power of nature lay readily at hand, not just for individuals but for the nation as well." Mosse continues, "The quest for the genuine through the power of nature became a search for the true soul of the nation as well."[37] Elgar located this quest vaguely in "an out-of-door sort of spirit," but other English contemporaries took this ideology a step further in the case of Sibelius: he became an avatar of the Finnish race through his presumed "pantheistic" identification with nature. Sibelius *was* Finland. In an obituary tribute, Ernest Newman declared forthrightly, "It is a case not of seeing Sibelius through Finnish eyes but of seeing Finland through the eyes of Sibelius."[38] For these critics, the influence of the Finnish composer's masculine "rootedness" offered a way of purging from English music the lingering perfume of post-Wagnerian decadence.

Predictably, Gray seeks to have his cake and eat it when discussing questions of national identity, casting Sibelius both as an international modernist and as the conflation of two distinct racial types. In his 1931 biography of Sibelius, Gray, having now visited Finland, helpfully informs his readers that—despite the "otherness" of a landscape dotted with prehistoric boulders—it is a modern country that exemplifies technological, architectural, educational, and political progress.[39] By so doing, Gray seems ready to place the composer in a decidedly contemporary context. He then makes a sharp and unexpected detour, for though Gray has honed his vocabulary since the publication of *A Survey of Contemporary Music*, he does not abandon altogether his "primitive" rhetoric of 1924. Instead, he articulates a similar point with greater subtlety through the use of racial stereotyping. Gray explains the dualities of Sibelius's personality as well as his music—the contrast between the ephemeral salon music and the profound symphonies—in terms of a putative bifurcation between the composer's supposed Swedish affability and essential Finnish nature. Gray, who despised Newman and constantly baited him, uses a geologic image similar to that employed by his nemesis:

> This aspect of his personality probably represents the Swedish element in him, both of race and culture, for the Swedes are justly famed among peoples of the north for their possession of . . . amiable social attributes . . . With Sibelius, however, one very soon becomes aware of another side to his personality, deeper and more fundamental, a substratum of Finnish granite, as it were, underlying the

polished and elegant Swedish surface. He unites in himself, in fact, the characteristic qualities of the two racial types; the traditional charm, affability, and *bonhomie* of the Swede and the fiercely independent spirit, the sturdy self-reliance, the love of isolation and solitude, the extreme reserve, of the Finn.[40]

Readers today cannot help but be disconcerted by the insouciance with which Gray bandies about racial profiling in such passages (and they are legion), but for Gray and his contemporaries, a dissection of a composer's inherent racial characteristics was both "progressive" and "scientific." After the popularization of Darwinian theory, such assertions were common in the writings of British music historians. Sir C. Hubert H. Parry (1848–1918), who was appointed Director of the Royal College of Music in 1895, is best remembered today as a composer, but during his lifetime he was revered as a distinguished scholar as well.[41] Parry was considered a political and social liberal: his celebrated volume *The Evolution of the Art of Music*, first published in 1896, reflects its author's admiration for the Victorian progressive Herbert Spencer (1820–1903).[42] The book is filled with authoritative racial pronouncements presented serenely as scientific fact. (The firm of Kegan Paul published Parry's book as one of "The International Scientific Series.") In his Hegelian chapter on folk music, Parry, whose ethnography was shaky at best, asserts, "Racial differences, which imply different degrees of emotionalism and imaginativeness, and different degrees of self-control in relation to exciting influences, are shown very strongly in the folk music of different countries. . . . The folk-tunes of England present much the same features as German tunes. There is next to no superfluous ornamentation about them, but a simple, directness, such as characterises most northern folk-tunes."[43]

Given such a background of racial discourse in English musical writing, it would be difficult to argue that the vocabulary of later British writers was the result of either unselfconsciousness or naïveté. Although Newman once wrote that he was not "a believer in rooted and inalterable race-characteristics," his practice contradicts that assertion, as when, in the course of a laudatory review of Ernest Bloch's *Sacred Service*, he opines, "The work . . . is of course Jewish at heart . . . . What gives this music its particularly moving quality is the cry throughout it all of a sorely persecuted race."[44] That Newman's colleague Gray was conversant with contemporary racial theory is clearly illustrated by a passage aimed at excusing Sibelius's compositional promiscuity. Gray writes defensively:

This immense fecundity, combined with a certain unevenness in quality, has always militated strongly against Sibelius in the eyes of

many superior persons who are disposed to regard these characteristics of his with the same stern disapproval as that with which
eugenists [*sic*] regard the unsystematic, uncontrolled proliferation of
the lower classes. According to them, the artist should so control his
creative urge as to permit nothing unworthy to escape into
existence.[45]

Just because Gray humorously uses eugenicists as a stick with which to
beat those censorious critics—he cites only Germans—who disapproved
of Sibelius's "immense fecundity" does not mean he disagreed with eugenic premises. In the next paragraph he clarifies his position: "It is
certainly better to produce one healthy and intelligent offspring than a
large family of weaklings and mental defectives, and better to write one
good composition than a vast horde of mediocre ones."[46] Indeed, his assertions represent the continuation of a strain of British thought that came
into sharp, dogmatic focus in the mid-Victorian period after the publication of Charles Darwin's *Origin of Species* in 1859. At this juncture, the
racial prejudices indispensable to imperial conquest were given new lus-
ter by the burnished imprimatur of science. Previously, religion—the
conversion of "savages" deprived of the tender mercies of Christianity—
was often ardently invoked in the pulpit as an excuse for colonial expansion.
As the doctrine of biblical inerrancy gave way to Victorian faith in technological progress, however, science was called on to provide a pretext for
the subjection of "lesser" races. Darwin's Theory of Evolution, embroi-
dered upon by such polymaths as Herbert Spencer and Sir Francis Galton
(1822–1911), led to a form of social Darwinism that posited "the survival
of the fittest" in racial terms.[47]

With a gift for publicizing his ideas, Galton was profoundly influential in
shaping racial theory. As Stephen Jay Gould wrote, "Independently wealthy,
Galton had the rare freedom to devote his considerable energy and intelligence to his favorite subject of measurement. . . . He even proposed and
began to carry out a statistical inquiry into the efficacy of prayer!" As Gould
relates, "Galton coined the term 'eugenics' in 1883 and advocated the regu-
lation of marriage and family size according to hereditary endowment of
the parents."[48] But Galton did not stop at such relatively modest measures,
for he argued that, just as the hardiness of domestic animals can be
enhanced by "preventing more faulty members of the flock from breeding, so a race of gifted men might be obtained, under exactly similar
conditions." Galton even hinted that it might be a positive development if
the modern state instituted the culling of its weaker members according to
the "social arrangements" favored by the ancient Spartans. Galton asserted
flatly, "Modern industrial civilization deteriorates the breed."[49]

It was a short step from Galton's hypotheses to a scientific racism that viewed the white races—to which all of these eugenicists and scientists belonged—as superior to other races such as Jews, Africans, African-Americans, Indians, Native Americans, Arabs, and Mediterranean peoples. Commenting on the American Civil War, distinguished English biologist T. H. Huxley (1825–1895) wrote:

> It may be quite true that some negroes are better than some white men; but no rational man, cognizant of the facts, believes that the average negro is the equal, still less the superior, of the average white man. And, if this be true, it is simply incredible that, when all his disabilities are removed, and our prognathous relative has a fair field and no favour, as well as no oppressor, he will be able to compete successfully with his bigger-brained and smaller-jawed rival, in a contest which is to be carried on by thoughts and not by bites. The highest places in the hierarchy of civilization will assuredly not be within the reach of our dusky cousins, though it is by no means necessary that they should be restricted to the lowest. But whatever the position of stable equilibrium into which the laws of social gravitations may bring the negro, all responsibility for the result will henceforth lie between Nature and him.[50]

Huxley's use of scientific terms ("prognathous") to justify racial taxonomy became a common stratagem for racial discrimination throughout the English-speaking world.

These British hypotheses of scientific racism found a ready welcome among the privileged upper crust of American society, as well as in universities, where classes on eugenics were added to the curriculum.[51] This development was due in large part to the tensions unleashed in America both by Reconstruction and the influx of immigrants; these fears reached a feverish pitch during the administration of Theodore Roosevelt, who was an ardent eugenicist.[52] In 1916, Madison Grant, who was a patrician conservationist, a friend of Roosevelt's, and a fanatical believer in eugenics, published *The Passing of the Great Race or the Racial Basis of European History*, a classic of scientific racism that, despite relatively modest sales, had an enormous impact both in America and Europe.[53] Following Deniker and others, Grant, who popularized the neologism *Nordic*, posits a hierarchy of races at the apogee of which he placed the hardy peoples of the Baltic region.[54]

A lifelong bachelor, Grant positively luxuriates in his fantasies about tall, virile Nordic men; he rarely describes, discusses, or mentions, women. For Grant, the Nordics are "a purely European type" that he apotheosizes as "*Homo europæus*, the white man par excellence." Grant describes these paragons of racial purity as "everywhere characterized by certain specializations, namely wavy brown or blond hair and blue, gray, or brown eyes, fair skin" also possessing a "narrow and straight nose."[55] Hypothesizing that the Nordic race developed around the shores of the Baltic sea, he posits that "the vigor and power of the Nordic race as a whole is such that it could not have evolved in so restricted an area as Southern Sweden." Admittedly, "the problem of the Finns is a difficult one," as they seemed to Grant not to have many racial connections to the other peoples settled in the Baltic region, but he observes brightly that "the coast of Finland, of course, is purely Swedish" and concludes that the Finns are a "thoroughly Nordic type."[56]

Grant hails Nordic men as a "race of soldiers, sailors, adventurers and explorers, but above all, of rulers, organizers and aristocrats." Furthermore, Grant proclaims, "The Nordic race is domineering, individualistic, self-reliant and jealous of their personal freedoms . . . The pure Nordic peoples are characterized by a greater stability and steadiness than are mixed peoples."[57] Influenced by Huxley and others, Grant lays this purity at the feet of geographical isolation abetted by nature in the form of an inclement climate: "The climatic conditions must have been such as to impose a rigid elimination of defectives through the agency of hard winters . . . such demands on energy if long continued would produce a strong, virile and self-contained race."[58]

With notable exceptions, such as those penned by the distinguished anthropologist Franz Boas and his students, Grant's tome—virtually unreadable today—received respectful reviews. The *New York Herald* lauded the volume as " a profound study of world history from the ethnological standpoint." (As Jonathan Peter Spiro points out, Emily Greene Balch, then a professor of economics and sociology at Wellesley, was the only reviewer "to object to Grant's statement that negative measures should ultimately be applied to 'worthless race types.'")[59] *The Passing of the Great Race* was published throughout Europe, in German, French, and Norwegian translation; all four of the book's editions appeared in Great Britain as well.[60] Among Grant's influential British admirers were the socially progressive novelist John Galsworthy and the distinguished Oxford geologist W. J. Sollas, who sent a letter of praise to Grant, declaring, "I hope your work will be widely read and that it may have some influence on our Statesmen."[61]

Though few, if any, British statesmen of the time seem to have been influenced by Grant's book, the vocabulary of eugenics became part of the lingua franca of many English writers, such as George Bernard Shaw and H. G. Wells, as well as those who wrote about Sibelius. However, it cannot therefore be assumed that any music critic was a passionate eugenicist, a doctrinaire scientific racist, or a political conservative. In his book *Breeding Superman: Nietzsche, Race and Eugenics in Edwardian and Interwar Britain*, Dan Stone aptly observes, "It is now fairly widely accepted that eugenics appealed to thinkers across the political spectrum. . . . Eugenics was not some kind of free-wheeling amorphous project, but was an aspect of generally held ideas about social reform. . . . For left-wing thinkers . . . it became an integral part of their conception of society, along with (indeed part of) schemes for public hygiene and education."[62] One of the reasons that eugenics became so popular during the First World War and after is that it provided a hygienic promise of a renewed world purged of defect; few had the foresight to discern the horrors into which this seemingly benign program would lead humanity. Discussions of eugenics were so pervasive in Britain during the interwar period that Gray, Newman, and others used both the vocabulary and assumptions of the eugenicists without a second thought. When *A Survey of Contemporary Music* was published in 1924, for example, Gray did not use the word *Nordic* to describe the Finnish composer; in the final chapter of his 1931 biography of Sibelius, he uses it several times and places the concept in relation to Sibelius's stylistic development: "The decade 1900–10 presents . . . a conspicuous decrease in the number and importance of the more predominantly nationalistic and Nordic works, and a corresponding increase in the number and importance of those which I have loosely designated as cosmopolitan and eclectic."[63] Furthermore, Gray does not hesitate to use racial profiling on Sibelius, applying an unattributed quotation from unidentified "ethnologists" that essentially offers Grant's Nordic type: "The typical Finn has been described by ethnologists as 'of middle height, muscular, broad-shouldered, with round head, broad face, concave nose, fair complexion, and blue or grey eyes.'" Gray continues, "This might almost be the passport description of Sibelius, so closely does he conform in physique to the national type."[64]

Notice that both Newmarch and Gray describe Sibelius's physical body in virtually the same terms, and that both pointedly observe how his features conform to assumptions about Northern manhood.[65] A more revealing aspect of this strain of criticism are the various ways that Gray and other writers use references to the male body to describe Sibelius's music. Nowhere is this focus more apparent than in descriptions of the Fourth Symphony. Gray, for example, compares the Third and Fourth symphonies both as sexes and bodies: "If the Third represents the result of a slimming treatment, a reduction of the adipose tissues and somewhat opulent curves of the symphonic muse as she appears in the first two examples, the Fourth is the outcome of a process of sheer starvation, of a fakir-like asceticism and self-denial. The Fourth Symphony is gaunt, spectral, emaciated almost; the question here is no longer one of superfluous flesh, but of any flesh at all—the very bones protrude."[66] In an article published two years after the appearance of Gray's biography, Newman echoed his colleague: "No other music that has ever been written is so spare of build as this: it is an athlete's body, without an ounce of superfluous flesh upon it, with most of the weight in the bones and with the bones and the muscles all tension and power."[67] In his comparison, Gray executes an awkward rhetorical pirouette starting from the voluptuous female body of Sibelius's first two lushly romantic symphonies, pivoting on the slimming classicism of the Third and landing akimbo in front of a male body stripped to its bare essentials—that of an Indian ascetic in loin cloth (if that) and stripped of "superfluous flesh." Having arrived at the image of an emaciated but powerful body, it was a short step for Gray to envision the Fifth Symphony as energy only, a massive, pulsating "Red Giant" star glistening in the dark of outer space. Newman prefers to see healthy flesh, comparing the symphony to the body of an athlete, a trained body that—taut with muscle and tension—is, like Gray's fakir, devoid of "superfluous flesh."

Whereas Gray's fakir is an image drawn from fantasies of the crumbling Raj, Newman's Sibelian athlete is a Nordic—or perhaps a Nietzschean—superman who anticipates those virile blonde young men who would pose, hurtle, and race through Leni Riefenstahl's 1938 film *Olympia*, and whose model may well have been the superstar Finnish runner Paavo Nurmi (1897–1973).[68] The other phallic metaphors mentioned above—the prehistoric stones rising out of the earth, the rising overwhelming climaxes, the rooted granitic substratum of the Finnish soil, fall into place as a homoerotic variant of the Lacanian "gaze." Here, indeed, is Grant's "great race" in its Nordic glory.

For all its potency, this virile body is serene due to its self-imposed restraint, the virtually superhuman poise that Gray found in the Sixth Symphony and, especially, in its successor: "The Seventh shows him at the summit of his powers in respect of fecundity of invention . . ." (Yet more Sibelian fecundity!) "It is not merely a consummate masterpiece of formal construction, however, but also a work of great expressive beauty, of a lofty grandeur and dignity, a truly Olympian serenity and repose which are unique in modern music, and, for that matter, in modern art of any kind."[69] But this serenity exacts a fearsome price. As Mosse observed, "Manliness was based upon the Greek revival which accompanied and complemented the onslaught of respectability and the rise of modern nationalism . . . Indeed, those rediscovering their bodies at the end of the nineteenth century would continue to invoke Greek models as examples of physical beauty stripped of all sensuousness and sexuality . . . Greece was conjoined with

nature. The urge to be natural, to integrate oneself with an unspoilt setting, was thought to free the human body of its sexuality."[70]

Gray's ambition to place Sibelius among the Olympians was just one
of several strategies used by critics to contain and even abjure the powerful eroticism in Sibelius's symphonies and tone poems, to which, as revealed
by the extravagant phallic metaphors that appeared in their writing, he
and his British colleagues were responsive. Any acknowledgment of this
eroticism must occur only through metaphor, or, better yet, be avoided
altogether: "No sex, please, we're British!"

Another common strategy was to deny that the symphonic tradition
allowed for the expression of sensuality in any form, for, as Gray opined,
"The symphonic style is averse to the picturesque, the opulent, the highly
coloured, preferring rather a certain austerity, dryness, asceticism even . . . .
The ideal symphony—the symphony in the mind of God, to speak Pla-
tonically—avoids as a rule the luscious, the sensuous, and impressionistic,
as foreign to its nature."[71] This curious statement hardly constitutes an isolated instance of such aesthetic premises, for Gray's construction of the
"ideal symphony" was extolled by many other British critics, as well as by
the practice of Edwardian composers such as Parry and Stanford. Furthermore, the laudatory critical reception of Sibelius's least ingratiating
symphony testifies to the general acceptance of this anhedonic view of the
proper symphonic style. As apparent from the terms of praise given to
austerity that pervade the critical reception of the Fourth Symphony, Gray
speaks for many other British critics when he regards the "complete
absence of sensuous appeal" as a *positive* virtue that elevates this score to
"Sibelius's greatest achievement."[72]

But the eroticism of Sibelius's music could not be conjured away
completely through appeals either to ancient Greece or to Platonic philosophy. Images of masculine potency have a way of reemerging even in
passages of musical analysis. Specific "scientific" terms used by eugenicists were employed as tools to elucidate the Finnish composer's
creative—or, one might say, generative—process. (This in turn was part
of a broader expropriation of language drawn from science that music
theorists used to legitimize the intellectual basis of their discipline
throughout the twentieth century: organicist metaphors drawn from eugenics were succeeded in the 1950s and '60s by positivistic terminology
loosely derived from higher mathematics.) When Cherniavsky, following
Gray, Simon Parmet, and, indeed, the composer himself, used the word
germ to characterize the melodic fragments from which he believed
Sibelius generated music by a process of elaboration and accretion, he is
not referring to microorganisms in general but to what the educated
knew was a stage in sexual reproduction.[73]

Writing shortly after the Second World War, and thus a member of the last generation that could do so with impunity, Cherniavsky expropriates for use in musical analysis the short form ("germ") of an organicist concept that eugenicists and early geneticists called "germ plasm."[74] This is an outmoded term that, as Spiro notes, "we know today as the genes inside the egg and the sperm cells." Husbanding the male germ plasm was an obsession of eugenicists, for they believed that "reformers who were serious about improving the human race . . . would do better to devote their efforts to eugenic programs that strove to eliminate defective germ plasm from the population."[75] Even artistic ability was determined by the germ plasm, and the American eugenicist Charles Benedict Davenport (1866–1944) posited that musical ability was the result of a single recessive gene.[76] In his theoretical musings, Cherniavsky used the terms "germ motives" and "thematic germs" to describe Sibelius's motives. The writer spins his unabashedly organicist—and sexual—musical metaphors further and further as the "thematic germs" replicate toward larger forms of musical "life," just as cells do to create large organisms. Cherniavsky reveals his reliance upon eugenics for theoretical models when he writes, "The influence of nature, which can be so strongly felt behind nearly all his works, is revealed not only in the impressionism, in the colour and mood awakened in his tone-poems, but also in the organic growth, in the vitality and elemental power of the music itself—music which often seems to have been inspired by that same natural force from which the organic world itself draws its unceasing life and fertility."[77]

For the British, Sibelius's cavalier treatment of his musical germ plasm was a cause for consternation. Gray found that anything that deviated from the healthy, masculine directness of the symphonic works—such as the "necrophilistic ardours" of the *Valse triste*—was unclean, the debased result of the Finnish composer's onanistic abuse of his creative germ plasm.[78] Sibelius's charming popular works clearly aroused Gray's revulsion even as he tried to explain away the composer's "immense fecundity" as "one of the signs of his true greatness."[79] Gray was also anxious to excuse any popular elements that might sully the aesthetic purity of the symphonies, as when he observes that the "Swan Hymn" theme of the Fifth Symphony is "almost note for note identical with a popular music-hall song of some ten years or so ago, but in Sibelius's hands it is endowed with a grandeur and a dignity that banish entirely from our minds its dubious associations." (If Sibelius has banished this "dubious association" so effectively, a skeptic might well wonder why Gray felt compelled to point it out in the first place.)[80]

Such inconsequential perversities as the *Valse triste* aside, Sibelius was lauded for his integrity as a symphonist. With an enthusiasm worthy of

Madison Grant hailing the racial homogeneity of his beloved Nordics, Gray proclaims, "Sibelius, in fact, alone in modern times, has preserved inviolate the purity and integrity of the true symphonic style." By setting up Sibelius's practice as a standard by which all others are to be judged, Gray weighs the achievements of the Finnish composer's contemporaries in the balance and finds them wanting: "It will be found that the symphonies of such composers as Bruckner and Mahler, Tchaikovsky and Elgar, and indeed of every important practitioner of the form in modern times, sin in one or more crucial respects against the symphonic spirit—either through the employment of the device of the thematic interconnexion of all or some of the movements, through the excessive sensuousness of harmony, melody, or orchestration, or through formal invertebracy and redundance, and sometimes through all of them."[81] For Gray, as for many of his colleagues, deviation from the "purity and integrity of the symphonic style" was tantamount to a moral failing—a "sin."

Coupled with the use of the word *germ* to describe the motives used by Sibelius is an insistence on the "simplicity" and "directness" of his finest work. Such adjectives are used to differentiate Sibelius sharply from effete decadent exoticism while attesting to his masculine probity. Unsurprisingly, these qualities, thought to be particularly masculine at the time, are often tied to Sibelius's racial origin, a rhetorical move that Gray in particular used as a way to sidestep the aesthetic problem posed by Sibelius's early, untrammeled nationalism. For differing reasons, Newman, Lambert, and Gray were uncomfortable with a musical expression of nationalism based on folk traditions. Despite their acutely individual outlooks, all shared a visceral reaction against the use of folk materials of any kind within art music, for anything extraneous to the composer's personal "germ plasm" would fatally sully the purity of a work's conception. Recall that Gray struggled to keep the distinction between "nationalistic" and "Nordic" when he described Sibelius's music; the "nationalistic" works were those that drew upon Finnish legends or some other overtly national source, and were thus to be faintly deplored, while the Nordic works were the essential expression of a racial homogeneity that arose from deep within the composer's psyche. These critics believed that an unselfconscious expression of racial consciousness irradiated Sibelius's "abstract" works as well his tone poems, no matter how often the composer protested, "My symphonies are music conceived and worked out in terms of music and with no literary basis. . . . A symphony should be first and last music."[82] Ernest Newman simply contradicted Sibelius: "The musical faculty does not exist in a watertight compartment, shut off from the rest of the mind and the nature and experience of the man." To Newman, as the final sentence of his obituary tribute makes clear, the nature of this particular man was bound up inextricably with his race: "No one could ever imagine any other signature, personal or racial, upon any page of his music other than that of Jean Sibelius."[83]

Finnish Modern

The only other composer who had previously possessed such control over his creative germ plasm was, of course, that *ne plus ultra* of compositional virility, Ludwig van Beethoven. Flattering comparisons between Sibelius and Beethoven abound in the writings of these English critics. Constant Lambert wrote that the "almost unbearable spiritual and technical concentration" exemplified by the coda of the finale of the Finnish composer's Fourth Symphony "may be held to form a modern parallel to the posthumous quartets of Beethoven."[84] Cherniavsky stated, "It was left for Sibelius to develop the really organic matter of imparting unity originated by Beethoven—the use of motivic germs."[85] Although this statement may be a touch hyperbolic, it pales in comparison to Gray's proclamation: "The symphonies of Sibelius represent the highest point attained in this form since the death of Beethoven."[86]

But Lambert's invocation of Beethoven was part of an agenda to position the Finnish composer as a modern, even prophetic, voice who would lead the way into the future. Throughout *Music Ho!* Lambert mocks the various fads of Continental modernism as well as the mere idea of nationalism (British or otherwise) as he seeks to refashion modernism through the construction of a new canon. He was hardly alone, for both Newman and Gray had their own ideas of what a twentieth-century British canon might contain. To position Sibelius as Beethoven's true successor allowed the British to jettison the decadent post-Wagnerian and post-Wildean aesthetics as well as the entire Teutonic symphonic tradition now tainted by German aggression. In an amazing display of historical insouciance, Gray blithely tosses the entire nineteenth-century repertory of German symphonies after Beethoven—including those of Brahms—onto the ash heap of history:

> [Brahms] achieved the symphonic style through a kind of self-immolation. One always feels with him, in the symphonies, a sense of effort and constraint, a continual striving after an ideal that was foreign to his innermost being. He was not a symphonist by natural aptitude or inclination, in fact, and on the whole this is true of all the most eminent German composers of the nineteenth century and of modern times. [87]

The most astonishing aspect of Gray's argument is that he couches the peroration in racial terms, with the sentimental Teuton defeated by the hardened Nordic who displays those very qualities of heroism, individuality, and power that were attributed to him by ethnologists like Madison Grant:

> The Teutonic genius in music, indeed, as in everything else, is preeminently lyric, contemplative, philosophic, and fundamentally opposed to the dramatic, the heroic, the epic, which constitute the essence of the symphonic style. The old academic theory of the superiority of the Teuton over all other races in respect of large-scale constructive capacity is simply a myth based upon one or two great exceptions such as Beethoven; but Beethoven was no more a typical German than Goethe. . . . The truth is, therefore, that the Germans are in reality the last people in the world who have the right to arrogate to themselves, as they do, the supremacy over all other races in symphonic music, and to claim that they alone possess the secret of musical construction on a large scale. It is the one thing of which, as a race, they are fundamentally incapable, and this makes their patronizing attitude towards the symphonies of Sibelius particularly laughable . . . His entire art, in fact, follows on straight from that of Beethoven, without intermediary influence of any kind; one can pass from one to the other without feeling that there is the intervening gap of a century.[88]

Such wholesale revisionism concerning German musical hegemony had begun well before the war, accompanied by the construction of a putative English Musical Renaissance. This loose confederation was in part a newfound resistance to German cultural imperialism and a reaction to the newly unified German nation's challenge to British political and economic domination. It was during precisely the most politically fraught period before the war that the man from the North, Jean Sibelius, stepped ashore at Dover and provided the British a very attractive alternative connection to the Beethovenian symphonic tradition. Just as Grant placed the Nordics at the apex of his bogus pyramid of races, so the British critics found in Sibelius the solution to the vexing problem of whom to place at the top of their reconstituted canon. Deliciously, according to the tenets of eugenics and scientific racism fashionable at the time, the Nordic genius Sibelius racially outranked composers who hailed from the adulterated Alpine and Teutonic races, who then could be put firmly in their place.

Gray's ambition to turn the tables on the German tradition through racial arguments of course proved futile. However, his invocation of race to create a new canon laid bare the aesthetic Social Darwinism inherent in the endeavor. Coincidentally or not, since the middle of the nineteenth century the accepted canon of Western art music has been organized as if designed by a musical Madison Grant. It is heavily weighted in favor of the superiority of white males from northern climes. Like Grant, who dismissed Mediterranean men as effete creatures who "can work a spindle, set type, sell ribbons or push a clerk's pen," the progressive Victorians, such as Parry and Sir George Grove (1820–1900), who created the prototype of the modern canon, relegated composers from indolent warmer climes to secondary positions. Certain exceptions might be made for the occasional Italian or Frenchman—or even a "primitive" Slav—but these could never reach the higher status accorded to Austrians and Germans.[89]

This bias toward composers from Northern Europe has never faded, but it was certainly in force when Gray, Lambert, and other British critics were writing in the years just after the First World War. A turn away from Germany toward a country whose population was adulterated by the Mediterranean races, such as France, was unthinkable. (Italy, whose composers wrote opera—a genre that Parry considered the musical equivalent of the Whore of Babylon—never came into serious consideration during this period; even Verdi was suspect.)[90] Although Vaughan Williams had taken the daring step of studying with Maurice Ravel for several months in 1907–8, such Francophilia was rare within the British establishment. In his chapter on Debussy in *A Survey of Contemporary Music*, Gray asserts, "This soft, enervating, female, boudoir prettiness has always been the disease against which French artists have had to fight."[91] Discussing Debussy as a "key-figure," Lambert announces confidently, "The French as a race have a remarkably poor sense of rhythm."[92] Just after stating unequivocally that he is "not a believer in rooted and inalterable race-characteristics," Newman declares, "It is the fact, however, that the French musicians have never shown much capacity for architecture on the great scale . . . Debussy and his fellows have laboured under the delusion that form could be replaced by style."[93]

So, with rare exceptions such as Edwin Evans (1874–1945) and M. D. Calvocoressi (1877–1944), British critics never considered the French as a replacement for the Teutons within the canon. By the 1930s, however, when Lambert published *Music Ho!* and Gray produced his biography of Sibelius, ominous developments within Germany made the need for an alternative to the German tradition even more urgent. Their books were prompted by an impulse similar to that which led Ernest Newman in search of a composer who promised continuity of the symphonic tradition, masculine health, and an alternative modernity. For these writers, Sibelius's modern renewal of the symphonic tradition was made possible because his innovative formal procedures employed Beethovenian motivic logic in reverse. From the Second Symphony onwards, Sibelius developed a technique in which thematic, rhythmic, and harmonic fragments accumulate power over longer and longer spans of music in a relentless forward trajectory. The English critics found in the eugenicist and organicist vocabulary an up-to-date language to describe Sibelius's technique of musical tension and release, and they wanted it to be a special sign of the repudiation of decadence after the devastation of the war.

But there was another reason that Gray and Cherniavsky reached for images borrowed from eugenics. In those days, it was so embarrassing for most British middle-class readers to contemplate the topic of sexual pleasure that it could find comfortably oblique expression only in scientific metaphors. Viewed through the lens provided by eugenics, there is an obvious analogy between Sibelius's creative process and that of heterosexual intercourse: tentative foreplay, increasingly sustained sexual engagement, orgasm, and, the ultimate teleology, a healthy new life generated from the male "germ plasm."

If a cultural squeamishness concerning the eroticism that saturates Sibelius's music twisted the British critic's arguments into knots of allusion, the need to tie Sibelius to Beethoven created equally vexing epistemological inconsistencies. The Victorian progressives and their successors prized several traits of Beethoven's practice and vaunted them as the standard by which all other composers had to be judged, regardless of whether this aesthetic Procrustean bed was appropriate or not. Beethoven, universally considered the manly paragon of composers, exemplified to perfection the desired masculine traits of rugged individuality, originality, abstraction, and ceaseless innovation. Sibelius was considered by Newman, Gray, Lambert, and the rest to possess all of these Beethovenian characteristics, examples of which appear like a ground bass throughout their encomiums. Unfortunately, Sibelius himself threw cold water on attempts to paint him as a self-consciously intellectual composer, insisting repeatedly that he composed instinctively; furthermore, he had the wisdom never to claim publicly Beethoven's mantle. In addition, the inherent contradiction between the discourse concerning race created by these authors around Sibelius—portraying him as transcending the mere provincialism of nationality to become a racial archetype—and their oft-repeated insistence on his iconoclastic individuality—one of a kind, belonging to no time—created an unbridgeable cognitive dissonance that was never addressed seriously, let alone reconciled.[94]

Above all, to insure Sibelius's supreme status as the true heir to the Beethovenian succession, the British had to insist on his modernity. They were untroubled that portraying Sibelius as a modernist might conflict

with their poetic evocations of the Finnish composer as a Nordic archetype who stood outside the boundaries of recorded history. In the opening
chapter of his biography, Gray places Sibelius in a modern setting by
strategically name-dropping some of the most innovative Finnish architects—Eliel Saarinen, Lars Sonck, and Armas Lindgren—as he observes
that the streets of Helsinki are "lined with large and sumptuous buildings
designed in an aggressively modernistic style of architecture."[95] In order
to present Sibelius's modernist credentials in the most effective possible
light, Lambert eschews organicist verbiage, explaining Sibelius's innovative conceptions of form through an inspired comparison to a particularly
contemporary form of popular fiction:

> Instead of being presented with a fait accompli of a theme that is
> then analysed and developed in fragments, we are presented with
> several enigmatic fragments that only become a fait accompli on the
> final page. It is like watching a sculptured head being built up from
> the armature with little pellets of clay or, to put it more vulgarly, it
> is like a detective story in which the reader does not know until the
> final chapter whether the blotting paper of the ashtray throws more
> light on the discovery of the corpse in the library.[96]

But Lambert's appeal to the devices used by such popular authors as
Agatha Christie and G. K. Chesterton as models for Sibelius's modernism
pales by comparison to the way in which machines were used as a metaphor
for Sibelius's music. Oddly enough, these mechanistic metaphors had their
origin in the staging of one of Sibelius's most popular works, *Finlandia,* composed to accompany a series of *tableaux vivants* that celebrated Finland's
propulsive entry into the twentieth century. As James Hepokoski observes:

> This busy tableau proclaimed a linear version of self-assertion pro-
> jected into the future—a new finally awakened Finland greeting the
> new century (only two months away) equipped with its own history,
> with its own poetry and legitimised language, with modern re-
> sources (education), and with modern technology (the unstoppable
> locomotive in this tableau, an image of industrial progress—a steam-
> propelled Finland racing, by implication, toward an even more
> modern form of eventual self-rule).[97]

This phallic locomotive, barreling through winter darkness toward the
light of a new century, was only the first time a modern machine would be
associated with Sibelius's work. Ernest Newman, for instance, compared
Sibelius's formal procedures to the huge propeller of a sleek ocean liner.[98]

It was of all people the musical analyst Donald Francis Tovey (1875–1940) who made the most suggestive evocation of a machine to elucidate a score by Sibelius, one that neatly situates the modern over the natural. While Tovey occasionally indulges in natural imagery to make points about music, he generally eschews the organicist vocabulary: no "germs" here. Furthermore, though Tovey worshipped Beethoven as much as anyone at the time, he pointedly refrained from comparing Sibelius to his idol. (In fact, Tovey never published an analysis of the Fourth Symphony.)

Tovey begins his remarks on Sibelius's Seventh Symphony with a juxtaposition of the natural with the technological:

> I confess that I was thrilled when, in its New-Year's-Eve review of 1933, the British Broadcasting Corporation used a gramophone record of parts of Sibelius's Seventh Symphony as "slow music" during the recital of the flight over Mount Everest. Let this sentence do duty for all further efforts to describe the austere beauty and rare atmosphere of Sibelius's mature style. Unlike mountain atmospheres, however, that of Sibelius is by no means lacking in oxygen.

Tovey leaves the natural phenomenon (Mount Everest, no less!) on the ground where it belongs, directly symbolic of nothing, while the modernist composer soars confidently overhead. Later in this admirably concise and consistent essay, Tovey enlarges upon his comparison of Sibelius's music to that most modern of technological advances for 1933:

> If the listener feels that unformed fragments of melody loom out of a severely discordant fog of sound, that is what he is meant to feel. If he cannot tell when or where the tempo changes, that is because Sibelius has achieved the power of moving like aircraft, with the wind or against it. An aeronaut carried with the wind has no sense of movement at all; but Sibelius's airships are roomy enough for the passengers to dance if they like: and the landscape, to say nothing of the sky-scape, is not always too remote for them to judge the movement of the ship by external evidences. . . . He moves in the air and can change his pace without breaking his movement.[99]

Tovey's essays on Sibelius sum up the prevailing British attitudes toward the Finnish composer without lapsing into hagiography, racial profiling, or special pleading. Tovey vividly presents the music, using images drawn from nature and mythology where appropriate. (In truth, it would be extraordinarily difficult to write about *Tapiola* without using a word such as *hurricane*.) Aside from his discussion of *Tapiola*, Tovey does not cite

Finnish mythology or the legends of the *Kalevala*, but rather those of the Norsemen. In his essays on both the Third and Fifth symphonies, Tovey invokes Thor, the god of thunder: "The bustling introduction," he writes of the opening of the finale of the Fifth Symphony, "provides a rushing wind, through which Thor can enjoy swinging his hammer."[100] Once again the Nordic is conflated with the Finnish: Sibelius the Viking composer steps onstage, portraying Thor, that most virile of Norse deities, suggestively swinging his hammer. Newmarch, who surely read this essay, must have been thrilled to her core.

Although it was all very well and good for these British critics to project their prejudices and cultural (and clearly psychological) anxieties upon Sibelius, one wonders whether all this comment had a positive or negative effect on the reception of his music over time. Both Newmarch and Gray knew the composer and were surely aware that personally Sibelius was no Viking. He was a habitually undisciplined, sybaritic connoisseur of potent spirits and expensive cigars, and his fastidiousness was reflected in his immaculate clothes. These characteristics are what Gray doubtless meant by "Swedish affability." The Finnish composer may have been patently heterosexual—he sired five daughters, after all—but he was hardly a "primitive."[101]

Contemporary British critical biases affected later reception of the music as well, and not in positive ways. Certainly, Sibelius would have had to have possessed superhuman equipoise not to have basked in the admiration of the English; at the same time, their often excessive praise may have contributed to the long creative silence that followed the Seventh Symphony. What sensitive and insecure composer could have lived up to such adulation? Aside from Tovey's unpretentiousness and Lambert's wit, the phrases used to describe this music were often sullied by both snobbery and racism. The jungle of organicist verbiage used by Cherniavksy, for example, gave the impression that Sibelius's music could only be understood in terms of "germ" analysis. The pernicious tendency toward aesthetic ranking long beloved by British critics did further damage, especially during the reaction against Sibelius that set in during the 1950s and '60s. At that time, the high claims made by Newman, Gray, and others were discredited largely as a result of the hyperbole in which those critics had indulged. One of the reasons that the Fourth Symphony remains rarely performed today is the undue stress that Newman, Gray, Lambert, and Cherniavsky laid upon its austerity, a critical trope that has been repeated lazily for decades. For all its seriousness, the Fourth displays considerable sonic allure and, in the finale, long passages of brightness and charm. Reading Gray's daunting descriptions, one would never guess that the gloom lifted for even a moment. (Dissenting from this conventional wisdom, Newmarch protested, "Surely it is impossible to write of the A minor Symphony as conceived in a dull, uniform and colourless scheme?")[102] By promoting the Fourth Symphony, along with the Seventh and *Tapiola*, as the summit of Sibelius's achievement, these critics were compelled by their own narrow standards to discredit other scores that are equally superb.

Of course, these writers were not entirely without discrimination: their enthusiasm for Sibelius's music, though ineptly expressed at times, was not misplaced. They were right about the quality of the works they praised. After a relatively brief eclipse during the darkest days of High Modernism, Sibelius's music has reemerged as a cornerstone of the orchestral repertory in the twenty-first century. The British critics rightly prized his music as a useful alternative to a Teutonic modernism they deemed, not without cause, as pretentious, decadent, amateurish, and sterile. They admired Sibelius's formal control as worked out in the persuasive if unorthodox progression of ideas in his symphonies; they honored him as an innovator whose originality was expressed in his own fashion. More controversially, they believed that through being an avatar of the "Nordic race" he channeled the voice of nature itself. In other words, the British admired Sibelius for precisely the opposite reasons—item for item—for which Adorno criticized him to Newman. The "urbane" Newman must have been bemused by the German philosopher's inversion of the British critical estimate: the diatribe must have seemed straight out of *Alice in Wonderland*. On the subject of Sibelius and England, as with Stravinsky and jazz (and so much else), Adorno got it wrong.

NOTES

The author wishes to thank Daniel M. Grimley, Aidan Thomson, Lauren Cowdery, Christopher H. Gibbs, Howard Pollack, and Marcus Desmond Harmon for their assistance in the preparation of this essay, which is dedicated to the memory of Felix Aprahamian, critic, bon vivant, mentor, and loyal friend.

1. Theodor W. Adorno, *Introduction to the Sociology of Music*, trans. E. B. Ashton (New York: Seabury, 1976), 172–3. Translation amended.

2. Ernest Newman (1868–1959, born William Roberts) was a music critic and biographer who served as chief critic for the (London) *Sunday Times* from 1920 until his death.

3. Adorno returned to the subject of Sibelius several times over the course of his career, echoing the opinions expressed to Newman. See Theodor W. Adorno, "Törne, B. de, Sibelius: A Close–Up," *Zeitschrift für Sozialforschung* 7 (1938), 460–63, repr. as "Glosse über Sibelius" in *Impromptus* (Frankfurt am Main: Suhrkamp, 1968), 88–92, and translated in the Documents section of this volume. See also "Difficulties" in Theodor W. Adorno,

Essays on Music, ed. Richard Leppert, and trans. Susan H. Gillespie (Berkeley and Los Angeles: University of California Press, 2002), 646–67; and Max Paddison's essay in the current volume.

4. Granville Bantock, Foreword to Rosa Newmarch, *Jean Sibelius: A Short History of a Long Friendship* (Boston: C. C. Burchard, 1939), 9.

5. *Daily Telegraph*, 15 December 1934, in Walter Legge, *Walter Legge: Words and Music*, ed. Alan Sanders (New York: Routledge, 1998), 74.

6. Newmarch, *Jean Sibelius*, 27.

7. Over four hundred performances of works by Sibelius were given at the Proms between 1901 and the year of the composer's death, 1957. See The Proms Archive, http://www.bbc.co.uk/proms/archive/.

8. Jean Sibelius to Rosa Newmarch, 2 May 1911, in Newmarch, *Jean Sibelius*, 36.

9. Frederick Delius to Granville Bantock, 3 June 1912, in Lewis Foreman, *From Parry to Britten: British Music in Letters 1900–1945* (Portland: Amadeus Press, 1987), 52. In his commentary on this letter, Foreman writes, "Wood was to have introduced Scriabin's *Prometheus: Poem of Fire* to England but it was cancelled after the programme had been announced." Conducting the Queen's Hall Orchestra, Wood introduced Scriabin's work to London audiences on 1 February 1913.

10. Barry Smith, *Peter Warlock: The Life of Philip Heseltine* (Oxford: Oxford University Press, 1994), 36.

11. Erik Tawaststjerna, *Sibelius*, vol. 2, *1904–1914*, trans. Robert Layton (Berkeley: University of California Press, 1986), 219.

12. Newmarch, *Jean Sibelius*, 46.

13. Ibid., 47.

14. Smith, *Peter Warlock*, 36. Author's emphasis added.

15. Quoted in Tawaststjerna, *Sibelius*, 2:220.

16. Ibid.

17. No Proms performances for Janáček took place during his lifetime: the first performance at a Proms of a work by Janáček was his *Valašské tance*, op. 2, conducted by Wood in 1930. See The Proms Archive: http://www.bbc.co.uk/proms/archive/.

18. Ursula Vaughan Williams, *R. V. W.: A Biography of Ralph Vaughan Williams* (Oxford: Oxford University Press, 1984), 159. The year of the ISCM Festival at which Vaughan Williams heard *Příhody Lišky Bystroušky* is incorrectly given here as 1925, but the Prague/Salzburg festival occurred in 1924, the year of the opera's premiere in Brno.

19. Peter Franklin, "Sibelius in Britain," in *The Cambridge Companion to Sibelius*, ed. Daniel M. Grimley (Cambridge: Cambridge University Press, 2004), 187.

20. Ernest Newman, *More Essays from the World of Music: Essays from the London "Sunday Times,"* selected by Felix Aprahamian (New York: Coward-McCann, 1958), 113–15.

21. Ernest Newman, *Essays from the World of Music: Essays from "The Sunday Times" Selected by Felix Aprahamian* (London: John Calder, 1956, repr. New York: Da Capo Press, 1978), 128–29.

22. Cecil Gray, *Sibelius*, 2nd ed. (Oxford: Oxford University Press, 1934), 10. The first edition of this biography was published in 1931, when the Proms were presenting such popular scores as *Finlandia* constantly; Gray is clearly speaking here about the Fourth Symphony, the Seventh Symphony, and *Tapiola*.

23. For a detailed discussion of the reaction by British artists to the Wilde Trials, see William Gaunt, *The Aesthetic Adventure* (New York: Harcourt Brace, 1945), 214–15, and Byron Adams, "The Dark Saying of the Enigma: Homoeroticism and the Elgarian Paradox," in *Queer Episodes in Music and Modern Identity*, ed. Sophie Fuller and Lloyd Whitesell (Urbana and Chicago: University of Illinois Press, 2002), 216–44.

24. Quoted in Jerrold Northrop Moore, *Edward Elgar: A Creative Life* (Oxford: Clarendon Press, 1984), 459.

25. See George L. Mosse, *Nationalism and Sexuality: Respectability and Abnormal Sexuality in Modern Europe* (New York: Howard Fertig, 1985), 30, 33–37.

26. Dan Stone, *Breeding Superman: Nietzsche, Race and Eugenics in Edwardian and Interwar Britain* (Liverpool: Liverpool University Press, 2002), 116.

27. Newmarch, *Jean Sibelius*, 16.

28. Ibid., 18.

29. Newman, *More Essays*, 114–15.

30. Gray, *Sibelius*, 143–44.

31. Constant Lambert, *Music Ho!: A Study of Music in Decline* (London: Faber & Faber, 1934; repr. London: Hogarth Press, 1985), 261.

32. David Cherniavsky, "Special Characteristics of Sibelius's Style" in *Sibelius: A Symposium*, ed. Gerald Abraham (London: Lindsay Drummond Limited, 1947; repr. Oxford: Oxford University Press, 1952), 168–69. (Author's emphases.)

33. Cecil Gray, *A Survey of Contemporary Music* (London: Oxford University Press, 1924), 186–88.

34. Ibid., 193.

35. Max Nordau (1849–1923) was an influential author whose major work, *Entartung* (Degeneration; 1892) is in part an attack on the decadence of the modern metropolis.

36. Mosse, *Nationalism and Sexuality*, 32.

37. Ibid., 183.

38. Newman, *More Essays*, 128.

39. Gray, *Sibelius*, 23–24. Describing the strangeness of the Finnish landscape, Gray uses the word *otherness*, which he mentions he has borrowed from D. H. Lawrence.

40. Ibid., 56. Most of Sibelius's later biographers dismiss Gray's racial bifurcation as incorrect; Robert Layton, for example, states that Gray's assumptions are "highly misleading," as "Swedish–speaking Finns possess a distinctive and highly developed culture which is purely Finnish." See Robert Layton, *Sibelius* (New York: Schirmer Books, 1992), 12n2.

41. Jeremy Dibble, *C. Hubert H. Parry: His Life and Music* (Oxford and New York: Oxford University Press, 1992), 206.

42. Ibid., 121.

43. C. Hubert H. Parry, *The Evolution of the Art of Music*, 4th ed. (London: Kegan Paul, 1905), 60–61, 74. Parry's racial assumptions are directed at individual composers as well, as when he writes, "Indeed, the Oriental love of display which is so frequently found subsisting in people of Jewish descent marked Meyerbeer as essentially a man for the occasion" (312).

44. Newman's abjuration of "unalterable race-characteristics" comes from an essay entitled "Wagner, Debussy and Form" originally published in an April 1918 issue of *The New Witness*, and reprinted in Ernest Newman, *The Testament of Music: Essays and Papers by Ernest Newman*, ed. Herbert Van Thal (New York: Alfred A. Knopf, 1963), 200. Newman's review of Bloch's *Sacred Service* appeared in the *Sunday Times*, 3 April 1938, and was reprinted in Newman, *Essays from the World of Music*, 139–40. This review is hardly the sole instance in which Newman resorts to racial essentialism. As he once wrote of Bruckner, "The basis of this music is a certain racial or ancestral mentality that is nourished by a strong feeling for nature." See Newman, *More Essays*, 60. It must be pointed out that Newman published a scathing condemnation of the Nazis' racial policies just after the Anschluss: see "Racial Theories and Music: Whither Is Germany Tending," *Sunday Times*, 20 March 1938, repr. in *Essays from the World of Music*, 185–88.

45. Gray, *Sibelius*, 170. On the very next page, Gray, who was clearly taken with prolific composers, pays tribute to "the exuberant fecundity of Sibelius" which he sees as "a positive quality, even if some of its by-products are purely negative; it is a necessary condition of the highest creative achievements" (171).

46. Ibid., 170.

47. Herbert Spencer first used the phrase "survival of the fittest" in his *The Principles of Biology*, vol. 1 (London: Williams and Norgate, 1864), 444–45. Sir Francis Galton shared a common ancestor, Erasmus Darwin, with the great biologist and was thus related, more distantly, to Darwin's great nephew, Ralph Vaughan Williams. For the cordial relationship between Darwin and Galton, see Jonathan Peter Spiro, *Defending the Master Race: Conservation, Eugenics, and the Legacy of Madison Grant* (Burlington: University of Vermont Press, 2009), 118–19.

48. Stephen Jay Gould, *The Mismeasure of Man* (New York: W. W. Norton, 1996), 107.

49. All quotes by Galton are found in Spiro, *Defending the Master Race*, 119–21. As Spiro notes pointedly, "Galton's ideas on eugenics were fully sanctioned by his admiring cousin. In *The Descent of Man*, Charles Darwin extolled the 'remarkable' and 'ingenious' work of Galton, and affirmed the central tenet of eugenics" (122). G. K. Chesterton was one of the few British intellectuals of the time to challenge the conclusions of the eugenicists. Eugenic programs were espoused by George Bernard Shaw, Beatrice and Sidney Webb, and H. G. Wells, among others. In a speech delivered at the Eugenics Education Society on 3 March 1910, Shaw publicly proposed the eventual use of a "lethal chamber" to prune humanity of the weak and disabled; see Stone, *Breeding Superman*, 127. Chesterton argued against eugenics from an ethical rather than a scientific position and thus found few supporters at the time; later historical and scientific developments proved him correct. See G .K. Chesterton, *Eugenics and Other Evils* (London: Cassell and Company, 1922).

50. Thomas Henry Huxley, "Emancipation—Black and White," originally published in the *Reader*, 20 May 1865, repr. in *Lay Sermons, Addresses and Reviews* (New York and London: D. Appleton and Company, 1910), 20. Notice that Huxley does not allow African Americans into the same genus as himself and his (presumably) white readers.

51. Spiro, *Defending the Master Race*, 168.

52. The staggeringly rich and powerfully connected widow of the railroad baron E. H. Harriman sponsored the Cold Harbor Project of the American eugenicist Charles Benedict Davenport (1866–1944); see Spiro, *Defending the Master Race*, 127, for Theodore Roosevelt's interest in eugenics, especially his fears of "race suicide" if the members of his own class did not overcome their "selfishness" and procreate like barnyard animals (Spiro, 99, 112). The Republican Party was anti-immigration and nakedly anti-Semitic during this era.

53. Like a surprising number of those eugenicists who urged the white races to procreate industriously, Grant lived in an exclusively male environment. A prominent Republican, an unwavering anti-Semite, and the founder of the American Galton Society, Grant was the guiding force behind the creation of the Bronx Zoo, several national parks, and the passage of draconian laws that imposed strict quotas upon immigration. See Spiro, *Defending the Master Race*, a volume that examines the history of the American eugenics movement through an investigation of Grant's life and career. For the sales of *The Passing of the Great Race*, see Spiro, 161. 355–56.

54. Spiro erroneously claims that few "people realized that the term 'Nordic,' which was universally accepted and employed by laymen and scientists alike, was a neologism introduced by Grant in 1916." See Spiro, *Defending the Master Race*, 167–68. This is incorrect: Joseph Deniker (1852–1918) expropriated the term from literary criticism and used the word *Nordique* in his racial classifications. The economist and ethnologist W. Z. Ripley used Nordic in a "scientific" context in 1898.

55. Madison Grant, *The Passing of the Great Race or the Racial Basis of European History*, 4th rev. ed. (New York: Charles Scribner's Sons, 1921), 167–68.

56. Ibid., 169, 236.

57. Ibid., 228.

58. Ibid., 170.

59. Emily Greene Balch (1867–1961) was a pacifist, a professor of sociology and economics at Wellesley College from 1896 to 1918, and the editor of *The Nation*; she was awarded the Nobel Peace Prize in 1946. For information on Balch and other reviews of Grant's book, see Spiro, *Defending the Master Race*, 158–61.

60. Ibid., 355,

61. Ibid., 158, 301–2. John Galsworthy (1867–1933), author of *The Forsythe Saga*, was awarded the Nobel Prize for Literature in 1934. W. J. Sollas (1849–1936), whom Spiro identifies as an anthropologist, was appointed to the Chair of Geology at Oxford in 1894.

62. Stone, *Breeding Superman*, 5–6.

63. Gray, *Sibelius*, 183.

64. Ibid., 55. I have been unable to trace the source of Gray's descriptive quotation, which may well be a composite of the author's own devising. These blithe comments on his subject's physique are particularly jarring as they are made immediately after Gray's declaration that it was unnecessary "to intrude in unmannerly fashion upon [Sibelius's] private life."

65. Not everybody was impressed with Sibelius's appearance, however: Bantock's daughter Myrrha was reminded of a "Nordic troll." Quoted in Tawaststjerna, *Sibelius*, 2:42.

66. Gray, *Sibelius*, 141–42.

67. Published in the *Sunday Times*, 1 October 1939, repr. in Newman, *More Essays*, 119.

68. Nurmi won his first medals at the 1920 Summer Olympics in Antwerp, and went on to win 12 Olympic medals in total. He was barred from competing in the 1932 Los Angeles Games because of claims he had received money for appearances—in other words, that he had become a professional. After he retired from athletics, he struggled with health problems, and later attacked the sporting establishment.

69. Gray, *Sibelius*, 151.

70 Mosse, *Nationalism and Sexuality*, 13, 49.

71. Gray, *Sibelius*, 157.

72. Ibid., 144.

73. Gray, for example, writes of the first movement of the Second Symphony: "One can detect several distinct groups of thematic germs. . . . [Sibelius] then breathes life into them, bringing them into organic relation with each other and causing them to grow in stature and significance with each successive appearance, like living things" *Sibelius*, 135–36). If Walter Legge's translation from the original German used in the interview is accurate, Sibelius claimed that "the germ and fertilisation of my symphonies has been purely musical" (Legge, *Words and Music*, 73). While earlier British composers and writers, such as Sir Charles Villiers Stanford (1852–1924), employed the word *germ* to denote a musical motive, only later was the term placed within the context of an organicist vocabulary and its meaning expanded significantly. See Sir Charles Villiers Stanford, *Musical Composition: A Short Treatise for Students* (London: Macmillan, 1911), 66.

74. Cherniavsky's early death was the result of complications to his health while on active service during the Second World War.

75. Spiro, *Defending the Master Race*, 124–25. Grant mentions the "germ plasm" as well, in *The Passing of the Great Race*, 15.

76. Spiro, *Defending the Master Race*, 129.

77. Cherniavsky, "Special Characteristics of Sibelius's Style," in Abraham, *Sibelius*, 144.

78. Gray, *A Survey of Contemporary Music*, 185.

79. Gray, *Sibelius*, 175.

80. Ibid., 146. Gray disdains to give the reader even the slightest hint of what this low music-hall song might be, but he may have been alluding to the similarity of the "Swan Hymn" to the American popular song "The Band Played On," written by Charles B. Ward (1879–1946) in 1895, that begins, "Casey would waltz with a strawberry blonde." Any

connection between Sibelius's "Swan Hymn" and this song seems to have originated in Gray's perfervid imagination. For the reasons why Sibelius himself called the great melody of the finale of his Fifth Symphony the "Swan Hymn," as well as a sketch analysis of the melody that casts severe doubt upon Gray's facile assertion, see James Hepokoski, *Sibelius: Symphony No. 5* (Cambridge: Cambridge University Press, 1993), 36–37.

81. Gray, *Sibelius*, 188–89.

82. Legge, *Words and Music*, 73.

83. Newman, *More Essays*, 124, 128.

84. Lambert, *Music Ho!* 272. The use of late Beethoven to complement Sibelius's music was a common device used by both Gray and Cherniavsky; see Gray, *Sibelius*, 201, and Cherniavsky, "Special Characteristics of Sibelius's Style," in Abraham, *Sibelius*, 146.

85. David Cherniavsky, "The Use of Germ Motives by Sibelius," *Music and Letters* 23/1 (January 1942): 2. It must be remembered that Cherniavsky was serving in the British armed forces, at one of the darkest moments in the Second World War, when his article was published: it was amazing he managed to write it, or, for that matter, that the valiant editors of *Music & Letters* managed to publish an issue at all.

86. Gray, *Sibelius*, 187, 201.

87. Ibid., 190.

88. Ibid., 190–91, 201.

89. Grant, *The Passing of the Great Race*, 209.

90. Parry denounced the contemporary operas of his day in no uncertain terms: "It is only in the crudest phases of modern theatrical music that mere appeals to sensation are dignified by the name of art. . . . In modern opera climaxes of sound are often piled up one after another without doing anything but excite the animal side of man's nature." See Parry, *The Evolution of the Art of Music*, 180.

91. Gray, *A Survey of Contemporary Music*, 110.

92. Lambert, *Music Ho!* 49.

93. Newman, *Testament of Music*, 200, 203.

94. Newman spoke for many of his critical peers when he opined, "Nationalism in music is like dialect in speech: the only means we have of detecting it, indeed, is by some peculiarity of melody or rhythm." See Newman, *Testament of Music*, 185. Predictably, such opinions brought Newman into conflict with Vaughan Williams.

95. Gray, *Sibelius*, 24, 28.

96. Lambert, *Music Ho!* 271.

97. James Hepokoski, "*Finlandia* Awakens," in Grimley, *The Cambridge Companion to Sibelius*, 89–90. The event at which the first version of *Finlandia* was performed to accompany these *tableaux vivants* was the Helsinki Press Celebrations that took place in November 1899.

98. Newman, *Essays from the World of Music*, 130–32.

99. Donald Francis Tovey, *Essays in Musical Analysis*, (London: Oxford University Press, 1939), 6:89–90.

100. Donald Francis Tovey, *Essays in Musical Analysis*, (London: Oxford University Press, 1935), 2:128.

101. Indeed, Sibelius had a marked distaste for disorderly dress: he recalled Brahms as "an unsavory-looking fellow, untidily dressed in a shabby suit that bore evidence of many a previous meal and grey with cigar ash." He was no more approving of Bruckner's slovenliness. See Legge, *Words and Music*, 72.

102. Newmarch, *Sibelius*, 74.

Jean Sibelius and His American Connections

GLENDA DAWN GOSS

Conventional wisdom has often held that Jean Sibelius's most vital musical connections outside Finland were primarily with the Austro-German world. Yet, as ever with topics both Finnish and Sibelian, the reality is far more complex. For one thing, two of Sibelius's greatest tone poems—*The Oceanides* and *Tapiola*—were composed for the United States of America. For another, there is evidence to suggest that this composer's only trip to the United States, in the year 1914, was among the high points of his professional life. And it seems never to have been pointed out that, throughout his adult life, Sibelius cultivated connections with musical Americans.

Unfortunately, the paucity of scholarship on this topic has reinforced an oversimplified view. One of the few scholars to deal with the theme during the composer's lifetime was Otto Andersson (1879–1969), the music professor who founded the Sibelius Museum in Turku (Åbo), in southwestern Finland. After two visits to the United States, in 1950 and 1954, Andersson published his *Jean Sibelius i Amerika* (Jean Sibelius in America).[1] Since then, there have been only two book-length forays into the subject, both under my authorship: *Jean Sibelius and Olin Downes: Music, Friendship, Criticism* (1995) and *Vieläkö lähetämme hänelle sikareja? Sibelius, Amerikka ja amerikkalaiset* (Are we still sending him cigars? Sibelius, America, and Americans; 2009).[2] Yet all three studies show that Sibelius's connections with Americans ran deep and suggest how much is still to be learned in this area.

The discussion that follows is too brief to afford an all-encompassing view of Jean Sibelius vis-à-vis American musicians, composers, music lovers, and the many aspects of American life on which the Finn exerted an influence. The purpose here is rather to establish a framework for the scope and quality of these connections and then to provide a few vignettes to illustrate something of the nature of this relationship. Just as a new route to a well-known place can refresh our outlook, a different approach to a familiar subject can reveal unsuspected connections between people on different sides of a vast ocean, show curious ways in which the histories of Finland and America have intertwined, and even suggest new ways of hearing Sibelius's music.

Early Links

Sibelius's links to the New World are usually associated with the year 1914, when the composer spent several weeks in North America. Yet his connections with Americans had their beginnings at least as early as 1889. In that year, a government stipend to study composition in Berlin brought the twenty-three-year-old Hämeenlinna musician into contact with other foreigners aspiring to musical careers and converging on what was probably the most famous capital in the world for their art. While these foreigners included such Nordic musicians as Alf Klingenberg, Christian Sinding (both from Norway), and Fini Henriques (of Denmark), Americans were also among them: a sister and brother, violinist Geraldine and cellist Paul Morgan, and the violinist Theodore Spiering, who, like Geraldine Morgan, was studying with Joseph Joachim at the Königliche Hochschule für Musik. Sooner or later, all of these young musicians would play a part in Sibelius's life and career.

A few months after Sibelius left Berlin in 1890, Paul Morgan wrote to remind him of a promise to send a copy of his G-Minor Piano Quintet, which Morgan wanted to play for Joachim. Whether Sibelius followed through on his promise is unclear, but on 15 February 1891, the two Morgans together with Spiering and Henriques did play Sibelius's Quartet in B-flat Major (op. 4, completed the previous September), prompting enthusiastic accolades from Sinding, who was in the audience.[3]

By the time Sibelius began to settle down in Finland after his study years abroad, an American had even stepped onto the musical scene in Helsinki. William Humphrys Dayas (1863–1903), one of Franz Liszt's American pupils, had succeeded Ferruccio Busoni as the piano teacher at the Helsinki Music Institute. Dayas, known among the Finns as a "competent and enthusiastic teacher," would teach in Finland from 1890 until the middle of 1894.[4] Among his pupils was Karl Ekman (Sr.), who with his wife, Ida, became a great interpreter of Sibelius's songs.

At the end of August 1891, Sibelius was planning to meet Dayas because "I want to consult with him about one or two things."[5] The "one or two things" may have had to do with his solo songs, because on 2 November 1891, Dayas accompanied the leading Finnish baritone Abraham Ojanperä (1856–1916) in the premieres of "Hjärtats morgon" (The heart's morning), "Drömmen" (The dream), op. 13, nos. 3 and 5, and "Fågellek" (The play of the birds), op. 17, no. 3.[6] The following year, on 16 December 1892, the same musicians premiered "Under strandens granar" (Beneath the fir trees of the shore) and "Till Frigga" (To Frigga), op. 13, nos. 1 and 6. Both times the composer was in the audience. After the first of these concerts, Sibelius was writing exuberantly to his fiancée, Aino Järnefelt, that hearing these songs performed gave him new life.[7]

At a surprisingly early stage, then, Sibelius's career was being advanced by American performers. But how much Sibelius in turn was exerting an influence on Americans is yet to be determined. Dayas, for one, was a composer as well as a pianist, and the importance of Sibelius's works to his music has not been explored. Certainly, the two men were, if not friends, at least colleagues. During 1892–93, Sibelius was playing the violin regularly with the Music Institute's string quartet, an activity that placed him on the same concert program with Dayas at least seven times. On one of these evenings, 17 March 1893, they even played together in a somewhat unusual work: Camille Saint-Saëns's Septet for trumpet, string quintet, and piano (op. 65).[8]

Among the most distinguished Americans to take up Sibelius's music in the first decade of the twentieth century was Maud Powell (1867–1920), another violinist who had studied with Joachim. Powell made her European debut with the Berlin Philharmonic in 1885 with Joachim conducting, and knowledgeable contemporaries eventually placed her in the same league as Fritz Kreisler and Eugène Ysaÿe. Only a year after Sibelius had revised his Violin Concerto, Maud Powell gave the work its American premiere. On 30 November 1906, she performed the concerto with the New York Philharmonic conducted by Wassily Safonoff (1852–1918). The reception was disappointing, but when she repeated the work in Chicago a few months later, the evening was "a triumph," as she put it; the conductor, Frederick Stock (1872–1942), she said, was completely in sympathy with her interpretation and with Sibelius's composition.[9]

Americans had even begun to perform Sibelius's vocal music—hardly a foregone conclusion, given the language question. Minnie Tracey (ca. 1870–1929), a native of Albany, New York, was one of the first foreigners to take up Sibelius's songs. In her article "Music Masters of Scandinavia," published in *Musical America* in 1912, Tracey declared that she had sung all of the Finnish composer's songs.[10]

Minnie Tracey made her career as an opera singer. The evidence for her success is somewhat checkered. She took on the mezzo-soprano role of Rosa Mammai in Francisco Cilea's *L'arlesiana*, a part in which she was acclaimed mainly for her "horrible pronunciation"; in 1909, she was hissed off a Geneva stage during a performance of *Tristan und Isolde*, an episode she put down to professional jealousy.[11] Yet when Tracey premiered

Sibelius's orchestral version of "Höstkväll" (Fall evening) in Paris, with Alfred Cortot conducting on 14 January 1905, *Le Figaro* reported that the work "made a deep impression."[12]

Sibelius came to know Tracey personally during a stay in Paris at the end of 1911. Their relationship was more fraught than that with Morgan or Dayas. In letters written from Paris to Aino (by now the composer's wife), Sibelius reported meeting Tracey several times; he first described her as not being as great an artist as a person; before long he was referring to her as *min fiende* (Swedish: my enemy) and eventually as *koko tiikeri* (Finnish: a real tigress).[13] At the very least, Tracey's letters to Sibelius show her to have been single-minded in her determination to arrange extravagant plans for concertizing with the composer, including a tour in the United States.[14] It would not be until another American diva, the contralto Marian Anderson (1897–1993), visited Ainola in the 1930s that the bitter experience with Minnie Tracey would, in a sense, be redeemed.[15]

During these years, the violinist Theodore Spiering (1871–1925) resurfaced in Sibelius's life. Appointed concertmaster of the New York Philharmonic under Gustav Mahler, Spiering stepped in to conduct the last seventeen concerts of the 1910–11 season after Mahler fell ill. Among these was the program on 13 March 1911 featuring "national geniuses": Johan Svendsen, Pyotr Tchaikovsky, Antonin Dvořák, and the Sibelius Violin Concerto.[16]

Spiering's conducting ambitions would benefit Sibelius in other ways. Failing to secure the permanent post as the New York Philharmonic's chief conductor, Spiering moved to Berlin in 1912. There he became the conductor and adviser to the Neue Freie Volksbühne, for which he had scheduled Sibelius's Fourth Symphony for the 1914–15 season. In January 1914 Sibelius too was in Berlin. He met Spiering and gave him instructions for conducting the symphony as well as *Finlandia*.[17] The outbreak of war put a stop to the Fourth Symphony plans, but not to Spiering's conducting of Sibelius's music. In 1925 when Spiering was appointed the conductor of the new Portland Symphony Orchestra, *Finlandia* was on his concert programs for school children.[18]

"Till America! Avay!"

In 1913 Sibelius began receiving correspondence from the American composer and Yale University professor Horatio Parker (1863–1919).[19] By this time, he had been personally acquainted with Americans for more than two decades. Parker initially approached Sibelius with a request to set three poems to music for American school children. And so the *Three Songs for*

American Schools were born: "Autumn Song," "The Sun Upon the Lake Is Low," and "A Cavalry Catch." All appeared in Parker's Progressive Music Series, a graded music instruction course published in Boston in 1915.

It was on Parker's recommendation that the wealthy music patrons Carl and Ellen Battell Stoeckel invited Sibelius to compose a work for their summer music festival in Norfolk, Connecticut (an event that continues today as the Norfolk Chamber Music Festival). When Sibelius accepted and began the tone poem that would become *The Oceanides* (or, in Finnish, *Aallottaret*, op. 73), the couple followed up their commission with an invitation to conduct his works in their modestly named "Music Shed." Carl Stoeckel wrote a detailed account of this visit, from the docking of Sibelius's ship in New York harbor to the tours of Niagara Falls and the Housatonic River to the unforgettable performance in the Music Shed and the honorary doctorate bestowed upon Sibelius by Yale University.[20]

During this visit Sibelius met some of the most outstanding figures in the musical life of the United States: the conductor and composer Walter Damrosch, who would later commission *Tapiola* and give its premiere in New York's Mecca Temple; Maud Powell, for whom the Stoeckels commissioned a work from the African-British composer Samuel Coleridge-Taylor; the soprano Alma Gluck; the choral conductors Arthur Mees and Richmond Park Paine; the composers Horatio Parker, George W. Chadwick, Frederick Shepherd Converse, Charles Martin Loeffler, and Henry Hadley; critics of the likes of Henry E. Krehbiel, Philip Hale, and Olin Downes; and, not least, the recent president of the United States, William Howard Taft.

In the aftermath of the exuberant reception he was accorded by these and other American luminaries, Sibelius composed the music that many people consider to be his greatest—Symphonies 5, 6, and 7, and *Tapiola*.

The World's First Sibelius Society

Meanwhile, the ripple effect of Sibelius's visit had only just begun to be felt in North America. Almost exactly one year after the composer's New World journey, a group of music-loving Finnish-Americans in the mill town of Monessen, Pennsylvania, began serious discussions about how to advance the cause of Finnish music generally in the New World.[21]

Monessen was not just a town of steel mills: its pride and joy was the Louhi Band, which had been established on 14 February 1900, only two years after the town itself was founded. By 1915, George E. Wahlström was the band's conductor, and as Monessen's population expanded—to more than 18,000 by 1920—the band under his direction also grew, from the twelve who had played with the first conductor, Axel Ruuti, to a respectable fifty-member ensemble capable of performing Beethoven, Rimsky-Korsakov, Tchaikovsky, Wagner, and Sibelius.

It is not known exactly how much their famous countryman's recent visit to their shores may have inspired the cause of Monessen's Finnish-American residents. What is known is that the outcome of their meetings in July 1915 led to the founding of a nationwide music society. Initially, the founders called their association the Finnish-American Musical Club, but soon they took a bold decision: to ask Jean Sibelius for permission to name the organization for him. On 4 August 1915, the principal officers signed their names to a letter addressed to Sibelius, requesting to call their new organization "Sibelius-klubi"—the Sibelius Club; their purpose, they explained, was to build a bridge between their Finnish homeland and their present place of dwelling. Sibelius agreed, and the world's first Sibelius society was born.

The Sibelius Society members were exceptionally active. They intended their organization to be the conduit for supplying Americans with scores and musical arrangements by Sibelius and other Finns and Finnish-Americans. They issued arrangements for a full military band version of Finland's national anthem *Maamme-laulu*, as well as patriotic works such as *Porilaisten marssi* and *Suomen laulu*. In 1916 the Society decided to undertake a series of songbooks for Finnish choral groups in America, and in 1917 began to publish a periodical called *Airut*.

Airut's debut volume was hugely impressive: large in size, expensively and handsomely produced, it included numerous photographs showing off Finnish-American brass bands and choral societies. Sibelius's letter permitting the Society to use his name was reproduced in facsimile. There was a poem, "Sibeliukselle" (To Sibelius) by Kalle Koski. And there were caricatures of the board members, which spruced up "serious" articles by Leevi Madetoja. *Airut* and the Society's activities were soon curtailed, however, apparently by America's entry into the Great War.

But after the war the Sibelius Society members, along with other Finnish-Americans of Monessen, in a sense, came home. In 1920 the Louhi Band announced a concert tour of Finland in honor of the newly independent nation. A contingent of some four hundred Finnish-Americans wanted to accompany the band. On 10 June 1920, when the steamship *Ariadne* arrived in Helsinki's south harbor, it bore the Louhi Band, members of the Monessen Sibelius Society, and the largest group of emigrant Finns ever to return to the homeland.

That evening in the National Theatre, the Louhi Band gave the first of its twenty-five planned concerts. Sibelius was in the audience. Afterward he came forward to thank the conductor in person. According to Louhi

Band lore, the wreath later on display in Monessen's Finnish Lutheran Church was a gift from the composer himself on that occasion.

Sibelius and the Eastman School of Music

After the Great War, many other Americans came knocking at Sibelius's door. In January of the same year as the Louhi Band's tour of Finland, the composer received a tempting offer from the Eastman School of Music in Rochester, New York. The director of this newly established institution was none other than Alf Klingenberg, Sibelius's friend from his student days in Berlin. Klingenberg had emigrated to the United States and eventually settled in Rochester. Along with two other musicians—Hermann Dossenbach, a prominent Rochester violinist, and a voice teacher by the name of Oscar Gareissen—Klingenberg had founded the D.K.G. Institute of Musical Art. After a few years the organization, which was floundering financially, was purchased by the wealthy George Eastman, the inventor of the Kodak camera and roll film. Eastman appointed Klingenberg director of the new school, and Klingenberg began to recruit faculty members.

A long-running fiction—that Sibelius was asked to be the Eastman School's director—was introduced into the Sibelius lore by Karl Ekman Jr. (the son of the pianist taught by Dayas), who in writing a biography of the composer in the 1930s either misunderstood Sibelius or was misled by him.[22] In fact, Klingenberg invited Sibelius to teach composition. His offer is very clear and its terms quite attractive: Sibelius was to teach "the up-and-coming geniuses in America" to compose, "a task that should not be too onerous," he promised.[23] Moreover, Sibelius was to have free time to travel as a guest conductor in order to perform his works with the "many excellent orchestras" in the United States.

Sibelius said maybe, then he said yes, and then he said he would need to have $20,000. Staggered, Klingenberg came up with that unheard of sum for the 1921–22 academic year. But then, after his acceptance had been announced in the *New York Times* (on 25 January 1921), Sibelius telegraphed his refusal.

The reasons seem to have been several, and the one Sibelius gave to Klingenberg—ill health, apparently Aino's—was perhaps the main one. And so the post of Composition Professor at Eastman was offered to another member of that long-ago Berlin circle, Christian Sinding (1856–1941). Sinding accepted, but vacated the position after some months, and Klingenberg again turned to Finland, recruiting Selim Palmgren (1878–1951), who taught in Rochester for several years.[24] Perhaps it was this beginning that disposed the Eastman School to a Nordic outlook, even when its Norwegian-born director was replaced by an American: Howard Hanson (1896–1981).

Born in Wahoo, Nebraska, a town half Swedish and Lutheran, half Bohemian and Catholic, Hanson belonged to the Swedish-Lutheran half, his parents having been brought to the United States as children from Sweden. Perhaps for that reason their son nurtured a particular fondness for Nordic music. Pulled between music and the ministry, Howard Hanson opted for music and headed to New York, then to Northwestern University in Evanston, Illinois. After graduation he taught at the College of the Pacific in San Jose, California, where he became the Dean of the Conservatory of Fine Arts in 1919. Then he spent three years in Italy.

It was in Rome that Hanson completed the first of what would be seven symphonies: the austere Symphony no. 1, op. 21, subtitled "Nordic," a work that, according to its composer, embodies "the solemnity, austerity and grandeur of the North." Like Sibelius's first symphony, Hanson's first is in E minor. Hanson himself conducted the premiere in Rome with the Augusteo Orchestra in 1923. Sibelius was also in Rome that year; in March, he too conducted the Augusteo Orchestra, performing his Second Symphony and movements of the *Lemminkäinen* Suite. It seems likely that the two composers met on this occasion, although for how long and under what circumstances remains unclear.[25] What is clear is that the "Nordic" Symphony brought Hanson to the attention of George Eastman when the composer conducted it in Rochester on 19 March 1924.

The result was the appointment of a young and untried musician, whose long and eminent tenure as the director of the Eastman School would be distinguished for its enthusiastic and empathetic cultivation of American music. The school also showed distinct Nordic sympathies, evident among a number of Hanson's faculty and students, one of whom was Gardner Read (1913–2005). Read, who went on to have a respected career as a composer and as the author of several widely used books on musical notation and orchestration, composed his first symphony as a student at Eastman. As he told Sibelius in private correspondence, he was directly influenced by his symphonies 2 and 4.[26] Read even chose the same tonality (A minor) as Sibelius's Fourth Symphony for his own first symphony, a work awarded first prize in a national contest sponsored by the New York Philharmonic Orchestra.

Another piece of fiction—widely circulated—is that Gardner Read "studied" with Sibelius.[27] Although Read's correspondence shows that he studied Sibelius's scores, studying with Sibelius himself was a more difficult proposition. Like hundreds of other Americans during the twentieth century, Gardner Read simply made a visit to Ainola one summer afternoon: the date was 31 July 1939. Read got a great deal of mileage out of that visit. The cachet of saying one had "studied with Sibelius" was so great that the claim appeared in books about American music, in Read's obituaries, in respected research works, and even on Read's official website.[28] The documentary evidence suggests that Sibelius's influence on Read may have been more distant than directly personal: there is no reason, however, to question Sibelius's musical legacy in Read's work.

Finlandia and Americans

The timing of Read's visit to Ainola and his enthusiasm for Sibelius's music was no coincidence. By the 1930s, Sibelius was at the height of his North American fame. There were many reasons, among them conductors in the United States dedicated to programming his music, men like Serge Koussevitzky, Leopold Stokowski, and eventually Arturo Toscanini; enthusiastic and influential music critics, especially "Sibelius's Apostle" Olin Downes, who was well placed at the *New York Times*; the prevalence and power of radio and the recording industry; and, not least, the musical soundscape of the twentieth century, a world in which the gulf that had opened between listeners and composers was becoming unbridgeable. In 1935, when listeners to radio broadcasts of the New York Philharmonic Orchestra concerts were asked to cast two votes—one for their favorite living composer and one for their favorite past composer—respondents voted Sibelius in first place as their favorite living symphonist, placing him on a par with Beethoven, their favorite symphonist from the past.[29]

Although the seven numbered symphonies were widely known, both inside the concert hall and on the radio waves, Sibelius was most often represented across the United States by two phenomenally popular works, *Valse triste* and *Finlandia*. It was *Finlandia* that Americans embraced as their own, and by the 1930s that embrace had reached extravagant dimensions.

Composed in 1899, at a time when Finland was still an autonomous Grand Duchy of the Russian Empire, *Finlandia* was first heard during the last of six *tableaux vivants* staged during the so-called Press Celebration Days, the ostensible purpose of which was to raise money for pension funds of journalists made redundant by the tsar's censorship and his systematic closing down of Finnish newspapers. The subtext of the event, however, was Finnish resistance to Russian restrictions on freedom of the press and freedom of speech. *Finlandia* is often referred to as an orchestral tone poem, yet its closing portion is in the unmistakable style of a Lutheran hymn. A few years after the first performances, words began to be written to that hymn. By the 1930s the number of versions, arrangements, and editions of that final section had grown by leaps and bounds.

So too had the numbers of texts associated with it. "Accept Our Thanks," "Beloved Land," "The Christian Life," "Dear Friend of Mine," "Lift Up Your Hearts," "O Mighty Land"—these were just some of the English words heard to the *Finlandia* hymn in North America.[30] By the end of that decade it was clear that *Finlandia* had become an established part of American life. Had anyone doubted it before, events in connection with the New York World's Fair, scheduled to open in 1939, eliminated all uncertainty.

Already in 1938, the fair's directors had begun to implement plans for an event that would surpass all previous world fairs. Howard Hughes (1905–76), the fair's aeronautics adviser, promoted the happening with a record-setting round-the-world flight in his Lockheed 14-N Super Electra, dubbed the *New York World's Fair 1939*. On 14 July 1938, Hughes landed his craft in Brooklyn, a mere 3 days, 19 hours, and 8 minutes after takeoff.

Buildings began going up on the fairgrounds to demonstrate a vision of the "World of Tomorrow." The Futurama, the Trylon, and the Perisphere would be among the most talked about. So would one of the fair's other major exhibitions, the Westinghouse Time Capsule. Made of cupaloy —an alloy of tempered copper, chromium, and silver believed to be indestructible—the time capsule was buried beneath the fairground at a depth of fifty feet, not to be opened for 5,000 years. To ensure that knowledge of the capsule would not be lost, the exact burial site was entered into *The Book of Record* with the information inscribed on permanent paper in special ink.[31] Some 3,000 copies of *The Book of Record* were distributed around the world, placed in libraries, monasteries, and other locations.

The Book of Record includes requests that its contents be translated into new languages as these supersede old ones; it has instructions for making instruments to locate the time capsule electromagnetically; and it contains an ingenious key to the English language to aid future archaeologists and linguists should knowledge of English be lost.

The Book of Record also explains that items for the time capsule were chosen for how well they represented American life in 1939. The items included ordinary things—a fountain pen, a pack of Camel cigarettes—and extraordinary things, such as statements from Albert Einstein and Thomas Mann. And they included "American" music: John Philip Sousa's *Stars and Stripes Forever*, the swing piece *Flat Foot Floogie*, and not least, phonograph recordings and scores of Jean Sibelius's *Finlandia*.

Finlandia has shown up time and again at America's most historic moments and has been integrated into the religious life of the nation. In the grieving aftermath of 9/11, the hymn from *Finlandia* was sung in services around the country.[32] The Mormon Tabernacle Choir—the choir of the Church of Jesus Christ of Latter-Day Saints and the ensemble Ronald Reagan called "America's Choir"—sings *Finlandia* as a staple of its repertory, sometimes to the words "On Great Lone Hills," and has recorded the work on the CD conspicuously titled *Faith of Our Fathers*. One of its arrangements, for voices and orchestra with unctuous harmonic twists, transforms the Sibelian sound into the unmistakable tone and style of an American church choir.

Americans have not all treated *Finlandia* with solemn veneration. William Saroyan (1908–1981), irreverent author and playwright (*The Daring Young Man on the Flying Trapeze* and the Pulitzer Prize–winning *The Time of Your Life*), visited Helsinki in 1935 and brashly decided to call on Sibelius. "Who am I to see Jean Sibelius? . . . I am a punk writer, and he is a great composer, Jesus Christ."[33] Yet visit he did, recording his impressions in an essay pointedly titled "Finlandia." Saroyan's first reaction on hearing Sibelius's *Finlandia*, he said, was to get up from his chair, push over a table, knock some plaster out of the wall, and yell, "Jesus Christ, who is this man?"[34]

Closer to home, both in time and space, was the appearance in Helsinki in July 2006 of "the most dangerous band in the world," as Guns N' Roses has been called. The band may well be dangerous: it has been dogged by controversy almost since its beginning in Los Angeles in 1985, criticized for its members' flagrant use of drugs and alcohol, their messy lives and offensive lyrics, and for founder Axl Rose's habit of wearing Charles Manson T-shirts. Yet it is also tremendously popular: Guns N' Roses is believed to have sold an estimated 100 million albums worldwide. On that July evening in 2006, the band's guitarist, Robin Finck, who grew up in Marietta, Georgia, the part of the country's Bible Belt saturated with the *Finlandia* hymn (to the words "Be Still My Soul"), treated the crowd to nothing less than a hard-rock version of Sibelius's *Finlandia*.[35] The crowd cheered. The Internet bloggers went to work. And one of them summed up the prevailing sentiment in two words: "Sibelius rules."

It is undeniable that Sibelius's "rule" over Americans has been aided in part by immigrant elements, certainly by immigrant Finns, but also perhaps by many others who find themselves in exile. For along with the extraordinary intelligence that shines through in works of stunningly original design, the power of Sibelius's music lies in its creator's ability to connect with listeners emotionally. Among American composers today, John Adams (b. 1947) has been foremost in his appreciation of that power. Adams has singled out Sibelius (along with Beethoven) for the exceptional skill with which the Finn so effectively achieves "a sense of emotional change when a modulation occurs."[36] Passages in Adams's works such as the gigantic harmonic struggle at the end of *Harmonielehre* (1985), which the composer ultimately resolves with a breakthrough into tonality (in this case, E-flat major), owe a serious debt to similar battles in Sibelius's music, most notably the Fifth Symphony. As an adolescent, Adams kept Yousuf

Karsh's brooding photograph of Sibelius from *Life* magazine taped on the wall facing his bed; as an adult, his music has been described as sounding "like Sibelius superimposed on a Eurorock rhythm track."[37] It seems somehow fitting that just as Sibelius made the most of diversity in his own music—setting both Finnish-language and Swedish-language texts, merging features of symphony and symphonic poem, amalgamating the resources of folksong, Lutheran hymn, fugal process, and Grieg-like orchestral techniques in his works—that some of his most creative American admirers have emulated his reach across musical and cultural barriers and forged new musical paths of their own.

NOTES

1. The book appeared in Finnish in 1960 as *Jean Sibelius Amerikassa* (Åbo: Förlaget Bro, 1955), but there is no English translation.

2. The Sibelius-Downes book was published in Boston by Northeastern University Press; the Finnish book was brought out by WSOY in Helsinki. Its text is currently being revised and expanded for publication in English. There is also a monograph on Sibelius and his Masonic music, which directly involved the composer with Freemasons in the United States. See Hermine Weigel Williams, *Sibelius and His Masonic Music: Sounds in "Silence"* (Lewiston, NY: The Edwin Mellen Press, 1998).

3. Paul Morgan's letter to Sibelius, dated 5 September 1890, National Archives of Finland (henceforth NA), Sibelius Family Archive, Box 23. On the quartet, see Fabian Dahlström, *Jean Sibelius: Thematisch-bibliographisches Verzeichnis seiner Werke* (Wiesbaden: Breitkopf & Härtel, 2003), 13–15. The evidence for the quartet's performance and the responses to it come from a letter written by Adolf Paul to Sibelius on 16 February 1891 (NA, Sibelius Family Archive, Box 25), with lavish tributes to Henriques and quotations of Sinding's fulsome praise of the composer; afterward, Morgan held a party for the musicians and their friends. On their return to the United States, the Morgans formed the Geraldine Morgan Concert Company with the soprano Inez Grinelli (see *New York Times*, 4 November 1894). Paul Morgan eventually became first cellist in the Minnesota Symphony Orchestra. When he heard that Sibelius was coming to the United States, he invited the composer to his country home in Westchester County, New York, both for old times' sake and hoping that they could go through the composer's cello and piano work, *Malinconia* (op. 20). These later Morgan letters, dated 27 May and 14 June 1914, are preserved in the National Library of Finland(Helsinki University Library, henceforth HUL, Collection 206.25).

4. For more about Dayas, see Carl Lachmund, *Living with Liszt: From the Diary of Carl Lachmund, an American Pupil of Liszt, 1882–1884*, edited, annotated, and introduced by Alan Walker (Stuyvesant, NY: Pendragon Press, 1995), esp. 236–38, 367–69. Fabian Dahlström gives details of Dayas's activities at the Music Institute (today the Sibelius Academy) in *Sibelius-Akademin 1882–1982* (Helsinki: Sibelius-Akademins pub., 1982), 358–61. Dayas was remembered fondly in Helsinki, both as a teacher and as a composer; when he died unexpectedly in 1903, although he was no longer in Finland, obituaries appeared in a number of Finnish newspapers, including *Päivälehti* and *Uusi Suometar* (both on 12 May 1903).

5. Sibelius to Aino Järnefelt, 27 August 1891, NA, Sibelius Family Archive, Box 94.

6. The other numbers on the program were Wagner's *Albumblatt*, David Popper's *Elfentanz*, op. 39; Beethoven's Quartet in E-flat, op. 74 and Sonata in G Minor, op. 5.

7. Sibelius to Aino Järnefelt, 2 November 1891, NA, Sibelius Family Archive, Box 94.

8. Dahlström lists the concerts and their programs in *Sibelius-Akademin 1882–1982*, 358–61. In 1892 the dates were 24 October, 7 November, 11 November, and 16 December; in 1893, dates were 7 and 26 April.

9. Powell's letters to Sibelius are preserved in NA, Sibelius Family Archive, Box 26. Her descriptions of both the New York and the Chicago performances come from a missive dated 17 June 1906.

10. *Musical America* 26/10; see Jean Sibelius, *Dagbok 1909–1944*, ed. Fabian Dahlström (Helsinki: Svenska litteratursällskapet i Finland/Stockholm: Atlantis, 2005), 386n242. By the end of 1911 Sibelius had composed approximately 80 of his more than 100 solo songs, although not all of them had been published. For biographical information on Tracey, see K. J. Kutsch and Leo Riemens, *Großes Sängerlexikon*, 4th rev. ed. (Munich: K. G. Saur, 2003), 7:4751.

11. See Alan Mallach, "*L'arlesiana*: Francisco Cilea," *Opera Quarterly* 11 (1994): 162–65; and Mallach, "American Singer Hissed," *New York Times*, 1 April 1909.

12. *Le Figaro* quoted in *Helsingfors-Posten*, 26 January 1905.

13. See Suvi Sirkku Talas, ed., *Syysilta: Aino ja Jean Sibeliuksen kirjeenvaihtoa 1905–1931* (Helsinki: Suomalaisen Kirjallisuuden Seura, 2007), 219, 260. Other letters mentioning Tracey are found on 211, 213, 218, 257, 260.

14. Tracey's letters to the composer (fourteen in all plus three postcards) are preserved in HUL Coll. 206.39. Sibelius's reactions are recorded in his diary; see *Dagbok*, 4 December and 19 December 1911; 26 August, 2 September, and 6 September 1912; 16 May and 28 August 1914; 15 August 1915.

15. Miss Anderson's accompanist, the Finnish pianist Kosti Vehanen, recalled Sibelius saying that the contralto's recording of "Kom nu hit, död!" (Come away, death!) was the most satisfying by any singer of any of his lieder; see Vehanen, *Vuosikymmen Marian Andersonin säestäjänä* (Porvoo: WSOY, 1949), 37. Anderson and Sibelius are dealt with in my *Vieläkö lähetämme hänelle sikareja? Sibelius, Amerikka, ja amerikkalaiset* (Are we still sending him cigars? Sibelius, America, and Americans) (Helsinki: WSOY, 2009), 177–83.

16. Reported in the *New York Times*, 14 March 1911. For biographical information on Spiering, see the extensive entry in the *Dictionary of American Biography*, ed. Dumas Malone (London: Humphrey Milford, Oxford University Press, 1935), 17:457.

17. According to the composer's *Dagbok*, 24 January 1914.

18. As he told Sibelius in a letter dated 21 June 1925; he also asked for a new work that could be performed for the first time in America. This and other Spiering correspondence is preserved in NA, Sibelius Family Archive, Box 30; two other missives as well as one from Spiering's wife, Frida Mueller Spiering, are found in HUL Coll. 206.36.

19. Sibelius, *Dagbok*, May 1914, 189.

20. Carl Stoeckel, "Some Recollections of the Visit of Jean Sibelius to America in 1914," *Scandinavian Studies* 43 (1971): 53–88. The article includes annotations by Prof. George C. Schoolfield and his transcriptions of the composer's correspondence with Horatio Parker.

21. This and the following vignettes on the Eastman School and *Finlandia* are drawn from my *Vieläkö lähetämme hänelle sikareja?* They are retold here with the kind permission of the publisher WSOY and *Finnish Music Quarterly*. In that publication a portion of the Sibelius Society essay appeared as part of "The World's First Sibelius Society" (no. 4 [2008]: 66–67). Paul Sjöblom appears to have been the first person to call attention to Monessen's historic society, in "Out of the Past: A Forgotten Chapter of Finnish-American History," *Suomen Silta*, no.1 (1970); his article has been reprinted in *Finland from the Inside: Eyewitness Reports of a Finnish-American Journalist, 1938–1997*, edited with introduction and commentary by Glenda Dawn Goss (Helsinki: New Bridge Press, 2000), 37–43.

22. Karl Ekman Jr., *Jean Sibelius: En konstnärs liv och personlighet* (Helsinki: Holger Schildts, 1935), 251. The English translation, *Jean Sibelius: His Life and Personality*, trans. Edward Birse (London: Alan Wilmer, 1936), 242, repeats the same misinformation.

23. Klingenberg to Sibelius, 19 January 1920, NA, Sibelius Family Archive, Box 22. The Eastman invitation is dealt with in the context of Sibelius's life in the 1920s in my *Sibelius: A Composer's Life and the Awakening of Finland* (Chicago: University of Chicago Press, 2009), 426–28.

24. See Kimmo Korhonen, *Selim Palmgren: Elämä musiikissa* (Helsinki: WSOY, 2009), 414–25.

25. Sibelius does not mention Howard Hanson in his diary. However, Andrea Sherlock Kalyn, in "Constructing a Nation's Music: Howard Hanson's American Composers' Concerts and Festivals of American Music, 1925–71" (PhD diss., University of Rochester, 2001), 79, mentions several "highly acclaimed musicians," including Sibelius, whom the young Hanson encountered during his Prix de Rome years. I would like to express my gratitude to David Peter Coppen, special collections librarian and archivist in the Sibley Music Library, for consulting this dissertation on my behalf.

26. Two letters of Gardner Read to Sibelius are preserved in HUL Coll. 206.31: in the first, dated 29 March 1939, Read introduces himself, asks permission to visit Sibelius, and tells about his own first symphony; the second, dated 1 August 1939, is discussed below in note 28. No letters from Read have been found in the National Archives of Finland.

27. See, for example, Virgil Thomson, *American Music Since 1910*, with an introduction by Nicolas Nabokov (New York: Holt, Rinehart and Winston, 1970), 167; and Mary Ann Dodd and Jayson Rod Engquist, *Gardner Read: A Bio-Bibliography* (Westport, CT: Greenwood Press, 1996).

28. See http://www.composergardnerread.org/biography/, and the obituary in *The Independent*, 14 December 2005. The purely social nature of Read's visit is clear from his letter of thanks written to Sibelius the following day (1 August 1939, HUL Coll. 206.31), in which Read expresses his gratitude for the composer's hospitality and also asks for a signed photograph. He mentions nothing, however, that could be construed as "studying," not even discussion of his own music, whose scores he allegedly brought along. Although Read seems to have maintained that he returned to Ainola at a later date, just when such a visit would have taken place or what its nature might have been is unclear. The outbreak of war in Finland on 30 November 1939 and the ongoing hostilities worldwide would have prevented any such visit until after 1945. By then Sibelius was eighty years old and had not taken on any composition students since 1916–17, when Bengt de Törne was his pupil. On Read's side, the correspondence preserved in connection with him in the National Library of Finland suggests that he was eager to connect his name with the greatest living composers; a courteous letter of reference on Read's behalf written to Sibelius by Ildebrando Pizzetti states that Read had studied with the Italian master "pendant quelques jours" (29 March 1939, HUL Coll. 206.29). Another letter of reference to Sibelius, this one from Read's benefactress Mary A. Cromwell (HUL Coll. 206.9, 30 March 1939), states that Read wanted to get to know Finland and show Sibelius two scores he had just published (in which case any corrective from Sibelius would be coming too late). Perhaps for Read, simply to meet and converse on music with a world-class composer was enough to constitute studying with the great man.

29. See "Sibelius, Composer, Leads in Radio Vote," *New York Times*, 2 December 1935.

30. For an idea of the astonishing number of *Finlandia* arrangements, see Dahlström, *Werkverzeichnis*, 113–21, where a "selection" takes up some eight pages.

31. *The Book of Record of the Time Capsule of Cupaloy: Deemed capable of resisting the effects of time for five thousand years, preserving an account of universal achievements, embedded in the grounds of the New York World's Fair 1939, September 23, 1938* (New York: n.p., 1938).

32. Jouni Mölsä, "Finlandian kaksoiselämä" (*Finlandia*'s double life), *Helsingin Sanomat*, 13 October 2002.

33. William Saroyan, "Finlandia," *The William Saroyan Reader* (New York: George Braziller, 1958), 130.

34. Ibid. Saroyan's essay was originally published the year after his meeting with Sibelius, in the volume *Inhale and Exhale* (New York: Random House, 1936). It has been reprinted in *The William Saroyan Reader* (New York: Braziller, 1958), 126–32.

35. Robin Finck's Helsinki performance of *Finlandia* was available on YouTube as of this writing (January 2010).

36. Adams's comment was made in an interview with Jonathan Cott, in liner notes to *John Adams Harmonielehre*, San Francisco Symphony conducted by Edo de Waart, Nonesuch Digital 7559-79115-2, 1985.

37. Adams's autobiography, *Hallelujah Junction: Composing an American Life* (New York: Farrar, Straus and Giroux, 2008), 19–20, is the source for the information about the Karsh photograph; see also 104, 129–30. The "Eurorock" comment is David Schiff's, in "Memory Spaces (*On the Transmigration of Souls*) (2002)," *The Atlantic*, April 2003; repr. in *The John Adams Reader: Essential Writings on an American Composer*, ed. Thomas May (Pompton Plains, NJ: Amadeus Press, 2006), 189.

Art and the Ideology of Nature:
Sibelius, Hamsun, Adorno

MAX PADDISON

The meaning of nature in almost every age is inseparable from social considerations.

—Leo Löwenthal, "Knut Hamsun"[1]

It is a long-established view that the music of Sibelius portrays nature and landscape, together with a specific sense of place and the spirit of its people—Finland, a land of sparsely populated forests and lakes. This view dominated the reception of the composer, particularly in Scandinavia, Britain, and the United States in the first half of the twentieth century; furthermore, as Tomi Mäkelä has shown, it was also the case in Germany in the early years of the century, and then, after a period of disdainful neglect between the wars, it surfaced again in the late 1930s, when it fitted conveniently with aspects of Nazi ideology. As Mäkelä has put it, Sibelius "was widely thought to represent the nature and people of the North," while the early twentieth-century reception of the composer in Germany emphasized "the link between Sibelius and Finnishness as a fundamental expression of the pure Nordic spirit."[2] There is plenty of evidence that the composer himself also thought of his work in this way. That great advocate of Sibelius in England, Ernest Newman, wrote in 1938 that the composer "has told us that the origins and the working-out of his musical thoughts are determined by 'mental images': that is to say, his work wells up from definite impressions of nature and of human life," although Newman was also careful to stress that Sibelius "develops the resultant musical ideas not in pursuance of any programme that could be put into words but according to their true nature as *music*."[3] The music of Sibelius is often seen as brooding and introspective, wherein a contemplative and lonely subjectivity is absorbed and overwhelmed by the immensity of nature, engendering an experience that borders on the sublime.

Three questions in particular emerge from any discussion of music and nature. The first concerns what we mean when we say that art can "represent" nature; the second concerns what we mean when we say that art in some way "is" nature, as, for example, drawing on material that is in some way natural, or even "embodying" nature in the sense of its processes or structures or systems as being "natural"; and the third concerns the transcendent meanings we ascribe to nature and in particular to its representation in art, such as feelings of mystery, profundity, awe, freedom, and hope, a sense of being at the origin of all things.[4] The first, art as the representation of nature, might appear to be the most straightforward, but is not so, of course, in the case of music, at least beyond the most rudimentary onomatopoetic level. In the case of Sibelius, there are undoubtedly examples to be found at this level—the tone poem *Tapiola* is an obvious instance, combining the impression of storm and wind in trees through the use of rapid interlaced pianissimo muted string figurations. The second, that music is, or can be "nature," or "natural," because its material and processes are in some sense "natural," is a position that can only be sustained if the artificially constructed aspects of music and its tonal systems are overlooked (that is, the reality that tonality as a system is a highly artificial construct based on a calculated interference in the natural intervallic relations of the harmonic series). Provided that this inbuilt artifice at the core of the Western tonal system can be put to one side, the most profitable way of understanding "music as nature" in relation to Sibelius is probably to regard the use of aspects of instrumental color and texture as in some sense standing in for nature, particularly through the preponderance of long sustained drones, or repeated ostinato figures over lengthy stretches of time, a distinctive use of sustained brass harmonies, especially in the horns, and the use of primary instrumental colors as simply "being" themselves in some elemental and natural sense, to mention just a few possibilities. Indeed, Sibelius's famous comment about his orchestration offering "pure spring water" as opposed to "cocktails" would appear to support this view.[5] The third, the transcendent meanings ascribed to nature and its portrayal in music, might be said to flow from the first two instances, so that the mysterious and the profound, or the elemental and overwhelming effects of the music might be said to be the direct result of the use of such devices and processes.

I suggest here that such transcendent ascriptions are ideologically loaded, and as a result have always been prone to political exploitation.[6] Although in this essay I address all three of these questions to varying degrees, my main emphasis is on the third, the ideological implications of the concept of nature—that is to say, to paraphrase Walter Benjamin, the ways in which each age projects its own needs onto the face of nature.[7]

Important aspects of the concept of nature in Sibelius, his reception in Germany, and specifically the negative role played by Adorno, to this day, in the reception of the composer there, have been addressed in recent years, in particular by Tomi Mäkelä.[8] I have gratefully drawn on his extensive and valuable work. Indeed, a substantial part of his book *"Poesie in der Luft": Jean Sibelius, Leben und Werk* (2007) is devoted to a consideration of the role of nature in Sibelius's music. My focus here, however, is on the concept of nature as an implicitly ideological, which is to say, historical and social notion, and in particular on philosophical aspects of the concepts of nature and the sublime in Sibelius and his literary contemporary, the Nobel Prize–winning Norwegian novelist Knut Hamsun.[9] It is for this reason that I have chosen to view the idea of nature in the music of Sibelius obliquely, and to do so by considering Adorno's interpretation of it in the two short essays he wrote as a critique of Sibelius in 1937 and 1938, which, for reasons that will become evident, I have read in conjunction with a celebrated essay by a Frankfurt School colleague of Adorno's, Leo Löwenthal, written as a critique of Knut Hamsun and published in 1937. I argue from the position that aesthetic judgments are not formulated in a vacuum, and that in particular a concept like "nature" cannot be understood apart from the historical and political context that gives it meaning. My aim is to reconsider Adorno's Sibelius critique in its context, show the centrality of the concept of nature, and to examine critically the claims Adorno makes in relation to the achievements of Löwenthal's Hamsun critique. Underlying both Adorno's and Löwenthal's positions, I propose, are pivotal arguments concerning nature, the sublime, and the position of the experiencing subject that can be traced back to Kant's *Critique of Judgment,* and which go a considerable way toward helping us understand the real motivation behind Adorno's polemical critique.

Adorno's Critique of Sibelius: Context

To Adorno's German musical sensibility the value accorded to Sibelius's music in England, where he arrived in exile in 1934, was difficult to fathom, and the great claims being made for it must have appeared irritatingly excessive, to a degree that made him determined to reveal what he saw as the emptiness of the kind of rhetoric that compared the composer to Beethoven. Indeed, both Erik Tawaststjerna and Tomi Mäkelä have pointed out that in all likelihood Adorno's barbed attack was really a direct response to Bengt de Törne's book *Sibelius: A Close-Up,* which had appeared in its English translation in London in 1937 and had added further fuel to the Sibelius adulation of the time.[10] In his brief article "Glosse über Sibelius" of 1938 (translated in the Documents section in this volume), Adorno ruthlessly identified what he considered to be the trivial and commonplace character of the thematic material in the symphonies, what he saw as the conventional and reactionary use of tonal harmony, the tendency to fall back on pedal points and to abandon harmonization completely for lengthy passages of unison or octave doubling, the meagerness of the orchestration and the amateur appearance of the scores themselves, which looked, he says, as if they were composition exercises done by a student. Sibelius had in fact studied composition in Germany and Austria in the early 1890s before returning to Finland, the "land of a thousand lakes," to become a symbol of the Finns' national aspirations. Adorno rather unkindly suggests that the composer "buried himself in the land of a thousand lakes in order to hide himself from the critical eye of his [Austro-German] schoolmasters."[11] And he goes on to say, regarding the composer's initial fame in Scandinavia, that "probably no-one was more astonished than he to discover that his failure had been interpreted as success, his lack of technical ability as necessity."[12] By this I understand Adorno to mean that what he regards as the technical shortcomings manifest in Sibelius's music quickly became the dominant feature of its distinctive identity, and were interpreted as part of the inner structural necessity that caused his works to unfold in the distinctive and original way they do. Adorno was not convinced by the claim advanced by sympathetic critics like Ernest Newman that the symphonies are highly original and truly integrated works, characterized by movement from an initial statement of fragmentary ideas as part of an organic process toward a final unifying apotheosis.[13] He maintained instead: "The resulting appearance of originality is ascribable only to the senselessness with which the motives are put together, without anything to guarantee their meaningful context other than the abstract passage of time."[14] Adorno further deplored Sibelius's failure to depart from the relatively traditional use of tonality: no doubt a factor that contributed to the Finnish composer's great popular success. For Adorno, to write tonal music in the twentieth century was an anachronism, and was interpreted as a sign of regression.

Adorno's own theory of new music, particularly as formulated in the book he began writing in 1941, *Philosophy of New Music*, was founded, of course, on a Schoenbergian notion of historical necessity, a historical dialectic driven by the convergence of the most advanced stage of expressive needs in relation to the most advanced technical means at any particular historical period. In principle this meant that tonality had been historically superseded, and that the attempt to employ tonal means in the twentieth century was a sign of reaction, implying an absolutist claim that tonality itself was the natural state of music—indeed, that the tonal system itself was "nature."

Regressing to tonality did not, however, offer an escape from the upheavals that characterized modernism, according to Adorno: the cracks and fissures that are a feature of the modernist work also find their place in those works that attempt to ignore its effects. The result, he claimed, is that under the new conditions even tonal works no longer retain their coherence and consistency. As he put it in "Glosse über Sibelius": "The earthquake that found its expression in the dissonances of the great works of the new music did not spare the little works that remained with the old-fashioned style. They became torn and false."[15] Whatever the claims made for the composer in Nordic and Anglo-Saxon countries, Sibelius's failure was, for Adorno, threefold. First was Sibelius's erroneous belief that the dialectic of musical material could be circumvented or ignored, and tonality restored. Second was what Adorno regarded as the sheer technical incompetence displayed by Sibelius in working with such regressive materials. Third, and perhaps most important, was the dangerous and overarching claim made by the music to heroic profundity and sublimity in its relation to nature—a claim that served both to mask the commonplace character of the music itself and the falsity and incompetence of its technical means, while at the same time placing itself at the service of the dominant authoritarian mythologies of its time, namely Fascism and Nazism. Adorno writes:

> His followers want to know nothing about this. Their song is stuck on the refrain: "It's all nature; it's all nature." The great Pan, and as required Blood and Soil too, appears promptly on the scene. The trivial is validated as the origin of things, the unarticulated as the sound of unconscious creation.[16]

And he continues:

> Categories of this kind evade critique. The dominant conviction is that nature's mood is bound up with awe-struck silence. But if the concept of "nature's mood" should not remain unquestioned even in the real world, then surely not in works of art. Symphonies are not a thousand lakes, even when riddled with a thousand holes.[17]

In Sibelius, Adorno saw the representation of nature as that which overwhelms and excludes critique and self-reflection. Clearly, he also had in mind the same points about such a use of the idea of nature made in Leo Löwenthal's article on Knut Hamsun published a year earlier, in 1937, in the *Zeitschrift für Sozialforschung*. Adorno had written what was in effect an extended footnote to that article, in which he said: "The obscurity, a product of technical awkwardness, feigns a profundity that does not exist."[18] In this he is referring especially to the similarity Löwenthal had identified between Hamsun's habit of creating characters in his novels who are types rather than individuals (the Peasant, the Vagabond, the Shepherd Girl) combined with his penchant for vague generalizations that evoke a sense of profundity, and what Adorno saw as Sibelius's use of generalized tonal materials: familiar and in themselves commonplace and reassuring but, being set in a vague and abstract context (that is, the peculiar structure of Sibelius's symphonies) evoking a similar air of the profound, the mysterious, and, indeed, "nature."

Adorno's claim that Sibelius seeks to represent "the sound of nature" through the use of materials and processes that are in themselves commonplace, trivial, and familiar, takes us back to the issues raised at the outset: I could reformulate these here as: (1) Can music represent nature? (2) If so, are the materials of music in some way inherently natural, so that they can "be" nature, and not simply mimic the processes of nature? And (3), are the transcendent meanings we ascribe to the experience of nature, for example mystery, profundity, freedom, and hope, a sense of being at the origin of all things, evoked by the very "naturalness" of such musical materials? In her *Elective Affinities* Lydia Goehr makes a number of points that are relevant here. Essentially, she characterizes Adorno's and Horkheimer's argument in *Dialectic of Enlightenment* as describing "a dialectic between nature and art, according to which nature came, in the civilized name of reason and art, to be dominated by humanity at the same time that it was reincorporated into an uncivilizing discourse of myth. Enlightenment . . . 'as [als] mass deception.'"[19] Adorno's and Horkheimer's account of the Enlightenment turning into its opposite is located in the 1930s and '40s, and pertains to the rise of Nazi Germany and of Fascism in Europe. Goehr's reading also places Adorno and Horkheimer in relation to another very different account of modernism—that of the American philosopher Arthur Danto. In the 1930s and 1940s, Goehr argues, the dominating motif characterizing the relation between art and nature was the heroic—something that survives in the ethic of the Darmstadt composers of the 1950s as heroic modernism. In the conceptualist and minimalist art of 1960s as interpreted by Danto, however, the dialectic between art and nature is nature "under the guise of the commonplace."[20] Danto's and Goehr's idea of the commonplace comes out of the 1960s, yet the concept is remarkably appropriate for considering Adorno's Sibelius critique, where the impression of the heroic is created, he claims, by banal means. As we have seen, Adorno argues that the commonplace dominates Sibelius's music, that it is employed to evoke "the sound of nature," presented as if it were nature itself, in a way that excludes and rejects the human. This equation of nature and the banal fits aptly with aspects of Löwenthal's critique of Hamsun, which Adorno introduces into the following passage from his "Fußnote zu Sibelius und Hamsun":

> The constructed opaque repetitions lay claim to an eternal rhythm of nature, which is also expressed by the lack of a symphonic consciousness of time; the nullity of the melodic monads, which is carried over into unarticulated pitches, corresponds to the contempt for humanity to which an all-embracing nature [*die Allnatur*] subjects the Hamsunian individual. In this respect Sibelius, like Hamsun, is to be distinguished from Impressionist tendencies, in that all-embracing Nature is formed from the dessicated remains of traditional bourgeois art, rather than seen as the primal vision of a protesting subjectivity.[21]

The Representation of Nature and the Evocation of the Sublime

Adorno recognizes that representing "nature" in music has much to do with what is *not* expressed, with what is *not* defined—in effect, what is *not actually presented*, as Jean-François Lyotard was to put it later.[22] Music is particularly good at this because of its lack of referentiality. At the same time, the "sound of nature" in art has to do with the silence of nature, even in the case of a "sounding art" like music. In the late *Aesthetic Theory* (1970) Adorno writes: "What in artworks is structured, gapless, resting in itself, is an after-image of the silence that is the single medium through which nature speaks."[23] As I have already suggested, Adorno is really referring not so much to the representation of *nature* in Sibelius as to the evocation of the *sublime*, even if his focus is almost exclusively on the concept of "nature." Indeed, it is difficult not to think of the identification of techniques designed to achieve the effects of the sublime in the different arts in Edmund Burke's 1757 compendium-like treatise, *A Philosophical Enquiry into the Origin of Our Ideas of the Sublime and Beautiful*. Burke refers, for instance, to the use of the color black, to darkness and obscurity, and above all to the need to create a sense of fear and terror through a use of indistinctness and vagueness. Obscurity, not clarity, is required if you want to create the effect of the sublime, insists Burke. Seen in such a context, Sibelius might appear to be a master of such effects in music. Yet strangely, though Adorno shows great awareness of the implications of the sublime in his *Aesthetic Theory*, particularly in relation to modernism, he does not emphasize the distinction between the representation of nature and the evocation of the sublime in the case of Sibelius in his two 1930s articles on the composer. Löwenthal, however, does just this in relation to Hamsun, and makes the point very clearly by contrasting Hamsun's evocation of the sublime in his description of a violent storm in his novel *The Last Joy* (1912) to Kant's famous description of the power of nature and the experience of the sublime in his *Critique of Judgment*.[24] Löwenthal writes, in comparing the words of Hamsun and Kant:

> At first sight there seems to be no essential difference between the two passages. For Kant, however, the sublimity of nature and the experience of man's helplessness before it are counterbalanced by the concept of nature as subordinate in the face of humanity. It is man's own knowledge and imagination which creates the conception of the grandiosity in nature that dwarfs him. In the end, the rational faculties of man are of a higher order than the elemental force of nature, and they allow him to see it as sublime, instead of simply terrifying. . . . For Kant, nature is not to console man for frustrations, but to stimulate his moral and intellectual development.[25]

Yet in Hamsun, Löwenthal argues, "the relation of man to nature takes on an entirely different cast." The differences he identifies, it seems to me, could be applied equally to Sibelius in Adorno's reading of his music, even though Adorno himself does not actually formulate these points with comparable clarity, and thus does not bring his argument to an equally convincing conclusion. Löwenthal, in referring to a passage from the novel *Pan* where the solitary narrator stands in the shelter of an overhanging rock, asking questions of the boiling and foaming sea, formulates the issue like this:

> The locus of knowledge has become nature itself, mysterious and beyond man's capacities to know. Hamsun's questions are framed so they cannot be answered; his tired individuals seek to silence themselves as quickly as possible. They really have nothing to say, and they welcome the storm that can roar loudly enough to drown out their own silence. The relationship of man to nature as seen by Kant is reversed; for Hamsun, the storm serves as an occasion for increasing the individual's awareness of his own insignificance.[26]

In Kantian terms, the experience of the "dynamic sublime" may be overwhelming and make us feel our insignificance, but we nevertheless retain a definite sense of self, a subject who is preserved and who does not disappear in the experience. The distinction is an important one, because it is the defining aspect of the human experience for both Löwenthal and Adorno.

Kant writes:

> Though the irresistibility of nature's might makes us, considered as natural beings, recognize our physical impotence, it reveals in us at the same time an ability to judge ourselves independent of nature, and reveals in us a superiority over nature that is the basis of a self-preservation quite different in kind from the one that can be assailed and endangered by nature outside us. This keeps the humanity in our person from being degraded, even though a human being would have to succumb to that dominance [of nature]. Hence if in judging nature aesthetically we call it sublime, we do so not because nature arouses fear, but because it calls forth our strength.[27]

According to Löwenthal, Hamsun's novels represent the retreat from modernity into the myth of nature. In Adorno's reading, Sibelius's music may be characterized in a similar way. The sacrifice of a historically hard-won autonomy to the mysterious and overwhelming aspects of nature is not "first nature," assert both Löwenthal and Adorno, but a "second nature" that is itself the projection of the helplessness of the individual capitulating to overwhelming and violent forces it does not understand. Adorno attempts, with only partial success, to discuss this in Sibelius in technical musical terms as the destruction of the hard-won technical control over the historically determined musical material. Sibelius's material, he claims, is arbitrary, lacks "historical necessity," and the clumsiness of his technique masquerades as nature. Adorno ends his essay: "But such destruction masks itself in his symphonies as creation. Its effect is dangerous."[28]

Problems with Adorno's Sibelius Critique

Adorno's evaluation of Sibelius's music has not worn as well as Löwenthal's evaluation of Hamsun. The criticisms of Sibelius are difficult to demonstrate and support musically in the convincing way that Löwenthal's critique of Hamsun has succeeded in literary terms. This has partly to do with the nature of music and any attempt to pin down its social or political content. But the accuracy of Löwenthal's critique of Hamsun's writing was borne out by history in a way that Adorno's of Sibelius was not. Löwenthal's 1937 analysis of Hamsun's novels concluded that his work showed motivic affinities with the symbolism of Nazi Germany. When the Nazi collaborator Vidkun Quisling came to power in Norway in 1941, Hamsun was quick to reveal himself as a Nazi sympathizer, much to the surprise and dismay of the many admirers of his novels.

Adorno made no such claims with Sibelius, although he warned that these are the implications, even in those areas of art-as-nature where we perhaps feel most justified in retreating from the stresses and responsibilities of modernity. In conclusion, I offer some observations on the problems I perceive in Adorno's attempt at musical ideology critique in these early essays on Sibelius (in some respects a sketch for what he was later to try again on a larger scale with the case of Stravinsky in *Philosophy of New Music*). I address four main issues.

First of all, I suggest that Adorno makes his task difficult from the outset by clouding his main aim, which is to indicate the ideological content (that is, *Gehalt*) of Sibelius's music by starting off with the emphasis on a musical-aesthetic critique of his work. He does this because on one level he insists that the aesthetic quality and technical consistency of a work is an indicator of its truth content (*Wahrheitsgehalt*), though he does not actually employ this concept in the Sibelius essays. Adorno had not greatly developed the idea of truth content at this stage, but it does nevertheless underlie his critique of Sibelius. Thus, because of what he claims are the music's aesthetic and technical flaws, it necessarily follows, from Adorno's point of view, that the composer's musical work is also ideological—either through the ease with which it will be appropriated by the culture industry, or by the forces of political reaction and domination, or indeed both.

Second, Adorno's attempts to support his claim that the music is aesthetically flawed because it is technically flawed are themselves seriously flawed. His examples are too general, too cursory, and lack convincing detail. Given a sympathetic reader who knows both Adorno and Sibelius's music, it is possible to deduce what he means and to fill in the gaps in his critique, and even to provide musical examples in support. However, this asks too much of any reader/listener, and suggests a do-it-yourself approach that would not find a sympathetic reception from most philosophers or from most musicologists or music analysts today.

Third, Adorno's claims, with or without evidence, are impossible to verify or validate in philosophical terms given the relativity of aesthetic values that became the norm in the second half of the twentieth century. Adorno came to witness this by the 1960s, when he acknowledged that the Schoenbergian notion of the historical dialectic of music driven by "historical necessity" had disintegrated. In such a context the fact that Sibelius wrote tonal music can simply be seen as part of the prehistory of such disintegration. After all, Schoenberg himself wrote tonal and tonally inflected works in his late period in the United States during the 1940s, which undermines the case Adorno made for a "dialectic" characterized by a process of the ever increasing rationalization of "musical material." The exclusiveness of Adorno's scheme has always depended for its justification on an accompanying aesthetics of modernism. Adorno allowed some well-known exceptions such as Bartók and Janáček (given special dispensation in a famous footnote in the 1949 *Philosophy of New Music*).[29] Less well known are the allowances made for Berg and Satie. Little allowance, however, was made for either Stravinsky or Sibelius.

Finally, it has to be recognized that Adorno's dialectical approach, whatever its shortcomings in any particular instance, always locates its claims in specific historical situations and conditions.[30] And so it is, I suggest, with his Sibelius critique. Debates on art and nature and their social and political implications took on a particular urgency in the period between the two world wars, when claims for the legitimacy of political systems became closely linked with claims for their rootedness in nature as some kind of "natural order" of things, and in associated ideas of folk, tradition, community, and their locatedness in ties of blood and soil, as well as in the naturalness of human beings if uncorrupted by "unnatural" or alien ideas such as those associated with modernism. Though the origins of this particular turn can be traced back to the beginnings of German nationalism in the early years of the nineteenth century, and especially in Herder, its ramifications in music were especially tied up with a combination of specific technical issues and of what constituted "natural musical material." To philosophers and critics with particular ways of listening and hearing music regarded in some way as "natural," aesthetic modernism posed a clear threat.

The striking point about the use made of the idea of "nature" in the period between the 1920s and the 1940s is that it is characterized culturally by a flight into nature as an escape from modern society. Given the long-standing tendency since the nineteenth century for art to act in a similar way as a point of escape from the difficulties of modern life, and as a retreat to *Innerlichkeit*, it is not difficult to see distinct affinities between nature and art in this respect. True, art, as artifact, is clearly not "natural." At issue here is precisely the appearance of nature, or *Schein*, and not nature itself. I suggest, furthermore, that music in particular has best exploited this affinity in representing the appearance of nature, even down to the detail of presenting us with the appearance of organic unfolding, and the imitation, as John Cage put it, of nature "in her manner of operation."[31] The height of Sibelius's popularity in the late 1930s coincided with the political obsession with nature that Adorno was quick to identify. The reception of Sibelius, whatever else it might have been, was undoubtedly part of this relapse into the myth of nature that accompanied the rise of authoritarianism in the first half of the twentieth century. I think it is to Adorno's credit, notwithstanding his failure to grasp other features of the composer's music, that he sought to identify why this was the case.[32]

NOTES

1. Leo Löwenthal, "Knut Hamsun" (1937), repr. in *The Essential Frankfurt School Reader*, ed. Andrew Arato and Eike Gebhardt (New York: Urizen Books, 1978), 320.

2. Tomi Mäkelä, "Sibelius and Germany: *Wahrhaftigkeit* Beyond *Allnatur*," in *The Cambridge Companion to Sibelius*, ed. Daniel M. Grimley (Cambridge: Cambridge University Press, 2004), 173.

3. Ernest Newman, Foreword, in Karl Ekman, *Jean Sibelius: His Life and Personality*, trans. Edward Birse (New York: Alfred A. Knopf, 1938), xx.

4. There is also a fourth question, which concerns what are claimed to be the natural physiological limitations of our organs of perception, as for instance our hearing apparatus. That is to say, if we are prepared to argue, as Roger Scruton has done, that some systems of music (e.g., tonality) and some ways of listening to music (i.e., dictated by the natural physiological limits of our ears and the way in which our brains process what we hear) are more natural, and therefore more "correct" than others. The latter condition is the state of what Roger Scruton calls "the natural bourgeois man," which, for some reason, he refuses to acknowledge as in any way historical, regarding it as the natural and absolute measure of how we hear music. Amusing and important as this might be, it will not be my focus here, though I have addressed it elsewhere in "Die vermittelte Unmittelbarkeit der Musik: Zum Vermittlungsbegriff in der Adornoschen Musikästhetik," in *Musikalischer Sinn: Beiträge zu einer Philosophie der Musik*, ed. Alexander Becker and Matthias Vogel (Frankfurt am Main: Suhrkamp, 2007), 175–236, at 177–78.

5. The originality of Sibelius's innovations in the timbral and textural use of the orchestra has been explored by Ron Weidberg, especially in his article "Sonic Design in Jean Sibelius's Orchestral Music," in *Sibelius Forum II: Proceedings from the Third International Jean Sibelius Conference, Helsinki, 25–29 November, 1995*, ed. Matti Huttunen, Kari Kilpeläinen, and Veijo Murtomäki (Helsinki: Sibelius Academy, 2003), 216–26.

6. I have addressed some of these issues in philosophical terms in my chapter "Nature and the Sublime: The Politics of Order and Disorder in Twentieth–Century Music," in Jonathan Dunsby, Joseph N. Straus, Yves Knockaert, Max Paddison, and Konrad Boehmer, *Order and Disorder: Music-Theoretical Strategies in Twentieth-Century Music* (Leuven: University of Leuven Press, 2004), 107–35.

7. Walter Benjamin actually wrote: "The word 'history' stands written on the countenance of nature in the characters of transience." Benjamin, *The Origin of German Tragic Drama*, trans. John Osborne (London: NLB, 1977), 177.

8. See Tomi Mäkelä, "Sibelius and Germany: *Wahrhaftigkeit* Beyond *Allnatur*," in Grimley, *The Cambridge Companion to Sibelius*, 169–81, and especially Mäkelä's book "*Poesie in der Luft": Jean Sibelius, Leben und Werk* (Wiesbaden: Breitkopf & Härtel, 2007).

9. Mäkelä records that Hamsun and Sibelius met in Helsinki in 1897–98. See Mäkelä, "*Poesie in der Luft*," 132.

10. Erik Tawaststjerna, "Über Adornos Sibelius-Kritik," in *Adorno und die Musik*, ed. Otto Kolleritsch (Graz: Universal Edition, 1979), 112–13. See also Tomi Mäkelä, "*Poesie in der Luft*," 360.

11. Theodor W. Adorno, "Glosse über Sibelius" (1938), in *Impromptus. Gesammelte Schriften*, vol. 17, ed. Rolf Tiedemann (Frankfurt am Main: Suhrkamp Verlag, 1982), 248. Translations in the essay are the author's own.

12. Ibid., 248.

13. This was the claim put forward by a number of British music critics and musicologists in the 1930s, including Cecil Gray, Gerald Abrahams, and Neville Cardus.

14. Theodor W. Adorno, "Fußnote zu Sibelius und Hamsun" (1937), in *Vermischte Schriften II. Gesammelte Schriften*, vol. 20.2, ed. Rolf Tiedemann (Frankfurt am Main: Suhrkamp, 1986), 804.

15. Adorno, "Glosse über Sibelius," 249.

16. Ibid.

17. Ibid.

18. Adorno, "Fußnote zu Sibelius und Hamsun,", 804; this note also appears in translation in the Documents section of this volume.

19. Lydia Goehr, *Elective Affinities: Musical Essays on the History of Aesthetic Theory* (Columbia: Columbia University Press, 2008), 81.

20. Ibid., 82.

21. Theodor W. Adorno, "Fußnote zu Sibelius und Hamsun," 804; this note also appears in translation in the Documents section of this volume.

22. See Jean-François Lyotard, *The Inhuman: Reflections on Time*, trans. Geoffrey Bennington and Rachel Bowlby (Cambridge: Polity Press, 1991).

23. Theodor W. Adorno, *Aesthetic Theory*, ed. Rolf Tiedemann, trans. Robert Hullot-Kentor (London: Athlone Press, 1997), 74. See *Ästhetische Theorie*. Gesammelte Schriften, vol. 7, ed. Rolf Tiedemann and Gretel Adorno (Frankfurt am Main: Suhrkamp, 1970), 115.

24. See Immanuel Kant, *Kritik der Urteilskraft* (1790), *Werke in Zwölf Bänden*, vols. 9 and 10, ed. Wilhelm Weischedel (Frankfurt am Main: Suhrkamp, 1957), sec. 28. In English as *Critique of Judgment*, trans. Werner S. Pluhar (Indianapolis: Hackett Publishing, 1987), sec. 28, esp. 120.

25. Löwenthal, "Knut Hamsun," 327–28.

26. Ibid., 328.

27. Kant, *Critique of Judgment*, sec. 28, 120–21.

28. Adorno, "Glosse über Sibelius," 252.

29. See Adorno, *Philosophie der Neuen Musik*. Gesammelte Schriften, vol.12, ed. Rolf Tiedemann (Frankfurt am Main: Suhrkamp, 1975), 41–42n3. In English as *Philosophy of New Music*, trans. Robert Hullot-Kentor (Minneapolis: University of Minnesota Press, 2006), 176n4.

30. I expand on this point in "Die vermittelte Unmittelbarkeit der Musik," 175–86.

31. John Cage, *Silence* (London: Marion Boyars, 1968), 173.

32. It needs to be emphasized that it was Adorno's intention to demonstrate how historical, social, and ideological tendencies manifested themselves in purely musical terms, whether or not the composers or their audiences were conscious of their significance. He was not interested in the political beliefs or affiliations of artists themselves, and whether, for example, Sibelius as an individual harbored any Nazi sympathies. In view of this, Adorno's claims should not be read as *ad hominem* arguments. Adorno, like Löwenthal in his critique of Hamsun's novels, focused on an ideology critique of art works "in themselves," not on the political views of the artists who had created them. This distinction is important.

Storms, Symphonies, Silence:
Sibelius's *Tempest* Music and the
Invention of Late Style

DANIEL M. GRIMLEY

The last thirty years of Sibelius's life have cast a long shadow over writing on the composer and our understanding of his music.[1] The creative silence that effectively followed the completion of his final tone poem, *Tapiola*, in 1926, remains a deeply ambivalent episode in Sibelius's career and his critical reception. For some contemporary English writers in the 1930s and '40s, most notoriously Cecil Gray and Constant Lambert, waiting (in vain) for the appearance of the long-promised Eighth Symphony, Sibelius's late works presented an elliptical spiritual language at its optimum point of refinement and expression, a *ne plus ultra* that permitted no form of imitation or further development.[2] For more recent critics, the silence has become a tragic gesture, an ultimate teleology: the irrevocable shading into nothingness of an earlier once virile phase of musical modernism.[3] This pattern of shadow and decline remains a problem of Sibelius biography. As Veijo Murtomäki, for example, has pithily expressed it, "Sibelius's late period contains an enigma."[4] For Glenda Dawn Goss, in the preface to her recent cultural history of the composer's life and work, the silence of the final years is presented in the form of a detective story: the "murderer" is unveiled in the final chapters not so much as Sibelius's own addictive personality (his fabled alcoholism and chronic self-criticism), but rather as the complex trace of a fading subjectivity and artistic milieu, one that had become increasingly strained and unsustainable in the face of a rapidly shifting political environment.[5] As Goss argues, Sibelius threatened to become an anachronism or monument in his own lifetime. But this image, Goss emphasizes, is problematic, not least given the prevalence of Sibelius's influence on more recent music in Finland and abroad. His legacy, in that sense, is acutely doubled-edged. And the idea of the monumentalized composer invokes a more complex narrative of musical creativity, meaning, and authorial intention. The extent to which, even in his apparent silence, Sibelius acted as an agent in his own reception remains provocative. Sibelius's silence serves both as a leave-taking and as a summation. But it also suggests a creative twist, one in which the idea of a "late style" emerges strongly as a performative category: a particular role or character that Sibelius played out reflexively in his work. "Late style" here is not concerned with a purely chronological sense of time, but rather, following Theodor W. Adorno, Edward Said, and others,[6] with an attitude or tone of voice: a mode of musical utterance that both engages with a rich critical legacy and also unfolds new creative space.

Greater insight into the nature of this late style, and into the possible meanings of Sibelius's "silence," can be gained from attending more closely to his music from the late 1920s, especially after the premiere of the Seventh Symphony in Stockholm on 24 March 1924. A key work here is Sibelius's music for a Danish production of Shakespeare's *The Tempest*, directed by Johannes Poulsen and premiered at the Royal Theatre in Copenhagen on 16 March 1926. Sibelius's *Tempest* music is one of his most evocative and enigmatic late scores. The music's stylistic diversity and range of expression, in contrast with the celebrated unity and concision of works such as the Seventh Symphony, has often puzzled and divided critics. Goss, for example, laments, "*The Tempest* is no symphony. Nor is it a tone poem. Despite flashes of brilliance, it is not a work of sustained inspiration."[7] The piece remains a rarity in live performance, despite the relative success of the concert suites that Sibelius drew from his own music. Yet the complete score, in terms of page length and performing duration alone, was by far Sibelius's most substantial work after 1900, and it demands critical reevaluation. Furthermore, many of the play's themes—artistic isolation, enchantment, nature mysticism, and Prospero's paternal bond with his daughter, Miranda—strongly appealed to aspects of Sibelius's creative imagination. As Erik Tawaststjerna suggests, "For Sibelius, Prospero became a symbol of the creative man and therefore of his own self, just as Ariel symbolized his inspiration and Caliban his demonic side."[8] The ambiguity of Shakespeare's text, especially the equivocal sense of closure in its final pages, seems closely attuned to the tone of much of Sibelius's later work, and to the idea of late style in particular. This essay will explore some of these themes in greater depth, examining the play's relationship with other late works including the Sixth and Seventh symphonies. Drawing on archival work in Denmark and Finland, this essay will shed new light on the genesis and realization of Sibelius's score, and suggest that, far from being a creative diversion or cul-de-sac, his music for *The Tempest* became one of Sibelius's most eloquent achievements, a summing up that offers unique insight into the problem of Sibelius's silence.

As Tawaststjerna notes, the idea of *The Tempest* as a musical subject was first suggested to Sibelius by his close friend and confidante Axel Carpelan. In a letter dated 28 February 1901, listing possible future projects for the composer, Carpelan wrote: "*The Tempest* would suit you ideally. Prospero (the sorcerer), Miranda, the spirits of earth and air, etc."[9] Though Sibelius had set two songs from *Twelfth Night* in 1909, it would be over two decades before he turned to *The Tempest* as a serious creative proposition. By then Carpelan had been dead for six years (he died on 24 March 1919). Yet Sibelius's enthusiasm for Shakespeare in the meantime is further suggested by a piece of evidence preserved in a box marked "Paris 1911, England 1912" held in the Sibelius Collection at the Finnish National Archive in Helsinki. The box contains a souvenir leaflet for Holy Trinity Church, Stratford-upon-Avon, including a guide to the stained-glass windows and the epitaphs of the Shakespeare Family memorial in the chancel.[10] Sibelius's tour of Shakespeare country was arranged by Rosa Newmarch in connection with his visit to conduct the British premiere of the Fourth Symphony at Birmingham. In a diary entry dated 18 September 1912, Sibelius noted: "Journey to England. London.—Stratford on Avon, Shakespeare's birthplace."[11] The timing of Sibelius's visit was significant, as his diary entries vividly reveal: he had begun to experience profound feelings of loneliness and isolation in connection with his composition of the symphony. This sense of alienation, as James Hepokoski and others have argued, was motivated partly by his creative struggles with the symphony, but more deeply by an awareness of a significant shift in the wider European musical climate circa 1910–11.[12] As early as 10 January 1910, two years prior to his England visit, Sibelius had noted: "My life's solitude begins. The trick is to keep working in spite of this 'Alleingefühl' [sense of isolation]."[13] Yet by 10 July, his mood had shifted significantly, and he wrote pessimistically in his diary: "Awoke with unpleasant worries about the actions of the warmhearted. Fear that one turns to people who are not worth it. Do you really have to endure this? Is it better to sit by the side of the Esplanade in Helsinki and hail the passing capitalists? You know yourself that it was hell. Your time went and your fantasy departed. Something for something. You have given music, so—?!"[14] Even when Sibelius could report more positive progress on the symphony, such moments of inspiration were increasingly bound up with a sense of banishment and withdrawal, eliding art and life in a manner that would become paradigmatic in much of his later work. On 5 November 1910 he noted: "Worked splendidly. Forged the finale in the Symphony. Wonderful day—typically Finnish—with 'snow upon the trees' branches.'. . . Must break with Helsinki. Never any peace. A symphony is not a composition in the ordinary sense. It is really a confession from different stages of life."[15]

Completion of the symphony, following its Finnish premiere preceding the England trip and colored by its mixed critical reception at home, brought little sense of relief. Writing on 19 April 1912 that "I've set my mind on a new symphonic mission!" Sibelius lamented, "How little, interminably little understanding and patronage my symphonies have received out in the wider world! It often strikes me now how this whole symphonic struggle is futile. But this work and this struggle have greater educational meaning for me. At present I find myself small and insignificant. A little, insignificant talent! Dear God! Now take bread unto the desert!—Today splendid, summer-like! In the evening—stars, stars!"[16]

Read retrospectively from the perspective of the *Tempest* music and the silence that followed in the later 1920s, it is easy to anticipate in such early diary entries Sibelius's propensity toward a Prospero-like exile, the merging of self and dramatic character that Tawaststjerna later identifies as one of the key components of his interest in Shakespeare's play. Even if this is not wholly unproblematic, taking into account the musically rich decade between the composition of the Fourth Symphony and the late works, a recurrent crisis of confidence, comparable to that experienced in 1910–12 but significantly intensified, certainly appears to have afflicted Sibelius in the years 1923–25, prior to his work on *The Tempest* and during composition of Symphonies 6 and 7. On 3 October 1923, for example, he wrote in his diary: "My life is now finished. If I'm sometimes happy and have a glass to drink, I pay for it a long time afterward. This terrible depression that not even Aino can understand, but which I've inherited. This 'sensitivity' or lack of self-confidence, which means that Aino and the children have never had proper support in their life. This hell upon the earth, which they encounter outside, never to escape. Woe am I, alone, alone!"[17] Again, Sibelius's diary entries suggest that such intense moments of self-doubt and loneliness could become an intrinsic part of his creative process. For example, on 17 February 1925 he confided: "It is blowing a gale outside. How infinitely richer is this [illegible word] unreflected gust than the poetry of Goethe or other gentlemen! I have begun to 'snap,' namely to drink in secret. This is one way to take a life. But—a few drinks, at midnight—have a wonderful effect! Those who survive shall see! But the poetry in all of this! Dear Lord! Reflection is intoxicating!"[18]

Sibelius's thoughts in the mid-1920s had increasingly turned toward questions of his own mortality. The death of his brother Christian in 1922, the fate of his sister Linda, who suffered from mental health problems throughout her life, and the early death of his father weighed heavily upon Sibelius's mind, especially following a painful operation on a throat tumor (related to his heavy smoking) in 1923. In 1923–25, Sibelius had no reason to foresee his own remarkable longevity. Yet, as Tomi Mäkelä

suggests, such preoccupation with death points back to an earlier symbolist existentialism, cultivated by Sibelius's association with the Symposium
circle in the 1890s. The following day, 18 February 1925, Sibelius explicitly
evoked in his diary his symbolist roots, and the mood of works such as
Valse triste and "The Swan of Tuonela" from the four *Lemminkäinen* Legends,
op. 22, with their brooding sense of the liminal boundary between life and
death: "The lemon table at the Kämp restaurant! The lemon, the symbol
of death—for the Chinese. And even here once. 'Buried with a lemon in
the hand,' sang Anna Marie L[enngren]. One would be hard-pressed to
find a more fitting epithet. . . . The whole of winter in summer's raiment.
A nature poetry that drives one mad! If only I will not succumb. I cannot
live this miraculously rich life. Must stimulate myself. Afterward remorse
[ångern]! Anguish [Ångesten]! I wonder if something lies beneath that
alliteration?"[19]

Sibelius's whimsical musings on death, isolation, and the natural world
had once more become bound up with an acute sense of his own creativity. But such thoughts had also been motivated by a sense of his own
mortality. In other words, they had become intrinsically linked artistically
with the notion of a "late style": not merely a chronological category, but
rather a whole aesthetic outlook. And here surely lies the attraction of *The
Tempest* as a source text. Such "lateness," as Gordon McMullen has argued
in his study of Shakespeare's later plays, is paradigmatically "a time of renewal which is also a recapitulation of earlier styles and subject matter,
expressed with a childlike simplicity and a certain looseness of painterly
technique indicative of a mythopoetic tendency, a whittling down to basics,
a return not only to the artist's youth but also to the youth of art which is
at the same time a looking forward to the future after the artist's death
and a kind of self-portraiture which is also a process of citation."[20]: a
process, I shall argue below, which is also characteristic of Sibelius's work
from the 1920s. As McMullen suggests, such late writing becomes a
"borderline activity, a creative response to death, a kind of eschatology."[21]
Therefore when Sibelius's Danish publisher Wilhelm Hansen approached
him on 1 May 1925 with the offer "Have you have written music to
Shakespeare's *The Tempest*?—The Royal Theatre intends to perform this
work, and would like to use your music,"[22] Sibelius may already have had
many of the play's themes and preoccupations at the forefront of his mind,
even though he had not yet written a single note of the score.

As Tawaststjerna suggests, "Hansen's letter came at the right psychological moment" for the composer. Drawing on his account of the creative
crises in the preceding years from Sibelius's diary entries, Tawaststjerna
explains how

for more than ten years almost without a break Sibelius had wrestled with the symphonic problem. He had refined his material and concentrated its form to an extreme degree in the attempt to attain the ideal of absolute music as he conceived it. Now an opportunity presented itself for him to give free rein to his thematic invention and depict the play's characters in kaleidoscopically shifting colors, the play of the naiads and spirits of the air, natural catastrophes and a mythological harvest festival.[23]

The *Tempest* music thus served as a creative release, and simultaneously acted as a focal point for gathering together and summarizing many of the ideas and processes Sibelius had so strenuously sought to develop in his symphonies from the Fourth onward. In this sense, theater music may indeed have offered a less immediately threatening or confrontational genre for Sibelius's work, one that was less explicitly bound up with a particularly weighty legacy and burden of aesthetic expectations than the early twentieth-century symphony. But writing music for one of Shakespeare's plays inevitably brought its own particular anxieties of interpretation and tradition. And, despite his initial attraction to the project, Sibelius's working relationship with the Royal Theatre's production in Copenhagen did not proceed entirely smoothly. The Royal Theatre followed Hansen's letter with a telegram dated 27 March 1925, inquiring whether Sibelius had previously written music for the play, and advising that the Royal Theatre's director, Johannes Poulsen, would travel to Helsinki to discuss the project with Sibelius in person.[24] Sibelius replied by return to accept and outline his financial terms for the music (3,000 Swedish kronor, plus 5 percent of the ticket receipts and future rights over the music).[25] The majority of the music was composed over a remarkably short period of time between the end of May and the beginning of September. As Tawaststjerna observes, Sibelius's manuscript score (now held in the Sibelius Archive in Helsinki University Library) was notated in a strikingly neat and confident hand, belying the nervous insecurity that marks the sketches for many of his later symphonic works.[26] The Royal Theatre's managing director, Wilhelm Norrie, acknowledged receipt of some of the *Tempest* material (presumably the songs and chorus music) in a letter dated 22 August, adding. "I expect, as we discussed, delivery of your score by 1 September, when rehearsals of *The Tempest* will be already under way and the premiere will preferably take place by 1 September [*sic*: Norrie presumably meant to write October] at the latest."[27] Sibelius finally delivered the manuscript by the middle of October, and in a letter acknowledging receipt, Norrie wrote that "music director [Georg] Høeberg asks me to send his greetings and expresses his pleasure with your splendid music, and I can add that artistic director Johannes Poulsen and the artists who will interpret your tones are greatly excited."[28] In the event, however, the premiere did not take place until 16 March the following year, and Sibelius's increasing frustration with the theater and associated delays with the production can be followed in an extended correspondence with Gunnar Hauch, music critic of the Danish newspaper *Nationaltidende* and a fervent supporter of Sibelius's music.

Hauch first mentioned the project in a letter to Sibelius dated 28 May 1925, the day after the Royal Theatre had telegraphed to canvas Sibelius's interest in the play.[29] And over the following months Hauch served partly as a distant confidant during Sibelius's work on the score and partly as a discreet intermediary between Sibelius and the Royal Theatre. Sibelius responded to Hauch's inquiry on 2 June 1925, writing: "Music to *The Tempest* interests me immensely. Waiting for Mr. Poulsen, who has not yet been in touch. With the Royal Theatre, things are never clear." As the delay began to accumulate, Sibelius wrote to Hauch on 2 October: "I now come to a highly discreet matter. It concerns music to *The Tempest*. I sent the first act two months ago. Now I have completed 34 numbers apart from 3, which I will send very shortly. This is dependent upon how my take on the material strikes the authorities. I have not heard a word, not even a reply to anything. Would you kindly 'sound out the territory' and see whether my music will be performed or not?"[30] Hauch replied on 8 October to explain, with a fine sense of journalistic diplomacy, the reasons for the postponement:

> Thank you for your letter about the situation regarding *The Tempest* and your music at the Royal Theatre. . . . I heard some time ago that Johannes Poulsen was very excited by the music that the Professor had sent, and in a conversation with Director Norrie on Tuesday he emphasized this strongly. I can truly say that we are exceptionally pleased, and grateful for the work that the Professor has accomplished, and that the theatre expects the premiere, which will take place between Christmas and New Year according to the latest decisions, to be a unique occasion. That it won't take place earlier is because in a month's time the theatre must perform Debussy's *Pelléas et Mélisande* and Stravinsky's *Petrouchka*. I find it amazing that the Professor has been able to create such a large work in a short space of time—and it will please me more than anything to get to know this work. Is it indiscreet to ask a little about the work's character? Whether there is an overture, the instrumentation, etc?[31]

Sibelius wrote again a month later, on 2 November, to say that he would attend the Copenhagen premiere incognito—if Hauch could confirm a date for the performance.[32] On 7 January 1926, as the New Year ticked past without further news, Sibelius wrote once more to Hauch, revealing his own anxieties with the project and offering a rare insight into his feelings about the text: "Now I must acknowledge that—despite all my attempts—I cannot recollect anything about Shakespeare. The following day whatever I wrote the previous day strikes me as weak and foolish. Thank God I am not a journalist. You must forgive me. *Timon of Athens* is dearest to me because of its humanity; *The Tempest* because of its musicality. Regarding *The Tempest*, when will it be performed? Will you kindly look into it down there and write to me about it?"[33] With the theatre clearly overstretched, Hauch was forced to admit on 2 February that "an unlucky fate has hovered over the preparation of this work,"[34] recounting the various accidents and misfortunes that had befallen the company in the meantime. In the event, Sibelius did not attend the premiere, even in disguise, and Hauch reported to the composer on 18 March:

> The performance at the Royal Theatre will be without doubt a great success. There were many extremely fine moments in the technical use of the stage, and the execution was supported by a particularly great effort. But it cannot be denied that the actors' powers at various points were not quite up to Shakespeare's heights. As a whole it seemed that the lyrical scenes worked least well because of the production's fragility. But the comic scenes came out well enough. And that the true tone of the play's poetry and fantasy was heard so often is due to the music.
>
> How wonderful, time after time, to observe how these tones opened up the word's true soul. The music was conducted by the young music director Johan Nye Knudsen, who is a much more talented music director than Høeberg.[35]

Despite Hauch's best efforts, it was hard to conceal the obvious shortcomings with the performance. Sibelius confided to his wife, Aino, at the end of the month that "I have forgotten the whole story with *The Tempest*. The blunder was that I threw in my lot with Poulsen. He can be fine, but certainly the stage production—as you wrote—is poor."[36] Sibelius subsequently attempted to salvage his music through two concert suites, and when the production was revived at the Finnish National Theatre in Helsinki the following year, his daughter, Ruth Snellman, played the central role of Ariel. Yet Sibelius's dissatisfaction with the Danish production may not entirely have been the result of the organizational tensions described in his correspondence with Hauch. Rather, his unease could equally have arisen from profound differences over the interpretation of

Shakespeare's play. As Tawaststjerna notes, "In none of the theater pieces he had written music for hitherto had he been able to live through one of the principal characters as intensively as he now identified himself with Prospero in Shakespeare's *The Tempest*."[37] But *The Tempest* offers a uniquely complex and ambivalent text. As David Lindley and others have stressed, *The Tempest* is marked by some of Shakespeare's most innovative and experimental theatrical effects, not least its use of masque in the fourth act. From its first recorded public performance on "Hallomas nyght," 1 November 1611, at the indoor Blackfriars Theatre in London, *The Tempest* must have presented an alluring dramatic spectacle. As Lindley observes, "In its dramatic shaping, and in its deployment of music and spectacle in particular, *The Tempest* breaks new Shakespearean ground"—a possible reason why it was printed at the head of the first folio of Shakespeare's plays in 1623.[38] Yet photographs and designs of Poulsen's Danish production of Edvard Lembcke's nineteenth-century translation at the Royal Theatre suggests a somewhat more conservative vision of the play: the pervading mood is of a stylized gothic fantasy or fairy tale, with expressionistically twisted rocks and trees to represent the enchanted island. Miranda is rendered as a chaste, pale pre-Raphaelite figure—similar in character to Maeterlinck's Mélisande (which was, of course, in repertory at the Royal Theatre in the 1925–26 season), and reinforcing her role as an essentially submissive agent under Prospero's dominion. More striking contemporary echoes of Debussy and Stravinsky can be found in Kai Nielsen's costume designs for the play (see Figures 1 and 2), including a Nijinskian faun's attire for Ariel with tabor and pipe (to accompany the catch "Flout 'em and scout 'em," Act 3, scene 2:120ff) and a Rusalka-style sketch for a winged naiad. Kai Nielsen's haunting sketch for a masked Caliban, seemingly neither fish nor beast, but closer to Shakespeare's "freckled whelp, hag-born, not honoured with / A human shape" (Prospero's description in Act 1, scene 2:283–84) assumed a more conventional bearded form in the production, heightening the comic effect of his dialogues with Stephano and Trinculo in Act 2, scene 2, but robbing Caliban of his threatening force elsewhere. The final tableau (Act 5, scene 1) presents a strange juxtaposition between the fairy-tale quality of Poulsen's staging and the more colorfully primitivist style of Kai Nielsen's masked spirits, suggesting the influence of Paul Gauguin (who had briefly been resident in Copenhagen in 1884–85 with his Danish wife) or Japanese ritual theater. Throughout Poulsen's version of the play, Prospero remains a seemingly statuesque presence, whose reserved formality suggests an emotional detachment from the proceedings. From photographs of the Copenhagen production, it is difficult to discern any of the tensions or ambiguities that motivate Shakespeare's character beyond a sense of stern authority alone. It was here, perhaps, that Sibelius

Figure 1. Kai Nielsen's sketch of costume design for Ariel, Sibelius's *Tempest*.

Figure 2. Sketch of costume design for winged naiad.

might have felt at greatest odds with Poulsen's interpretation. With his strong symbolist leanings, and his urgent desire to understand art and life as troubled and darkly merged, Sibelius is unlikely to have been sympathetic to Poulsen's more one-dimensional reading of Shakespeare's principal character.

Sibelius's reading of the text, and his idea of Prospero in particular, may rather have been informed by an existing Scandinavian academic tradition of Shakespeare scholarship, especially through the work of Danish literary critic Georg Brandes, whose three-volume study of Shakespeare was published in Copenhagen in 1895–96 and widely read across the Nordic region.[39] The basis for Brandes's interpretation, as Niels B. Hansen has observed, lay partly in his studies of European literature, particularly Hippolyte Taine's *Histoire de la littérature anglaise* (1863), and the German translations of Schiller and A. W. Schlegel.[40] But the most important source of information for Brandes was Edward Dowden's seminal *Shakespeare: A Critical Study of His Life and Art* (1875), which exerted a strong influence over all late-Victorian readings of Shakespeare up to and including writers such as George Bernard Shaw and A. C. Bradley. Like Sibelius after him, Brandes visited London and Stratford-on-Avon, making the same journey to Holy Trinity Church to view the Shakespeare memorials. But, as Hansen suggests, it was his close reading of Shakespeare's play texts that distinguished Brandes's study: "The Shakespeare [Brandes] looked for and found in the texts was a personality who in many respects reflected Brandes's concept of himself. In constructing the psychobiography of the Renaissance genius, he was in a sense working in an autobiographical vein, or at least engaged in a process of identification—a poetic rather than a scientific project."[41] Shakespeare, through this process of self-reflection, became a model for the modern man: a central category in Brandes's literary criticism. And the defining characteristic of modernity, as Brandes understood it and defined it elsewhere, lay precisely in its sense of belatedness: the cultivation of a late style that was somehow out of step with its time and sought to break the boundaries or barriers of its own epoch, yet was simultaneously marked by a melancholic sense of loneliness or self-exile. Hence the opening of Brandes's third volume, starting discussion of the late plays with *Hamlet*, begins a section pointedly titled "Discord and Scorn" by echoing the lines of the play itself, eliding Shakespeare (as both autobiographical subject and author) with Brandes's own worldview: "Out of tune! Out of tune! Out of tune the instrument whereon so many enthralling melodies had been played—glad and gay, plaintive or resentful, full of love and full of sorrow. Out of tune the mind which had felt so keenly, thought so deeply, spoken so temperately, and stood so firmly 'in the very torrent tempest, and as I may say, whirlwind of your passion.'"[42] For Brandes, *Hamlet* was marked both by a creative rage and also a turning-away from the world: a new ludic sensibility in Shakespeare's work that signaled a significant change of emphasis in his writing. *The Tempest* occupies an even more privileged position in Brandes's discussion, as in other nineteenth-century surveys, principally on account of its assumed historical status as Shakespeare's last single-authored work. For Brandes, however, *The Tempest* served as both a carefully calibrated summation and a farewell. "Never, with the exception of *Hamlet* and *Timon*," Brandes argued, "had Shakespeare been so personal." Brandes read the work partly through a Darwinian-Nietzschean lens, claiming, "In Caliban we have the primitive man, the aboriginal, the animal which has just evolved into the first rough stages of the human being. In Prospero we are given the highest development of Nature, the man of the future, the superhuman man of spirit."[43] Prospero thus becomes a Zarathustra-like figure, both a prophet at the dawn of a new age (or "brave new world," whose imminence Miranda famously announces in Act 5, scene 1:183) and also a lone wanderer: roles that Sibelius himself would also happily embrace at various points in his diary entries. In a critical turn characteristic of Shakespeare's other later plays, notably *Cymbeline* and *The Winter's Tale*, Brandes argued that "tired by suffering, Prospero proves its strengthening qualities. Far from succumbing to their blow, it is not until it has fallen that he displays his true, far-reaching, and terrible power, and becomes the great irresistible magician which Shakespeare himself had long been."[44]

For Brandes, and other late nineteenth- and early twentieth-century critics, Prospero merges with the biographical figure of Shakespeare himself, and with the condition of modernity. "It is Shakespeare's own nature which overflows into Prospero," he maintains, "and thus the magician represents not merely the noble-minded great man, but the genius, imaginatively delineated, not, as in *Hamlet*, psychologically analyzed." Both Prospero and Shakespeare dissolve into mere manifestations of the will, a creative force whose ebb and flow can be felt through the shifting tensions of the drama almost like a tidal current. "Audibly and visibly does Prospero's genius manifest itself, visible and audible also the inward and outward opposition he combats."[45] This sense of a tidal stream also runs powerfully through the play's seasonal setting. "The scenery is autumnal throughout, and the time is that of the autumn equinox with its storms and shipwrecks," Brandes observes. "With noticeable care all the plants named, even those occurring merely in similes, are such flowers and fruit, &c., as appear in the fall of the year in a northern landscape. The climate is harsh and northerly in spite of the southern situation of the island and the southern names. Even the utterances of the goddesses, the blessing of Ceres, for example, show that the season is late September—thus answering to Shakespeare's time of life and frame of mind."[46] For Brandes the play thus becomes a last act, audibly and visually delineated, the spirit of Prospero's "Ye elves of hills, brooks, standing lakes and groves" speech (Act 5, scene 1:35–57), read as Shakespeare's own departure from the stage, comparable in tone to the mood of the Night watchman's song, "O Mensch, gib acht!" (Oh mankind, take heed!) in Nietzsche's *Also sprach Zarathustra*, 4:12 (1883–85).

Sibelius responds to this richly late vision of the play on several levels. His music for the production falls broadly into four archetypal categories or modes (listed in Table 1), which correspond to different groups of characters and strategic moments in the plot, as well as fulfilling the more familiar dramatic functions of supplying mood, continuity, or commentary upon the drama. The first, and most prominent of these modes is nature music, which sounds either wild and untrammeled (as in the opening prelude and the interludes accompanying Ariel's arrival and departure from the stage), or hushed and barely audible (the "Chorus of the Winds" in Act 1, scene 2:224). Such aeolian (wind-based) sounds, whether high-pitched and intense or subdued, permeate much of the music throughout the play, serving

Table 1. Sibelius *The Tempest*, op. 109.

NO.	TITLE	SOURCE (ACT, SCENE, LINE)	CATEGORY
1	Overture	1.1	Nature
2	Miranda is lulled to slumber	1.2.186	Archaic
3	Ariel flies in	1.2.187	Nature
4	Chorus of the Winds	1.2.224	Nature
5	Ariel hastens away	1.2.305	Nature
6	Ariel's First Song "Come unto these yellow sands"	1.2.377–87	Pastoral
7	Ariel's Second Song "Full fathom five"	1.2.396–403	Pastoral
8	Interlude: Prospero	entr'acte	Archaic
9	The Oak Tree (Ariel plays the flute)	2.1.184	Pastoral
10	Ariel's Third Song "While you here do snoring lie"	2.1.301	Pastoral
11	Interlude: Caliban	2.2	Orientalist
12	Stephano's Song	2.2.41–54	Pastoral
13	Caliban's Song	2.2.176–81	Orientalist
14	Interlude: Miranda	entr'acte	Archaic
15	Humoresque	3.2.40	Pastoral
16	Canon	3.2.121	Pastoral
17	Dance of the Shapes	3.3.18	Orientalist
18	Melodrama (Ariel as Harpy)	3.3.52	Orientalist
19	The Shapes dance out	3.3.82	Pastoral
20	Intermezzo: Alonso mourns	entr'acte	Archaic
21	Ariel flies in	4.1.33	Nature
22	Ariel's Fourth Song "Before you can say 'come'"	4.1.44–48	Pastoral
23	The Rainbow	4.1.58	Nature
24	Melodrama: Iris	4.1.60	Pastoral
25	Juno's Song "Honour, riches, marriage blessing"	4.1.106–117	Pastoral
26	Minuet: Dance of the Naiads	4.1.134	Pastoral
27	Polka: Dance of the Harvesters	4.1.138	Pastoral
28	Ariel flies in	4.1.164	Nature
29	Ariel hastens away	4.1.188	Nature
30	Ariel flies in	4.1.193	Nature
31	The Dogs	4.1.254	Pastoral
31bis	Overture: Ariel	entr'acte	Pastoral
32	Prospero's monologue "Ye elves of hills, of brooks"	5.1.33	Nature
33	Ariel's Fifth Song "Where the bee sucks"	5.1.88–94	Pastoral
34	Cortège	[5.1]	Pastoral
34bis	Epilogue	[5.1]	Archaic

almost as an auditory background or grain for the whole score. Closely related is the second category, which consists of a stylized, archaic music, usually modal (Dorian) in color and associated with aristocratic figures such as Miranda (Act 1, scene 2:186), Prospero (the entr'acte between Acts 1 and 2), or Alonso (the intermezzo between Acts 3 and 4, illustrating the King's grief for his drowned son). For Robert Layton, the slow sarabande meter and restrained dynamic level of this music gains a "Purcellian grandeur," but Sibelius might equally have been thinking of Fauré, or his own music for Maeterlinck's *Pelléas et Mélisande* (1905). The third, broadest, category is pastoral music, associated both with spirits and the masque (Act 4, scene 1:60), and also with the comic scenes in Acts 2 and 3. The conventional affective connotations of the pastoral (images of Arcadia, idyll, and a lost golden age) strengthen the play's autumnal tone. But the pastoral also provides one of the characteristic modes for Ariel's songs, especially the first, "Kom herhid på gule sand" (Come unto these yellow sands, Act 1, scene 2:37–87) and the fifth, "Med bien drikker jeg af krus" (Where the bee sucks, there suck I, Act 5, scene 5:88–94), which serves also as an overture to the final act. The last category is associated principally with Caliban, whose two solo numbers (the Interlude, Act 2, scene 2, and his mock-triumphant song of independence, "Farvel, min husbond" [Farewell, my master], Act 2, scene 2:176–81) are characterized by a greater degree of chromaticism, strong rhythmic ostinato figures, and heavy percussion scoring: qualities conventionally associated in much nineteenth-century theatrical music with stereotypical evocations of the Orient. At a crude level, Sibelius therefore reinforces the received image of Caliban as a primitive subhuman savage or animal, as Brandes and other critics suggest. But Sibelius blurs the immediate boundaries of this stereotype by bleeding elements of such musical Orientalism into other numbers, notably the whirling "Dance of the Shapes" that provides the high point of Act 3, scene 3:18. Caliban's bestiality, it seems, points toward a more general (base) level of the human condition, one that is no less essential than Prospero's elevated detachment elsewhere and whose presence can be felt across the island.

Closer attention to the individual numbers in Sibelius's score of *The Tempest* offers further insights into his reading of the play. Though extensive sketches do not survive, the Sibelius archives in Helsinki University Library do contain an early draft of no. 4, "The Chorus of the Winds," which conflates material that eventually appeared in no. 2 (Miranda, Act 1, scene 2:186), as well as a version of the "Winds" music that differs significantly from its final form (see Example 1).[47] The music is directed to be played "Hoch oben, über d. Bühne" (High above the stage), a marking that occurs at several comparable points throughout Sibelius's manuscript score, suggesting a physical as well as figurative evocation of distance.

Sibelius's striking scoring, for wordless chorus, *con bocca chiusa* (with closed mouths), accompanied by harp and harmonium, which he retained in one version of no. 2 and the final version of no. 4, suggests both enchantment and also the nature sounds that form the play's basic acoustic background.

Example 1. Unpublished draft for nos. 2 and 4, "Miranda" and "Chorus of the Winds," Sibelius's *Tempest* (National Library of Finland).

Example 1 continued

Example 1 continued

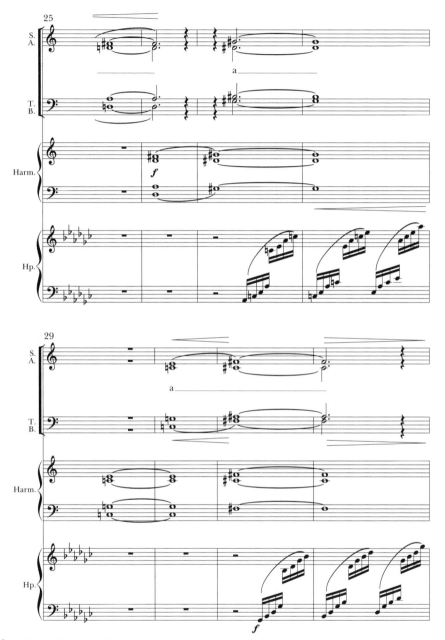

Example 1 continued

Example 1 continued

Example 1 continued

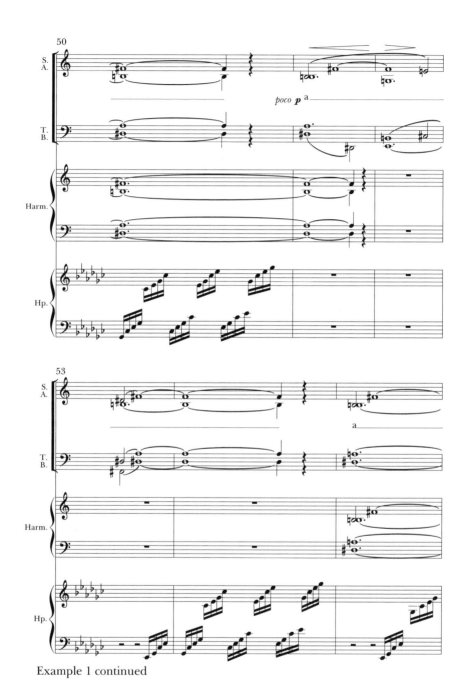

Example 1 continued

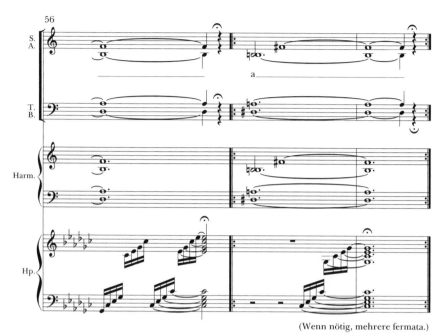

(Wenn nötig, mehrere fermata.)

Example 1 continued

Both voices and harmonium here become "wind instruments," a hybrid aeolian harp, intaking and exhaling air alternately in a wave-like manner whose undulation is reinforced by Sibelius's envelope hairpin dynamic markings and melodic contours. The harmonium might equally well evoke memories of its use in some of Schoenberg's early works, notably *Herzgewächse*, op. 20 (1911), where it assumes a more sultry, breathy quality. Harmonically, this preliminary draft is remarkable for the sudden enharmonic shift in measure 17 (C♯-D♭), prompted by the incursion of the E♭'s into the Dorian context in mm. 13–16, and the haunting tritone progressions descending by whole tones of the following page (D–G♯, mm. 26–28; C–F♯, mm. 29–32; B♭–E♮, mm. 33–36). Sadly, none of this affective sequence of diminished-fifth steps was retained in the final version. No less notable is the allusion to the swinging fifths of the "Swan Hymn" from the finale of the Fifth Symphony in mm. 37–37, underpinned by shadowy bass notes in the harp (the C♭ in mm. 46–48 is especially effective and, en-. harmonically reinterpreted once more, becomes the grounding tone for the B⁷ chord with which the number gradually fades away into nothingness). Was the directness of this allusion to the symphony perhaps the reason Sibelius eventually reconceived the passage, dividing Miranda's restrained aristocratic berceuse and the "Chorus of the Winds" into separate numbers? The "Swan Hymn" fifths recur elsewhere as a fingerprint, not least in the swirling gale that accompanies Ariel's dramatic entries and exits from the stage.

The first of Ariel's songs, "Kom herhid på gule Sand," is essentially a pastoral in D major, the key of the Second Symphony and *The Oceanides*, but the music's radiant diatonicism is increasingly clouded by the incursion of B♭, a chromatic element that points back toward the (predominantly flat-side) storm music of the Overture. Ariel's dramatic association with the elements, and with the wild nature sounds of the opening number, is therefore made harmonically explicit. After an orchestral play-over, the first strophe is sung by the "Chorus of the Winds" alone, reinforcing precisely the association established by Ariel's flat-side chromaticism. Sibelius's autograph manuscript marks the chorus "Hinter d. Bühne" (Behind the stage), once again suggesting a literal and figurative distancing, whereas the harmonium is marked *Come coro* (Hoch oben, über d. Bühne), so that the overall impression would almost have created a surround-sound effect: a glowing aura of noise rather than a sharply focused timbral signal. Ariel's first entry is almost parenthetical, the mood darkened by the presence of a rolling wave-like chromatic figure in the cellos and basses—more an undertow than a functional harmonic element (a musical illustration of the evocative line "the wild waves whist," though, as Lindley notes, "whist" here refers to "becoming silent," one of the recurrent thematic tropes in Sibelius's music).[48] Ariel's stanza is harmonically and texturally cut short at rehearsal letter C (measure 51), *Poco a poco stretto,* by the entry of the chorus as watchdogs: this is sparked by a moment of chromatic disruption, the heavy brass and percussion audibly recalling the wave-tossed storm sonorities of the Overture. It also serves to negotiate an awkward moment in Shakespeare's text: line 380, "And sweet sprites bear the burden/the burden bear," can be read alternatively as a lyric in Ariel's song, or as a stage direction marking the entry of the chorus, "the burden."[49] Sibelius, presumably unconsciously, thus highlights a moment of textual as well as dramatic rupture: the revelation that beneath the idyllic pastoralism of Ariel's lyric a much darker layer is constantly present.

This more shadowed tone is even more evident in Ariel's second song, "Fem favne dybt" (Full fathom five, Act 1, scene 2, 396–403). Sibelius's use of the trombones here suggests a funeral solemnity rather than the raw nature sounds of the Overture. Similarly, the music's angular melodic contour (with prominent flattened second and raised fourth—the Locrian mode characteristic also of passages in *Tapiola*) likewise evokes an atmosphere of mourning, loss, and painful remembrance: "Slet intet af ham er spildt eller tabt" (Nothing of him that doth fade). As in Ariel's first song,

Sibelius again exploits the expressive potential of the chorus: the voices of the sea nymphs who "hourly ring his knell" become a drone in the second half of the setting, underlying Ariel's inverted pedal (which moves at half speed).[50] The strange disorienting effect of the chorus's swinging bell sounds is intensified by Sibelius's metrical modulation—the expansion of the initial common-time meter into a more spacious 3/2 creates the illusion of stretching time, even while the underlying pulse remains constant. Closure is signaled by a descending chromatic sequence (Ariel's symbolic B♭ pitch from the first song is resolved by register displacement in the strings), and by a gradual shading into silence: Ariel's vision sinking once more into the gloom.

A similar expressive and textural arc is traced by no. 23, "The Rainbow" (Act 4, scene 1:58), which serves as an overture to the masque (which Sibelius sets as a melodrama) and Juno's song that follows. Tawaststjerna comments on Sibelius's use of a pitch collection that Messiaen would later describe as one of his "modes of limited transposition": octatonic collection II.[51] In reality, the pitch organization is more complex and subtle. The number begins with a bass drone or pedal (bassoons, horns, double basses) that strongly recalls the opening of the Fourth Symphony: the prominent pitch classes C, D, and G♭ refer explicitly to the symphony's basic motto. This dark timbral layer provides an acoustic ground while simultaneously blurring any firm sense of tonality: as in the symphony, the low scoring creates a rich spectrum of overtones and resonant upper partials. The imitative entries of the cellos and upper strings fill in the C–G♭ pitch space with the whole step–half-step pattern of octatonic collection II; the double basses, however, invert this intervallic space, descending toward G♭ in purely whole-tone steps. Sibelius thus establishes a distinct modal layering (octatonic above, whole tone below) to emphasize the symmetry of the underlying tritone pair C–G♭ (see Example 2). The enharmonic transformation of this G♭ (F♯) in measure 12 marks the approximate midpoint of the number, and the beginning of the rainbow's brightening (intensified by the entry of the timpani, trombones, trumpets, and upper wind). The rising upper string figure now ascends from F♯, while the bass descends toward C, although, characteristically, the final measures remain anchored on a first inversion chord, suspending any definitive sense of tonic arrival: indeed, the whole number is properly a study in modal contrast, intervallic space, and timbral modulation.

"The Rainbow" exemplifies, in highly compressed form, a structural and formal dynamic that is characteristic of much of Sibelius's later music. For James Hepokoski, such structures suggest "the bypassing of traditionally mediated thought and external control in favor of more potent, archetypal urges that were believed to strike more deeply than the

Example 2. "The Rainbow" (opening), no. 23, Sibelius's *Tempest*.

schematic methods of an 'artificial' rationality—the trusting embrace of
the apparently mythic or pre-rational claims of intuitive impulse, blood,
and nature (including raw sound itself)."[52] The modal-timbral design of
"The Rainbow" is indicative of this urge to access or uncover a more elemental sense of sonority, or *Klang*. The revelatory atmosphere of the
closing measures is both an enigmatic moment of withdrawal and also a
gateway to the mythic ritual of the masque that follows. Yet one of the most
powerfully modernist characteristics of Sibelius's music is the tension between such apparently intuitive structures and their carefully calibrated
musical design. As Sibelius's *Tempest* music repeatedly reveals, the invoca-

tion of such mythic or pre-rational claims to impulse and intuition is rarely straightforward or trusting. On the contrary, any appeal to blood, nature, or raw sound, Sibelius's music insistently suggests, swiftly becomes threatening or destabilizing. Indeed, one of the central dramatic themes in *The Tempest*, which Sibelius's music brings vividly into the foreground, is the extent to which notions of creative agency and control are stretched to breaking point by the incursion of such natural forces or elemental powers: a dissolution of self toward which the whole score constantly returns.

This sense of a structural and expressive breaking point is rendered most clearly audible in two numbers that effectively frame the play's dramatic action: the Overture with which the play begins and the "solemn music" that accompanies Prospero's monologue in the final Act 5, scene 1:33–57. As previous commentators have noted, Poulsen followed the nineteenth-century convention of omitting the opening scene's dialogue and substituting Shakespeare's text for an independent tableau vivant, illustrating the storm and shipwreck that initiates the play's action.[53] At one level, Sibelius's music can be heard as a naturalistic portrait of the storm itself, a genre piece in the tradition of earlier nineteenth-century Romantic dramatic music such as Berlioz's "Royal Hunt and Storm" from *Les Troyens*. At a deeper level, however, the piece can be understood as a timbral study in wild aeolian sonorities: the rushing sounds of wind, rain, and crashing waves. The Overture's percussively edged chromatic saturation, its roaring plenitude of white noise, can thus be heard as a kind of musical meteorology, an attempt to move beyond simple illustration toward a more phenomenologically grounded engagement with the nature and affect of the shifting weather—a reading to which we shall return below. At a third level, Sibelius's Overture reveals the extent of his debt to Debussy, and in particular to works such as "Voiles" and "Ce qu'a vu le vent d'Ouest" from the *Préludes*, Book 1, pieces similarly concerned with spectral sonorities and complementary modal collections. The shifting emphasis between the two basic transposed collections of the whole-tone scale, allied to larger-scale variations in textural, melodic, and dynamic density, provides the music's wave-like sense of structure and drama: spiraling in increasingly tight curves toward a plunging climax, and then gradually unwinding once more to an unsettled, but near-static conclusion.

In this sense, the work exemplifies, to an especially condensed and intensified degree, Hepokoski's three-stage model of rotational form in late Sibelius: "1) a gradual ripening or phenomenological Coming-into-Being; 2) an attainment of a peak followed by an immediate overripening; 3) crisis, distortion, and decay."[54] At a more immediate level, however, the work initially resists a straightforward teleological reading. Indeed, it is hard for the listeners to orient themselves within the music's whirling textural density. On closer listening, the rich micropolyphony of the opening measures presents different ways of partitioning the complete chromatic aggregate using whole-tone scales. The individual string parts, for example, articulate the complete chromatic set horizontally, rising and falling in a complex series of local wave shapes that rapidly generate a reflective contrary motion and imitative counterpoint. The way that the double basses turn downward a beat early in measure 1, echoed by the upper strings a beat later as the basses turn upward again, for example, reveals the music's characteristic undulating weave of interlocking patterns, falling and dipping to create an animated curtain or tapestry of sound. But the figuration is assembled vertically from stacked whole-tone groups (four-note [0268] tetrachords), which alternate the two basic transpositions of the whole-tone set (collections I and II). These tetrachords can also suggest octatonic patterns—an important modal resource elsewhere in *The Tempest* music. The initial emphasis here, through rhythmic stress alone, is on whole-tone collection I, which effectively serves as a modal "tonic." Reinforced by bass B♭ in the timpani, and the subsequent entry of lower brass in measure 2, the music accumulates a resonant E^7 sonority with a strongly Lydian flavor—a modal coloring similar to that which later opens "The Rainbow."

The next textural layer (introduced from measure 3, rehearsal letter A), is a more readily perceivable horizontal-melodic element: a strict two-part canon in the wind. This process of textural accumulation through imitation is borrowed from the opening string figuration, but the wind lines offer a purer form of whole-tone collection I (at least until the decorative sixteenth-note cadential tail at the end of measure 4). The eruptive entry of the horns is initially dissonant, but similarly lands on collection I. From here, the music commences its second rotational cycle or strophe: the canon and eruptive horn figure is repeated, mm. 6–11, but this time the music's wave energy overshoots, and the Overture dramatically plunges onto whole-tone collection II for the first time, at measure 12. This is a moment of decisive modal reorientation, signaled by the curling woodwind fanfare in triplet thirty-second notes. The tuba slips down to E♭ and builds a new harmonic foundation, until the music begins to mix collections more playfully, lurching back to whole-tone collection I on the final dotted quarter-note beat of measure 13.

The central section of the Overture (rotation 3) is a sickening swaying between the two whole-tone collections, with associated brass chromatic glissandi and shrill woodwind fanfares (like thunderbolts or the crackling discharge of St. Elmo's fire, as described by Ariel in Act 1, scene 2:195–206), the opening tetrachords climbing upward threateningly in augmentation in the heavy brass. It is at the start of precisely this phase of greatest struc-

tural crisis or activity that Sibelius notes the curtain up (*Tæppe*) in his manuscript score: Poulsen's tableau vivant was therefore synchronized carefully
with the Overture's most vertiginous plunge between whole-tone collections I and II in measure 15, initiating the final approach toward the
Overture's registral and dynamic 'breaking point' in measure 21. From
here, the music gradually begins to subside in a reflective echo of the
accumulative first half. The two-part woodwind canon begins again in
measure 22 (rehearsal letter F), led by the upper rather than lower parts,
but the Overture's energy irresistibly drains away like a retreating storm
or ebb tide. The slow repeated E–D–C descent in the tuba grounds the
music at the very bottom of the brass register. On the final page, from rehearsal letter H, the music is reduced to its elemental component parts:
the string figuration finally gives way to a shivering tremolando and distant sustained bell-like chords in the brass and woodwind. The Overture
closes on a mysterious spectral chord: a "root" form of the earlier aeolian
sounds built from whole-tone collection I, but scored so that it suggests a
softly glowing spectral harmony: an E-major triad plus raised fourth, flattened seventh, and major ninth degrees (Example 3). Closely related again
to the Overture's opening tetrachord, the final measures do not so much
offer a resolution of the music's unstable modal tensions as settle on a ref-
erential sonority associated both with nature and also with the idea of the
supernatural.

The illustrative quality of *The Tempest* Overture serves an obvious dramatic function in Sibelius's response to Shakespeare's play. But it is
instructive to compare the music's structural and expressive qualities with
similar storm passages in Sibelius's other closely contemporary works,
notably the Sixth and Seventh symphonies and *Tapiola*. In the Sixth, the
strongly circular rotational cycles of the opening half of the finale are concerned with a gradual process of textural and harmonic accumulation,

Example 3. Sibelius's *Tempest* Overture, conclusion, mm. 36–39, "spectral"
chord (brass, strings doubling).

driven, as Hepokoski notes, by the instability of the symphony's underlying Dorian "tonic" and the various modal, diatonic, and chromatic pressures that the work brings to bear upon its basic material. The finale opens in a straightforwardly ballad-like manner, with a series of eloquent antiphonal exchanges that seem to promise a renewed sense of modal cadential order: the timpani's hollow "V–i" in D Dorian in mm. 36–37 apparently signals a regained musical balance. But the sequential cycles that follow from measure 53, struggling to reattain this D-Dorian collection in its full range and depth of expression, swiftly become overburdened with chromatic elements, and the final cycle, from measure 114, reaches saturation point, overshooting its intended goal and landing on a formidably dark B♮ in measure 144, a point that corresponds exactly with a parallel moment of harmonic arrival in the symphony's opening Allegro. As Hepokoski suggests, "The most compelling telos of this [symphony's] finale, it seems, is one of crisis, not one of affirmation."[55] The storm here, as in *The Tempest* Overture, presages a decisive moment of rupture in the musical fabric, a point at which the work's underlying processes and patterns appear to break down, even as they are foreshadowed by an earlier, seemingly more stable event (that point of arrival in the first movement). Indeed, it is not until measure 205 that the finale is able to reach its originally intended target: a subdued climactic statement of the opening measures in D Dorian. What follows is a gradual decline, or dying of the light: a slow acceptance of a seemingly inevitable harmonic goal rather than its triumphant accomplishment. As Hepokoski concludes, "Sibelius might have been pleased for us to meditate upon the process structure of the Sixth as a kind of elemental archetype: a natural cycle rising to a peak (and into a centered tonic, D Dorian), then declining into extinction, in the manner, perhaps, of a day, a season, a year, or a person's life. In thus contemplating the general shape of rise, full flowering, and inevitable decay, Sibelius, as nature-mystic, may have been inviting us to brood on the elemental cycles that structure our own lives."[56] The Sixth thus charts a broad narrative arc similar to that which many critics (including Brandes) have read in Shakespeare's *The Tempest*, and which may powerfully have informed Sibelius's response to the text.

The Seventh Symphony offers an even more complex working-through of these structural and expressive tensions. The underlying structural issue is not the fragility of a basic D-Dorian collection, as in the Sixth, but rather the idea of C major as a tonal and symbolic reference point, embodied in the noble trombone theme first heard at measure 60. The symphony opens characteristically with a "misfired" cadence: an interruptive A-flat minor sonority (measure 3) whose local implications Sibelius temporarily resolves via chromatic stepwise voice-leading progressions, but whose modal coloring (particularly the "dark" shade of the A♭ and C♭ components) inflects much of the music that follows. When the trombone theme emerges for the first time, it serves both a symbolic and tonal-harmonic function: emblematic, perhaps, of an aristocratic Prospero-like presence within the work, surveying the symphony's domain as if from an elevated height or distance. This reading is strengthened by an obvious (though previously unnoted) intertextual reference to the Alphorn theme in the finale of Brahms's First Symphony—a work likewise concerned with the structural-expressive idea of C major and associated chromatic tensions (especially A-flat). This reference is also closely bound up with the idea of late style, since, for Reinhold Brinkmann, Brahms's symphony is already a profoundly "late" work, one shaped not just by the symphony's relationship with its inherited musical tradition or legacy, but by a wider aesthetic outlook or sense of belatedness. For Brinkmann, the full weight of this historical burden can be felt when the Alphorn theme returns at the end of the development (measure 284). "This passage is not only the structural culmination of a purely thematic process" Brinkmann notes, "it marks the dynamic climax of the evolution of the entire form, and the alphorn call is sounded at the point where, as a result of the development, one expects the start of the recapitulation, and with it, in line with the orchestral climax, a powerful main theme heard in the full orchestra."[57] What should follow is the reprise of the string's broad melody from the start of the Allegro non troppo, ma con brio, measure 61, the idea that famously invoked comparisons with the "Ode to Joy" theme from Beethoven's Ninth Symphony. But crucially, as Brinkmann points out, "instead of reappearing it is emphatically replaced. Here the alphorn call transcends an adaptation of a Beethovenian theme, quelling it, effacing it."[58] Brahms's finale hence becomes a "taking-back" of the Ninth, to adopt Thomas Mann's phrase, a moment of historical return that is simultaneously a rewriting, erasure, or withdrawal—a gesture, Brinkmann suggests, that points to the essential condition of Brahms's modernity. In Sibelius's symphony, the initial return of the Alphorn/Prospero trombone theme (measure 221) is swept away in a swaying storm of chromaticized string figuration: an expected moment of decisive structural realignment hence becomes a crisis, much like the deflected climax at measure 144 in the finale of the Sixth. When the theme returns a second, and final time, in measure 475, signaling the symphony's closure, it is therefore already marked by a strongly retrospective quality—the poignant awareness of previous events and the earlier sense of a profound structural misalignment or loss. For Brinkmann, this kind of gesture, in Brahms, evokes what Ernst Bloch described as the "melancholy of fulfillment":

Moreover there is everywhere a fissure, indeed an abyss in the very realizing, the actuated-actual arrival of that which was beautifully foreseen and envisioned; and this is the abyss of uncomprehended existence itself. Thus the surrounding dark also provides the ultimate basis for the melancholy of fulfillment: there is no earthly paradise which does not have, at its entrance, that shadow which the entrance still casts.[59]

The closing measures of Sibelius's Seventh offer a similarly melancholy vision, despite their seemingly radiant tone: a sense of harmonic and tonal order is restored, but at considerable expressive and emotional cost. The storm or tempest at the heart of the Seventh Symphony, whose rushing winds can be heard even in the strained, high-string writing of the prepenultimate page (measure 500), resolving the symphony's disruptive A-flat elements for almost the final time, abates to offer the glimpse of an enchanted island, a domain of "marvelous sweet music" (Act 3, scene 3:18) embodied in the Prospero-like tone of the trombone theme. But it is a vision already shadowed by the awareness of its own contingency, a melancholy that, following Brinkmann, "signifies more than just a personal self-diagnosis, private and artistic. It is—as well as that—a historical signature."[60]

This sense of rupture, which Brinkmann suggests marks the idea of late style in Brahms, and which, I've argued above, can be heard also in Sibelius's Sixth and Seventh symphonies, is most forcibly expressed in *The Tempest* by Prospero's monologue in Act 5. For many commentators, including Brandes, Prospero's "Ye elves of hills, brooks, standing lakes and groves" speech is an autobiographical window that serves as both a summation and also a farewell to the dramatic stage, Shakespeare's evocative drawing down of the blinds on his own creative career. For Sibelius, however, the process becomes an anguished and enraged leave-taking, a snarling sequence of chromaticized nature sounds—the most dissonant music in the whole work—interrupted suddenly at measure 11, the moment when Prospero breaks his staff and resigns his magic powers, returning ambivalently to his former role as Duke of Milan (see Example 4). The music that follows is a 16-measure adagio, the simplest music in the whole score, a cadential hymn in B major, and a passage that returns to the austere aristocratic mode associated with Prospero in the entr'acte between Acts 1 and 2 (no. 8). Yet the passage is already marked by a strongly retrospective tone: the music might be heard as a threnody as much as a celebration of humanity regained. This unexpected hymnic turn exemplifies in almost schematic form one of the principal qualities of late style as understood by Gordon McMullen. "Late period work is typically

Example 4. Sibelius's *Tempest*, Prospero's monologue, no. 32, mm. 8–15.

depicted not as a steady development towards an epic climax in the way of the Virgilian model," McMullen explains, "but as a kind of coda, a supplementary phase of the creative life manifesting itself at the same time as a renewal, a rediscovery, a renaissance, characterized in particular ways by a looseness of facture, a tendency toward intense color or expression, a certain difficulty and abstraction of manner, and by a distinct style which is in a way childlike and yet at the same time—and this is frequently the key authenticator of true lateness—predicative of styles yet to be established by the artist's successors, of future developments in the particular art-form in question—as work, in other words, that stands outside its own time."[61] Sibelius's setting of Prospero's monologue can be heard in precisely this vein—as a coda that is already a rediscovery of earlier sounds and modes of utterances in the work. It combines textual density and remarkable concision with a sense of looseness—of being, in some ways, little more than a sketch for a much larger, imaginatively conceived but physically unrealized work. But it also marks a point of closure: the music is followed by Ariel's song, and the final cortège (incongruously, a polonaise) that Sibelius borrowed is taken wholesale from his music for Kaarlo Bergbohm's retirement from the Finnish National Theatre. Even the closing epilogue (no. 34bis) that Sibelius supplied for the 1927 Finnish production is reworked from his earlier orchestral work *Cassazione*. To all intents and purposes, in other words, the final measures of the monologue mark the actual end of the whole work just as the end of Prospero's monologue in a sense marks the end of the play's principal drama.

Yet it could be argued that the restful B-major triads at the close of the monologue do not wholly succeed in banishing memories of the violence with which the number begins, nor definitively resolve the music's tensions and instabilities. The pervading aural impression of the score surely remains the wild nature sounds of the Overture and the storm with which Prospero's monologue opens, not the more dignified aristocratic music with which it concludes, just as the audience's imagination remains with the barely controlled fury of Prospero's "Ye elves" speech, even after the festive reunion of the play's final pages. Ironically, given his profound antipathy to Sibelius's music, assessed elsewhere in this volume, it is Theodor Adorno who best captures this Sibelian sense of instability and rage. Adorno wrote dismissively of Sibelius's "Caliban-like destruction of all the musical results of mastery over nature" in his infamous Gloss of 1938, explicitly equating the nature symbolism of Sibelius's score with the most bestial reading of Shakespeare's dramatic character. Yet Adorno's penetrating analysis of late style in Beethoven arguably offers more compelling insights into Sibelius's *Tempest* music and the two last symphonies. Writing of Beethoven's late style, Adorno argues that "the force of subjectivity in late works is the irascible gesture with which it leaves them. It bursts them asunder, not in order to express itself but, expressionlessly, to cast off the allusion of art. Of the works it leaves only fragments behind, communicating itself, as if in ciphers, only through the spaces it has violently vacated. Touched by death, the masterly hand sets free the matter it previously formed."[62] Late work, according to Adorno, thus remains fundamentally fissured, stubbornly fractured and incomplete, even as it tends toward silence. This would account for the beat's rest that Sibelius places at the heart of the monologue in measure 12, or the reverberant after-echo once the strings' resonant chord has died away at the close of the Adagio (significantly, there is no pause over the held chord of the final two measures). In Beethoven's late work, Adorno suggests, "he no longer draws together the landscape, now deserted and alienated, into an image" invoking the idea of landscape both as an imaginary and as a physically perceived world. "The fragmented landscape is objective, while the light in which alone it glows is subjective." Yet, Adorno continues, "[Beethoven] does not bring about their harmonious synthesis. As a dissociative force he tears them apart in time, perhaps in order to preserve them for the eternal. In the history of art, late works are the catastrophes."[63]

A similarly wasted landscape frames Sibelius's *Tempest* music, and his other late works, from the Sixth and Seventh symphonies to *Tapiola*. Following the principles of Adorno's Beethoven analysis, this might have pointed to the music's underlying tendency toward fracture or collapse, a sense of cataclysm realized most vividly in the storm with which *Tapiola* concludes. It is hard to retain any sense of Prospero-like authority at the end of this work, even though it concludes with precisely the same B-major chords as his monologue in *The Tempest*. Yet these passages also bring into sharp focus questions of agency and intention in Sibelius's music. They force us to reconsider ideas of nature and the natural world in Sibelius's work not as an ideologically conceived mold for deeply regressive notions of purity and elementalism, as Adorno insisted in the closing page of his critique. Rather, landscape, and particularly the storm, emerges as a mode of immanent critique. It is concerned precisely with the dissolution and breaking apart that Adorno believes Sibelius's music attempts to conceal. Sibelius's late works repeatedly evoke forms of spatial perception, imaginatively shaping our perception of auditory space by tracing an expressive arc that curves initially upward (and outward) from an opening feeling of concealment or veiling toward moments of rupture, luminescence, or actualization, and leading ultimately to a distant, intangible horizon or point of dissipation in their final measures. This basic trajectory, charting a process of emergence, arrival, and redeparture across parallel but contrasting time frames, is shared by the two last symphonies, *Tapiola*, and the

Tempest music. All of these late works, in other words, suggest different journeys across the same basic terrain. But they also suggest a sense of instability or flux, of a continual motion to and fro: the symbolism of the shifting tides to which Shakespeare's *The Tempest* repeatedly alludes.

This sense of motion leads us away from Adorno's analysis of late style toward social anthropologist Tim Ingold's recent critique of sound studies and the notion of soundscape.[64] For Ingold, sound, and by extension music, is akin to visual perception. But just as sight is more properly a function of light and illumination, rather than of objects themselves, Ingold claims, so sound "is not the object but the medium of our perception. It is what we hear *in*." Sound, Ingold writes, "is neither mental nor material, but a phenomenon of experience—that is, of our immersion in, and commingling with, the world in which we find ourselves." This immersion prompts a fundamental shift of perspective or attitude, away from questions of materiality or ground, toward something more mobile: the shifting patterns of the weather. For Ingold, "Weather is no mere phantasm, the stuff of dreams. It is, to the contrary, fundamental to perception." Hence, "we do not touch the wind, but touch in it; we do not see sunshine, but see in it; we do not hear rain, but hear in it. Thus wind, sunshine and rain, experienced as feeling, light and sound, underwrite our capacities, respectively to touch, to see and to hear." From his phenomenological standpoint, Ingold argues that "we should therefore turn our attention skywards, to the realm of the birds, rather than towards the solid earth beneath our feet. The sky is not an object of perception, any more than sound is. It is not a thing we see. It is rather luminosity itself. But in a way, it is sonority too." In a remarkably Prospero-like gesture, Ingold thus turns us back toward a more mythic account of the origins of music, in the Orphic sounds of nature: the rushing of the wind, the crying of birds, and the flow of water across the landscape. But in proposing his musical meteorology, Ingold suggests that "the wind is not so much embodied as the body *enwinded*." By extension, "we should say of the body, as it sings, hums, whistles or speaks, that it is *ensounded*. It is like setting sail, launching the body *into* sound like a boat on the waves or, perhaps more appropriately, like a kite in the sky."

Ingold's idea of enwindment offers a radical new reading of *The Tempest*, one in which Prospero is revealed not as a magus, or superhuman being, far less as a dramatic representation of Shakespeare himself, but rather as a mere agent for a more powerful and elemental medium: the rushing winds of the storm. By turning our gaze upward and attending to the sounds of the weather around us, we also become aware, like Prospero, of our own contingency and transience. We are shaped by the meteorological environment just as much as we seek to control the elements around us. Sibelius seems to have shared precisely this perception in his recurrent crises of confidence and moments of self-doubt and creative angst, and in his repeated descriptions of the natural world and his fascination with landscape. This is perhaps the defining quality of Sibelius's "late style." In a diary entry dated 23 November 1924, the year before he began his *Tempest* music, he wrote: "How infinitely difficult it is to age as an artist—above all as a composer." Turning again to a landscape metaphor, he added: "It is perhaps wise not to have friends. One dies alone and that is certainly easier. It might be that I should 'descend from the mountain'—life is little other than waiting for death."[65] Here is the key to Sibelius's reading of Prospero, in his resignation as he descends to the earthly sphere from the exalted heights and "cloud-capp'd towers" of his creative imagination. But it prompts an even deeper act of self-reflection and abandonment. As we listen to the closing measures of Sibelius's setting of Prospero's monologue, or the conclusion of the Seventh Symphony or *Tapiola*, it is as though we ourselves inhabit Prospero's mind as he waits to leave the desert island—his stage—at the end of Shakespeare's *Tempest*. Nothing lies beyond except obliteration. Yet for a seemingly infinitely prolonged moment, before the silence begins, we hear intensely the crashing of the waves against the shore, the roaring of the wind among the pines.

NOTES

I would like to thank the staff of the National Archives of Finland (NA) and the Music Manuscript Reading Room in the National Library of Finland (HUL) for their assistance with research for this essay. I am indebted to Glenda Dawn Goss, Gitta Henning, Timo Virtanen and Lilo Skaarup at the library of the Royal Theatre, Copenhagen. Haydon Lorimer first brought Tim Ingold's work to my attention, and Tiffany Stern read a preliminary draft of the essay and made many corrections and improvements.

1. The idea of a shadow is problematic and is invoked cautiously here, since it suggests both a sense of anxiety and also a patrilineal model of inheritance and tradition that demands further critical scrutiny. Sibelius's "shadow" is frequently cast in writing about more recent Finnish music, for instance in Ilkka Oramo's essay "*Sub umbra Sibelii*: Sibelius and His Successors," in *The Cambridge Companion to Sibelius*, ed. Daniel M. Grimley (Cambridge: Cambridge University Press, 2004), 157–68.

2. Cecil Gray, *Sibelius* (Oxford: Oxford University Press, 1934), 150–51; and Constant Lambert, *Music Ho! A Study of Music in Decline* (London: Penguin, 1934; repr. 1948), 237–41. The date of the two volumes, the same year as the death of Elgar, Holst, and Delius, is itself significant given currents in English music at the time. See also Byron Adams's essay in the present volume.

3. For a trenchant example, see Arnold Whittall, *Musical Composition in the Twentieth Century* (Oxford: Oxford University Press, 1999), 64.

4. Veijo Murtomäki, liner notes to *Sibelius: The Tempest*, Finnish Radio Symphony Orchestra, cond. Jukka Pekka Saraste, Ondine, ODE 813–2 (1993), 7.

5. Glenda Dawn Goss, *Sibelius: A Composer's Life and the Awakening of Finland* (Chicago: Chicago University Press, 2009), 3–6 and 438–41.

6. The key texts are Theodor W. Adorno, *Beethoven: The Philosophy of Music*, ed. Rolf Tiedemann, trans. Edmund Jephcott (Berlin: Suhrkamp, 1993; repr., Cambridge: Polity, 1998), and Edward W. Said's posthumous *On Late Style: Music and Literature Against the Grain* (London and New York: Bloomsbury, 2006). For other musical discussions of late style, see Rose Rosengard Subotnik's seminal article, "Adorno's Diagnosis of Beethoven's Late Style: Early Symptom of a Fatal Condition," *Journal of the American Musicological Society* 29/2 (Summer 1976), 242–75, and, for a more recent survey, Marianne Wheeldon's *Debussy's Late Style* (Bloomington and Indianapolis: Indiana University Press, 2009).

7. Goss, *Sibelius*, 424.

8. "För Sibelius blev Prospero en sinnebild för den skapande Människan och därigenom för honom själv, liksom Ariel fick symbolisera hans inspiration, Caliban åter hans demoni." Erik Tawaststjerna, *Jean Sibelius*, vol. 5: 1919–1957 (Stockholm: Atlantis, 1997), 204. All references to Erik Tawaststjerna's Sibelius biography in this essay are drawn from his 5-volume Swedish original (published in Stockholm and Helsinki), rather than Robert Layton's heavily abridged (3-volume) English edition. All translations below are mine unless otherwise acknowledged.

9. "Just Stormen borde ligga för Er. Prospero (Trollkarlen), Miranda, jord—och luftandar m.m." Tawaststjerna, *Sibelius*, 5:202

10. The box includes a visiting card for H. Orsmond Anderton, head of the Midland Institute, Birmingham, in addition to the guide leaflet (ticket no. 28676). Box 52, "Pariisi, 1911, Englanti 1912," Sibelius Family Archive, National Archives of Finland (henceforth NA), Helsinki.

11. "Resa till England. London.—Stratford on Avon Shakespeares födelsebygd." Jean Sibelius, *Dagbok 1909–1944*, ed. Fabian Dahlström (Stockholm: Svenska litteratursällskapet i Finland, Atlantis, 2005), 153.

12. As early as 21 May 1909, in Berlin, Sibelius had remarked "En stilförändring?" (A change of style?; ibid., 35), prefiguring, as Hepokoski suggests, the later crisis of identity that would occur the following year. James Hepokoski, *Sibelius: Symphony No. 5* (Cambridge: Cambridge University Press, 1993), 10–18.

13. "Mitt lifs solitude *börjar*. Konsten är att hålla arbetsmodet uppe trots 'alleingefühl.'" Sibelius, *Dagbok*, 39.

14. "Vaknade med de ohyggligaste grämelser öfver de varmhjärtades åtgöranden. Fruktar att de vände sig till personer, hvilka icke äro värda förtroendet. Skall du verkligen lida af detta! Är det bätre att sitta på esplanadesofforna i H:fors och preja an förbigående kapitalister. Du vet sjelf att det var helvetet. Din tid gick og din fantasi led. Något för något. Du haf gifvit musik, alltså—?!" (ibid., 48). As Dahlström notes, Sibelius alludes here to the famous point at which Lear begins to dismiss his daughter Cordelia— "Nothing will come of nothing, speak again"—in *King Lear*, 1.1.94.

15. Sibelius, *Dagbok*, 59

16. "En ny symfonisk uppgift leker mig i hågen! Huru liten, oändligt liten förståelse och uppmuntran har ej mina sinfonier erhållit ute i store verlden! Ofta förekommer det mig numera som vore hela denna sinfoniska sträfvan lönlös. Men deta arbeta och denna sträfvan har nog sin stora uppfostrande betydelse för mig. För närvarande finner jag mig liten och obetydlig. En liten, obetydlig talang! Herre Gud, ja! Ta nu bröd i öknen!—Dagen härlig, sommarlik!—Om aftonen stjärnor! Stjärnor!" *Dagbok*, 134.

17. Lifvet är nog slut för mig. Är jag nå'ngång glad och tar mig ett glas, får jag lida långa tider efteråt. Denna fruktansvärda depression—hvilken Aino ej kan förstå, men som jag nog har ärftlig. Denna "blödighet" eller att man saknar själftillit, som gör att Aino och barnen aldrig får rigtigt stöd i lifvet. Dette helvete på jorden, som de råkat uti, aldrig slippa. Ve mig ensamma, ensamma!" Ibid., 319.

18. "Det blåser ute. Huru oändligt rikare är icke [illegible word], denna orefleterade blåst än Göthe's och de andra herrarnas poesi! Jag har börjat 'knäppa' D.v.s. supa i hemlighet. Också ett sätt att ta lifvet av sig. Men—några supar, midnattstid—ha en förunderlig verkan! Den som lefver får se! Men poesien i allt detta! Herre Gud! Reflexionen är bedårande!" (ibid., 324). As Tawaststjerna notes, Sibelius's alcoholism eventually prompted an ultimatum from his wife, Aino, that had a significant rebalancing effect upon their relationship and also, Tawaststjerna implies, may have impacted Sibelius's creativity during the later 1920s and early '30s.

19. "Citronbordet på Kämp! Citronen, dödens sinnebild—hos kineserna. Äfven här fordom. 'Gravlades med citron i hand' sjunger Anna Maria L[enngren]. Ett mera passande epitet får man leta efter. Etta skrev jag äfven i går [diary entry 17 February]. Hela vintern i sommarens tecken. En poesi i naturen som gör en galen! Måtte jag ej gå under. Kan ej lefva detta underbara rika lif. Måsta stimulera mig. Efteråt ångern! Ångesten!! Ligger det något under alliterationen?" Sibelius, *Dagbok*, 324–25.

20. Gordon McMullen, *Shakespeare and the Idea of Late Writing: Authorship in the Proximity of Death* (Cambridge: Cambridge University Press, 2007), 26.

21. Ibid., 10.

22. "Ang. Shakespear 'Stormen'/Kære Sibelius,/Vi tillader os hermed at forespørge, om Du har skrevet Musiken til "Stormen" af Shakespear.—Det Kgl. Theater agter at opføre dete Stykke og vilde da eventuelt benytte Din Musik.–/Vi hører derfor gerne fra Dig desangaaende og tegner/Med venlig Hilsen/[signed] Wilhelm Hansen." Box 45, NA.

23. "Hansens brev kom i det psykologiskt riktiga ögonblicket. Under mer än tio år hade Sibelius nästan oavbrutet brottats med det symfoniska problemet. Han hade sovrat sitt material och koncentrerat formen till det yttersta i syfte att uppnå den absoluta musikens ideal sådant han uppfattade det. Nu yppade sig för honom ett tillfälle att ge fritt utlopp åt sina tematiske ingivelser och i kalejdoskopiskt växlande musikaliska visioner karakterisera dramats personer, luftandars och najaders spel, naturkatastrofer och mytologiska skördefester." Tawaststjerna, *Sibelius*, 5:202.

24. "KONGELIGE THEATER FORESPŒRGER VIL DE KOMPONERE/MUSIK TIL SHAKESPEARES STORMEN DERES/BETINGELSER UDBEDES MA HAVE MUSIKKEN FŒRSTE/AUGUST JOHANNES POULSEN REJSER OP FOR NÆRMERE AFTALE OMGAAENDE SVAR UDBEDES=NORRIE." Box 52, Folder "Myrsky/Stormen," NA.

25. "Direktor Norrie/Kongelige Teater/Köbenhavn/Villig komponera Stormen mina betin–/gelser tretusen kronor genast samt fem prosent av bilettoinkomsten kompositionen/min egendom." Undated draft of telegram, Sibelius to the Royal Theatre, Copenhagen, torn leaf brown paper (Box 52, NA). The theatre cabled and accepted Sibelius's terms on 29 May.

26. Tawaststjerna, *Sibelius* vol. 5, caption accompanying Figure 8. Unfortunately, the image published in the Atlantis edition is in fact a page from the second movement of the Sixth Symphony, not from *The Tempest*.

27. "Jeg forventer som aftalt Deres Partitur til 1 Septem–/ber, da Prøverne paa 'Stormen' allerede er i fuld Gang og/Premieren gerne skulde finde Sted sidst 1 September./ Med venlig Hilsen/Deres ærbodigste/Wm Norrie." Box 52, Sibelius Family Archive, NA.

28. "Kapelmester Høeberg beder mig hilse Dem og udtale hans/Glæde over deres herlige Musik, ligesom jeg ogsaa kan med–/dele, at Sceneinstruktør Johannes Poulsen og de Kunstnere,/der skal fortolke Deres Toner, er i allerhøjeste Grad be–/gejstrede." Box 52, Sibelius Family Archive, NA.

29. Hauch wrote on 28 May: "I disse dage har Johannes Poulsen talt meget med mig om den eventuelle Mulighed för at formaa Professoren til at skrive Musik til Shakespeare's 'Stormen," som indstuderes paa Det Kgl Teater. Han tænkt paa at rejse op til Finland og bede dem derom—men om den bliver noget af det ved jeg endnu ikke. Men var det ellers en Sag som kunde interesse?" (Johannes Poulsen has recently told me much about the eventual possibility of asking the Professor [Sibelius] to write music for Shakespeare's *The Tempest*, which is being staged at the Royal Theatre. He is thinking of traveling up to Finland and asking you about it—but whether anything will actually happen I don't know. But is this something that would be of interest?) Box 20, Sibelius Family Archive, NA.

30. "Jag kommer till Eder med en mycket diskret Sak. Det gälder musiken till Stormen. Redan föra circa två månader sände jag de första scéneren. Nu åfinstå af 34 endnast 3, hvilken jag med det snareste skal sände. Detta dock beroende på om mitt gripp på ämnet slagit om på vederbörande. Jag har ej med ett ord, ej med ett teckan fått besked om något./Ville Ni nu godhetsfullt 'sondera terraine' D.v.s. taga moda på om min musik äfvenhufvudtaget kommer till utförande, eller ej." National Library of Finland (HUL), Collection 206.61.

31. "Tak fordi De hensendte Brev til mig angaaende Situationen vedraaende "Stormen" og deres Musik til det Kgl Teater. . . . Allerede for nogen Tid siden har jeg hört af Hr. Johannes Paulsen hvor aldeles begejstret han var over de Musik Professoren har sendt, og under en Samtale jeg på Tirsdags havde med Direktor Norrie bekræftede han ganske dette Ledsagen. Jeg have trygt sige, at man er usædvanlig glad, taknemmelig over det Værk, Professoren nu har skabt, og Teatret ventes sig en enestaadende Begivenhed af Premieren, der efter den seneste Bestemmelse skal findes sted i Tiden ved Jul og Nytaar. Naar den ikke kommer tidligere skydes det at teatret nu i Maaneder maa fremföre Debussy"s Pelleas et Melisande, og Stravinskys Petrouchka. Jeg finder det aldeles beunderingsværdigt, at Professoren i saa kort Tid har medfört et saa stort Værk—og mere end nogen glæde mig til at lære dette nye storværk af Dem at kende. Er det indiskret af spörge lidt om Værkets ydre Karakter? Om der er Ouverture, og Instrumentation, etc.?" Box 20, Sibelius Family Archive, NA.

32. "Om Ni kunde få beda forå när Stormen oppföres, skall jag försöke komma till Köbenhavn. Men incognito om ej till Premiären." HUL Coll. 206.61.

33. "Nu måsta jag bekänna mig—trots alle mina försök—ej ha fått ihåg något om Shakespeare. Följande dag har det jag skrivit foregående dag, förefallit fattigt och dumt. Gudskelof att jeg ej är journalist./Ni måsta tillgifne mig. Timon från Athén är mig kärest på grund af dess mänsklighet; Stormen i dess musikalishhet. Beträffande Stormen, när uppföres den? Ville Ni vänligen ta medd derpå och skriver till mig några om den." HUL Coll. 206.61.

34. "En ulykkelig Skaben har hidtil hvilet over Indstuderingen af dette Værk." Box 20, Sibelius Family Archive, NA.

35. "Opförelsen par den kgl. Teater bliver uden al Tvivl en meget stor Success. Der havde adskille ydre pragtfulde Momenter i Anvendelsen af den sceniske Teknik, og Udförelsen var mærkbart baaret oppe af en stor Indsats. Mens det kan ikke nægter at Skuespillernes Kræfter paa afgörende Punkter ikke just var paa Shakepeareske Höijder. Som Helhed gælder det at de lyriske Scener virkede for svagt paa grund af Fremstillernes Spinkelhed. Mens de komiske Situationer bredte sig mere end rimeligt. Naar Poesiens og Fantasiens sande Tone dog ofte klang, skyndtes det saa afgjort Musiken.

"Hvor forunderligt Gang paa Gang at mærke disse Toners Aabenbaring af Ordens sande Sjæl. Musiken blev dirigent af de unge Kapelmeter Johan Nye-Knudsen, der er et adskilligt större Kapelmester–Talent end Höeberg." Box 20, Sibelius Family Archive, NA.

36. "Hela Historien med Stormen har jag glömt. En dumhet var det att jag sog mig i slang med Poulsen. Han kan nu nog vara bra, men säkert är iscensättningen—som du skref—dårlig." Tawaststjerna, *Sibelius*, 5:219.

37. "Inte i något av de teaterstycken han dittills skrivit musik till hade han dock kunnat leva sig in i huvudpersonerna like intensivt som han nu identifierade sig med Prospero i Shakespeares Stormen." Ibid., 204.

38. David Lindley, Introduction, *The New Cambridge Shakespeare: The Tempest* (Cambridge: Cambridge University Press, 2002), 1–83, at 3.

39. Georg Brandes, *William Shakespeare* (Copenhagen, 1895–96). The prominence of Brandes's writing in European literary circles is evidenced by its remarkably early translation into English (in two volumes) by William Archer, Mary Morrison, and Diana White (London: William Heinemann, 1898), French and German. Some of the Shakespearean allusions in Brandes's text are lost in Archer, Morrison, and White's translation (see below).

40. Niels B. Hansen, "Observations on Georg Brandes's Contribution to the Study of Shakespeare," in *Shakespeare in Scandinavia*, ed. Gunnar Sorelius (Newark, DE: University of Delaware Press, 2002), 148–67.

41. Ibid., 151.

42. Brandes, *William Shakespeare*, 160, translation altered. The allusions are to Ophelia's description of Hamlet's apparent madness: "Like sweet bells jangled, out of tune and harsh" (3.1.161), and as Hamlet is directing the players in his dumb show on how to perform (3.2.6–7).

43. Ibid., 378.

44. Ibid., 380.

45. Ibid., 380.

46. Ibid., 386.

47. HUL Sibelius Archive, Manuscript 0935.

48. Lindley, *The New Cambridge Tempest*, 121.

49. See Lindley's illuminating discussion of the confusing typography in the first folio, ibid., 247–50, and the contrasting solution offered by the most recent edition of *The Arden Tempest*, ed. Virgina Mason Vaughan and Alden T. Vaughan (London: Methuen, 2000 [1998]), 177. Lembcke's Danish translation is, characteristically, less richly ambivalent than Shakespeare's original: "Aander synger koret med" literally means "The spirits sing along with the chorus."

50. For a discussion of the folio text and the surviving seventeenth-century settings of the song, see Lindley, *New Cambridge Tempest*, 248 and 252.

51. Tawaststjerna, *Sibelius*, 5:209. Octatonic collections are symmetrically ordered scales, organized in alternating half-tone/whole-tone steps, and can be transposed only three times before the initial collection repeats itself. They are especially common in early twentieth-century music because of their ability to suggest familiar diatonic functions (such as dominant-seventh chords) without conclusively indicating a stable diatonic root.

52. James Hepokoski, "Rotations, Sketches, and the Sixth Symphony," in *Sibelius Studies*, ed. Timothy Jackson and Veijo Murtomäki (Cambridge: Cambridge University Press, 1997), 322–51, at 322.

53. Tawaststjerna, *Sibelius*, 205. Tawaststjerna describes the music's whole-tone quality as a representation of Ariel's "demonic" side, but it might be more illustrative to compare it with similar whole-tone and octatonic collections in Russian dramatic music, which are frequently concerned with ideas of enchantment and the supernatural. See Richard Taruskin, "Chernomor to Kashchey: Harmonic Sorcery; or, Stravinsky's Angle," *Journal of the American Musicological Society* 38/1 (Spring 1985): 72–142.

54. Hepokoski, "Rotations, Sketches, and the Sixth Symphony," 329.

55. Ibid., 346.

56. Ibid., 351.

57. Brinkmann, *Late Idyll: The Second Symphony of Johannes Brahms*, trans. Peter Palmer (Cambridge, MA: Harvard University Press, 1995)

58. Ibid., 40.

59. Ernst Bloch, *Das Prinzip Hoffnung* (*The Principle of Hope*), vol. I, chapter 20: the translation is Brinkmann's own and is quoted in *Late Idyll*, 132, but the passage can be found in the English edition, trans. Nevill Plaice, Stephen Plaice, and Paul Knight (Oxford: Basil Blackwell, 1986), 299.

60. Brinkmann, *Late Idyll*, 46.

61. McMullen, *Shakespeare and the Idea of Late Writing*, 26.

62. Adorno, *Beethoven: The Philosophy of Music*, 125.

63. Ibid., 126.

64. Tim Ingold, "Against Soundscape," in *Autumn Leaves: Sound and the Environment in Artistic Practice*, ed. Angus Carlyle (Paris: Double Entendre, 2009), 10–13.

65. "Huru oändligt svart är det ej att åldras som konstnar och—framför alt som komponist. Det är nog klokast att ej ha vänner. Man dör ensam och då är det ju lättare. Måhända måste jag 'stiga ned från berget'–lifvet blir ju annars ett väntande på döden." Sibelius, *Dagbok*, 323.

Waving from the Periphery:
Sibelius, Aalto, and the Finnish Pavilions

SARAH MENIN

In 1900, Jean Sibelius accompanied a delegation of Finnish cultural figures to the Paris World Fair, where he performed a series of pieces
including his recent work *Finlandia*—under the politically expedient title,
La patrie.[1] This event marked a breakthrough in Sibelius's international
career. But it was simultaneously an important milestone in Finland's
attempts to gain cultural independence from Russia—a prelude to the
political independence that it would seize at the outbreak of the Russian
Revolution in 1917. Four decades later, at the 1939 New York World's Fair,
Finland's cultural heroes met again to draw the world's attention to their
nation's plight while the Soviets were making aggressive overtures toward
Finnish territory. At the opening of the Finnish Pavilion on 4 May, the
tones of Sibelius once again joined the cultural vanguard, urgently an-
nouncing the perilous state of the small nation, its young democracy
teetering on a knife edge. The New York Pavilion, designed by Finland's
leading architect, Alvar Aalto (1898–1976), did not celebrate the nation
with pomp and circumstance, but rather offered what some found to be
a more disturbing view of a wild hinterland—not only one of Europe's
farthest outposts, but also a wilderness of the human mind. This essay will
address the development of Sibelius's music in the years between these
two pavilions and its congruence with Aalto's architectural output, exploring the reasons why *Tapiola* (which was not performed) might have
been the most appropriate parallel in New York in 1939. The discussion
will shed light on the cultural roles of the two men, but also on the genesis
of their creativity and their experience of Finland's natural environment
and its significance as a cultural stimulant.

A Stylistic Cocktail Party:
The Symposium and National Romanticism

Sibelius's close friendship with the Järnefelt brothers, painter Eero, composer Armas, and writer Arvid, brought him to the heart of Nuori Suomi, or Young Finland—the progressive, liberal pro-Finnish group that led the movement that first turned cultural attention toward the Karelia region in the east of the country.[2] Today, two locations remain that are particularly associated with members of this group—the famous Kämp Restaurant on the Esplanade in Helsinki, where they regularly met, and the studio-villa complex at Hvitträsk, less than twenty miles west of the city, built by the architectural trio of Herman Gesellius (1874–1916), Armas Lindgren (1874–1929), and Eliel Saarinen (1873–1950). A dinner-party seating plan from Hvitträsk included the Järnefelt brothers, their sister Aino and her young husband (Sibelius), the conductor-composer Robert Kajanus, as well as the architectural hosts and their wives.[3] Members of the group were united in seeking to create a sense of what being Finnish meant in the arts, echoing the famous words of the nineteenth-century Finnish statesman Johan Vilhelm Snellman: "Swedes we are not, Russians we cannot become. Let us be Finns!"[4] The architects, in particular, sought to break away from the grand symmetry of the Russian-funded empire style that had gripped Helsinki in the nineteenth century, and promoted instead a localized art nouveau, or Jugendstil.[5] Many were caught up fully in the art nouveau movement, and whole new areas of Helsinki were redesigned in a style that moved beyond neoclassicism toward something altogether more primitive and radical. Stone dressing was added to brick structures to give the illusion of medieval massiveness, symbolic of the individual breaking out from the strictures of tradition. Indeed, many of the Symposium circle explored spiritualism and challenged social, cultural, and religious taboos. As Salme Sarajas-Korte has written, "The symbolists in fact believed in the coming of a new age of spiritual depth . . . [each] engrossed in the mystical being of his own self."[6]

Sibelius's music must have seemed particularly closely attuned to the work of Saarinen, Lindgren, and Gesellius at the 1900 Paris World's Fair. The pavilion has been described as "the unprejudiced mingling of international influences with original splashes of local color," and, from the outside, resembled a simple chapel, with stone massing and a steep roof, like much medieval architecture in Finland.[7] (See Figure 1.) Although the pavilion's entrance was carved in granite and soapstone, the other walls were made of lighter, cheaper materials. The simple rectangular building had one rounded end that was top-lit, allowing light to flow into the heart of the building. It also had a tower at its center, which offered the chance to

Figure 1. Exterior of Paris Pavilion, designers Gesellius, Lindgren, and
Saarinen, National Board of Antiquities, Helsinki.

have a vaulted interior. The pavilion's whole conception had a certain
clarity, despite its rather eclectic detailing, with features borrowed from
many parts of the world. The building was thus highly charged: "The
entire pavilion and its interior design created such a coherent and compact atmosphere[, a] unified expression of the 'creative soul' of this
strange country."[8] It was something of a stylistic cocktail party, mingling
art nouveau gestures with aesthetic references borrowed from the Finnish
forests.[9] Fellow symposium member Akseli Gallen-Kallela provided a
pictorial narrative for the pavilion with frescos based on scenes from the
Kalevala (Canto XIX) that decorated walls and vaults with the imagery of
what, at the time, was thought to represent Finnishness, its history and
current reality (see Figure 2). In depicting the magical smith Ilmarinen
ploughing a field of vipers dressed as a soldier, for example, Gallen-Kallela
invoked folk mythology while presenting a political allegory of the Finnish
struggle against the Russians.[10]

Everything was designed to boost Finland's artistic and political self-
confidence. The public relations triumph was secured when Anatole
France wrote approvingly in *Le Figaro* of the serene chapel-like building;

Figure 2. Vaulted interior of the Paris Pavilion, Gallen-Kallela frescos

it was, he concluded, "étrange et charmant," and more modern than many other things at the fair.[11] Ironically, the building's rich cocktail of styles and ornamental details, like Sibelius's music, owed as much to Russian traditions as to the Finnish backwoods—the medieval castles to which the pavilion referred were originally built by the city state of Novgorod, ancestors of the Russians who had seized Finland from Sweden in 1809. Yet the Paris Pavilion demonstrated to a young nation the importance of creating a national image that it could embrace as its own. Many sympathetic observers sensed the building's "Finnishness." Sibelius's friend, the photographer I. K. Inha, wrote:

The shingle roof reminds us of the shingle roofs of our ancient stone churches. Its walls and windows resemble original country dwellings— stone cowsheds, as they have been called. The tower on the roof is like a belfry, and the outside ornamentation is a vivid reminder of Finnish nature. The huge hulking bears stalking the foot of the tower, the bears' heads and squirrels on the arches of the main corridor, the giant pine cones that support the side turrets of the corridor and the water lily leaves on the outside walls all tell of the flora and fauna of our land. The material of the walls depicts Finland's endless supply of granite. The points of the cupola on the tower depict the sun's shimmering rays—a metaphor for the endless daylight of the northern summer and for the brightness of the nation's hopes, which will never be dimmed even in the face of the most severe hardships.[12]

Inha's response demonstrated what Finns had invested in the building— the form and content of which became inseparable in their desire for nationhood. The renaissance that Gallen-Kallela and others had called for in the 1890s had come to full fruition, and the architects had not only assimilated the new artistic currents from Europe, they had added their own Finnish color. In Paris at the turn of the new century their design was understood as distinctively Finnish, whatever that slightly peripheral and exotic sense of otherness might have meant to cosmopolitan tourists in the French capital as they visited the fair.

The organizers of the musical tour to accompany the Paris Pavilion were keen not to antagonize the Russian authorities, and therefore avoided using *Finlandia*'s more politically provocative title openly. Yet Sibelius's name had already become associated in Finnish circles with resistance, and his role in Paris was primarily as a musical ambassador—with two programs, including *La patrie*, some of the *King Christian II Suite*, the "Swan of Tuonela" and "Lemminkäinen's Homeward Journey" from The *Lemminkäinen* Legends, op. 22, alongside the First Symphony, conducted by Robert Kajanus. As Erik Tawaststjerna suggests, Kajanus recognized that Finland's success depended upon Sibelius's music.[13] Prince Vyacheslav Tenishev, the Russian commissioner at the exhibition, kept a close eye on proceedings, and ensured that the Finnish Pavilion was labeled "Section russe": no separatist sentiments would be tolerated. In the event, however, both he and the French minister of culture applauded the concert warmly. Sibelius himself was concerned about the *entente cordiale* between Russia and France, and how pro-Russian papers "are bound to heap abuse upon us all, above all me, as I am so nationalistic."[14] However, many of the key protagonists in French musical life, including critics and artistic contacts, were away from the city at the time of the concerts. Although the overall impression of the

Finnish delegation in Paris drew attention to Finland's plight, it did not immediately appear to the Russians as a threat.[15] But such sounds of romantic patriotism were designed, in part, to stir Finland to awake and arise. Sibelius's music, like Gesellius's pavilion, established the idea of Finland in the mind of many who had been unfamiliar even with its existence, and, as Inha put it, struck "the brightness of the nation's hope" upon an international stage.

"Fresh Springs" or "Absurd Birch Bark Culture"?

Following the Paris Pavilion's success, art nouveau gained strength in Finland. But this approach to design frustrated more forward-looking Finns, such as the critic Gustaff Strengell (1878–1937) and architect Sigurd Frosterus (1876–1956), who had been frequent visitors to Hvitträsk in the 1890s. They had traveled abroad and become increasingly dissatisfied with the parochial nature of Finnish architecture at a time when other international architects and designers were building in a more austerely modernist idiom. In 1904, they issued an open challenge to the supposed decadence of the animal and plant carvings that adorned the massive stone edifices that were such a characteristic feature of the buildings designed by the Hvitträsk trio in and around Helsinki. Their particular target was the competition for the city's new railway station. Such stylized or naturalistic details were irrelevant in their eyes, and they ridiculed "the quasi-nationalistic, archaic archaeological romanticism" of such buildings, lamenting that "Finnish architecture, divorced from reality, is like soap bubbles floating in the air."[16] They even likened the massive stone edifices in Helsinki to "program music . . . a sonnet in stone."[17] Despite the fact that this stylistic richness had been used to herald Finland's existence to the world in Paris, Strengell and Frosterus felt it had become a local self-indulgence, out of kilter with fast developing aesthetic tastes elsewhere. They demanded "fresh springs" from architects and others—something more authentic and less redolent of what they described as "mindless romanticism."[18]

Sibelius, of course, had exploited the programmatic potential of the *Kalevala* in works such as his early *Kullervo* Symphony and the *Lemminkäinen* Legends, as well as in his music for the series of *tableaux vivants* in the 1890s from which *Finlandia* emerged.[19] Yet as early as 1904, Sibelius's creative journey toward his most individual and arguably profound music naturally took him increasingly away from the national romantic agenda. As he himself is supposed to have put it much later: "Whereas other composers are engaged in manufacturing cocktails of various hues, I offer pure spring water."[20] Strengell and Frosterus's challenge had been made just as Sibelius first began to confront the distillation and abstraction of large-scale form in his First and Second symphonies, but many of his architectural colleagues were still flavoring their designs with the heady mix of motives drawn from local flora and fauna. Strengell recognized this trend, writing:

> The history of music is one long series of extending the rules. All its pioneers overstepped the contemporary rules of harmony, and here in Finland we have Sibelius, and he too, in many respects, points to the future by stretching the limits currently accepted for harmony.[21]

The image of pure spring water that Sibelius later channeled into his music was especially emotive: a landscape of lakes and the snow of the long, harsh winters, where, as Aleksis Kivi expressed it in his influential poem "Bear Hunt," "a harsh wind blows."[22] The correlation between Finland's meteorological climate and the increasingly frigid tone of political suppression in the early 1900s undoubtedly led to periods of deprivation among the wider Finnish population. During Finland's long winters, extending from October to March, temperatures could regularly dip below −30 degrees F and effectively rendered preindustrial Finland into a state of hibernation. Indeed, Finnish ethnologists have cited how cold winters and failed crops brought tragedy to the lives of many thousands of peasants, enshrining hardship or "lack" as the hallmark of their lives. In 1865, the nationalist poet Zachris Topelius wrote: "Although a humble people, our guard against the powers of barbarianism and darkness is humanity's own endless struggle for light and life." There is little doubt that the manner of survival in the forests had become an important theme for the cultural elite—who tiptoed in their galoshes through the mud, uttering awkwardly in newly learned Finnish, as they began to define what being Finnish meant. Pushkin had understood this when he described Finland as "harsh nature's poor abandoned child." Up until the later part of the nineteenth century, the majority of Finnish-speaking Finns had been slaves to the rigors of their natural environment—but the independence movement brought the more wealthy Swedish-speaking elite alongside them to discuss aspects of common hardship at the heart of their country. Even Sibelius bought a sheepskin coat in order to look more like a true peasant.[23]

Although a sense of opulence had characterized Carl Friedrich Engel's 1830s imperial architecture in Helsinki, creating a model town for French visitors to visit en route from Paris to St. Petersburg, a simpler backwoods classicism of pole and pediment had appealed to Finns in the "hard unrelenting nature of the country that the architecture clearly reflects."[24]

Worked tree trunks replaced ornate classical columns. It was not a lack of beauty that characterized such native classicism, but rather a lack of superfluity dictated by a lack of choice or resources. The congruence between the poverty and simplicity embraced a Lutheran asceticism, and somehow sanctified the reality of a harsh existence: "A lack of materials and of economic possibilities made simplicity in its classical meaning a natural solution."[25] In contrast, the extraordinary fecundity of springtime as the winter snow recedes could bring a huge sense of release. Thus the clarion cry of "Let us be Finns!" heard in the vaults of the Paris Pavilion, pointed not toward art nouveau symbolism but toward a new modernist spring—an aesthetic of renewed energy and vitality. Strengell and Frosterus had opened a window to a new, modern Europe. Their call for "fresh springs" was both a reaction to the heady stylistic cocktail party of Saarinen, Lindgren, and Gesellius and a desire to become more "honest" and less superficial.

Alvar Aalto, who was taught by Lindgren but belonged to a younger artistic generation than the Hvitträsk trio, grew up in architectural reaction to their art nouveau, preferring a more sober neoclassicism. Yet even here was a superficiality of style and idea he would later come to challenge. When Aalto began designing in the early 1920s, Sibelius had traveled a long way from the stirring patriotism of *Finlandia*. Finland had grasped its chance at independence and leapt forward, albeit with jerky and at times faltering steps, into the modern industrialized community of nations. It was now time, Aalto felt, for a new mode of architectural expression. Sibelius, too, seems to have undergone a similar moment of aesthetic transformation or realignment. The trauma surrounding his throat tumor in 1909 amplified Sibelius's preexisting fear of death, and coincided with a deep musical crisis. In the Fourth Symphony, this involved moving toward the borders of atonality and exploring the realms of the unconscious. He turned away from the world, and the overt national romanticism of friends such as Gallen-Kallela. What followed creatively was a pared-down, elliptical orchestral form through which Sibelius allowed himself to concentrate and condense musical ideas. As for Aalto, neoclassicism was "a point of departure" for Sibelius, not a formal goal.[26] Indeed, Sibelius's shift away from romanticism toward a new, streamlined creative expression was a deeply personal journey, what he called his "ethical line."[27] More recently, the English psychiatrist and writer Antony Storr has suggested that a work of art is "a positive adaptation, whereas neurosis is a failure to adapt." Indeed, Storr suggests that "creativity is one mode adopted by gifted people of coming to terms with, or finding symbolic solutions for, the internal tensions and dissociations from which all human beings suffer in varying degrees,"[28] that is, the sense of "otherness" in art.[29] Crucially, Sibelius's work never lacks discipline—even though Tawaststjerna suggests it may be a "psychological symphony," the Fourth Symphony is not "neurotic" art in the sense defined by Storr.[30] Rather, the Fourth demonstrates clearly Sibelius's musical journey toward greater symphonic unity. Sibelius's motivation became increasingly personal, addressing deep inner conflicts through the creative exploration of ways of relating symbolic musical forms. Hearing Schoenberg's music brought Sibelius to an exploration of the boundaries of tonality, and face to face with his own creative crisis. Yet, though Sibelius did not follow Schoenberg into atonality, he greatly admired the work.[31] As Tim Howell has explained, to move forward Sibelius had to look back—toward the backwoods of Karelia, and indeed to his own past in provincial Hämeenlinna.[32] "The impressions of childhood form our most precious inheritance in life. The more I live the more I come back to them, and they remain an inexhaustible source of inspiration."[33]

Alvar Aalto's career began not with the imperative sense of national romanticism that had motivated Sibelius and his immediate architectural contemporaries, but rather within this neoclassical discourse. Like many determined young people, Aalto did not lack self-conviction, and he held a deep animosity toward his tutor's generation, writing of "the absurd birch bark culture of 1905, which believed that everything clumsy and bleak was especially Finnish."[34] But as soon as the modernists sounded their clarion call, heard decisively in Scandinavia at the 1930 Stockholm Exhibition, Aalto was keen to relinquish his earlier classical garb and follow the herald. Critically, however, he was to do this with a Finnish accent. This stylistic change in the late 1920s saw him denude his neoclassical design for the Viipuri Library (1927–35) shortly before it was built (see Figure 3). The frieze that had previously adorned his designs for a sunken Pompeian reading room was jettisoned in the name of modernist clarity. Aalto was ridiculed for challenging the neoclassical vogue by leading figures in Helsinki, such as the vociferous Bertel Jung, for whom Nordic classicism had become the style of nationhood. Stark white modernity, which would later become synonymous with Finnish design, was perceived as a threat, and Aalto even came to blows over the issue before it gained wider acceptance as the way forward for a new Finnish idiom.[35]

Rather like Sibelius's ambiguous feelings toward the New Music of Schoenberg, Stravinsky, and others in the 1920s, Aalto from the very start both sought to align himself with the high priests of the Congrès Internationaux d'Architecture Moderne (CIAM) yet also felt a deep ambivalence about inherent aspects of their way of being modern. Most famously epitomized by Le Corbusier's statement "The house is a machine for living in," modernist architects believed that engineering and the machine held the

Figure 3. Alvar Aalto, Viipuri Library, interior.

epoch's salvation.[36] Aalto could never worship the machine in the way that his erstwhile colleagues Le Corbusier and Walter Gropius did. On the contrary, he still tended to look to nature's growth processes for his work's genesis. Aalto's aim was to discover how to make standardization work flexibly for human life, not vice versa—real functionalism, Aalto maintained, starts from the human point of view, not the other way around.[37]

The reasons for this position go to the heart of the correlation between Aalto and Sibelius. Unlike those who followed Le Corbusier's modernism blithely into the International style, believing they had a universal solution that could be transplanted to all design contexts, Aalto believed strongly that it was important to relate to the local milieu and root a building in its immediate context. Although he had stripped his Viipuri Library of unnecessary ornamentation and used pallets of whitewashed rectilinear form in good modernist fashion, Aalto simultaneously mocked the epoch-shifting, machine-orientated worldview, challenging the principal tenets of mainstream modernist architecture. Aalto had designed an acoustic ceiling in the form of an amorphous wave for the library's long lecture room. This was a critical moment: he had apparently gone modern. Yet on closer inspection he had somehow undermined the very basis of the style. Indeed, this clever architectural move signaled an alternative modernist tradition,[38] one that asked questions not about the nature of the machine, but about how to make architecture a warm invitation for the "little man," as he affectionately described his building's intended users. The undulating ceiling "waves," so to speak, at the "little man" in a gesture of faith. However modern and ascetic Aalto's buildings appeared to be to his Finnish colleagues, they constituted a pointed response to his machine-worshipping colleagues elsewhere. The response took the form of a wave, constructed out of that most Finnish of materials—wood.

Children of the Forest God

The question nevertheless arises: Why was Aalto's "wave" wooden? The answer lies both in the congruence between geographical and physical narratives of deprivation in Finnish history and the profound connection between Aalto's own early life and his work's consequent asceticism. Similar arguments can be advanced toward Sibelius's life and work. The fact that the wave was made of wood is of primary significance. The etymology of wood in Latin is *materia*, closely related to the word *mater*, meaning mother and maternal love. Aalto sought to use forest material in order to offer a "primary embrace"—one associated with this sense of "mater" or the maternal. He wrote:

> Of course I primarily mean substance, and yet the word material means more to me, for it translates purely material activity into related mental process. . . . Matter is a link. . . . It has the effect of making a unity. . . . The links in material leave open every opportunity for harmonious synthesis . . . wood is the natural material closest to man, both biologically and as the setting of primitive civilizations.

Interestingly, Aalto continued, "I do use wood, but not for sentimental reasons." Rather, he suggested that it was a tool for mediation, "as a timeless material with an ancient tradition wood is readily available, and not merely for constructive purposes but also for psychological and biological ones."[39] Although written in 1970, toward the end of his life, this explanation epitomized both Aalto's manner of relating the material and psychological, and importantly, how he utilized nature (more specifically wood) in his work. The desire to mediate, to create a bridge or bond between material and human worlds, was an agenda that had placed him at odds with many of his modernist colleagues. And the reason for this concern with the material/maternal may be related to Aalto's close relationship with his mother, who died when he was only eight years old.

The question his architecture subsequently posed was about how to accommodate the "little man" through his work—both the eventual "users" of his buildings and himself. Aalto repeatedly linked architecture to metaphysics when he suggested that the root of "disharmony" in architecture arises at "the break with the individual's genuine psychological needs."[40] Again, this is close to what Sibelius called "the ethical line."[41]

Such breaks or points of disruption are a matter of historical fact in the early lives of both Sibelius and Aalto. Sibelius's impulsive father, Christian Gustaf, lived at the mercy of "self-destructive forces."[42] A doctor and an alcoholic, he married Maria Charlotta Borg, a priest's daughter who was nearly twenty years his junior. Weakened by drink, he died in an epidemic when Sibelius was just two. Sibelius's mother was left pregnant, in debt and destitution. She was a fervent Lutheran, cold, unaffectionate, and completely incapable of showing either the vital emotional warmth or physical closeness that her three children demanded, the youngest of whom, Sibelius's brother Christian, became a psychiatrist, while the oldest, his sister Linda, ended her life in a mental institution.

Aalto's family was also familiar with early death and illness. His mother, Selma Mathilda Hackstedt, came from an educated Swedish-speaking family and was keenly interested in issues of women's emancipation. Aalto's father, a caring but emotionally cold man, was from a farming background, and educated himself to become a land surveyor. Aalto's mother bore five children, of which Alvar was the second, before dying in their early childhood in 1906. Her first child died in infancy; the last, Selma, remained weak throughout childhood. Aalto's younger brother Einar killed himself at the start of the Winter War, in 1939.

Both Sibelius and Aalto's biographies suggest they experienced considerable psychological distress. As if speaking for them both, Sibelius confessed to his brother Christian on 21 November 1893: "I am often afraid of dying."[43] Nonetheless, both Sibelius and Aalto crucially had a childhood refuge—the realm of the Finnish forest—something that remained a creative stimulant throughout their lives. And arguably both addressed their biographical conflicts by creating (or one might argue by borrowing) a natural growth process through which to articulate complex unities or difficult wholes. Indeed if, as Freud suggested, creativity is a tool with which to adapt or relate to the external world, creative struggle may also be able to defend against anxiety and depression, pushing it from the foreground of conscious life. Thus the psyche may choose a creative defense as a mechanism for self-regulation, seeking to ameliorate or even resolve such conflicts in the long term, or simply fill (or at least plaster over) the divide. This is a less painful solution than the deep restlessness that characterizes the mass of repressed feelings in the "maternally deprived." As

Anthony Storr has suggested, "Creative people may be more divided than most of us, but . . . have an especial power of organisation and integrating opposites within themselves."[44] Given the trauma of their childhoods, to which they both referred in later life, Sibelius and Aalto's common desire to piece together small fragments into more complex wholes is a vivid example of self-maintenance or homeostasis: the positive adaptation in their art may also be a mechanism for the symbolic resolution of deep personal trauma rooted in insecurities surrounding childhood bereavements. Sibelius and Aalto used their inherent creativity to address, and even reorder these gaping deprivations of inner reality in symbolic form, informed by their tendency to syncretize disparate elements and to relate to the deprivation of the past. It can be argued that for both men the Finnish forest and nature's growth process was the bridge. Indeed, Aalto was later to discuss the fecundity of "continual renewal and growth" in his architectural creativity—in his case he also recognized this as something psychology demanded.[45]

The nature of the refuge or retreat that Sibelius and Aalto sought in the Finnish backwoods seemed to attract their interest again later, and retained a central place in their creative and personal lives. As adults, they both chose to explore forest culture. In the *Kalevala*, Sibelius had found an epic composed of fragments of individual runes: the seemingly endless lines Elias Lönnrot had recorded and synthesized were taken from an oral culture, created on the spur of the moment by singers from received narratives or folk tales, which they spontaneously wove into song: what the ethnologist Milman Parry called "composition in performance."[46] There was an attractive flexibility in this process—a way of enabling something larger to grow from small parts depending on the individual circumstance of its performance.

Aalto sensed something very similar in the backwoods way of making buildings—particularly as he was working for the Propaganda Office during the Second World War, when he began to be increasingly interested in the observation that deeper into the forest (and farther east in Finland) settlement patterns were less geometric and more "organically living and flexible forms." He also noted that in the east, the Swedish influence of the Lutheran Church (which resulted in buildings clustered in rectilinear formations as a sign of civilization) had noticeably less influence. Instead, an Orthodox, or even pagan influence remained.[47] Aalto challenged the views of some who maintained that the Euclidean logic of the Western tradition was inherently superior to the "chaotically fragmented" and "wretchedly disorganized" grouping of vernacular settlements in the East.[48] In eastern Finland, he believed, settlements tended to be determined through dialogue with their environmental context and more subtle indigenous or circumstantial forces. The Finnish architectural writer Juhani Pallasmaa has developed this idea and suggested: "Finns tend to organize space topologically on the basis of an amorphous 'forest geometry' as opposed to the 'geometry of town' that guides European thinking."[49] This is congruent with Aalto's repeated claims that a properly progressive modernism should be conceptually rooted in the nuances of nature, the symbolism of the natural world (that is, growth)[50] and its materiality (wood, stone, and water).[51] His model and inspiration, as his writings and designs testify, was the forest.[52] To Aalto, this way of connecting elements was an organic process resulting from the changing needs and character of inhabitation—responding to nature and to need.

Though Aalto's creative output has been described as "illogical,"[53] and Sibelius's turn to the natural world, for Adorno, was "deranged,"[54] there was an undeniable urge in both men to evolve an order from the content inherent in their work—resulting, perhaps, in a congruence between the backwoods forms they found in the Finnish forest and their own deeply psychological motivation. After his personal crisis and his sojourn to the Koli hills in 1909, Sibelius seemed to begin to look further backwards, beyond Lönnrot's *Kalevala* to the runes from which it had grown, to something about the way in which folksingers composed the lines in their minds as they rowed, sawed, or spun laboriously in the backwoods. The creative flexibility they demonstrated—the continual adjustment of words and runic fragments to their performing context and the circumstantial needs of the moment—particularly attracted Sibelius. He began to be interested in allowing a whole to grow from the parts, variously described as motives, germs, cells, or kernels: tiny fragments of sound that are allowed to grow, twist, mutate, and weave together into a larger whole. This process is exemplified best in his final large-scale composition, *Tapiola*. Scholars have debated whether *Tapiola* is a unity grown from a single theme, or whether indeed the core motive can be considered a theme at all. Erkki Salmenhaara, for example, has argued that "the starting point for total variation is not a theme unit but a germ motive," and that this "core" motive develops into at least four central, interconnected basic motives, which then branch into "around thirty highly characteristic, original and inimitably Sibelian musical motives."[55] In 1915, Sibelius described his creative process as one of assemblage: as though "God the Father had thrown down mosaic pieces . . . and asked me to put them back as they were."[56] He reported collecting fragments of musical ideas from various sources (including the color of new leaves and the cry of a passing crane), but he also suggested the presence of an overarching vision, allowing "their development in my spirit to fashion the formal shape of the piece."[57] From Sibelius's sketches, it seems as though a lengthy "trance-like" gestation was often necessary before the musical form suggested itself, a process that often coincided with deep depression.[58] The divine vision of Sibelius's "God the Father" was more often occluded than revealed. It is also significant that in his diaries Sibelius equated God with "the divine logos." One translation of logos is "to relate," and thus Sibelius may be associating God with the process of relating—whether in composition or in life.

In "The Trout and the Mountain Stream" (1947) Aalto similarly wrote of the importance of an incubation period in his creative process: "For a moment I forget all the maze of problems . . . I begin to draw in a manner rather like abstract art. Led only by my instincts . . . sometimes even childish compositions . . . I eventually arrive at an abstract basis for the main concept."[59] Here Aalto suggests that there must be a complete vision, one that draws together all of the fragmentary ideas; a notion, indeed, that Tawaststjerna and others have applied to Sibelius's work on his Fifth Symphony (1915–19).[60] Aalto, like Sibelius, was interested in exploring the crystallization of a whole form from its individual parts. Yet this consciously organicist approach to architecture, with its loose curves banishing all thought of parallel lines and perpendicular angles, is often thought to be at odds with the rational frame of Euclidean geometry. Aalto's practice was more complex and exacting, and resulted in a tightly governed compositional form that sought to wed functional rectilinearity with a more freeform approach to space in which the essence of the building was accommodated and revealed. Aalto attempted to understand the inner content of the architectural space itself, and allow the overall form to grow from this. In 1925 Hugo Häring (1882–1958), a modernist on the far edges of the CIAM (from which he was then excluded), said, "We want to examine things and allow them to discover their own images. It goes against our grain to bestow a form on them from outside."[61] Häring and his colleague, Hans Scharoun (1893–1972) called this *Leistungsform,* an undogmatic inquiry into what buildings "wanted to be." James Hepokoski has similarly identified the idea of 'content-based form' as central to Sibelius's work.[62] Indeed, Sibelius himself suggested the notion of such content-based forms by repeatedly referring to the "musical themes" or "thoughts" or "motives," which he felt "must create the form."[63]

Symphonies in Wood and Steel

The World's Fair in New York in 1939 came at another critical moment for Finland. When the Finnish Pavilion opened on 4 May, the Soviet Bear was making threatening noises toward its young neighbor. Finland urgently needed to demonstrate how far the nation had traveled, in political

and economic terms, since it had escaped the tsar's clutches in 1917. At
this moment, the creativity and fame of Finland's two greatest cultural
ambassadors, Aalto and Sibelius,[64] were called upon to direct the world's
attention to the plight of their remote land.[65] The imagery with which
Aalto chose to adorn the wall of the pavilion illustrated an army of
machines hauling logs from the backwoods for the pulp industry that provided Finland's most important source of external income (see Figure 4).
The symbolism was striking, as the majority of the rural Finnish population still wrestled a subsistence existence from the forest floor, and that
survival knowledge astonished the world as much as the Finnish spirit of
independence. Despite being grossly outnumbered in 1939, the Finns
held back the invading Red Army throughout the frigid conditions of the
Winter War, deep within the forests on Finland's eastern border. Alvar
Aalto was not among their number. At the outbreak of war, Aalto had run

Figure 4. Alvar Aalto, Finnish Pavilion, New York World's Fair, 1939.

away to Sweden, but he was subsequently found and ordered back to his post; he soon pulled strings to orchestrate his move from the regular army into the Propaganda Office in Helsinki, and from there he traveled to the States. His brother, a regular soldier, then committed suicide. Aalto's actions were perceived as cowardice by many, and eventually Aalto was ordered back from the States to resume his post. His personal terror was palpable, and his creative escape route out of this lifelong angst was already evident in his design for the New York pavilion.

Aalto and his wife and architectural partner, Aino, worked on the pavilion design together after winning between them the first three places in the design competition. Finland could not afford to construct a free-standing building from scratch, so the competition brief called for the design of an interior for one of a series of restrictive rectangular box-like enclosures within a large building rented from the New York Exposition Committee. The fact that a wooden wave had been chosen by the competition judges to represent Finland a year before underlined the urgency of such (expedient) conceptions of "Finnishness"—a political necessity for the nation's existence at that time. Indeed, the title of Aalto's winning competition entry, "Land, People, Work, Products," became the dominant motif throughout. The creation of an "image" for the nation was crucial in attracting attention to its fragile fledgling state. It is difficult now to conceive of there being no "image" of Finland, so deep has been the impact of Finnish image making today. Yet Aalto's capacity in 1939 to fantasize may have been pivotal in creating an "image" of Finland that the world could embrace and would at the same time draw attention to the threat of Soviet military intervention. It is interesting to note a comment from Aalto's biographer, Göran Schildt, regarding Aalto's "tendency to confuse his own wishes with reality," something that had a fundamental impact upon the pavilion interior.[66] Yet the forest fantasy in New York was yoked to an economic reality; the wave ceiling's undulating curve yielded just enough to Euclidean geometry to hold off the critics, and was emotive enough to stir the hearts of American visitors at a time of national crisis. Here, at least, Aalto's imaginative free reign simultaneously led him toward a new creative pragmatism.

The essence of Aalto's New York design was a kind of contrapuntal thinking: the desire to undermine the containing rectangularity of the rented "box" he was given while working within its geometrically ordered space. In answer to the brief, Aalto's introverted, top-lit solution cut an undulating line through the "box," and projected it upward to create an imposing serpentine wall that was adorned with enormous photographic images. The wooden waving wall was inclined toward the visitor in what some felt was a threatening way, although for others the effect was embracing and reassuring. Practically, the angle was intended as an aid to viewing the walls from a low level. However, it also served to create a sense of envelopment. Archive sketches show that Aalto drew the wall as though it were sliced through the wood, as if to inhabit it. These sketches seem to show that he thought of this structure as a forested wall as much as a representation of the northern lights—and that the inclined angle of the wall further supported its embracing gesture.

Aalto's form evolved architecturally using techniques developed from the philosophical notion of *symphysis*. Aalto's yearning for "synthesis" is revealed in the earliest sketches for the undulation in the New York "box"—an "argument" central to Aalto's compositional technique, according to Colin St. John Wilson, who suggests that it "can be epitomized by drawing two forms—an ideograph of two lines—one straight, the other serpentine . . . a complementarity between the rigorous plane of analysis and the turbulent wave-like surge of fantasy."[67] (See Figure 5.) Wilson argues that the horizontal "bar" and its formal partner (the wave) in Aalto's design create an "an axis of difference."[68] Aalto himself described this as "the simultaneous reconciliation of opposites."[69] In practical terms, these oppositions bring the dynamic and auxiliary functions of life together in many of his buildings. Aalto's sketches for the pavilion demonstrate that

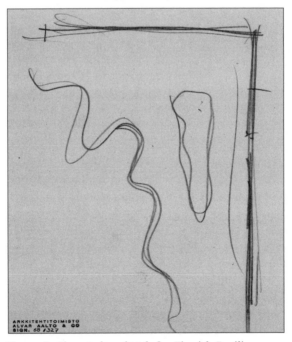

Figure 5. Alvar Aalto, sketch for Finnish Pavilion.

his notion of the "organic line" is never an unmitigated undulation, but is confined, in this case, by the "box" that anchors its exuberance, balancing the need for both containment and a capacity to reach out.[70] He felt that this required any "organic" gesture to hold firm within a Euclidean framework. But the undulation of the wave ceiling came to signify Aalto's humanist agenda, gesturing to the "little man," as he expressed it. Shallower still is the notion that the "wave" was self-referential since the word *aalto* means "wave" in Finnish, something Aalto, with his irreverent sense of humor, was happy to play on. (Sibelius's 1914 tone poem *The Oceanides* has the cognate Finnish title *Aallotaret*.) If we only read such totemic meanings in his compositions we miss his deeper, more challenging agenda—one that is gesturally close to Sibelius's intense dialogue between the pedal bass (or base) in his orchestral textures and the undulating, sometimes frenetically waving strings or woodwinds above.

Three significant elements can be identified in Aalto's design: a personal agenda, the wider socio-cultural context; and the formal composition. These elements are joined together by a continuum—the symbolism of a haven or refuge, in this case the forest or *Tapiola*. By 1939, such "forest geometries" were well established in Aalto's oeuvre, but in New York he inaugurated the wooden wave as a multivalent force.[71] It is no longer merely a design feature, but has become the primary sculptural tool for "carving" space out of the very nature of the wood—its tectonic malleability and its symbolic embrace becomes the mechanism for *symphysis*. Indeed, by suggesting that the pavilion had its own interior face or countenance,[72] Aalto revealed his desire to explore interiority—the visitor is immersed in Aalto's imaginary forest domain, much as listeners are immersed in the sound world of *Tapiola*, and as a result are invited to enter inside their own unconscious. In other words, Aalto's wave became a means of modeling the sense of interiority and psychological enclosure or containment he associated with the Finnish forest world.

Aalto was especially interested in the ideas of the classical world. As Leo Spitzer has shown, the ancient Greeks held that "the healthy soul is 'symphonic,' i.e., harmonious," and that this had a profound influence upon their notion of society. Aalto's pavilion has been described variously as "a harmonious whole," or like a "symphony."[73] We can better understand Aalto's reference by digging beneath the Greek etymon *sum*, which is an assimilated form of *sun* (with), relating it through *sumphonos* (sounding together) to *sumphusis* (growing together), a more suitable coupling in architectural terms. Importantly, the principles of harmony that Aalto repeatedly invoked are based on the Heraclitian idea of "mutual adjustment," the forging of a balance between consonance and dissonance.[74] The key to this principle is the idea of *harmos*—the etymon of *harmonia*, meaning "joint"—which, for Aalto, brings an abstract philosophical notion back to the physical realm, the joining of dissimilar and disparate elements in a more concrete sense. This idea became central to Aalto's compositional technique in New York and beyond. Indeed, it seems to become an ideal mode of thought toward which Aalto strove increasingly. To this end, he developed the notion that "architecture is thus a kind of supra-technological form of creation, and the harmonization of many disparate forms of activity is central to it."[75]

This principle of the "the harmonization of many disparate forms of activity" also relies upon the Heraclitian notion of *harmonia,* the mechanism through which the disparate elements are joined or coupled together. Heraclitus wrote that "what is at variance is in agreement with itself: a back-turning (*palintropos harmonia*)." This definition of *harmonia* calls for a form or structure to illustrate it by comprising "mutual adjustment" and conjunction (Frag. 10), where the relationship of consonance and dissonance together illuminate different aspects of God or the divine (*logos*). It is important that for neither Heraclitus nor any other Greeks did such systems function like a law or a rule, since the overarching *kosmos* (natural order) was the scene of a constant struggle between opposed forces. But not everyone experienced Aalto's New York pavilion as a modernist "integrated presentation," let alone a unified "symphony" of elements.[76] The correspondent for the *Architectural Review,* for example, found that too much was "crammed" in, creating a "general confusion," reminiscent more of a cacophony than a symphony.[77] Indeed, it might be said that the pavilion was a demonstration of the tension within and between forms—a dialogue between radically different elements.[78] The pavilion thus could be said to have created a more precarious symbolic resolution of the tension, argument, or relationship between its conflicting parts.[79] Here, the building evokes a "tension of betweenness," to borrow Colin St. John Wilson's phrase.[80]

On Forest Paths: Aalto, Sibelius, and *Tapiola*

The common urge to relate the disparate, shared by Sibelius and Aalto, is especially apparent in their mature works. The two Finns draw unlike elements into a complex whole—small elements "grow" into complex entities where, for some, any loose sense of harmoniousness is absent. Critically, an idea of harmony rooted in the Greek word *harmos* is the essence of the composition, and these difficult joinings are often the most profound moments of their work. The precise form of that "joint," or coming together of the disparate, is critical to the overall success of the whole—be it the rising and falling strings against a pedal bass, or a waving ceiling against rectilinear walls and floor. Indeed, these joinings often comprise extraordinary boundaries, junctions, and interfaces between compositional elements.

After 1925, Finland and the world waited for Sibelius to compose a path beyond *Tapiola*—in vain. It could be said that he was lost in Tapio's realm, having found a fully integrated sound world in his final tone poem. Aalto's 1939 pavilion demonstrates a moment when, in aesthetic and symbolic terms, he joined Sibelius in the forest domain. In 1900, Gallen-Kallela's frescos had evoked a powerfully national romantic portrait of Finland's mythological past. But in 1939, Aalto's massive black and white photographs represented the contemporary reality of an industrialized, resource-based economy. Aalto's expressive turn was crucial, both economically (through the projection of the natural and commercial abundance of the forest) and creatively (the pavilion interior demonstrated the germ of his maturing creative genre). Sibelius's contribution was emotionally moving in a more traditional way: it was not *Tapiola* that wafted through the Finnish Pavilion, but a more modest piece, the Andante Festivo. Sibelius was called out of retirement twice to conduct performances of the Andante in Finland, both of which were broadcast in the United States—once by Olin Downes on New Year's Day 1939, and again on 4 May the same year for the opening of the New York pavilion.[81] By the time the pavilion opened, "American enthusiasm for Sibelius reached a peak." Yet the choice of the Andante Festivo to accompany Aalto's creative vision at the opening ceremony was probably not Sibelius's own, and it arguably failed to do either Sibelius or Aalto justice.[82] The work's stirring patriotism meant that it had already been adopted for state occasions, and this added a more conventional formality to the proceedings. Had *Tapiola* been played instead, Finland would have offered a work as mystical and as disturbing as many found Aalto's pavilion. But it might also have repelled listeners, instead of stirring their hearts, and tightened the purse strings of the free world at an acute time of crisis for the young nation-state.

Sibelius is reported to have maintained that "if you don't create an artificial pedal for your orchestration there will be holes in it." He explained that "the orchestra . . . is a huge and wonderful instrument that has got everything—except the pedal." Without the artificial pedal, "some passages will sound ragged."[83] Sibelius's "basic formula" of melodic decoration—his characteristic scalar figures and "circular motives" or melodic impulses—is invariably heard against such pedal points, creating a complex undulating wave or tapestry of sound. As James Hepokoski has argued, such pedal points can control large expanses of musical time and space, energetically underpinning the music's teleological sense of cadential motion in counterpoint with the more localized tendency toward circular stasis.[84] Like Aalto, Sibelius sought to ground such activity in the constant combination and development of smaller melodic gestures or ideas. Such "pedals" are apparent in virtually all of his work, and can be equated with the strong horizontal emphasis—the "base lines"—in Aalto's work, or even the box in which the New York pavilion had to be conceived. This led to formal diversity in which the anchor element (Sibelius's pedal or Aalto's horizontal beam) acts as a "plane of analysis."[85]

From Viipuri Library (1927–35) onward, Aalto explored the relationship between waving contours and straight lines as expressions of the diverse functions in buildings. The "pedal" for Aalto is a unifying, grounding edge, a rationale from which the tangential, expressive walls may grow. Indeed, it could be argued that the wall permits the undulating form of the waving wall to expand, like an anchor that grounds the building in order to avoid chaos or drift. The pedal is demonstrated most clearly in Baker House (1946–49), the House of Culture (1955–58), and the Neue Vahr Apartment Block (1958–62). Most of the cross-sections through Aalto's buildings indicate his careful manipulation of their respective heights and depths. He used changes in floor levels to emphasize the distinct symbolic character of spaces within open plan areas. The section of the New York pavilion shows the use of different levels to distinguish different functions (see Figure 4)—a three-dimensional manipulation of space. In some instances Aalto used the pedal as a vertical as well as a horizontal anchor. Indeed, just as Aalto's anchoring horizontality changes levels with the content (or function) of the space (the restaurant above the ground floor exhibition area in the pavilion, looking across the full height space toward the inclining wooden wall), so Sibelius's pedal mechanism is rarely rooted on a single pitch. The function of the pedal remains constant whatever the change in its position relative to the activity around it. In other words, it is an element of stasis in relation to which other activity is dynamic. For example, in the Seventh Symphony, between rehearsal letters H and I, the brass presents a pulsating pedal that is tonally ambivalent but "firm" (rooted) in its dissonance (see Example 1). In *Tapiola* there are long passages of undulating strings "weaving their magic"[86] above the long pedal bass line that changes pitch (for example, between rehearsal letters K and L), the "land of shadows" between the perpetual oppositions of tonality, form, and structure.[87]

Aalto's work is frequently characterized by spaces that expand and contract, whether or not they are "waving." Changes in the floor level (the anchor or pedal in an architectural section) are often calculated in response to a shift in another level of the form, creating a kind of syncopation. In his library design at Viipuri, for instance, Aalto manipulated the roofline in accordance with the lighting requirements for the shelving and reading

Example 1. Sibelius, Seventh Symphony, from rehearsal letter H.

spaces below. In other words, the differentiation of the spatial functions is articulated both at roof and at floor level; a diminution or expansion of the resultant space between the two levels serves to create and manipulate the existing spatial tension. Sibelius's music is similarly characterized by musical passages that grow and compress, often at an extremely fast tempo. In some instances this occurs through the use of contrary motion (analogous to Aalto's syncopated floor levels), or the simultaneous rising and falling, crossing of instrumental lines over a stabilizing, grounding pedal in the bass. In the Allegro at the end of *Tapiola* (measure 513; see Tomi Mäkelä's discussion of this passage, Example 5, in his essay in this volume), a hectic oscillating motion begins in the strings, from which a crescendo rises in the brass at letter Q, attempting to establish an anchoring pedal episode. There is no immediate resolution, however, and the strings continue in a fantasy-like frenzy: the famous storm sequence with which the tone poem concludes. Here they are again challenged by an extended pedal: after finally being anchored in measure 564, they are yoked back into a long falling passage, after which the whole of the orchestra's power is discharged by a new pedal leading to rehearsal letter R.

At an intuitive level, therefore, both the pavilion and *Tapiola* became experiences of mediation: the phenomenological evocation of a space (in architecture or music) within which one may access a personal (inner) reality or gain an externalized representation of Finland and its modern forest industry. In this way, both Aalto's Finnish Pavilion and Sibelius's tone poem can be understood as "transitional objects" through which the inner life of an individual and their outer world can be simultaneously related: "Those damned realities which make up our work," as Aalto put it.[88] Here is an example of Aalto's penchant for connecting the practical with the personal—something that he had honed during his many episodes of personal collapse in which (he intimates) he learned the importance of "humanism" (the presence of psycho-social elements) in the built environment.[89] This capacity to trigger the inner world of the individual and thus allow aspects of the self to bleed into the experience of the outer place adds to the richness of the architectural experience, and of Sibelius's greatest music. In New York, one of Aalto's greatest achievements was to use this imagery of the forest, with all its practical and symbolic associations, to speak not only to the Finns but also to humanity as a diverse whole.[90]

Journeys End

In the 1900 Paris pavilion, Finland had sought to create a "window open to Europe," drawing on an established set of cultural agendas from the center to the northern periphery. But in New York in 1939, Aalto was happy to be offered a windowless edifice in which the Finnish Pavilion could dwell, generating its own, unique forest geometries. It is interesting to ask why Aalto's creative "idea" needed to be "scientifically" based, and not simply justified in its own creative, metaphorical terms. Just as the pedal binds the raging undulating strings in Tapiola, so, in a way, the pavilion could "hold" itself "together." The "box" in which the undulation occurs gives structure to the experience. Aalto believed form and content should be indivisibly melded together in the minds of architects,[91] and in this case the melding was deeply rooted in the use of wood—the material (from mater) that best meets the human need for "primary comfort."[92] It is at this level that Aalto challenges the limited rationalism of architectural modernism, suggesting that such functionalism must be "enlarged to cover even the psychological field."[93] In the New York pavilion he addressed this architectural imperative directly with a "disquieting," "threatening" forested interior that leans in toward visitors, engulfing them, somehow, in the hinterlands of their own minds.

It is telling that Aalto's New York pavilion was not widely reported in Finland, and only later did the Finns recognize that Aalto's architectural gestures were intended to serve as signifiers of themselves, their experiences, and their place in the world. In many senses, what Aalto created in the pavilion, like Sibelius in *Tapiola*, was a spatial drama of universal relevance and appeal: a complex set of gestures that spoke to many strata of the human condition, and not merely the physical experience of dwelling in Finland's northern climate. Although the pavilion seemed to be waving, desperately, to the free world, Finland itself was largely oblivious to its gesture. It was nonetheless an effective piece of political propaganda. Moments before his retreat from active war service, Aalto's pavilion threw down a gauntlet to international modernism, offering a significant conjunction of creativity and personal vulnerability. Similarly, by presenting a multileveled representation of contemporary Finland in the late 1930s, rooted in aspects of the forest culture past and present, collective and personal, conscious and unconscious, Aalto sought to yoke Finnish culture both backwards to the heart of the woods and forward to the heart of the twentieth century. Thus, on his nation's urgent behalf, Aalto waved to the wider world before retreating to a Stockholm hotel to escape the war, just as Sibelius, a decade earlier, had remained trapped in the silence of *Tapiola*'s wake. *Tapiola*, not the Andante Festivo, would have been the most appropriate accompaniment to Aalto's pavilion—and a mirror of Aalto's own deep affiliation with nature. But perhaps *Tapiola* would have been too risky, too disturbing a symbiotic cry from the deep—and the romantic air of Andante Festivo was more effective in moving sympathetic citizens to donate their money and support to Finland's cause. Yet the profound psycho-spiritual resonances between Aalto and Sibelius's work acknowledges a deeper level of existence—however difficult or disturbing such journeys may become.

NOTES

This paper is dedicated to the memory of two friends and mentors, Dr. Antony Storr and Prof. Sir Colin St. John Wilson.

1. Glenda Dawn Goss quotes Karl Flodin's description of how Sibelius's music conveyed "the peaceful, profound, serious, and melancholy splendors of Finnish nature and the national epic," going on to cite contemporary reviews in which observers saw "Finlanders who literally shook with musical power, and thereby roused the entire audience. . . . The soul of Finland was palpable." Goss, *Sibelius: A Composer's Life and the Awakening of Finland* (Chicago: University of Chicago Press, 2009), 284–85.

2. See Salme Sarajas-Korte, "Visual Arts at the Turn of the Century: From Paris to the Backwoods of Karelia," in *Suomen tekijät: Finland Creators*, ed. Kerttu Karvonen-Kannas and Kirsi Kaisla (Punkaharju: Taidekeskus Retrietti, 1992), 53–83; see also Erik Tawaststjerna, *Sibelius*, vol. 1, *1865–1905*, trans. Robert Layton (London: Faber and Faber, 1976), chaps. 6–10; and Aimo Reitala, *From Folklore to Applied Arts: Aspects of Finnish Culture* (Lahti: University of Helsinki, 1993), 72–73.

3. In Juhani Pallasmaa, ed., *Hvitträsk: The Home as a Work of Art* (Helsinki: Museum of Finnish Architecture, 1987), 124.

4. Goss, *Sibelius*, 35–37.

5. See Riitta Nikula, *Architecture and Landscape: The Building of Finland* (Helsinki: Otava, 1993), 87–93.

6. Sarajas-Korte, "Visual Arts," 62. See also Paula Suhonen, "A City and the Call of the Wilds," in Karvonen-Kannas, *Finland Creators*, 21–51; and Pekka Korvenmaa, "Forest and Metropolis," in *Finland Creators*, 123–49.

7. Vilhelm Helander and Simo Rista, *Modern Architecture in Finland* (Helsinki: Kirjayhtymä, 1993; repr. 1987), 17

8. Kerstin Smeds, "The Image of Finland at the World Exhibitions 1990–1992," in *The Finland Pavilions*, ed. Peter B. McKeith and Kerstin Smeds (Helsinki: Kustannus Oy City, 1992), 20.

9. Sarah Menin, "Aalto, Sibelius and Fragments from Forest Culture," in *Sibelius Forum: Proceedings from the Second International Jean Sibelius Conference, Helsinki, 25–29 November 1995*, ed. Veijo Murtomäk, Kari Kilpeläinen, and Risto Väisenän (Helsinki: Sibelius Academy, 1998), 347–55; also Menin, "Fragments from the Forest: Aalto's Requisitioning of Forest Place and Matter," *Journal of Architecture* 6/3 (Autumn 2001): 279–305; and Menin, "'Soap Bubbles Floating in the Air': Why Jean Might Drink 'Spring Water' with Alvar Not 'Cocktails' with Eliel," in *Sibelius Forum II: Proceedings from the Third International Jean Sibelius Conference, 7–10 December 2000*, ed. Matti Huttonen, Kari Kilpeläinen, and Veijo Murtomäki (Helsinki: Sibelius Academy, 2003), 8–14.

10. Smeds, "The Image of Finland," 17.

11. Tawaststjerna, *Sibelius*, 1:223.

12. I. K. Inha, "Commentary," in *The Village Library Illustrated Magazine* (1900), quoted in Riitta Nikula, *Wood, Stone and Steel: Contours of Finnish Architecture* (Keuruu: Otava, 2005), 100.

13. Tawaststjerna, *Sibelius*, 1:225.

14. Sibelius, letter to Aino dated 27 July 1900, quoted in Tawaststjerna, *Sibelius*, 1:230.

15. In her analysis of Finnish-French musical relations at this time, Helena Tyrväinen suggests many Finnish events were more politically than culturally motivated; in "Sibelius at the Paris Universal Exposition of 1900," in Murtomäki, *Sibelius Forum II*, 114–28, quote at 124.

16. Gustaf Strengell and Sigurd Frosterus, "Arkkitehtuuri: taistelukirjoitus" (Architecture: A Challenge), in *Abacus 3*, ed. Asko Salokorpi and Maija Kärkkäinen (Helsinki:

Museum of Finnish Architecture, 1983), 49–81. The article is a Finnish and English translation of the Swedish "Arkitektur: En stridskrift våra motståndare tillägnad" (Helsinki: Euterpas Förlag, 1904).

17. Strengel and Frosterus, "Arkkitehtuuri," 59.

18. Ibid., 70.

19. Tawaststjerna, *Sibelius*, 1:98.

20. Sibelius in conversation with a German publisher, quoted in Cecil Gray, *Sibelius* (London: Oxford University Press, 1931), 11. See also the opening lines of Erik Furuhjelm's biography, translated in the Documents section of this volume.

21. Strengell and Frosterus, "Arkkitehtuuri," 51.

22. Aleksis Kivi, "The Bear Hunt," in *Odes*, ed. and trans. Keith Bosley (Helsinki: Finnish Literature Society, 1994), 33.

23. See Sarah Menin, "'Let Us Be Finns': The Conquest of the Backwoods Front (The use of folkloric music and architecture by elite aesthetes in 1890s Finland in their search for Finnishness)," in *Cultural Conquests 1500–2000,* ed. Tim Kirk and Luda Klusakova (Prague: Karolinum, 2009), 121–32.

24. James Maude Richards, *800 Years of Finnish Architecture* (London: David and Charles, 1978), 9.

25. Matti Klinge, *Let Us Be Finns* (Helsinki: Otava 1992), 143.

26. Tawaststjerna, *Sibelius*, vol. 2, *1904–1914,* trans. Robert Layton (London: Faber and Faber, 1986), 67.

27. Sibelius, 20 May 1918, in Karl Ekman, *Jean Sibelius: His Life and Personality* (New York: Knopf, 1938), 154–55.

28. Anthony Storr, *The Dynamics of Creation* (Harmondsworth: Penguin, 1972), 252.

29. Adrian Stokes, "Form in Art," in *New Directions in Psychoanalysis* (London: Tavistock, 1955), 413–18

30. Tawaststjerna, *Sibelius*, 2:177.

31. Ibid., 2:262.

32. Tim Howell, *Jean Sibelius: Progressive Techniques in Symphonies and Tone Poems* (London: Garland, 1990), 74.

33. Sibelius, quoted in Bengt de Törne, *Sibelius: A Close-Up* (London: Faber and Faber, 1937), 94.

34. Alvar Aalto, unpublished, undated article in Aalto Archive, Helsinki.

35. Aalto was accused of being a Bolshevik by conservative architects in Helsinki, and responded, rising and giving the individual who voiced this view "a box on the ear," according to Aalto's biographer, Göran Schildt, *Alvar Aalto: The Decisive Years* (New York: Rizzoli, 1986), 87.

36. Le Corbusier, *Towards a New Architecture* (London: Architectural Press, 1982), 10.

37. Alvar Aalto, "The Humanizing of Architecture" (1940), repr. in *Alvar Aalto: Sketches,* ed. Göran Schildt (Cambridge, MA: MIT Press, 1985), 76.

38. Colin St. John Wilson, *The Other Tradition of Modern Architecture* (London: Academy, 1995).

39. Alvar Aalto, "The Relationship," in *Alvar Aalto in His Own Words,* ed. Göran Schildt (New York: Rizzoli, 1998), 267–68.

40. Alvar Aalto, "The Reconstruction of Europe Is the Key Problem for the Architecture of our Times" (1941), repr. in Salokorpi, *Abacus 3,* 121–42.

41. Sibelius, 20 May 1918, quoted in Ekman, *Jean Sibelius,* 154–55.

42. Tawaststjerna, *Sibelius*, 1:7.

43. Sibelius, 21 November 1893, quoted in ibid., 1:149.

44. Storr, *The Dynamics of Creation,* 282

45. Aalto, "Rationalism and Man," lecture at the Swedish Crafts Society, 9 May 1935, in Schildt, *Sketches,* 47–51, quotation at 50.

46. Milman Parry, *The Making of Homeric Verse: The Collected Papers of Milman Parry*, ed. Adam Parry (Oxford: Clarendon Press, 1971).

47. Aalto, "Architecture in Karelia" (1941), in Schildt, *Sketches*, 82.

48. Lars Sonck, "The Arrangement of Our Small Towns" (1904), repr. in Salokorpi, *Abacus 3*, 42. Sonck was a leading Finnish architect at the start of the twentieth century and the designer of Sibelius's villa, Ainola.

49. Juhani Pallasmaa, "Tradition and Modernity: Feasibility of Regional Architecture in the Post-Modern Society," *Arkkitehti* 3 (1993): 17–30.

50. Aalto, "Finland as a Model for World Development" (1949), in Schildt, *Alvar Aalto in His Own Words*, 171.

51. Aalto, "The Architecture of Karelia" (1941), in Schildt, *Sketches*, 80–83. Although he claimed not to have a feeling for folklore, Aalto admitted feeling that "the traditions that bind us lie more in the climate, in the material conditions, in the nature of the tragedies and comedies that have touched us." Conversation between Aalto and Schildt (1967), in Schildt, *Alvar Aalto in His Own Words*, 171.

52. See Sarah Menin, "Fragments from the Forest: Aalto's Requisitioning of Forest Place and Matter," *Journal of Architecture* 6 (Autumn 2001): 279–305.

53. Sigfried Giedion, *Space, Time, and Architecture: The Growth of a New Tradition* (Cambridge, MA: MIT Press, 1942), 77

54. Theodor W. Adorno, "Glosse über Sibelius," *Zeitschrift für Sozialforschung* 6 (1938), repr. in *Impromptus* (Frankfurt am Main: Suhrkamp, 1968), 247–52. A translation appears in the Documents section of this volume.

55. Errki Salmenhaara, *Sibelius* (Helsinki: Tammi, 1970), 124.

56. Tawaststjerna, *Sibelius*, vol. 3, *1919–1957*, trans. Robert Layton (London: Faber and Faber, 1997), 18.

57. Ibid.

58. Santeri Levas, *Jean Sibelius* (Porvoo: Werner Söderström, 1972), 82.

59. Aalto, "The Trout and the Mountain Stream," in Schildt, *Sketches*, 96.

60. Tawaststjerna, *Sibelius*, vol. 3, chap. 2.

61. Hugo Häring, "Die Wege zur Form," *Die Form* 1 (October 1925): 16–17.

62. James Hepokoski, *Sibelius: Symphony No. 5* (Cambridge: Cambridge University Press, 1993), 21.

63. Sibelius, 22–23 April 1912, quoted in Ferrucio Tammaro, *Jean Sibelius* (Torino: ERI, 1984), 139.

64. This was the one and only meeting of the creative energies of Finland's two most famous creative sons. See Sarah Menin, "The Profound Logos: Creative Parallels in the Lives and Work of Aalto and Sibelius," *Journal of Architecture* 8 (Spring 2003): 131–48, and Menin, "Aalto, Sibelius and Fragments from Forest Culture."

65. Finland was a pawn between Germany and the USSR at this time. A secret agreement between Hitler and Stalin, signed on 23 August 1939, gave Finland to the Soviets and Poland to the Nazis. Russia invaded Finland on 30 November 1939. See Eino Jutikkala and Kauko Pirinen, *A History of Finland* (Helsinki: Weilin and Göös, 1984), 247–49.

66. Göran Schildt, *Alvar Aalto: The Mature Years* (New York: Rizzoli, 1991), 47.

67. Colin St. John Wilson, "Alvar Aalto and the State of Modernism" (1979), in *Alvar Aalto vs. the Modern Movement*, ed. Kirmo Mikkola (Helsinki: Rakennuskirja, 1981), 121.

68. Douglas Graf, "Strange Siblings—Being and No-Thinness: An Inadvertent Homage to Ray and Charles Eames," *DATUTOP 14* (Tampere: Tampere University of Technology, 1991), 14. See also Gareth Griffiths, "The Polemical Aalto," *DATUTOP 19* (Tampere: Tampere University of Technology, 1997).

69. Aalto, "Art and Technology," in Schildt, *Sketches*, 125–29, at 127.

70. In the Lapua Forest Pavilion of 1938 (designed during the construction of the Finnish Pavilion), there is no such argument, since the whole pavilion, carried out by Aalto's

assistant Jarl Jaatinen, has become a pure undulation, unchallenged by any Euclidean frame—and consequently, it may be argued, loses its power.

71. Pallasmaa, "Tradition and Modernity," 17–30.

72. Aalto, quoted in Schildt, *Decisive Years*, 173.

73. See Karl Fleig, *Alvar Aalto*, 3rd ed. (Zurich: Architektur Artemis, 1992), 74; and Fleig, *Alvar Aalto: Complete Works, 1922–1962* (Basel: Birkhauser Verlag, 1990), 1130.

74. See Heraclitus, *The Cosmic Fragments* (Cambridge: Cambridge University Press, 1962), Frag. 51. See also Edward Hussey, *The Presocratics* (London: Duckworth, 1972), 44–47.

75. Aalto, "The Reconstruction of Europe," 154.

76. Richard Weston, *Alvar Aalto* (London: Phaidon, 1995), 113.

77. Anon., "Finnish Pavilion, New York World's Fair," *Architectural Review* (August 1939), 64.

78. Aalto, "Art and Technology," lecture on installation into the Finnish Academy, 3 October 1955, repr. in Schildt, *Sketches*, 125.

79. Aalto and Fleig refer to "synthesis" in reference to the New York pavilion. Indeed, Aalto increasingly used the word in later essays and interviews: for example, in conversation with Schildt in 1967, Aalto suggested that "what is needed is synthesis." Published as "Conversation," in Schildt, *Sketches*, 170.

80. Colin St. John Wilson, "The Natural Imagination," in *Architectural Reflections* (Oxford: Butterworth, 1992), 16.

81. Ironically, a radio engineer accidentally broadcast a rehearsal led by a different conductor, and not Sibelius's own performance as intended. Glenda Dawn Goss, *The Sibelius Companion* (London: Greenwood Press, 1996), 278.

82. For Robert Layton, the work is "indifferent." *Sibelius* (London: Dent, 1978), 90.

83. Sibelius, in de Törne, *Sibelius: A Close-Up*, 30–31.

84. Hepokoski, *Sibelius: Symphony No. 5*, 280

85. Wilson, *Architectural Reflections*, 91.

86. Taken from the quatrain printed at the head of the *Tapiola* score.

87. Similar activity in *Tapiola* and the Sixth is underpinned by extreme stasis, "a deep-current slow motion." Hepokoski, *Sibelius: Symphony No. 5*, 28.

88. Aalto, letter to Giedion, Autumn 1930, quoted in Schildt, *Decisive Years*, 66.

89. Aalto, "The Humanizing of Architecture," 76–79.

90. Aalto, "World's Fair," in Schildt, *Sketches*, 65.

91. It is significant that when he fled to New York in 1940 and began to compose the book *Finland Builds* (which accompanied the reopening of the pavilion), Aalto was also preoccupied with reconstructing Finland. His subsequent concept of "the growing house," rooted in his (partly erroneous) understanding of the adaptability of Karelian houses, was explored in his propaganda article "The Architecture of Karelia," *Uusi Suomi* (2 November 1941), repr. in Schildt, *Alvar Aalto in His Own Words*, 115–19.

92. Alvar and Aino Aalto, "Suomen New Yorkin näyttelyn rakenne ja yleissuunnitelma" (Finland New York the exhibition design and master plan), n.d., "New York 1939–40" file, Finnish Fair Corporation Archive (Helsinki).

93. Aalto, "The Humanizing of Architecture," 76.

Old Masters:

Jean Sibelius and Richard Strauss

in the Twentieth Century

LEON BOTSTEIN

Music, Language, and the Visual:
The Divergent Paths of Sibelius and Strauss

Jean Sibelius and Richard Strauss were born a year and a half apart, in December 1865 and June 1864 respectively. They were contemporaries within the same generation of European artists and musicians. Both lived remarkably long lives and survived two world wars. By the outbreak of World War I they were well established as leading figures not only in their respective regional and national communities and throughout Europe, but also in North America—which Strauss visited in 1904, and Sibelius in 1914, to great acclaim.

For Sibelius and Strauss, the years immediately preceding World War I and the war years themselves were a watershed. The radical changes in politics and society the war had sparked deepened a process of self-criticism and dissatisfaction that had already begun before 1914. The year 1911 marked a turning point for both composers. Sibelius completed his more overtly innovative and modernist sounding Fourth Symphony. *Der Rosenkavalier* had its premiere. The opera came to be regarded as marking Strauss's turn away from modernism onto a reactionary path of compositional practice in which he flaunted, cynically, a historicist aesthetic.

The period between the outbreak of war and 1926 witnessed many of Sibelius's finest works. But by 1930 Sibelius had begun what would be a startling thirty-year period of silence. Strauss, in contrast, kept composing through the 1930s and early '40s against the grain of the self-consciously modern. He continued to write music in the wake of the physical and moral destruction of World War II. For Strauss, the period between 1945 and 1949 (the year of his death) were an "Indian summer." Using an overt neoclassical strategy evocative of the eighteenth century, he produced an array of bitter-sweet, nostalgic, and intimate works. Sibelius died in 1957 as a revered national icon more than seven years after Strauss. His reputation, however, rested on music composed a half-century earlier, in which he perfected an unmistakable style and sound. The meaning and cause of the silence that came afterward have remained hidden from view.

Sibelius and Strauss enjoyed an embarrassing and, to varying degrees, self-inflicted popularity during the Third Reich. From 1933 to 1945 they were both ideological symbols of nationalist cultural pride and did little to deter official patronage, despite their personal misgivings about politics. Strauss's contempt for musical modernism and resentment for his status during the 1920s as marginal and outmoded led him to embrace the Nazis' call for a restoration of "healthy" musical culture. Strauss served as president of the Reichsmusikkammer, the State Music Bureau, despite the vulnerability of his daughter-in-law under Nazi racialist law. Strauss's shocking opportunism with respect to his own career, which made collaboration reasonable, also led to his falling into disfavor and isolation under the regime. After 1945 he was forced to confront his awkward collaboration with the Nazis. In contrast, Sibelius, enshrined as a Finnish national symbol well before the rise of fascism in Europe, emerged unscathed by his connections to and relative prominence in the cultural politics of Nazi Germany.[1]

Sibelius deliberately cultivated an image as elegant, severe, and bald.[2] Ironically, he came to embody modern Finland even though he identified with the beleaguered Swedish-speaking minority from which he came. He was not overtly political. A supporter of the "White" side during the Finnish Civil War of 1918, he feared mass democracy, nationalist populism, and the political Left. He harbored nostalgia for the social and cultural legacy of the monarchical and aristocratic nineteenth century in which he came of age. Strauss's attitude to politicians and politics, which dated from the 1890s, was far more derisive. He never wavered from a cynical focus on the advantages or disadvantages a regime offered his own career, standing, and income. As the symbol of a "non-degenerate" aesthetic tradition, he was flattered to be at the center of controversy about the future of German culture before and after the Nazi seizure of power. Statistics on repertoire performed during the Nazi era reveal that Strauss was the most often performed living German composer, and Sibelius the most popular foreign living composer.[3] Neither objected or complained.

Even before their accommodation to German fascism became a factor, Strauss and Sibelius shared the distinction of hostility from modernists and their apologists. This strain in criticism flourished pointedly after 1945. Both earned the scorn of T. W. Adorno.[4] Strauss was accorded grudging respect for his craft and achievements before 1911. Sibelius, in contrast, was dismissed as at best a local northern novelty, limited in his abilities as a composer. His music was too facile, simplistic, and popular.[5] Astonishing longevity earned both Strauss and Sibelius the reputation of having outlived their time. They were relics of a bygone age. Worse, for different reasons their music was viewed as affirmative of, if not complicit with, an aesthetic suggestive (if not supportive) of ethical indifference to injustice, human exploitation, and exclusionary ideologies of community. Such criticism never had much impact on the public. Sibelius and Strauss— particularly Sibelius—remained wildly popular well into the 1950s, especially in England and America, much to the chagrin of competitors, notably Stravinsky, Schoenberg, and Copland.[6]

Having receded into the background as old-fashioned and politically suspect during the heyday of midcentury modernism, Sibelius and Strauss emerged at the end of the twentieth century as dominant figures of influence. No longer marginal, they became representative figures of the twentieth century, harbingers of postmodernism, and suggestive of music's future. Sibelius in particular offered a model of an alternative modernism. Together they vindicated the potential of a tradition of an accessible and expressive eclectic musical discourse in contemporary life.

The most striking similarities and parallels between Sibelius and Strauss concern biography and reception. What justifies a closer look at these two composers together, however, is their shared musical inheritance, particularly the legacy of Liszt. Like Liszt, Sibelius and Strauss experimented in their orchestral music with the nature of form. They utilized tonality and a musical rhetoric derived from the classicism of the late eighteenth century and the Romanticism of the nineteenth. They continued Liszt's effort to transcend a purely formalist conception of instrumental music and extend music's capacity to narrate and communicate "poetically," albeit uniquely, alongside philosophy, literature, and the visual arts.

As members of a post-1848 generation, they were compelled to ask: how should one write music after Wagner and Brahms? Wagner's charismatic originality in harmonic usage, instrumentation, and the use of musical motives as signifiers extended the narrative power of music, but his conceit that there was a progressive trajectory in history explicitly devalued classicism and the traditions of instrumental music. Brahms, representing the anti-Wagnerian, revealed the crippling burden of classicism and a daunting self-conscious sensibility of lateness, one that overwhelmed Brahms himself.[7] How can a composer respond in a moment in history that seems at the end of a cultural tradition yet is suffused with palpable material and social change and the unmistakable imperatives of the present moment?

Strauss was forced to ponder these issues, given his contact with Brahms and such Wagnerians as Hans von Bülow and Alexander Ritter, let alone his father and his closest contemporaries and rivals, from Mahler and Pfitzner to Schoenberg. The attempt to segregate Sibelius from the currents of European culture because of his unique status as the voice and representative of the youthfully self-aware Finland and unique landscape (often described inaccurately) is not persuasive, as many recent scholars have noted.[8] Sibelius's awareness of European trends, from his encounter with Ferruccio Busoni in Helsinki to his studies in Berlin and Vienna and his frequent travels abroad, contradict any reductive construct of him as provincial or naïvely Finnish. He came of age confronting the same cosmopolitan musical culture Strauss faced and was forced to deal with the same issues Strauss struggled with after the end of the nineteenth century.

The central challenge posed by the realities of the pre– and post–World War I period was the sense that one was living, spiritually and philosophically (in terms of epistemology, if not ethics and politics), at a historical moment of decay, decline, and confusion, in a world beset with consternation and fear about culture, civility, and fundamental questions of meaning and value. Progress in everything but the most crassly material seemed to have ground to a halt. Industry and science may have been sufficient to transform everyday life, but their radical success left a spiritual vacuum. Artists in all fields, whether music, literature, or the visual arts, felt required to respond to questions on the nature and purpose of art with more than a dutiful continuation of past practice defended in terms of historical tradition. The sense of discontinuity and philosophical emptiness prevailed after 1918.[9]

Sibelius and Strauss sensed the disintegration of old assumptions and realities keenly, and their music reflected their struggle to continue their callings and commitments as composers. They were both prone to a thinly veiled pessimism, often masked by nostalgia or self-indulgence, particularly at the end of their careers, as Strauss's 1943 wind sonatina, "From the Workshop of an Invalid," and Sibelius's 1925 miniature melodrama, "The Lonely Ski Trail," suggest. Both sought refuge in an idiosyncratic reassertion of classicist ideals in their last works. Strauss used extended classical form and thematic figuration, punctuated by romantic expressiveness, as in the 1945 Oboe Concerto. Sibelius employed rich chorale-like textures reminiscent of Mendelssohn's own appropriation of baroque models in the affirmative 1922 Andante Festivo.

The paths of Strauss and Sibelius crossed, although without much frequency or intensity. Strauss performed the premiere of the revised Sibelius Violin Concerto in 1905. In 1901 he conducted two of the four *Lemminkäinen* Legends, "The Swan of Tuonela" and "Lemminkäinen's Return," remarking that the music showed genuine melodic inspiration and vitality. Later on, in his characteristic manner, Strauss came to regard his Finnish contemporary with condescending respect as the lesser of evils among living non-German composers. Strauss was a staunch cultural chauvinist regarding German music—a commonplace disease among his contemporaries and shared by Schoenberg and Heinrich Schenker. But Strauss recognized, with sympathy, the authenticity, depth, and greatness in the music of Sibelius, even though he considered his own skills as a composer decidedly superior. Strauss was not the only German who conceived of Sibelius as the voice of a yet unspoiled Northern Europe, a region still capable of naïve enthusiasms about nature, language, and myth. Strauss's view was an expression of envy as well as contempt. He sensed that Sibelius's gifts extended beyond being a voice of the exotic.[10]

No one understood with such clarity the cost and consequences of being German as Strauss. An heir to cultural sophistication and the exponent of an advanced rather than backward cultural heritage (although one that appeared endangered at the turn of the twentieth century), Strauss was a master of ironic detachment.[11] Polemical and ideologically consistent approaches to modernity, whether overtly progressive (Schoenberg) or reactionary (Pfitzner) did not appeal to him. Despite his pessimistic sense of the contemporary predicament, beginning with *Der Rosenkavalier* Strauss sought ways to communicate through music the allure and sentiment of mortality and intimacy as well as the elusive ideals of simplicity and eloquence. He appropriated markers of the eighteenth century, an era he cherished, distorting them without making the surface of his art explicitly mirror the radical turn in history that overwhelmed his generation.

Sibelius seems never to have been drawn to the revolutionary compositional example Strauss set in the 1890s as a young star composer. Unlike many near contemporaries—Bartók, Elgar, Schoenberg, Enescu, and Szymanowski—he did not engage Strauss's orchestral music deeply or use Strauss's meteoric career as a marker for himself. Rather, Sibelius's originality and significance as a composer are more striking because of the relative absence of Straussian influences in his early work. Sibelius's distance from Strauss, however, was offset by contact with Busoni and Mahler and an interest in the music of Debussy and the influence of musical romanticism from Russia.

Sibelius found his own path out of the dominant directions of post-Wagnerian composition. He did not imitate or emulate his contemporaries. Sibelius's appeal to audiences and composers began first in England and America in the first half of the twentieth century and then spread in the 1970s, despite the legacy of snobbery under which his reputation suffered at midcentury. This popularity becomes more explicable when his music is placed alongside that of the music Strauss wrote after 1914, when what has become termed—all too conveniently—the "long nineteenth century" came to an abrupt end. The exotic Finnish element, the aspect that provided the allure early in his career (in part through Sibelius's use of the *Kalevala*, the national epic), led to fundamental innovations in form and content that were not, as in the case of Strauss, explicit stylistic deconstructions of history and tradition.

The turn-of-century consciousness of a new and uncharted historical moment—confirmed brutally after 1914—led Strauss and Sibelius, for whom music deserved a central place in culture, to ponder three issues. The first was the relationship between music and language. Second was the connection between music and nature, an issue that implied a polemical contrast between nature and the machine, in which nature was an idealized romantic category and the machine representative of a dehumanizing modernity visible in cities and industry that grew at the expense of a vanishing rural landscape.[12] The third issue was the potential utility of literary and visual expressionism and naturalism against the radical, self-consciously contemporary aesthetic fashions that emerged from the rubble of world war.

Strauss and Language

Strauss was, if anything, a literary composer whose sensibility about language was acute and whose instincts regarding parallels between the musical and the linguistic was intensely cultivated. The semantic and rhetorical intent of the musical devices he developed and utilized, primarily in the orchestral music written before 1904, was literary in the Lisztean sense. Beginning in 1886, he sought to augment the potential of prose and poetic narrative in music through the use of form and orchestration. By fusing Wagnerian practices with the procedures of classical and Romantic instrumental music, Strauss generated a musical equivalent to the illusionism of literary hyperrealism (as exemplified in the novels of Flaubert, Theodor Fontane, and Thomas Mann, and audible in the 1903 *Symphonia domestica*) in terms of narration per se and the illustration of external events.[13] Language also inspired Strauss's virtuosic capacity to characterize, in music, conscious and unconscious meaning within the human psyche.

Strauss was inclined to think purely in music, absent text or image, in a narrative and mimetic manner parallel to language. Initially his music developed in the direction of mere illustration, allusion, and correspondence to linguistic meaning.[14] But later in his career Strauss chose to confront the skepticism regarding the character and power of language in an era of mass literacy that preoccupied his contemporaries, particularly Hofmannsthal and the postwar generation of philosophers that included

Wittgenstein. Faced with a deepening recognition of the abuse and limits of language, Strauss turned to more elaborate, indirect, and devious but still linguistically inspired musical strategies, using metaphor and artifice as understood in literary terms.

As Strauss responded to music and language, his visual imagination led him to the eighteenth century, during which the issue of the capacity of language and music to construct meaning and achieve a truthful correspondence to reality had been hotly debated. With that debate came intense speculation about the nature of music, a problem he explored in his final opera, *Capriccio*. Was music meaningful in a semantic manner analogous to language and therefore capable of attaining ethical and moral status as thought? Might music be superior, as a signifier of passion and sensibilities, with a reach beyond language? If so, music needed a logic and grammar rendering it subject to interpretation in words.

Strauss privileged music over language in a characteristic eighteenth-century fashion. Music retained a quasi-linguistic structure, but its nature allowed it to transcend ordinary thought. Strauss rejected Eduard Hanslick's formalism, not because he did not regard music as autonomous, but because he thought music was communicative precisely because it was distinct as a life-form, however analogous to language, generating identifiable meaning about emotion, ideas, and external reality.[15]

An aesthetic of realism as illusion (a precursor to magic realism) emerged in the late 1880s that depended on formal conventions derived from music's unique semantics and syntax. It led Strauss to the allegorical, decorative, and intricate practice of eighteenth-century rococo landscape and genre painting. Watteau, in particular, exemplified a subtle integration of artistic convention with covert narratives masquerading as stylized realism.[16] Strauss embraced as well an eighteenth-century construct of Hellenic classicism defined in aesthetic terms by Johann Joachim Winckelmann and in politics by the Enlightenment's recourse to Greece (and Rome) as metaphors and models. Strauss (as Brahms did in the 1870s) absorbed the mid-nineteenth-century German intellectual romance with ancient Greece (as opposed to Rome) and its identification of the nineteenth-century renascence in German culture as equivalent to the monumental achievement of ancient Greek civilization.[17] Nietzsche and Goethe, whom Strauss cherished, were authors with highly cultivated Hellenic sensibilities. Their affinities in the use of the German language appealed to him. Despite Strauss's veneration of Wagner, Nietzsche and Goethe offered a welcome contrast to the faux archaic and medieval diction of Wagner, which Strauss, after *Guntram*, did not choose to emulate.[18] Strauss's philosophical outlook was intensely secular and modern, free of metaphysical speculations.

By the early 1920s Mozart emerged for Strauss as representative of the ideal eighteenth-century musical achievement. Grace, transparency, and a classical sense of form and candor existed alongside philosophical and emotional depth, if not a genuine, albeit restrained romanticism. The comparison of Mozart with Goethe was also persuasive. Strauss's career, like Goethe's, had two overarching moments: the first, from 1886 to 1908, was dominated by the examples of Liszt and Wagner; the second, from 1908 to 1949, was marked by a return to Mozart and a classical ideal. In the predicament of post–World War I Europe, the aesthetics of Mozart pointed the way toward the baroque and neoclassical as sources of cultural survival and renewal.[19]

The primacy of the neoclassical, the rococo, and the baroque in Strauss's music after 1911 coexisted in an uneasy alliance with the nineteenth-century naturalism and realism that dominated his earlier work. After *Der Rosenkavalier*, however, artifice in language and music became Strauss's essential tool. This explains Strauss's deep attachment to Hugo von Hofmannsthal, whom Harry Kessler poignantly described in 1929 as the "last of the great baroque poets." Hofmannsthal's approach to the expression of feelings and ideas was ceremonial and indirect, dependent on the "grafting of genuine feeling on consciously artificial matter."[20]

The key to Strauss's affection for the elaborate twists and turns in Hofmannsthal's libretti after *Elektra* as the basis for music (explaining Strauss's dismay at librettist Joseph Gregor's inability to emulate Hofmannsthal) was the consistent elegance and classical restraint of Hofmannsthal's language, no matter how complex its rhetoric.[21] The baroque structure of the libretti he insisted on in two post-Hofmannsthal operas in the years between 1911 and 1941, *Die schweigsame Frau* and *Capriccio*, permitted Strauss free reign in the appropriation and manipulation of the widest arsenal of inherited musical semantics, syntax, and rhetoric. The emulation of baroque literary style enabled Strauss to evoke, in his scores, intimacy and psychological perception. Within his elaborate musical fabric, Strauss constantly used wistful and ironic invocations of recognizable past musical traditions. Thus recast into a contemporary idiom, their appearance functioned as sharp cultural criticism of the modern age. In the end, musical thinking preceded language, even if music remained tethered to it.

For Strauss, the visual offered no refuge from the link between music and language. His visual sensibilities were rather restricted, limited, and nostalgic. The visual element in culture was not Strauss's strongest suit, a trait he shared with Wagner. His lifelong affection for the baroque and mannerist in the visual arts was refined and paralleled his neoclassical taste in German prose and poetry. But, throughout, the visual remained subordinate to music and language, despite Strauss's enthusiasm for great eighteenth-century painting.[22] Strauss's visual imagination and taste, so striking in the surroundings he created in the villa in Garmisch (Figure 1), hinted at the consequence of his prejudices and his stylistic shift after 1911: the eighteenth century became for him a metaphorical refuge from which modernity could be approached.[23]

The breakthrough in Strauss's utilization of a baroque literary tradition in music to negotiate the expression of authentic thought and feeling in modernity begins at the point where most observers regarded the composer as having abandoned modernism and lost his originality, if not his muse—with *Der Rosenkavalier*. Alongside the much-maligned 1915 *An Alpine Symphony*, *Der Rosenkavalier* marks Strauss's recognition that realities of the present moment could not be responded to by art in an unmediated manner. Like the young Hofmannsthal, who confronted the limits of language early in his career, Strauss by 1911 had found he could no longer use music in the unabashedly representational, evocative, descriptive, and expressive manner to which he had become accustomed.[24] Only through the tortured formal procedures of baroque theatricality, and through the ironic distortion of evident markers of tradition, including myth, naturalism, classical form, and farce, could the truth about the ethical and aesthetic bankruptcy of modern age be revealed by music and language.[25]

The "iron cage"—the existential trap of advanced Western civilization— could not tolerate the direct illusionism of realism or expressionism, the

Figure 1. Interior of Richard Strauss's villa in Garmisch, Germany.

unselfconscious continuation of a late Romantic idiom, the modernist neo-classicism of the 1920s, or even a disarmingly ascetic radical musical system such as Schoenberg's. Even though Schoenberg's intent was a reassertion of the autonomy of musical logic and thus neoclassical in ideology and formal ambition, it would not, for Strauss, carry meaning or reach the public.

The musical modernism of the 1920s rejected Romanticism and monumentality in favor of directness and simplicity. Structure in music, art, and architecture was privileged at the expense of ornament. This modernist credo sought to reassert art's function as essential to truth-telling, transcending art's function as mere decoration and affirmative entertainment. Strauss's response to this modernist impulse was less dismissive than ironic and contrarian. He offered a return not to the sound world of either late nineteenth-century post-Wagnerian Romanticism or early twentieth-century expressionism, but to tradition revised. He embraced ornament as a crucial part of a complex, ritualized, indirect, textured, and multilayered approach to authenticity and the truth-telling function of art, as exemplified by baroque architecture and eighteenth-century neoclassical painting and design. Decorative detail, including an almost filigree-like use of complex orchestral texture, without sacrifice to transparency, and a lightness suggestive of Mozart, became hallmarks of Strauss's orchestration in his later operas, as he openly confessed in his "Preface" to *Capriccio*.[26] Strauss shunned the lean, ascetic quality of modernist sonority, even in his most neoclassic final period in the years after 1945. He explicitly retained the seemingly incompatible expressive intensity of a nineteenth-century Romantic sensibility, whose impact he managed to heighten within the unexpected context of an eighteenth-century framework replete with the lavish use of inflected and brilliant detail.[27]

In retrospect, Strauss's most inspired and intellectually provocative period, the high point of his critical engagement with modernity, was not his so-called modernist period, the era between *Don Juan* and *Elektra*, when Strauss was in the European vanguard. Rather, it was the years between 1911 and 1941. At the close of these, his most derided and neglected decades, the composer completed *Capriccio*, in which he proposed the eighteenth century and its framing of the relationship between music and language as a way of approaching the historical place of modernity.[28] This was the composer's most trenchant, honest, and persuasive period. A scathing critique of modernism and its conceits was offered with a profundity masked in irony, including the use of self-quotation. Strauss's most philosophically powerful and personal works are not *Salome* or *Ein Heldenleben*, but rather *An Alpine Symphony* and the three last Hellenic operas —*Die ägyptische Helena*, *Daphne*, and *Die Liebe der Danae*.

Sibelius and the Visual

The challenges to art and culture in the same decades that prompted a decisive shift in the mature Strauss's aesthetic strategy also triggered a comparable transition in Sibelius's case. The works Sibelius composed from 1907 on are representative of his last and most productive period.[29] In the Third Symphony, begun in 1904 and completed in 1907, and *Pohjola's Daughter*, op. 49, an explicitly programmatic work from the same time based on a legend from the *Kalevala*, critics and scholars observed something "more organic" at work, a harbinger of "an increasingly organic way of welding movements together."[30] This tendency toward an organic formal unity would make an even more dramatic appearance beginning with the Fourth Symphony and especially in the Fifth and Seventh symphonies.

With the Third Symphony, Sibelius turned away from a reliance on programmatic inspiration, whether explicit or implied. Veijo Murtomäki suggests that the Third Symphony is an affirmative response to Busoni's polemical 1905 call for a modernist reaffirmation of Hanslick's view of music as autonomous and absolute, as an art form without a literary or poetic idea but defined by the interplay of moving forms.[31] Whether or not one concedes this explanation of the composer's intent (in view of the overt classicism of the work and its more economical and non-Romantic use of the orchestra), Sibelius's renewed attention to formal design would project him from his niche as little more than a Finnish composer, a representative of the North, into broader European currents.

Sibelius's path came not through language, but as the term "organic" suggests, through the visual.[32] He experimented with how musical form fundamentally transforms the spatial experience of time and the construction of meaning, particularly in the visual imagination. Sonority—the materiality of orchestral timbres—rather than the use of motivic development as a linguistic equivalent, emerged as the basic constituent of form. Structure seemed to arise from a repetition of rhythmic figures tied to instrumental colors inserted sequentially along a single dominant and purposeful arc. An unmistakable effort to mimic, in compact fashion, a dynamic quasi-naturalistic temporal process, a visual sense of extended structure over time, became audible. The thematic and motivic materials of all the movements in the Third Symphony were interrelated in the sense not of a literary, but of a visual construction.

In 1945 Ilmari Krohn, in a much maligned attempt to link Sibelius's Third Symphony with Wagner, despite its somewhat smaller orchestra, located leitmotifs in the first movement, many of them visual in nature: that of the forest, sunrise, and the cuckoo.[33] But the plausible suggestion of nature did not rely on such quasi–tone painting. In the Third Symphony as well as *Pohjola's Daughter*, Sibelius realized that he was fashioning something new—a "fantasy," his own "genre," neither a symphony nor a literary Liszt-style tone poem, but a form that would permit him to break free from "the weight of tradition."[34]

This new direction, strikingly audible in the coda to *Pohjola's Daughter*, alters the listener's anticipated visual image as suggested by the literary program. Instead, the music subordinates linguistic meaning to harmonic and instrumental timbre, foregrounding an atmospheric mental picture conjured by the eerie sound and deliberate pace of the coda. With these works, as Daniel Grimley has observed, Sibelius began to make the visualization of the landscape inform the musical and structural process.[35] "The temporal perception of the listener" becomes "analogous to the visual perception of the viewer." In *Nightride and Sunrise*, from 1908, completed shortly after the Third Symphony and *Pohjola's Daughter*, Grimley locates a "temporal-spatial" strategy: "The organization of musical events in time suggests a structural parallel with the placement of landscape objects in visual space." Of the 1914 tone poem *Oceanides*, Erik Tawaststjerna, Sibelius's biographer, noted that the work "seems to mirror nature itself."[36]

Early in his career, nature became an explanatory device to define Sibelius's uniqueness. But it was construed as contingent on something substantive in the Nordic and Finnish character. Sibelius, eager to make his mark as more than a Finnish celebrity and keenly attuned to the modern crisis regarding the proper path for music, turned for inspiration to a strategy and sensibility closest to himself: his predisposition for silent contemplation in nature. This inclination to the visual and material environment, to nature and a sense of the organic, went well beyond illustration. For all of his engagement with the *Kalevala* early in his career, Sibelius, unlike Strauss, never aspired to become a literary composer.[37] His only opera was a failure. And he himself recognized the centrality of the visual in his music. In 1915 he mused in his diary, "It is as if Father God had thrown down pieces of mosaic from heaven's floor and asked me to determine what kind of picture it was. Maybe a good definition of composing. Maybe not. How would I know?"[38]

Sibelius's self-doubt notwithstanding, the "pieces of mosaic" in his music consistently possessed attributes of spatiality, the organic, and the visual. Tawaststjerna notes that Sibelius, in his twenties, reported having dreamt as a boy of a new art form that combined sculpture and music, an art form "where matter, line and shape would be given life by sound and thus enabled to move. To the three dimensions of sculpture he wanted to add the fourth: time."[39] Painting was not crucial. There are those who hear color-sound symbolism, *Klangfarbensymbolik,* in the earlier *Lemminkäinen* Legends, op. 22. Such symbolism linked Sibelius with his contemporaries M. K. Čiurlionis and Alexander Scriabin, for whom the color-sound connection was structural and whose implications for form extended beyond the painterly correspondence between musical gesture and pictorial image.[40] The visualization of time in nature guided Sibelius's assembling of mosaic fragments—"pieces" of musical form—and after the Third Symphony led to a self-conscious search for self-evidently "simpler" elements. Instrumental music based on thematic transformation seemed more artificial, less "natural," less congruent with the experience of the organic. Large-scale form demanded reinvention. To give life to form through time called for events of sonic assemblage occurring in succession. In the sequential passage of time, sound and the sensuous particularity of the materials of sound emerged as units of structure.[41]

Sibelius's notion of the nature that gave life to form through sound was certainly influenced by the relatively "backward" (in Alexander Gerschenkron's brilliant non-pejorative usage) economic and industrial character of his native Finnish surroundings.[42] Early twentieth-century Finland fit with an image of nature as rural, uncorrupted by man, and therefore original in some theological sense. This sensibility coincided with Sibelius's increasing penchant for simple, transparent elements and harmonic motion that privileged static and slow-moving textures as structural components. These elemental, almost primitive, evocations of space and time in turn appeared congruent with the cult of myth and antiquity surrounding the *Kalevala* and helped define the uniquely "Finnish" as derivative of a premodern and more authentic natural landscape.[43]

When juxtaposed to the cosmopolitan and individual, however, the substantive construct of the natural and organic that can be associated historically with Sibelius generated darker political overtones. The natural and organic became aligned in early twentieth-century politics with a reactionary definition of authentic community, placing the modern, individual, and cosmopolitan vision of society as a differentiated, diverse, collective reality on the defensive as alienated and bereft of spiritual cohesion. The ideal of restoring a natural, organic community within modernity dissolved easily into apologies on behalf of homogeneous race-based nations and (ironically) futuristic visions of universal classless solidarity, further isolating notions of democratic individualism as abstract and materialistic.[44]

The duality between nature and man explicit in myth, and its attendant contrast between modern industrialization and the rural landscape that first inspired Sibelius to use the natural and organic as a visual metaphor for writing music, represented just one factor in shaping the late nineteenth-century concept of nature. Equally significant were nineteenth-century scientific obsessions with dynamic processes in nature, both cyclical (mitosis) and progressive (evolution). These explained how nature caused differentiation and regulated the cycle of birth, growth, and decay. The idea of nature implied temporal vectors of momentum without finite boundaries. Organic forms found in nature were known to be economical, symmetrical, and implicitly revelatory of their purpose. For that reason, late nineteenth-century theories of history frequently appealed to the scientific, dynamic character of the organic and of nature.

The natural, including disease and evolution, was understood as contingent on time and therefore temporal in experience in a way that the mechanical and inorganic were not. The philosophical fascination with the organic as a dynamic force was enhanced by the perception that nature generated differentiation in a manner compatible with uniformity. Natural phenomena such as multiplicity and individuation were consistent with unity, recurrence, cycles, repetition, and sameness. The natural world as understood in the late nineteenth century reconciled a dynamic surface of difference with a deep, shared structure of stasis. All this suggested an implicit unifying purpose in nature, perhaps a divine plan, compatible with a metaphysical belief in the invisibility of infinity and the boundlessness of the cyclical.

Sibelius gradually translated into music this reconciliation of diversity and unity in nature. For the listener, the persuasive musical expression in the later Sibelius symphonies derives from a visual conceptualization of spatiality, not a narrative one. The frequency with which pictorial explanations were made about Sibelius's music, particularly by English and American critics, suports this claim. The third movement of his Fourth Symphony suggests that "Sibelius's design is primarily a dynamic or cumulative one, like tiny ripples on a lake which expand into rolling waves."[45] Predictably, images from urban landscapes, industry, and the machine are rarely used in evoking the sound of Sibelius's mature orchestral music.

Sibelius's reliance on visual constructs of nature and the organic is most audible in the breadth, duration, and the specific materiality of sound. The harmonic structure is organized to emulate the emergence of single causes with dominant features. Characteristic elements in the discussion of Sibelius's music include the compression of form, the emphasis on sameness and not motivic contrast as a structural device, the use of cyclical "rotational" devices, and the focus on entropy and disintegration toward the end of works. Such features are routinely contrasted with the classical-Romantic model of symphonic procedure with its manipulation of heterogeneous motivic elements, or the narrative logic of the symphonic poem. Thematic development, variation, and dramatic culmination based on the synthesis and recapitulation of multiple contrasting variables are placed in opposition to music suggestive of the temporal experience of nature and the organic.[46]

In *Luonnotar* (1913), a "tone poem for soprano and orchestra," the striking aspect is not the text from the *Kalevala* or the setting of the creation myth from its first canto, but rather the economical transparency, the intensification of sound itself in which the materiality of each group of instruments, strings, winds, and brass, assists separately in evoking the strange distant landscape of divine creation. There is the unmistakable sense of a single line of experience or argument—a single formal arc. Repetition with slight nuanced variation evokes the illusion of extended duration in a short piece. Whether the "image" of nature suggested by *Luonnotar*'s sound world is dark, Dionysian, or seemingly "unconcerned with, and standing apart from any human perception of it" (as Hepokoski suggests), Sibelius's approach to temporality and musical form in the work is influenced by an effort at translation of a visual sensibility or image, even given the absence of a human observer.[47]

The pacing of the work, its steady motion, its grandeur, and its intricate but integrated sound world balance detail with the long line. This suggests a visual architectural logic—the use of sonority per se (open fifths) as a structural element, punctuated sparsely by detailing: ornament in the form of brief contrasts in instrumental coloration against a monochromatic background. In a vision of primeval chaos, sudden eruptions and waves of melodic exclamation fit within a commanding, stable, and atmospheric sensibility. The piece's visual sense of landscape is explicitly implied by the composer's admonition to the singer to sing, at letter L, "visionarico."[48]

Readings of *Luonnatar* that foreground ideological programmatic meanings in the work as opposed to its strikingly original use of sound and time invite a direct comparison to Strauss's *An Alpine Symphony*, completed early in 1915—his last major symphonic and large-scale independent orchestral work. Strauss, too, evokes the spatial expanse and grandeur of the landscape. But he does so by a thematic narrative, suggesting an observer and human subject. Strauss's techniques are illustrative. The work is explicitly reminiscent of Mahler, whose death in 1911 spurred Strauss to resume work on the piece, which he had begun years earlier. *An Alpine Symphony* can be heard, in fact, as a tribute to Mahler. Strauss unleashes a Mahlerian instrumental array, including cowbells and wind and thunder machines, along with his own signature use of horns and tenor tubas. Strauss employs this overwhelming arsenal descriptively, albeit sparingly. The listener follows at a distance, experiencing as an observer or the reader of a novel the awe, loss, return, and memory of the leading character. The perspective remains painterly: a species of narrative and an expression of philosophical realism.[49]

The visual element in *An Alpine Symphony* is explicit, but it is pictorial, not architectural. The music depicts the landscape, and the program suggests a story through Strauss's explicit evocation of past symphonic tradition. He satisfies the anticipation of a listener whose appreciation has been honed by familiarity with conventions of thematic exposition, development, and recapitulation (as in Rubinstein's *Ocean Symphony*, Goldmark's *Rustic Wedding Symphony*, Mahler's Third, Smetana's *Má vlast*, Liszt's *Dante Symphony*, and Beethoven's *Pastoral*). The music inspires in listeners an inner dialogue of a novelistic character, and the recollection of their own encounter with nature. The sensibility inspired in listeners is operatic, foregrounding the human character against a scenic backdrop—a brilliantly realized visual tableau.

The contrast between Strauss and Sibelius becomes acute when one compares *An Alpine Symphony* to Sibelius's two major orchestral works from 1911 and 1915, the Fourth and Fifth symphonies. Sibelius's Fourth has been said to "enshrine the essential Sibelius"; it reveals "a searching intensity" and a "purity of utterance."[50] Although praised by critics as Sibelius's most modernist work, it never captured a public the way the Second had or the Fifth would. Sibelius, perhaps offering a direct alternative to Mahler, suggested that the Fourth had a confessional aspect. Despite its surface of astringent modernism, the bleak sonorities, the elusive harmonic motion, the use of the tritone, the dominant innovative aspect of the symphony—its "free self-determining structure"—is formal.[51] Form is implied by elements linked to sonic materiality and is experienced as an evolutionary process. This is audible even in the tightly argued and more neoclassical first movement. The architectural shape of an arch in the last movement can be inferred.[52]

The polemical intent of the symphony, according to Sibelius's friend Axel Carpelan, was to expose the mechanistic "musical civil-engineering" of German composers and the "inner emptiness behind an enormous mechanical apparatus."[53] Sibelius's challenge was spiritual in the sense of the organic. Line and form—musical design as visual architecture—predominate, not the conventional functionality of motivic and harmonic relationships. Sibelius's architecture is organic in the use of cyclical procedures and recurrent patterns. Sibelius reconciles, in the Fourth, the technique of organic form-building already present in *Luonnotar* with a Beethovenian symphonic scale. The concentration on coordinating sonority with structure in the Fourth forces the listener to think musically and respond not to an implied narrative or philosophical argument as might be appropriate with Strauss and Mahler. The musical logic is not painterly, but suggestive of shape and design in a more abstract manner—visual three-dimensionality conceived and realized temporally in music.

In the Fifth, the work with which Sibelius most struggled, he mastered the musical equivalent of organic unity. After the popular Second, it was his most successful venture into symphonic form. The architecture of the work has been described by Hepokoski as based on "slow, rotational transformations toward a stronger and deeper principle." The form emerges from "an implicit essence" audible at the start.[54] Sibelius moves beyond evocations of sonata form and classical procedure by managing sound in time visually through space as if sound were light changing over time. But the symphony moves in one direction, leading to an "apotheosis" that is systematically prepared and implied from the beginning. Although Olin Downes thought the work rather "pastoral," that feeling is not achieved by an implied narrative, despite Krohn's elaborate argument on behalf of a "North Spring" that ends in a "Journey to Church" and the entrance into paradise in the presence of God. But even Krohn, faced with the "uniqueness" in the closing measures, retreats, suggesting a "symbolic effect."[55]

Sibelius's musical solution appears directly and pointedly responsive to Strauss. If musical meaning can be constructed along the lines suggested by language, then its form must somehow approximate the functions of words and utterances. Thematic significance is contingent on grammar and syntax that regulate usage and anticipate meaning, even in poetry, where convention can frame meaning.[56] For Sibelius, expositions, developments, and recapitulations defined by themes, cadences, variations, harmonic motion, and counterpoint, understood in traditional terms, no longer seemed persuasively meaningful. Just as the logic and power of language had been eroded in modern times, so too had the musical traditions rooted in conventions based on an analogy with language. In Sibelius's Fifth, to use Hepokoski's terms, teleological genesis, rotational form, content-based fantasy, and a focus on sonic materiality as an expressive element all contributed to an original construct of a unified organic-sounding form. The symphony was a response to decaying cultural practice represented, ironically, by *An Alpine Symphony*, itself a nostalgic and implicitly pessimistic reprise of tradition.[57]

By 1919, when the third and final version of the Fifth was premiered, Sibelius had arrived at a new approach to musical architecture, justifying his quip that in comparison to what was happening in Europe beyond Finland's borders "my music has infinitely more nature and life."[58] The Fifth has been said to have a "revelatory effect," the result of an "organic" expansion achieved through simplification and distillation.[59] The temporal experience in Sibelius assumes a spatiality that appears balanced and economical, in which content and function emerge sequentially, accumulate, and define in retrospect a single dominant formal logic.

Sibelius's experiments with form as sounding visual shapes and structures were elaborated and surpassed in three late works: the Sixth Symphony (1923), the Seventh Symphony (1924), and *Tapiola* (1926). The Sixth is perhaps the most personal and nostalgic, given its modal references to a premodern past. But it is also the most daring and unusual.[60] It proceeds directly in the path charted by *Luonnotar*. In the sequence of events, Sibelius intersperses silence and space within repetition, fragmentation, augmentation, and diminution, using highly simplified motivic and thematic units. The architectural line is elegant and restrained, generated by a single formal gesture that builds and then recedes. But the sonorities yield a succession of sharp contrasts, fleeting episodes, echoes of history, and fragments, often without evident symmetry. This detail is subsumed into an ethereal, mystical, and overarching harmonic sensibility, suggesting distance and contemplative interiority. The suggestion of a narrative argument has become weaker. Admirers of Sibelius have heard in the controversial Sixth Symphony an organic expression of Finnish identity, the most Finnish of the symphonies, "pure and cold water," a spiritualized expression of an ancient Finnish landscape, a wintry February; others have heard a "Nordic summer" that ends in a "midsummer night's dream."[61]

The Seventh, widely regarded as the greatest of the Sibelius symphonies, is more a symphonic fantasy than heir to the formal tradition dating back to Beethoven.[62] In the Seventh, Sibelius addresses the problem of unity in symphonic form with which nineteenth-century composers struggled. Consisting of a single movement, the Seventh represents a compressed structure. Donald Tovey invoked the metaphor of a mountain peak—flying over it, being on it—to characterize this densely argued work. The symphony, for Tovey, mirrors the logic of the visual experience of time: "The beginning is in darkness. . . . Dawn grows into daylight" before the composition ends, somberly, "in tones of noble pathos." The work's intensely condensed musical structure grows like an organism, from seeds that suggest immanently its form and design. In this way it is similar to the Sixth, heard as an "organism that grows with the same irresistible force and logic as the leaf stalks."[63] Both works reveal "the intuitive necessity of nature."[64]

The Seventh Symphony in particular invites a comparison less to sculpture, for which Sibelius maintained a lifelong enthusiasm, than to principles of modernist architecture that flourished after 1918 and were based explicitly on nature and the organic. So too does the far more static *Tapiola*, where music transforms one's sense of space and perspective by breaking the listener's sense of time as conventionally defined. The transparent and clear integration of the sound materials with their elaboration over extended duration—the link between form and function—is unitary, disciplined, elegant, evolutionary, directional, and strangely eloquent, entirely reminiscent of nature in a proto-minimalist manner.[65]

In *Tapiola* Sibelius makes clear the consequences of utilizing the visual and a conception of nature and the organic as alternative metaphors for musical logic. Having moved away from the long eighteenth- and nineteenth-century tradition of conceiving of music and language as interdependent, Sibelius at mid-career began functioning much like a modern architect and sculptor of sound, constructing new forms he thought evocative of nature. He recast the experience of space in time and derived his own vocabulary of design from the experience of space, time, and the sonic materials of construction. Sibelius's inspiration may have come from the crisis of his age, his sense that, in an era defined by technological and scientific progress, the existential needs of his metaphorical clients—the modern listening audience—might require a new kind of instrumental music that reconnected them with the essence of nature.

Many of Sibelius's closest friends and colleagues in Finland were painters and architects.[66] Throughout his life he felt drawn to the visual experience. The mature Sibelius remarked, "When I consider how musical forms are established I frequently think of the ice-ferns which, according to eternal laws, the frost makes into the most beautiful patterns."[67] In his mid-twenties, he wrote his uncle Pehr about imagining a C-major chord upon which a first inversion D-flat-major chord was superimposed, generating three pairs of minor seconds. With irony and humor he spoke about the beginning of a "new musical age" in which "one imagines a city with several factories"—cotton, timber, and iron, each represented by a pitch or an interval.[68] Where Strauss heard distinct tonalities while reading, Sibelius translated from sound to image and image to sound. More than one commentator has remarked that *Tapiola* suggests a frozen landscape.

Using architecture as a visual metaphor by which to understand musical form in Sibelius is justified by the frequency of references to an "architectural" aspect in his music, particularly the symphonies. In 1947, Gerald Abraham evoked the image of a cathedral in attempting to characterize form in late Sibelius. The metaphor of architecture has been expressed in terms of organic forms, cells, and even trees. Architecture has long been used as a theological image for inferring a rational, purposeful, and intentional beauty in nature. Abraham's emphatic description of the Seventh Symphony as "organic" suggests that in Sibelius one might hear the teleological vision of the composer unfold in a manner analogous to the way nature, in its designs, reveals the design logic of a divine creator.[69]

This implicit spiritual but not narrative dimension suggests Bruckner, whose music made such an impression on Sibelius during his short period of study in Vienna.[70] Bruckner transformed the spatial dimension of musical form, using regularity of pulse and the extended use of musical sequences. He generated a musical mirror of spiritual contemplation and celebration. These were appropriated and adapted by Sibelius to evoke, much in the spirit of Beethoven's *Pastoral*, a musical articulation of the response to the natural world. In Sibelius's case, a vast landscape marked by extremes of light and dark defined his idea of nature. The visual experience of nature untamed by humanity functioned as a vague program, offering existential awe, grand simplicity, and the terror of human insignificance. Sibelius appropriated Bruckner's sense of how music evokes space in time, retaining Bruckner's spiritual conceits as he transposed and compressed them.[71] At the same time, Sibelius's concentration of musical space led him beyond Bruckner.

Sibelius responded to the widespread sense of the inadequacy if not corruption of ordinary language in modernity by exploring the link between language (and therefore musical traditions rooted in language) and nature.[72] This led him, intuitively, to ponder the natural priority of the visual over the linguistic, a subject of nineteenth-century speculation along lines first suggested by Jean-Jacques Rousseau.[73] Among the most eloquent elaborators of this problem was Ralph Waldo Emerson, one of the few thinkers and writers Nietzsche admired. For Emerson, nature remained the refuge from the shortcomings of modern civilization: "In the woods we return to reason and faith. There I feel nothing can befall me in life—no disgrace, no calamity (leaving me my eyes), which nature cannot repair. Standing on the bare ground—my head bathed by the blithe air and uplifted into infinite space—all mean egotism vanishes. I become an all transparent eyeball; I am nothing; I see all; the currents of the Universal Being circulate through me."[74] At the core of truth, reason, language, and therefore art was nature. Sight—the visual—was the primary bridge between man and nature, not speech. For Emerson, as for Sibelius, the faculty of sight was fundamental in any effort to conjure up the inspiration of nature.

Meaning in music, as in all art, was contingent on nature, the source of the "symbolic" and "picturesque" foundations of language. "As this is the first language, so it is the last," Emerson wrote. Once it rises "above the ground line of familiar facts," a thought "clothes itself in images." Visual images are the "vestment" of thought. The visual generates in language "perpetual allegories" whose imagery is "spontaneous."[75] Vision links truth to nature. To realize this connection between thought, human experience, and nature, a modern musical discourse of significance had to be independent of language yet still be one of ideas. The visual—sight—suggested an alternative logic, one closely allied with nature.

Sibelius developed a new modern approach to musical form as the result of visual thinking transposed into music. While Strauss stuck steadfastly to the medium of language, working against the modern corruption of language with music based on sophisticated literary sources, Sibelius located the "transparent eye-ball" in himself. Using what Emerson termed "simplicity," the composer found the means to convert the truth-telling potential of the visual into sounding forms.[76] The closest visual analogue to music in Sibelius's lifetime was architecture.[77]

Music and Architecture:
Nature, Form, Modernity, and the Legacy of Schelling

The notion that architecture in modernity needed to connect to nature and the organic first appeared around 1900 in Finland and America. The particular challenges to the Finnish architects of Sibelius's generation resembled those faced by Sibelius as a Finnish composer. His artist-architect contemporaries did not grow up in cities defined by many prior generations of urban growth. There had been no defining mid-nineteenth-century historicist architectural consensus marked by a transformative intervention as in Paris, Berlin, and Vienna.[78] In Finland in 1900, as in much of the United States, cities and industry were relative novelties. The answers to how one should design modern cities, how to build homes, factories, and public buildings, were inevitably different by virtue of real contrasts in landscape, population, and economics.

Given the relative absence of a visible built urban landscape, the architect in turn-of-the-century Finland and America might bypass patterns previously inscribed in older cities. Neither the young Sibelius nor his architect contemporaries in Finland were as overwhelmed as their German contemporaries by the tremendous momentum of European late nineteenth-century historicism. They were not heirs to the radical erasure of history. They had no cultural memory of the destruction of the old urban Vienna to make way for the Ringstrasse, or of Haussmann's traumatic rebuilding of Paris. Nor was their situation comparable to that of Ödön Lechner, the leading Hungarian architect during Béla Bartók's youth, who participated in the massive building expansion in Pest and on both banks of the Danube in Budapest.[79] Some Finnish architects, such as Lars Sonck (1870–1956), responded by developing their own version of historicism: a "national" romantic style whose hint of originality derived from the explicit evocation of a premodern national heritage.[80]

Sibelius's aesthetic development as a modernist innovator parallels most closely the career of the most innovative Finnish architect of his generation, Eliel Saarinen (1873–1950). A towering figure in the history of modern architecture, he was a friend of the composer.[81] Much like Sibelius, Saarinen solved the challenges of modern times by both borrowing freely from and bypassing the twentieth-century's mainstream modernist confrontation with architectural historicism. Saarinen, like Sibelius, turned to the model of nature, whereas modernist architects in

France, Germany, and Austro-Hungary, faced with an overwhelming historicism, took a radical rationalist turn. This led to the so-called International style most famously associated in the 1920s with the Bauhaus. Saarinen was as skeptical of this trend in architectural modernism as Sibelius was of Schoenberg, Stravinsky, or the *Neue Sachlichkeit* (New Objectivity) in Germany. Their reasons were similar.[82]

After flirting with a romantic invention of a historical Finnish national style, Saarinen turned to the idea of nature and the ideal of the organic. Form had to be based equally in nature and on the specific requirements of the historical moment. All designed spaces, from houses to cities, had to take into account modern engineering, materials, and patterns of life. But the logic and method of design and architecture had to be organic, reflecting and revealing nature. This recourse to nature and the organic by Saarinen (and Sibelius) coincided with the ideas and designs of another iconoclastic modernist, the quintessentially American Frank Lloyd Wright (1867–1959). Like Saarinen, Wright distanced himself from the dominant modernist strategy of a rigorous alignment between structure and function in the early twentieth century. Instead, Wright defined his own modernism as rooted in the natural and the organic. Sibelius's popularity was at its height in America at the same time Frank Lloyd Wright's influence and reputation were at their peak. Wright and Saarinen were deeply invested in music. Both used musical analogies to defend their ideas. Wright was particularly fond of Beethoven, with whom Sibelius, in his lifetime, would be frequently compared.[83]

The idea of architecture in music and music in architecture reflects an influential nineteenth-century philosophical tradition. Music and architecture invite comparison in terms of how humans mediate between nature, the objective external world, and their imagination and subjectivity. In both, the expression of the aesthetic as it affects the conduct of life seems to demand the creation of intentional forms and structures that abstract from the natural and organic experience of time and space. Music and architecture transcend mere representation and description, the mirroring of external reality. As art they exemplify the Platonic idea of form, suggesting abstraction and permanence.

The human capacity to distill and articulate imagined space parallels the way time is experienced and refashioned into music in artificial forms that suggest meaning and coherence. Neither a painting or a sculpture, nor a work of poetry or prose share this basic capacity of breaking free from evident correspondences to human experience. To be understood, both music and architecture demand to be experienced primarily as structures, not as narratives tied to the human capacity for language. They define the human sense of time and space, absent language. Music and architecture rely for coherence on small elements repeated along patterns augmented, elaborated, and miniaturized in the service of an overarching form. A self-contained structural logic in a given work provides detail with a context of relationships. In both art forms one can speak of a foreground (a façade) as well as layers of underlying structure (organization of space, footprint, elevation, foundation, mechanical systems).

In music and architecture, both discrete elements and the whole assume symbolic meaning as they are perceived and lived with over extended time. Time reveals form and can alter meaning and function, deepening the relative independence of music and architecture from history and linguistic usage. Yet despite their artificiality, both art forms influence subjective consciousness and even appear capable of reconciling subjectivity with objective reality. They inhabit public space and transcend the private and the individual. Both are fundamental aesthetic elements for the definition of community and the formation of social cohesion.

The locus classicus with regard to parallelisms between music and architecture is Friedrich Wilhelm Joseph Schelling's *Philosophy of Art*, written between 1801 and 1804 and published in 1859.[84] Schelling's premise is that music, because it deals with sonority, is allied with the other arts that create form out of material nature. But music's nature concerns time itself—the succession of sound in time. Its elements are "manifest" in the cosmos, making it the most elemental art form and the deepest source of human self-awareness. Music is therefore uniquely capable of unifying the real and ideal, the subjective and the objective. Through its form-giving capacity and its dependency on rhythm, music creates unity out of diversity, linking human experience with the universal, temporal basis of nature.[85]

Music's dependence on one of the universe's "real" dimensions—temporality—makes its truth-value independent of human subjectivity. Its fundamental formal logic is dependent on nature. However, its components—rhythm, harmony, and melody—are not derived directly from nature, making direct imitation impossible. Because of this duality—the underlying dependence of music on nature, through time, and its evident aesthetic artificiality and dependence on the human imagination and capacity to attribute meaning—music is "anorganic."[86] This strange word, coined by Schelling, suggests that music, as an art, has a reality beyond art forms based on language and visual mimesis because it transcends subjectivity without losing its link to nature.[87] Music mirrors the structure of the cosmos beyond the framework of organic life in an objective ideal manner. The anorganic signals that music as an art form escapes from the impermanence of the organic and assumes infinitude. The logic of music suggests that the aesthetic can remain true beyond history, mortality, entropy, and the cycle of life.

As anorganic art, music, through its forms, takes up the task of "the informing of unity into multiplicity as such." By making music, humans can unify fundamental objective reality with human experience. We lend ourselves symbolic meaning through an art that itself mirrors the identity between concept and object. Music, as "anorganic" human art, offers an "allegory of the organic." The objectivity of nature and the ambitions of human subjectivity find infinite and unbounded opportunity in music. Music's "closed" and self-contained artificiality, "comprehends forms still within chaos and without differentiation." Music is "boundless" because it draws out of nature and the material "pure form" in sound, using rhythm, harmony, and melody.[88]

Schelling's most famous phrase about music and architecture defines architecture as "solidified" or "frozen" music (*erstarrte Musik*).[89] Architecture, like music, takes external reality—nature—and, through human form-giving, provides it with conceptual meaning. It transcends the mere subjective and quotidian by abstracting from human experience. Its ideal presence as art is "anorganic" through its reliance on forms compatible with nature. Architecture takes the plant organism as its model and through its form-giving anorganic character as art becomes understood symbolically. Although responsive to human needs, it must, as a fine art, always remain an "allegory of the organic." If architecture corresponds to the "organic form in its perfection" it can express ideas, thereby bridging the real with the ideal. Architecture, like music, is contingent on a fundamental normative logic—temporality, succession, and causality—yet it is also free. Architecture's autonomy, like music's, rests on its dependence on form. Its functionality and contingency as a material object placed by humans into external reality within nature are transcended by its aesthetic potential as form. Architecture's formal properties are comparable to harmony (proportion), rhythm (in the temporal experience of space), and melody (shape). These generate a subjective, aesthetic mirror, as in music, tied to the objective character and interrelationships of space and time.

Architecture is music frozen in time in that it gives aesthetic formal *permanence* to imaginary subjectivity in such a way as to alter the human experience in ways painting, poetry, and sculpture cannot. Architecture is lived with and alters the landscape. But music retains, inevitably, a philosophical and ethical priority. As Schelling argues, "Music, to which architecture corresponds among the various forms of the plastic arts, is freed from the requirement of portraying actual forms or figures, since it portrays the universe in the forms of the first and purest movement, separated from matter. Architecture, however, is a form of the plastic arts, and if it is music, then it is concrete music. It cannot portray the universe merely through form; it must portray it simultaneously in essence and form."[90]

In Schelling's system, music becomes a philosophical art form with an objective logic that defines form and structure. Its symbolic and emotional meaning—its utility as an expression of human subjectivity—is contingent on its fundamental character as non-arbitrary and derivative of the nature of time and sound.[91] Like architecture, it is essential to human life but remains consistent with the truths inherent in nature. The architect provides human form-giving to materiality while the composer provides the same to sound and time; both are analogous expressions of human needs consistent with nature and its fundamental laws. As humans create art, extending the logic of nature yet liberating it through the free human aesthetic impulse, the sharp distinction between the organic and inorganic, or mechanistic, is transcended.

This heritage of philosophical speculation, which already had a powerful history prior to Schelling, left a distinct legacy in the discourse about music that occupied young artists, writers, and musicians of Sibelius's generation in the 1880s and 1890s. The link between nature and art had occupied Kant earlier in his *Critique of Judgment*, particularly as related to the issue of causality and the idea of purpose in art. Goethe, too, was obsessed with nature, urging artists to study the process of development in plants as a prelude to cultivating a sense of form and style. Schelling's placement of music at the center of the arts, not at its periphery, and not subordinate to language, inspired Hanslick's argument on behalf of "absolute" music. By the same token, the new prestige Schelling lent music as the art form with the greatest power to transcend dualities—particular and universal, subjective and objective, real and ideal—also inspired Wagner and his notion of the *Gesamtkunstwerk*, the "total work of art," in which music provided the core with its capacity to integrate the experience of time and space.[92] By linking music with architecture, Schelling heightened the prestige of architecture as well. For Schelling they were both public art forms actualized in space and time, and thereby symbolic of collective ideals contingent on but beyond the organic. They were truthful as more than passing expressions of human individuality.

Schelling's association of music with architecture, in terms of criticism and public reception, was vindicated during the late nineteenth and early twentieth centuries when music and architecture as public arts became tied to politics and issues of national identity.[93] In the public sphere at the turn of the century, music and architecture defined the modern. The tension between historicism and modernism in the controversy in Vienna over the music of Schoenberg between 1906 and 1913 repeated itself in the furor over Adolf Loos's 1910 Goldman & Salatsch building on the Michaelerplatz. The controversy around Klimt in Vienna was architectural: it centered on his *Beethoven Frieze* for the 1901 Secession Klinger exhibition. And the cultural politics surrounding architecture in Vienna—debates about the work of Loos, Otto Wagner, Josef Hoffmann, Joseph Maria Olbrich—ran parallel to those about the music of Mahler and Schoenberg's pupils Berg and Webern, and to a lesser extent Alexander Zemlinsky and Franz Schreker.

Nature and Form: Saarinen, Wright, and Sibelius

The parallel between Saarinen's architectural ideas and realizations and Sibelius's use of orchestral sonority and time in the construction of musical form in the symphony rests in a common quest grounded in Schelling's alignment of architecture and music: How can art be truthful to nature, be universal and transcend specificity, and yet respond to the subjective needs of a moment in history?

Saarinen was born in 1873. His family, unlike Sibelius's, was part Finnish-speaking (his father, a Lutheran pastor), part Swedish-speaking (his mother). To make matters worse in terms of the conflicting linguistic currents in the formation of Finnish identity, Saarinen grew up in the Finnish part of Russia, beyond the Finnish border on the southeast of the Gulf of Finland. He spoke Russian and spent time in St. Petersburg, where he developed his initial ambition to be a painter. Influenced by his father, Saarinen, like Sibelius, became caught up in the rise of Finnish cultural nationalism that centered on an enthusiasm for the *Kalevala*. By the late 1890s he had begun working as an architect in Helsinki, employing visual elements from Finnish myth and history in interiors and exteriors. These decorative elements and figures in untreated stone walls corresponded to stories from the *Kalevala* about the hero Lemminkäinen and the tragic Kullervo.[94] Saarinen's breakthrough to prominence came with the Finnish Pavilion at the Paris Exposition of 1900.[95] In 1902 he built his legendary home Hvitträsk, a studio-home at which Sibelius spent many evenings.[96]

Both these structures are laden with markers of *Heimatkunst,* "homeland art," a term made notorious by Walter Niemann in his writing on Sibelius—explicit markers of a romanticized Finnish sensibility.[97] Comparable terms, e.g. *Provinzkunst,* were used in Vienna and Budapest to describe a similar architectural style in Central Europe around 1900. This style reflected an explicit break from architectural tradition in that it used highly stylized, rural folk traditions. Saarinen, in the 1900 Paris pavilion and his beloved Hvitträsk, emphasized local materials and evocations of the landscape. But in these projects, a sense of organic dynamism and formal unity was visible. Saarinen broke the distinction between façade and interior, giving the viewer and user a sense of a nearly monothematic arrangement of space that betrayed a single defining logic. Detail emerged from an all-encompassing flow in the design.

This strategy was indebted to Saarinen's devotion to the appropriation in design theory of the Wagnerian ideology of *Gesamtkunstwerk*, a quality characteristic of his generation of artists and architects. All the elements—fixtures, surface detailing, furniture, fireplaces, windows, and fabrics—were of a piece, creating an organic, unified, temporal experience for those using the building or living in it. Parallels between music and architecture were greatest in the immediate post-Wagnerian period, when architects and composers attempted to integrate every detail, overwhelm the user and spectator, and obliterate the quotidian and ordinary in an enveloping aesthetic that transformed the experience of time and space simultaneously. (Consider, for example, the apocryphal response Mahler gave Sibelius about the symphony needing to encompass the whole world.)

The closest architectural equivalent to Sibelius's *Finlandia* (1900) or *Lemminkäinen* Legends was Saarinen's 1899 building for the Pohjola Insurance Company in Helsinki. Indeed, although Saarinen built a series of great villas and houses before 1910, it is his public buildings that offer the precise analogy to Sibelius's sense of form in works for large orchestra. The Pohjola building, named for the land of the north in the *Kalevala*, was consistent in its footprint and layout with historicist models of urban multi-story buildings. But distinctly Finnish elements are visible from the start in the exterior: the use of large stone, the tower, and the softer roofline are all suggestive of Finnish rural architecture. Much of the stone façade is patterned in a naturalistic manner, evocative of craggy surfaces and characteristic wood construction. The modernity of construction (the iron columns bearing the weight) remains concealed, but the design draws a history in fantasy and does not pay homage to classical, Renaissance, or baroque models.[98]

The most visible sign of Saarinen's instinct for form based on an explicitly organic notion of movement over time can be found in the interior of the Pohjola building, in which he created sweeping but gentle curves and guiding vectors. The most startling element is the staircase, with its premodern-looking arches, intense carvings, asymmetrical patterning, and elaborate but modernist grillwork and fixtures (Figures 2 and 3). The reconciliation of form, function, and detailed, intensely symbolic decoration can be seen in the front door, down to its hinges. The elements of explicit Finnish symbolism and narration are unmistakable. After 1900, however, Saarinen began experimenting, moving away from late nineteenth-century Romantic and neoclassical impulses, just as Sibelius distanced himself from the lavish illustrative realism of Liszt and Wagner or its synthesis with sonata form and thematic transformation found in Strauss's tone poems of the 1890s.

Figure 2. Eliel Saarinen, staircase spiral in the Pohjola Insurance
Company Building, Helsinki, 1899–1901.

Figure 3. Eliel Saarinen, staircase detail in the Pohjola
Insurance Company Building, Helsinki, 1899–1901.

Saarinen's two most important, path-breaking buildings were the Finnish National Museum (1900–12) and the Helsinki Railway Station (1904–19). The museum reveals a greater distance from the mythic symbolism and nationalist impulses of the Pohjola building. Saarinen allowed himself more liberty in the detailing of the façade, filling it with geometric as well as illustrative decoration. Abstract forms were juxtaposed with narrative symbols. Saarinen exploited the flexible setting of the museum, which was not surrounded by other buildings, allowing him to unify function and design in the flow and footprint of the building. The entrance is placed parallel to the street and indented, softening the building's inherent monumentality. Saarinen achieved a balance between the vertical and horizontal, a more intimate and compact space than implied by the building's function.

Saarinen's other major accomplishment, the contemporaneous equivalent to Sibelius's 1902 Second Symphony, was the Helsinki Railway Station (Figure 4). Saarinen now integrated the structure of the façade with function, revealing a single formal entity. The building was given a defining

Figure 4. Eliel Saarinen, main entrance to Helsinki Railway Station (1904–19), 1939.

sweep. Ornament and symbolic allusion were muted, replaced by decoration that is geometric and functional. The graceful balance between right angles and round arch-like forms in such a large building, Saarinen's tapered layering of the massive structure, his theatrical and grand use of light and fenestration, combined with the sparse but powerful use of monumental sculpture, permitted him to retain a distinctive Finnish symbolism. But the character and content of that symbolism were resolutely modern. Saarinen projected a disciplined integration of form and function that utilized, with the suggestion of natural shapes, the character of the materials of construction. Saarinen's simplified vocabulary of modernism was not mechanical or ascetic. Rather, it communicated a monothematic line of organic form that, in a new way, used an abstract aesthetic to define a modern national identity.

The Helsinki Railway Station revealed a shift in Saarinen's architecture toward an integrated and simplified monumentality based on massive structural forms that seemed to emerge dynamically in space, diminishing the unavoidable static artificiality of architecture. Three Saarinen designs produced after the railway station can be understood as running parallel to Sibelius's development during the same period: the 1908 Parliament House project, the 1912 Lahti Town Hall, and the 1921 Kalevala House, which was never realized.

The Parliament House design (Figure 5) suggests the architect's intent to link the natural and the human. The building appears to emerge out of the incline in the site. The massive simple form—one gesture integrated by material and geometry—is differentiated subtly but consistently on the surface of the structure. The design can be read as stressing the ideal of unity in democratic politics, avoiding any clear architectural references to political models as had become traditional in European parliament designs during the second half of the nineteenth century. (In Budapest, for example, the English example of Westminster was adapted, and in Vienna, the Greco-Roman heritage was employed in an unabashed homage to classical antiquity).

Lahti Town Hall is more suggestive of Sibelius's use of transparent textures and sonorities.[99] It reveals a flirtation with a modernist aesthetic of simplicity. Saarinen uses a leaner vocabulary, fewer massive elements, and generates a more elegant vertical and delicate geometry. But the impressive integration of the curved and the straight, bringing the ornamental and the functional together into one gesture, is striking. Saarinen provides the user with a single vector of time. The entrance with its protruding fenestration and arched entryway implies the elegant staircase with its mix of curved fluidity, delicate vertical elements, and beautifully lit spatial stateliness.[100]

Figure 5. Eliel Saarinen, winning design for Parliament House competition, 1908.

The Kalevala House design (Figure 6), stark and lean, is a modernist evocation of a rural past. It is the most reminiscent of the sonorities of Sibelius's later works—the use of open intervals, the massing of the brass sound, and the nearly static stability of time generated by the use of tonal pedals and measured, slow, harmonic motion. Saarinen's design suggests an ancient fortress, but all symbolic signifiers are subordinated to the dominant shape of the structure that frames a tower at the center. The tower repeats, as if by variation and diminution, the ascending roof angle. Like Schelling's image of architecture as solidified music, the Kalevala project is Sibelius's sound world rendered concrete. It captures the experience of time created by musical form and structures that temporal experience spatially.

After distinguishing himself in the 1922 competition for the Tribune Tower in Chicago, Saarinen moved to the United States where he remained until his death in 1950. In America, Saarinen built buildings, taught, and wrote. Two of his American buildings are of particular interest with respect to a comparison with Sibelius: the Tabernacle Church of Christ from 1940 and Kleinhans Hall, built for the Buffalo Philharmonic in 1938, the only building for music Saarinen completed.[101] The Indiana church reveals the strong influence of the more ascetic attitude to ornament characteristic of the International style and the Bauhaus. Furthermore, the massing is leaner and the reference to organic rounded shapes, perhaps reminiscent of Finland, is gone in favor a more puritan American angularity.

Saarinen was influenced in his earlier work by European trends, including the Arts and Crafts movement and Otto Wagner and the Vienna Secession. In America he encountered modernist trends, particularly the work of Louis Sullivan. But his distinctive aesthetic survived these various influences. In the Indiana church one sees a striking austerity of line and simplification of form. But Saarinen's instinct for light and the gradual unfolding of a spatial framework make the interior of the church strikingly grand and uplifting. Despite its sparse, disciplined, and straightforward skin, the building integrates symbolic decorative motifs into the exterior, often functionally as fenestration.[102] The materials and transparent use of a single idea create a minimalist and static composition, an architectural equivalent of *Tapiola*.[103]

Kleinhans Hall in Buffalo, New York, built just a few years before the Tabernacle Church, offers the most suggestive analogue between music and architecture in the late work of Sibelius and Saarinen. Here Saarinen once again linked the organic with the geometric. The hall is both curved and impressively linear. The brick exterior highlights the simplicity of form, yet offers subtle decoration. Saarinen's brickwork suggests beauty and detail in a quite musical way. Throughout the building, larger simple structural elements work dialectically with design details, subthemes, and rhythmic counterpoint. The lobby staircases and public spaces have organic curved shapes created with a refined sense of wood detailing, all suggestive of the flow of time. Once again Saarinen builds ornament into a single line.

In the main hall Saarinen achieves his closest architectural equivalent to late Sibelius. White stucco and wood alternate in the undulating curved

Figure 6. Eliel Saarinen's rendering of Kalevala House, 1921.

ceiling, creating the sense of a hall that emerges dynamically like a wave of water from the stage: architecturally realized sound projected in space (Figure 7). The organic unity and simplicity of the design are breathtaking, as is the use of wood. The closest musical analogue is Sibelius's Seventh Symphony, where the composer's single-movement structure offers an arc of continuity with a nearly neoclassical "noble severity" and "grandeur," as one critic has observed.[104] Saarinen's achievement in Kleinhans Hall is a vindication of his special adaptation of modernism. Much like the Sibelius Seventh, its warmth and inviting simplicity can be experienced as a "single indivisible organism."[105]

The link to the organic and to nature suggested by Saarinen's brand of modern design represented a distinct philosophical ideology about architecture. Saarinen devoted much of his career in the United States to teaching at the Cranbrook School, which he also designed. He wrote two major books, *The City: Its Growth, Its Decay, Its Future* (1943) and *The Search for Form: A Fundamental Approach to Art* (1948), in which he gave voice to a philosophy of design that articulates the connection between nature and modernism in a manner comparable to the connection expressed in Sibelius's music, particularly in the symphonic form.

For Saarinen, nature provided the logic for all aesthetic structures. The human imagination must shape art along lines that reflect the inexhaustible potential inherent in nature. Furthermore, "organic order" is "the all-governing principle in the universe" requiring architecture to

Figure 7. Eliel Saarinen, ceiling of the concert hall in Kleinhans Music Hall, Buffalo, New York, 1938–40.

respect it. The organic defines the "whole world of forms." Like a piece of musical composition, a building must follow "the fundamental principle of organic order." Saarinen reconciles this notion with the imperatives of modernism by offering a corollary that "no man . . . is . . . timeless" and therefore no civilization can be "timeless." He generates a "categorical imperative"—namely, that every historical age must develop a style and personality in accord with its "place in time" and therefore evolution, with its inherent "potentialities" and "outside influences."[106]

Nature is understood as a constant variable, though its manifestations change with time and place. History determines the specific character and attributes that aesthetic forms must assume at any moment in time. Nature, for Saarinen, is an idea and reality that reconciles the particularity of history with normative principles of form. As formal arts and distinct from language and images, architecture and music are ideally suited to this synthesis of the objective and subjective.

Saarinen offers a brilliant account of how he, as a Finn, utilized the particularity of his historical circumstance to exploit the specific, while developing a valid international mode of expression. It required the distillation of design principles: "The more slowly form develops toward international expression, the safer the development." His unique brand of modernism, capable of international emulation, reconciled ornament and function, natural materials with modern industrial components; he redefined function as a dynamic temporal principle and deviated from the canons of the modernist International style by focusing on a mono-thematic, continuous, visibly organic sense of form that transcended the implications of function. He continued to believe in the symbolic meaning of architectural gesture. Sibelius's refusal to emulate the currents of Internationalist modernism can be understood in an analogous manner. Like Saarinen, his forms were unique, but naturally emergent from tradition. The emphasis on rotation, repetition, stasis, sonority, and symbolically powerful simplicity resulted in a distinctive originality. The once "local" natural setting bred a distinct pattern of formal design, while the expressive use of time no longer betrayed its origins, rendering it international.

Saarinen skirts the distinction between style and idea dear to many apologists for modernism. He defines style as "a form-language" expressive of a civilization in time. Therefore style is derivative of and dependent on form making. Since forms must be in accord with nature, every element must have a function, as in a cell or organism. Every note or chord in music must have a function within a formal design, just as every detail must in a building design. The task of the artist is not therefore the free play of the imagination. Rather, the freedom is defined and limited by fundamental natural principles that include the necessity of a purposeful logic for every element in a structure. When the "principle of organic order" is violated in a period of history, particularly in the design of cities, as it appeared to be the case for Saarinen with modernity's uncritical embrace of the International style of the Bauhaus, Le Corbusier, Breuer, and Gropius, the result is a dangerous disintegration, a disease analogous to "cancer."[107]

Art cannot tolerate the arbitrary. Yet the variety of valid original formal solutions to very particular challenges and problems in any age is great, as it is in nature. Saarinen describes artistic creativity and originality in architecture as a problem-solving process called "modulation." Saarinen observed, in a manner directly suggestive of Sibelius, that "since the problems are many and different, so must the solutions of these problems be many and different: sometimes simple and modest, sometimes vivid and playful, sometimes serene and elevated. Andante. Vivace. Festivo. It is up to the imagination to master the modulation."[108] Saarinen offered an apt characterization of the compositional procedure of the late Sibelius in which the formal architecture, derivative of a perception of the local and the natural, evokes a dynamic, organic logic focused on the functionality of sound, the sequential impact of motivic elaboration, pace, gesture, and material sonority. Sibelius defined an organic architectural music of modernity that reconciled tradition with the imperatives of contemporary existence, and a music that could communicate in an arresting manner as the impotence of language seemed ever more apparent.

Saarinen's ideology—the appeal to nature and the organic, reconciled with the requirement to reinvent tradition in accord with the specific demands of the historical moment, rejecting the slavish imitation of past styles and procedures—bears an uncanny resemblance to the ideas of Frank Lloyd Wright, his American contemporary. Like Saarinen, Wright invoked the primacy of nature and the idea of an "organic architecture." Key to Wright's usage of the concept of nature was its debt to Emerson. For Emerson, a "moral law" was at the center of nature, making every natural process "a version of a moral sentence." Like Swedenborg, nature represented the synthesis of the scientific and the aesthetic, since "nature is always self-similar" and infinitely self-generating, making creativity go on, unwearied, "adapted to infinity."[109]

Wright, like Saarinen, took this notion of nature as an overarching framework that could be reconciled as a normative principle with the variability and specificity that came with the passage of time. For Wright, nature meant the true "essential significant life of the thing, whatever the thing is."[110] For architecture that meant becoming true, as a moral precept, to the immanent truths in the materials and methods of modern life. Modernism, by expressing the specific character of modern life, would create structures that were simultaneously coherent with a transcendent definition of the organic and nature. The laws of nature were dynamic and continuous. Organic architecture in modernity meant "coming out from within ourselves to an outside that we've learned to understand as harmonious and *true* and beautiful, *true* to the *nature* of materials, *true* to the methods of our day, *true* to the life of our time, *true* to the best of ourselves."[111] Self-realization demanded the search for inherent harmony and unity within an honest confrontation with historical discontinuity.

Wright reversed the conventional appeal to nature as something that limited change and adaptation to historical developments. Nature was not a conceptual barrier against historical relativism and modernist innovation. But as with Saarinen and Sibelius, the appeal to nature offered Wright the artist a discipline of an almost religious character against imitation, fashion, and thoughtlessness. Modernism in Wright's usage may seem radical on the surface, but it was, as with Saarinen and Sibelius, a vindication of classicism. By linking the modern with nature, Saarinen, Sibelius, and Wright's break with past practice assumed the status of a vindication of eternal truths that simultaneously required a candid acceptance of progress in history. "Organic" modernism was a powerful answer to the accusation against modernism that it was either "degenerate" or nihilistic.[112]

An emphasis on "organic simplicity" links Wright with Sibelius.[113] For Wright, simplicity was inherent in nature and held the key to harmony, making the task of the artist a balancing act between elaboration and elimination. A piece of music, like a piece of architecture, reconciled form and function with simplicity. Simplicity was inherently modern, a consequence of rationalization and efficiency. It was the essence of the machine and modern technology. Wright objected to the derision of ornament in certain modernist circles and the notion that form should rigidly follow function. For him, they were "one" like a tree.[114] For Wright, the form of a building and plasticity in the use of space (like Sibelius's use of sonority to help define orchestral form), as well as the development of an aesthetic—a genuine style, in Saarinen's terms—all required a fundamental emancipation from inherited models. It required recognizing the particular implication of nature in modernity that privileged simplicity in plasticity and form consistent with the realities of modern life. Lending any church structure nobility, monumentality, and light demanded that the modern means equivalent to the materials and design of a Gothic cathedral be distilled with a traditional allegiance to "old ritual." Architecture—and all modern art—must create works that were "an adequate ideal for our general culture," creating no false distinctions hindering the natural, organic integration between form and function.[115]

The uncanny symmetry between Wright's work and Saarinen's suggests parallels in landscape and culture between fin-de-siècle Finland and the

American Midwest, notwithstanding the scale of the differences. This is visible in Wright's years in Oak Park, Illinois. Wright's own house, particularly the playroom, and the Dana House, bear key similarities to Saarinen's villas from the early 1900s.[116] The design of the Dana House reveals a shared emphasis on a single successive line of motion.[117] As in Saarinen's designs, ornamental elements and contrasts are integrated between the linear and the curved; the arched entrance to the Dana House and its vertical fenestration, for example, are both reminiscent of Saarinen's Lahti Town Hall.[118] Wright's Unity Temple[119] (Figure 8) and the Larkin Building for Buffalo[120] reveal a handling of exterior surfaces and the creation of large-scale interior spaces comparable to Saarinen's Helsinki Railway Station and his plans for the Parliament and the Kalevala House, even though the massing and the materials are different.[121] The similarities between Wright's project in Wisconsin, Taliesin, and Saarinen's studio-home complex, Hvitträsk, are particularly striking.

Figure 8. Frank Lloyd Wright, ceiling detail in Unity Temple, Oak Park, Illinois, 1905–08.

But Wright's later works—Fallingwater (1937), the Johnson Wax Building (1939; Figure 9), the Marin County Civic Center Administration Building (1957; Figure 10), and the Guggenheim Museum (1959)—are the most powerful examples of his use of the metaphor of nature and organic simplicity to fashion a modernism whose principles referenced the claims of tradition and classicism but whose vocabulary and resolution of form and function were distinctly and resolutely contemporary. Wright's late work went in a direction not dissimilar from Saarinen's last projects, particularly Kleinhans Hall. The resultant designs dispose of the notion of style as surface phenomenon. The legacy from these buildings invites a comparison with Sibelius. Sibelius's economical use of tonality, time, linear continuity, and orchestral sonority in his last works represent an original "organic" modernism, itself anticipatory of later composers such as Morton Feldman, George Crumb, and Magnus Lindberg.

Fallingwater represents the most eloquent modernist reconciliation of the manmade and nature characteristic of Saarinen and Sibelius.[122] The nature in which Wright's house is placed is clearly distinct from a manmade environment. But the fluid unifying integration of the two is not illustrative or governed by any priority of the natural, just as Sibelius's sound world in *Tapiola* fuses time created by music with the natural pace of time. Wright's integration of the resolutely modern manmade with a

Figure 9. Frank Lloyd Wright, interior of Johnson Wax Headquarters (1936–39), Racine, Wisconsin, 1939.

more innocent, pristine concept of nature is formal and seamless. This reconciliation of man and nature in modernity is best appreciated from the interior of Fallingwater.[123] It has its more modest parallel in Saarinen's Kingswood School (1929).[124] Like Fallingwater, the Johnson Wax Headquarters uses continuity achieved by repetition and regularity reminiscent of Sibelius in a manner that subsumes all detail within one formal gesture.[125] The same unifying effect is achieved in the Guggenheim Museum and in the Marin County Civic Center.[126] One sweeping successive line, a single organic natural gesture, creates a sense of space in which classical monumental grandeur and intimacy are reconciled with one dominating set of materials and structural shapes.

Figure 10. Frank Lloyd Wright, traffic entrance to the Marin County Civic Center Administration Building (1957–62), San Rafael, California, 1963.

The lean, condensed forms used by Sibelius in his last symphonies could well be described in Wright's self-justifying language; they turned "their backs on antique rubbish heaps with which classic eclecticism has encumbered new ground" by "going back to learn from the natural source of all natural things."[127] That turn to nature, understood in the terms of architectural polemic in his own time, opened up for Sibelius a path for innovation and simplicity that was relatively free of nostalgia. Strauss, in contrast, turned to irony, sentiment, and memory. Beginning in 1911 and even more so in the 1930s and '40s, Strauss utilized a dark-hued candor about human nature and history far removed from Wright's and Saarinen's persistent optimism, which was located in their appeal to nature. With a deep pessimism, Strauss turned away from shaping new forms and matching them with novel sonorities as he had done before 1908—an approach that had earned him a wide-spread reputation as a radical, eloquently endorsed by Schoenberg, who once quipped that Strauss, not he, had been a true revolutionary.[128]

Between 1911 and 1926, it was Sibelius who took a different path, and designed new shapes with distinct sonorities. Wright's designs, like Saarinen's, suggest the architectural analogue to Sibelius. The fact that Wright's designs invite a similar complementary juxtaposition vindicates the claim that Sibelius's originality and his debt to nature cannot be tied reductively to Finland, the North, and its landscape. Sibelius's approach to the challenge of modernity ran along lines comparable to a transnational "organic" strain in architectural modernism that included Saarinen and Wright, who worked without reciprocal influence at the exact same time. Both insisted on unifying form and function without lending function priority, thereby retaining an independent role for the aesthetic defined as integral to function. Experimenting with organic shapes and welcoming ornament, they defied the International style's clarion call for "objectivity" and the rejection of ornament as arbitrary and dishonest.

Saarinen's and Wright's adherence to ideas about the organic and the natural lent their work a relevance to contemporary postmodernism lacking in high modernism from the mid-twentieth century. That relevance holds for Sibelius as well, but quite differently from Strauss's ironic, self-conscious use of tradition. Sibelius sought and developed a resolution of the demands of modernity by conceiving of nature as suggestive of new ways of shaping sound and musical form and time. Sibelius created a musical analogue of architecture because, unlike Strauss, he distrusted language as a metaphor for composition or as a medium for himself. Yet he did not retreat, like Stravinsky, into the belief that music is an art in the non-objective sense, bereft of symbolic meaning.[129] While Stravinsky maintained a steadfast allegiance to an absolutist aesthetic of self-referential musical formalism, Sibelius linked his musical inspiration and ambition with nature and visual forms defined not by painting but by architecture. Doing so, he retained a belief in the capacity of music to express something of significance.

Sibelius's resolution of the challenge to the artist in modernity retained for music the same conceit of significance inherent in architecture. Designed space has function and is responsive to human experience. Sibelius sought to extend a classical tradition of art-making in which the aesthetic experience mirrored, in Wright's terms, life and nature at a particular historical moment. Sibelius reconciled a conservative impulse—his allegiance to a classical heritage that prized harmony with nature—with the imperatives of modernism. The startling simplicity and originality with which he employed the materiality of sound and the experience of time in music brought him a persuasive, popular influence in his lifetime and after, his critics notwithstanding.

Conclusion

In the end, Strauss, not Sibelius, expressed the most terrifying and troubling view of modernity and its relationship to art. Despite the seeming conservatism of his music after 1911, Strauss was radical in questioning the viability of any sustainable direct communication through the aesthetic in modern times. Faced with the bankruptcy of notions of progress and meaning, the collapse of language, and the atrophy of culture, Strauss embraced indirection, the manipulation of fragments, the construction of memory, and the primacy of irony and resignation, strategies located both in the artificiality of music's material and its susceptibility to connections and analogies with the linguistic. If Sibelius in his maturity appropriated a constructive modernist architectural model for writing music, Strauss shied away from any affirmative effort to embrace modernity.

Yet both artists reached a similar verdict about the future. Strauss, overcome with pessimism at the end of his career, used music as an instrument of recollection and nostalgia. Sibelius, after his breakthrough to a persuasive modern response to the exhaustion of past practice, came to realize the futility Strauss had discovered regarding the construction of meaning and truth-telling in modernity. As Ludwig Wittgenstein observed, a candid observer of modernity had to confront the limits of language and be consoled that what was truly significant demanded silence. Like architecture, music's shape and character could elude the linguistic. The conceit of music's capacity to communicate remained ingrained in Sibelius for a time. Retaining a visualized sense of nature to guide him, he turned to the possibilities of symbolic meaning in music and architecture. "It is impossible to define a religion—least of all in words," Sibelius noted during World War I, "but perhaps music is a mirror."[130]

Ultimately, Sibelius's recognition of the impotence of communicating in words would extend to music. Later in life he confessed, "Life is full of enigmas and the older I grow the more I perceive how precious little we actually know. The mysteries are always increasing." In response to the daunting reality of modern life, he fell silent, leaving his final works to inspire those less overcome with the profound anxiety and pessimism with which Strauss struggled to the end.

NOTES

I would like to thank those who helped with this essay: Daniel M. Grimley, Christopher Gibbs, Susan Gillespie, Bruce Matthews, Franz Kempf, Lynne Meloccaro, Irene Zedlacher, and Nina Stritzler-Levine.

1. On Sibelius and the Third Reich, see Ruth-Maria Gleissner, *Der unpolitische Komponist als Politikum: Die Rezeption von Jean Sibelius im NS-Staat* (Frankfurt: Peter Lang, 2002); and Timothy Jackson, "Sibelius the Political," in *Sibelius in the Old and New World*, ed. Timothy L. Jackson, Veijo Murtomäki, Colin Davis, and Timo Virtanen (Frankfurt: Peter Lang, 2010), 69–123. On Strauss's involvement, see Gerhard Splitt, *Richard Strauss, 1933–1935: Ästhetik und Musikpolitik zu Beginn der nationalsozialistischen Herrschaft* (Pfaffenweiler, Germany: Centaurus, 1987); Fred K. Prieberg, *Musik im NS-Staat* (Frankfurt: Dittrich, 2000); and Michael Walter, "Strauss in the Third Reich," in *The Cambridge Companion to Richard Strauss*, ed. Charles Youmans (Cambridge: Cambridge University Press, 2010), 226–41.

2. Sibelius's strikingly clean-shaven head dates from the time of his Fourth Symphony and parallels the austere stylistic shift it undertakes. Only later, perhaps, would it come to be associated with more extreme right-wing aesthetics. I want to thank Daniel Grimley for sharing this information with me.

3. See Gleissner, *Der unpolitische Komponist als Politikum*, 202.

4. See Theodor W. Adorno, "Richard Strauss: Zum 60. Geburtstage: 11. Juni 1924," in *Gesammelte Schriften*, ed. Rolf Tiedemann (Frankfurt: Suhrkamp, 1984), 18:254–62; and "Richard Strauss: Zum hundertsten Geburtstag: 11. Juni 1964," in *Gesammelte Schriften*, 16:565–606.

5. Tomi Mäkelä has discussed and refuted the modern reception history of Sibelius that portrays his work as essentially kitsch. However, in the case of Strauss the suspicion remains. Hermann Broch's famous distinction between kitsch and art pursued a common thread in fin-de-siècle Vienna thought about the need for the aesthetic to achieve an ethical status and transcend mere beauty and sensuous pleasure. By those measures Strauss's achievement, notably after 1911, does not qualify as kitsch. It represents an open, original, and eccentric approach to musical composition that breaks boundaries and rules and eschews any form of imitation. See Broch, "Einige Bemerkungen zum Problem des Kitsches," in *Gesammelte Werke: Dichten und Erkennen*, vol. 1 (Zurich: Rhein, 1955), 295–309; translated as "Notes on the Problem of Kitsch," in *Kitsch: The World of Bad Taste*, ed. Gillo

Dorfles (New York: Universe Books, 1969), 49–76. In this sense, the effort to see Strauss's works of art between 1911 and 1945 as inherently connected with evil is misplaced, even in Broch's framing of the problem (itself an extension of Schiller's aesthetic philosophy).

6. On Sibelius in America, see Glenda Dawn Goss, *Jean Sibelius and Olin Downes: Music, Friendship, Criticism* (Boston: Northeastern University Press, 1995), 39–74, as well as her essay in the current volume. Sibelius's influence during this period can be felt in the early work of Samuel Barber. See Barbara B. Heyman, *Samuel Barber: The Composer and His Music* (New York: Oxford University Press, 1992), 140–41; and Gian Carlo Menotti's comments in Peter Dickinson, *Samuel Barber Remembered: A Centenary Tribute* (Rochester, NY: University of Rochester Press, 2010), 62. With respect to Sibelius's reception in Great Britain, see Laura Gray, "Sibelius and England," in *The Sibelius Companion*, ed. Glenda Dawn Goss (Westport, CT: Greenwood Press, 1996), 281–95; Peter Franklin, "Sibelius in Britain," in *The Cambridge Companion to Sibelius*, 182–95; and the essay in this volume by Byron Adams.

7. See Reinhold Brinkmann, *Late Idyll: The Second Symphony of Johannes Brahms*, trans. Peter Palmer (Cambridge, MA: Harvard University Press, 1995), 199–228.

8. See Tomi Mäkelä's *"Poesie in der Luft": Jean Sibelius. Studien zu Leben und Werk* (Wiesbaden: Breitkopf & Härtel, 2007), 11–73. Mäkelä's indispensable monograph is perhaps the finest comprehensive analysis of Sibelius in the literature.

9. It is interesting to compare the sense of crisis in the realm of music and musical aesthetics with that in philosophy in the decade after World War I, particularly concerning issues of the human condition—being in the world—notably subjectivity and the perception of space and time in modernity. See, for example, Peter E. Gordon, *Continental Divide: Heidegger, Cassirer, Davos* (Cambridge, MA: Harvard University Press, 2010), 204–34.

10. Gleissner, *Der unpolitische Komponist*, 135–38. Perhaps the leading voice in this strain of criticism was Walter Niemann, whose 1917 monograph on Sibelius exercised considerable influence on his German reception.

11. A classic example can be found in Strauss's 1890 letter to Cosima Wagner, written after playing *Don Juan* for her on the piano—it had already been a sensational success— and being counseled by her to let his "heart" speak without his sharp intellect getting in the way. Strauss replied that it had been easier for Haydn, Mozart, and Schubert to write "naïvely," but for him and his generation the task was no longer so simple, even though in the end the "heart" must pierce through or "burn" beyond the intellect. He and his peers had to digest the gigantic advancement of all the arts in order to understand classicism, much less produce something to follow it, and that required that we "have to really strain our minds in a disciplined way." See *Cosima Wagner–Richard Strauss: Ein Briefwechsel*, ed. Franz Trenner (Tutzing, Germany: Richard Strauss, 1978), 28–30.

12. See, for instance, Walter Rathenau's *Zur Mechanik des Geistes* (Berlin: Fischer, 1917) and *Zur Kritik der Zeit* (Berlin: Fischer, 1919), esp. 45–101. See also Stefan Zweig, "Die Monotonisierung der Welt" (1925), in *Zeit und Welt* (Frankfurt: Fischer, 1981), 64–71; Georg Simmel, "Die Grosstädte und das Geistesleben" (1903), in *Brücke und Tür*, ed. Michael Landmann (Stuttgart: Köhler, 1957), 141–52; and Martin Heidegger, "Die Frage nach der Technik" (1953), in *Gesamtausgabe*, vol. 7, *Vorträge und Aufsätze*, ed. Friedrich-Wilhelm von Herrmann (Frankfurt: Vittorio Klostermann, 2000), 7–36. On Heidegger and modernity, see Charles R. Bambach, *Heidegger, Dilthey, and the Crisis of Historicism* (Ithaca, NY: Cornell University Press, 1995), 193–224.

13. See, for example, Charles Ives's view of Strauss's musical realism in *Essays Before a Sonata, The Majority, and Other Writings*, ed. Howard Boatwright (New York: W. W. Norton, 1971), 83–85.

14. Two examples stand out: *Don Quixote* and *Also sprach Zarathustra*. See Charles Youmans, "The Private Intellectual Context of Richard Strauss's 'Also sprach Zarathustra,'" *19th-Century Music* 22/2 (1998): 101–26.

15. On the subject of language and music, see Daniel K. L. Chua, *Absolute Music and the Construction of Meaning* (Cambridge: Cambridge University Press, 1999), 3–7, 167–70, 177–82, 221–90; John Neubauer, *The Emancipation of Music from Language: Departure from Mimesis in Eighteenth-Century Aesthetics* (New Haven: Yale University Press, 1986); and Garry Hagberg, *Art as Language: Wittgenstein, Meaning, and Aesthetic Theory* (Ithaca, NY: Cornell University Press, 1995), 91–98. The most useful synthetic consideration of this subject can be found in Ruth Katz's *A Language of Its Own: Sense and Meaning in the Making of Western Art Music* (Chicago: University of Chicago Press, 2009), particularly 134–92 and 315–29.

16. Strauss was so enamored of Watteau's 1719 *Embarquement pour Cythère* that he contemplated writing a ballet based on it; see Hugo von Hofmannsthal to Richard Strauss, 23 July 1912, in Hofmannsthal and Strauss, *Briefwechsel*, ed. Willi Schuh (Zurich: Atlantis, 1978), 187. Years later he reminded Joseph Gregor of this never-realized plan: see Strauss to Gregor, 14 January 1945, in Strauss and Gregor, *Briefwechsel*, ed. Roland Tenschert (Salzburg: Otto Müller, 1995), 262–63.

17. See Ulrich Tadday, ed., *Richard Strauss: Der griechische Germane* (Munich: Edition text + kritik, 2005).

18. Strauss did admire in Wagner the way he had fashioned an exemplary and appropriate integration of text and music.

19. See Leon Botstein, "Nineteenth-Century Mozart: The Fin-de-Siècle Mozart Revival," in *On Mozart*, ed. James M. Morris (Cambridge: Cambridge University Press, 1994), 204–25.

20. See Harry Kessler, *In the Twenties: The Diaries of Harry Kessler*, trans. Charles Kessler (New York: Holt, Rinehart, and Winston, 1971), 366.

21. One thinks of *Ariadne auf Naxos*, for example. On this point see two letters, Hofmannsthal to Strauss, 15 June 1911, and Strauss to Hofmannsthal, 24 July 1911, in *Briefwechsel*, 129–30 and 140–42.

22. See Romain Rolland's recollection of taking Strauss in 1900 to see the eighteenth-century galleries in the Louvre in *Richard Strauss and Romain Rolland: Correspondence, Diary, and Essays*, ed. Rollo Myers (Berkeley: University of California Press, 1968), 129–130.

23. See the illustrations in Kurt Wilhelm and Paul Sessner, *Richard Strauss persönlich: Eine Bildbiographie* (Munich: Kindler, 1984), 134–139 and 424–25, as well as the set designs for the first performances of Strauss's operas in *Richard Strauss: Autographen, Porträts, Bühnenbilder*, ed. Hartmut Schaefer (Munich: Richard-Strauss-Archiv, Garmisch; Theaterwissenschaftliche Sammlung, University of Cologne; and Deutsches Theatermuseum, Munich; in association with Bayerische Staatsbibliothek, 1999).

24. Hugo von Hofmannsthal's problems with language are eloquently expressed in his 1901 "Letter to Lord Chandos." See Hofmannsthal, *Gesammelte Werke* (Frankfurt: Fischer, 1951), 2:7–22.

25. The most trenchant analysis of Hofmannsthal and the problem of language at the turn of the century is Hermann Broch's *Hofmannsthal und seine Zeit: Eine Studie* (Frankfurt: Suhrkamp, 1974).

26. Strauss explicitly pointed to another late eighteenth-century model, Schiller, as exemplary with regard to communicating with the audience from the stage. See Richard Strauss, *Capriccio*, libretto by Clemens Krauss, arr. by Ernst Gernot Klussmann (Mainz: Schott/London: Boosey & Hawkes, 1942), 1–4.

27. For more on Strauss, the following works are recommended: Norman Del Mar, *Richard Strauss: A Critical Commentary on His Life and Works*, 3 vols. (Philadelphia: Chilton, 1962–1972); Bryan Gilliam, *The Life of Richard Strauss* (Cambridge: Cambridge University Press, 1999); Charles Youmans, *Richard Strauss's Orchestral Music and the German Intellectual Tradition* (Bloomington: University of Indiana Press, 2005); and Bryan Gilliam, "'Frieden im Innern': Außenwelt und Innenwelt von Richard Strauss um 1935," in *Richard Strauss und die Moderne*, ed. Bernd Edelmann, Birgit Lodes, and Reinhold Schlötterer (Munich: Henschel, 2001), 93–111.

28. Leon Botstein, "The Enigmas of Richard Strauss: A Revisionist View," in *Richard Strauss and His World*, ed. Bryan Gilliam (Princeton: Princeton University Press, 1999), 16–21; and Botstein, "Strauss and Twentieth-Century Modernity: A Reassessment of the Man and His Work," in *Richard Strauss und die Moderne*, 113–37.

29. James Hepokoski and Tomi Mäkelä have illuminated Sibelius's entire development as a composer through the lens of wider European historical developments and their attendant cultural politics. See Hepokoski, *Sibelius: Symphony No. 5* (Cambridge: Cambridge University Press, 1993), 2–3, 10–18; and Mäkelä's "*Poesie in der Luft*," 269–74.

30. Veijo Murtomäki, *Symphonic Unity: The Development of Formal Thinking in the Symphonies of Sibelius*, trans. Henry Bacon (Helsinki: Hakapaino Oy, 1993), 59.

31. Ibid., 59–84, esp. 79.

32. On the history of the appeal to organicism as a metaphor for musical form, see Mark Evan Bonds, *Wordless Rhetoric: Musical Form and the Metaphor of the Oration* (Cambridge, MA: Harvard University Press, 1991), 141–49.

33. Quoted in Eero Tarasti, "Sibelius and Wagner," in *The Sibelius Companion*, 71.

34. Ilmari Krohn, in his massive exploration of the symphonies, placed emphasis on the visual perception of form and sound, even though each had some "extra-musical" sensibility—in the Third the presence of the divine, in the Fourth the vain efforts of humanity. See Krohn, *Der Stimmungsgehalt der Symphonien von Jean Sibelius* (Helsinki: Suomalainen Tiedeakatemia, 1946), 2:404–05.

35. Daniel M. Grimley, "The Tone Poems: Genre, Landscape and Structural Perspective," in *The Cambridge Companion to Sibelius*, ed. Daniel M. Grimley (Cambridge: Cambridge University Press, 2004), 107–10.

36. See Erik Tawaststjerna's seminal biography, *Sibelius*, trans. Robert Layton, 3 vols. (Berkeley: University of California Press, 1976/London: Faber and Faber, 1997), 2:267. Those interested in the composer's life and music should also consult Glenda Dawn Goss's *Sibelius: A Composer's Life and the Awakening of Finland* (Chicago: University of Chicago Press, 2009), which is particularly strong on the Finnish context of Sibelius's career, and Andrew Barnett's *Sibelius* (New Haven: Yale University Press, 2007).

37. This generalization, of course, has to be understood as such, given Sibelius's many songs, melodramas, text settings (in *Kullervo* and *Luonnotar*), and the extensive music for the theater. But in the latter case, the music is largely incidental, not combined with text.

38. Quoted in Timo Virtanen, "*Pohjola's Daughter*—'L'aventure d'un héros,'" in *Sibelius Studies*, ed. Timothy L. Jackson and Veijo Murtomäki (Cambridge: Cambridge University Press, 2001), 174.

39. Tawaststjerna, *Sibelius*, 1:36.

40. On Čiurlionis and Scriabin, see Dorothea Eberlein, "Čiurlionis, Skrjabin und der osteuropäische Symbolismus," in *Vom Klang der Bilder: Die Musik in der Kunst des 20. Jahrhunderts*, ed. Karin v. Mauer (Munich: Prestel, 1985), 340–46; and Viacheslav Ivanov, "Čiurlionis and the Synthesis of the Arts," in *Čiurlionis: Painter and Composer*, ed. Stasys Gostautas (Vilnius: Vaga, 1994), 74–95, as well as other essays in this collection.

41. It is interesting to speculate about Sibelius's search for a new template for musical form as a response to a path whose character has been provocatively and brilliantly charted by Karol Berger in *Bach's Cycle, Mozart's Arrow: An Essay on the Origins of Musical Modernity* (Berkeley: University of California Press, 2007).

42. See Alexander Gerschenkron, "Economic Backwardness in Historical Perspective," in *Economic Backwardness in Historical Perspective: A Book of Essays* (Cambridge, MA: Belknap Press of Harvard University Press, 1962).

43. Lars Sonck's design of Sibelius's home Ainola reflects the composer's preference for simplicity and proportion. See Tawaststjerna, *Sibelius*, 2:18–22.

44. This fear is implicit in Adorno's critique; see Max Paddison's essay, "Art and the Ideology of Nature: Sibelius, Hamsun, Adorno," in this volume.

45. See Edward Laufer, "On the Fourth Symphony (Third Movement)," in *Sibelius in the Old and New World*, 185; and Goss, *Jean Sibelius and Olin Downes*, 39–74.

46. This summary derives from the original and provocative analyses of James Hepokoski, particularly in his *Sibelius: Symphony No. 5* and "Rotations, Sketches, and the Sixth Symphony," in Jackson and Murtomäki, *Sibelius Studies*, 322–51.

47. See Hepokoski, "The Essence of Sibelius: Creation Myths and Rotational Cycles in *Luonnotar*," 121–46.

48. Jean Sibelius, *Luonnotar* (Wiesbaden: Breitkopf & Härtel, 2005), 34, measure 189.

49. On *An Alpine Symphony*, see Mathias Hansen, *Richard Strauss: Die sinfonischen Dichtungen* (Kassel, Germany: Bärenreiter), 212–24; and Youmans, *Richard Strauss's Orchestral Music*, 217–30.

50. See Robert Layton's excellent *Sibelius* (New York: Schirmer Books, 1992), 77, 82.

51. Murtomäki, *Symphonic Unity*, 96.

52. Ibid., 118.

53. Tawaststjerna, *Sibelius*, 2:172.

54. Hepokoski, *Sibelius: Symphony No. 5*, 60

55. Krohn, *Der Stimmungsgehalt der Symphonien*, 144–45 and 206–09.

56. Leonard B. Meyer, "Music and Ideology in the Nineteenth Century," in *The Tanner Lectures on Human Values*, ed. Sterling M. McMurrin (Salt Lake City: University of Utah Press/Cambridge: Cambridge University Press, 1985), 6:23–52, esp. 38–45.

57. See Hepokoski, *Sibelius: Symphony No. 5*, 23–30.

58. Quoted in ibid., 17.

59. See Antonin Servière, "Twenty Measures of Sibelius's Fifth Symphony: A First Attempt at Stylistic Characterization," in *Sibelius in the Old and New World*, 236; and Hepokoski, *Sibelius: Symphony No. 5*, 26, 30.

60. On the Sixth Symphony, see Michael Steinberg, *The Symphony: A Listener's Guide* (Oxford: Oxford University Press, 1995), 601–10.

61. See Murtomäki, *Symphonic Unity*, 194–95; Hepokoski, "Rotations, Sketches, and the Sixth Symphony," 325; and Krohn, *Der Stimmungsgehalt der Symphonien*, 317–18.

62. The Seventh Symphony's original title was *Fantasia sinfonica*.

63. Putnam Aldrich quoted in Murtomäki, *Symphonic Unity*, 241.

64. See Donald Francis Tovey's analysis of Sibelius's Seventh Symphony in *Essays in Musical Analysis: Symphonies and Other Orchestral Works*, a collection of essays first published between 1935 and 1939 (Oxford: Oxford University Press, 1981; repr. 1989), 501–3. I thank Daniel Grimley for pointing out that Tovey's essay was inspired by a 1933 BBC radio account of an airplane flight over Mount Everest sonically illustrated by a recording of Sibelius's symphony, a work of "austere beauty and rare atmosphere." On the "organic" character of the work, see Gerald Abraham, "The Symphonies," in *The Music of Sibelius*, ed. Gerald Abraham (New York: W. W. Norton, 1947), 35; Marc Vignal, "The Sibelius Seventh as a One-Movement Work," in *Sibelius Forum: Proceedings from The Second International Jean Sibelius Conference, Helsinki, 25–29 November 1995*, ed. Veijo Murtomäki, Kari Kilpeläinen, and Risto Väisänen (Helsinki: Sibelius Academy, 1998), 311–14; and Murtomäki, *Symphonic Unity*, 241, 278.

65. See Veijo Murtomäki, "'Symphonic Fantasy': A Synthesis of Symphonic Thinking in Sibelius's Seventh Symphony and *Tapiola*," in *The Sibelius Companion*, 153–58.

66. For example, Akseli Gallen-Kalella, Eero Järnefelt, Pekka Halonen, Eliel Saarinen, and Lars Sonck, who designed Ainola, for no fee.

67. Quoted in Hepokoski, *Sibelius: Symphony No. 5*, 22.

68. Jean Sibelius, *The Hämeenlinna Letters: Scenes from a Musical Life, 1874–1895*, ed. Glenda Dawn Goss, trans. Margareta Örtenblad Thompson (Esbo, Finland: Schildts, 1997), 98–99.

69. Gerald Abraham, "The Symphonies," 35.

70. See Harmut Krones, ed., *Jean Sibelius und Wien* (Böhlau: Vienna, 2003), particularly Peter Revers, "Wien 1890: Jean Sibelius, Anton Bruckner, Carol Goldmark, Robert Fuchs," 15–21; also Glenda Dawn Goss, "Vienna and the Genesis of Kullervo: 'Durchführung zum Teufel,'" in *The Cambridge Companion to Sibelius*, 25.

71. One can compare the Sibelius symphonies, from the Fourth on, to Bruckner in a manner reminiscent of Reinhold Brinkmann's discussion of Schoenberg's op. 9 *Kammersymphonie* in relationship to prior models of nineteenth-century symphonic practice, e.g., Brahms. See Brinkmann, "Die gepresste Sinfonie: Zum geschichtlichen Gehalt von Schönbergs Opus 9," in *Gustav Mahler: Sinfonie und Wirklichkeit*, ed. Otto Kolleritsch (Graz: Universal Edition, 1977), 133–56; an English translation by Irene Zedlacher, "The Compressed Symphony: On the Historical Content of Schoenberg's Op. 9," appears in *Schoenberg and His World*, ed. Walter Frisch (Princeton: Princeton University Press, 1999), 141–61.

72. See Mäkelä, *"Poesie in der Luft,"* 69–73, 161–74.

73. Jean-Jacques Rousseau, "Discours sur l'origine, et les fondements de l'inégalitié parmi les hommes" (1755), in *Oeuvres complètes*, vol. 3, *Du Contrat social; Écrits politiques*, ed. Bernard Gagnebin and Marcel Raymond (Paris: Gallimard, 1964), 148–51.

74. Ralph Waldo Emerson, *Essays and Lectures*, ed. Joel Porte (New York: Literary Classics of the United States, 1983), 10.

75. Ibid., 23.

76. Ibid., 22.

77. Mäkelä, *"Poesie in der Luft,"* 245. See Hepokoski on the Sixth Symphony in Jackson and Murtomäki, *Sibelius Studies*, 324–25.

78. This hypothesis does require a concession to a distinction between the European "center" and a "periphery."

79. See Leon Botstein, "Out of Hungary: Bartók, Modernism, and the Cultural Politics of Twentieth-Century Music," in *Bartók and His World*, ed. Peter Laki (Princeton: Princeton University Press, 1995), 3–63.

80. See Pekka Korvenmaa and Lars Eliel Sonck, *Innovation Versus Tradition: The Architect Lars Sonck, Works and Projects, 1900–1910* (Helsinki: Suomen Muinaismuistoyhdistys, 1991).

81. See Jean Sibelius, *Dagbok, 1909–1944*, ed. Fabian Dahlström (Stockholm: Atlantis, 2005), 47, 149, 158, 296, 319. Tawaststjerna reports that the first thing Sibelius saw when he woke in the morning was an architectural drawing by Saarinen titled *Castle in Air* (*Sibelius*, 1:36).

82. In this volume, Sara Menin discusses connections in the work of Sibelius and a younger contemporary, Alvar Aalto, the great Finnish architect and an admirer of Saarinen. The discussion in this essay centers on Saarinen and Wright as more direct contemporaries of Sibelius and should be understood as complementary to Menin's essay.

83. On Wright's fondness for Beethoven, see Frank Lloyd Wright, *Frank Lloyd Wright: An Autobiography* (1943; repr. Warwick, UK: Pomegranate, 2005), 422–23.

84. See Friedrich Wilhelm Joseph von Schelling, *Philosophie der Kunst*, in *Sämmtliche Werke*, ed. Karl Friedrich August Schelling, vol. 5 (Stuttgart: J. G. Cotta, 1856–61; 1859), 355–736, English translation: *The Philosophy of Art*, ed., trans., and introduced by Douglas W. Stott, foreword by David Simpson (Minneapolis: University of Minnesota Press, 1989).

85. See Carl Dahlhaus, *Klassische und romantische Musikästhetik* (Laaber: Laaber, 1988), 248–56.

86. Schelling, *The Philosophy of Art*, 163–69.

87. Schelling's term attracted Goethe's ridicule. See Johann Wolfgang von Goethe, *Sämtliche Werke*, vol. 28, ed. Karl Goedeke (Stuttgart: J. G. Cotta, 1895), 416–17.

88. Schelling, *The Philosophy of Art*, 118.

89. Ibid., 177.

90. Ibid., 166.

91. See Berbeli Wanning, "Schelling," in *Music in German Philosophy: An Introduction*, ed. Stefan Lorenz Sorgner and Oliver Fürbeth, trans. Susan H. Gillespie (Chicago: University of Chicago Press, 2010), 95–119; and Bruce Matthews, *Schelling's Organic Form of Philosophy: Life as the Schema of Freedom* (Albany: State University of New York Press, 2011).

92. On Wagner's influence on Saarinen and his generation, see Marika Hausen, Kirmo Mikkola, Anna-Lisa Amberg, and Tytti Valto, *Eliel Saarinen: Projects 1896–1923*, with translations by Desmond O'Rourke, Michael Wynne-Ellis, and the English Centre (Helsinki: Otava, 1990), 21. On Wagner and Sibelius, see Eero Tarasti, "Sibelius and Wagner," in *The Sibelius Companion*, 61–75; Daniel M. Grimley, "The Tone Poems: Genre, Landscape and Structural Perspective," in *The Cambridge Companion to Sibelius*, 100; and Veijo Murtomäki, "Sibelius's Symphonic Ballad *Skogsrået*: Biographical and Programmatic Aspects of His Early Orchestral Music," in Jackson and Murtomäki, *Sibelius Studies*, 95–138.

93. The analogy between architecture and music was further elaborated by Hugo Riemann in *Wie hören wir Musik? Grundlinien der Musikästhetik* (1887), 6th ed. (Berlin: Hesse, 1923), 43–47.

94. For example, the Tallberg Building (1897) and the Suur-Merijoki Villa (1903). See Hausen, *Eliel Saarinen*, 18–19, 25, 106–16.

95. He beat out, among others, Sonck. Ibid., 32–33, 84–87.

96. See Albert Christ-Janer, *Eliel Saarinen: Finnish-American Architect and Educator*, rev. ed., with a foreword by Alvar Aalto (Chicago: University of Chicago Press, 1984); and Hausen, *Eliel Saarinen*, 48–55, 116–26.

97. See Walter Niemann, *Jean Sibelius* (1917; repr. n.p.: BiblioLife, 2009).

98. On the Pohjola Insurance Company building, see Hausen, etc., *Eliel Saarinen Projects 1896–1923*, 88–97.

99. On Lahti Town Hall, see Saarinen et al, *Saarinen Projects*, 182–84.

100. A curious mix between Lahti Town Hall and the Kalevala House project is the 1913 St. Paul's Lutheran Church in Dorpat, Estonia. See the photograph in Christ-Janer, *Saarinen: Finnish-American Architect*, 145.

101. The initial design of Tanglewood, the summer home of the Boston Symphony, with its 1938 shed and the 1944 opera facility, was first conceived by Saarinen, but not fully designed, built, or completed by him.

102. For photographs of the Tabernacle Church of Christ, see Christ-Janer, *Saarinen: Finnish-American Architect*, 89–92.

103. See Tim Howell, "Sibelius's *Tapiola*: Issues of Tonality and Timescale," in *Sibelius Forum: Proceedings from the Second International Jean Sibelius Conference*, 237–46.

104. Sibelius's Seventh was described in explicitly architectural terms by Simon Parmet in 1959 as a "dome mounted on the granite structure of the earlier symphonies." Quoted in Edward Laufer, "Continuity and Design in the Seventh Symphony," in Jackson and Murtomäki, *Sibelius Studies*, 352.

105. Abraham, "The Symphonies," 35.

106. Eliel Saarinen, *The Search for Form in Art and Architecture* (New York: Dover Publications, 1985), 47, 158–59. See also Eliel Saarinen, *The City: Its Growth, Its Decay, Its Future* (Cambridge, MA: MIT Press, 1943), 15–19.

107. Saarinen, *The City*, 15.

108. Saarinen, *The Search for Form*, 305.

109. Emerson, *Essays and Lectures*, 29, 668–69.

110. Frank Lloyd Wright, *Truth Against the World: Frank Lloyd Wright Speaks for an Organic Architecture*, ed. Patrick J. Meehan (New York: Wiley & Sons, 1987), 28.

111. Wright, *An Autobiography*, 162.

112. See ibid., 332–39, 344: and Wright, "This Is American Architecture," in *Truth Against the World*, 28–31.

113. Frank Lloyd Wright, *The Natural House* (New York: Horizon Press, 1954), 15.

114. Wright, *An Autobiography*, 146–47.

115. Ibid., 338.

116. On the Wright House playroom, see Neil Levine, *The Architecture of Frank Lloyd Wright* (Princeton: Princeton University Press, 1996), 24–26.

117. For Wright's design for the Dana House, see his *Drawings and Plans of Frank Lloyd Wright: The Early Period (1893–1909)* (Mineola, NY: Dover, 1983), plate 31a.

118. For photographs of the Dana House entrance, see Levine, *The Architecture of Frank Lloyd Wright*, 34–36.

119. Ibid., 40–46.

120. Ibid., 37–40.

121. Wright, *Autobiography*, 153–56.

122. On Fallingwater, see Levine, *The Architecture of Frank Lloyd Wright*, 224–40.

123. Ibid., 233–34, 247.

124. On the Kingswood School, see Christ-Janer, *Saarinen: Finnish-American Architect*, 70–78.

125. On the Johnson Wax Administration Building, see Levine, *The Architecture of Frank Lloyd Wright*, 303–5.

126. See photographs of the Guggenheim Museum and Marin County Civic Center in ibid., 363 and 411–13, respectively.

127. Wright, *Autobiography*, 344.

128. Arnold Schoenberg, *Style and Idea: Selected Writings of Arnold Schoenberg*, ed. Leonard Stein (New York: St. Martin's Press, 1975), 137.

129. See Daniel Albright, ed., *Modernism and Music: An Anthology of Sources* (Chicago: Chicago University Press, 2004), 4–13; and Daniel Albright, *Music Speaks: On the Language of Opera, Dance, and Song* (Rochester, NY: University of Rochester Press, 2009), 3–14.

130. This and the following quote can be found in "Jean Sibelius: Observations on Music and Musicians," compiled by Glenda Dawn Goss, in *The Sibelius Companion*, 231.

PART II
DOCUMENTS

Selections from Adolf Paul's
A Book About a Human Being

TRANSLATED BY ANNIKA LINDSKOG
INTRODUCED BY DANIEL M. GRIMLEY

After Sibelius graduated from the Helsinki Music Institute in the summer of 1889, where he had taken instruction with Martin Wegelius and the young Ferruccio Busoni, he decided to continue his studies not in Finland, where educational opportunities were ultimately limited, but in Germany, at the very center of the European musical marketplace. Having received a government stipend of 2,000 Finnish marks in May, Sibelius left Helsinki in September to begin lessons in harmony and counterpoint in Berlin with Albert Becker (1834–1899), director of the Königlicher Domchor and composer of numerous vocal, orchestral, and liturgical works including a *Reformation* Cantata (1878) and the ceremonial oratorio *Selig aus Gnade* (1890), dedicated in honor of Kaiser Wilhelm II.[1] By traveling south, Sibelius was following a well-worn path: other Nordic musicians, including Edvard Grieg and Johan Svendsen, had also studied in Germany, although Leipzig had been their preferred destination. Berlin, however, offered a more diverse and cosmopolitan milieu now, as well as the opportunity to hear many of the current trends in contemporary European music. Sibelius's studies with Becker appear to have focused almost exclusively on strict compositional technique—especially fugue—and the immediate benefits from Becker's lessons in his developing musical language are not easy to identify. The most important work from Sibelius's Berlin year—namely the remarkable Piano Quintet in G Minor, premiered in October 1890 in Turku—is more striking for its expressive handling of modal harmony, rugged texture, and rhythm than for its contrapuntal complexity. Berlin seems rather to have been a vital sensory and artistic stimulus for Sibelius—in other words, it served as a crash course in late nineteenth-century decadent aesthetics. Arguably, it was Sibelius's association with a close-knit group of Nordic writers, artists, and musicians at Zum schwarzen Ferkel (The Black Piglet), a tavern at the corner of Unter den Linden and Neue Wilhelmstraße in downtown Berlin, that left a lasting legacy on his later creative output. Here Sibelius came into formative contact with other leading lights of the Northern European avant-garde, including Edvard Munch, Richard Dehmel, and August Strindberg.

The most vivid, and problematic, account of Sibelius's time in Berlin can be found in the pages of Adolf Paul's lightly fictionalized novella *En bok om en Människa* (A book about a human being).[2] Paul (1863–1943), a former student at the Helsinki Music Institute, has generally received a poor press in the Sibelius literature, not least on account of his extreme right-wing aesthetics—he was later sympathetic to the Nazi regime and an admirer of Hitler. As an ambitious young man in the 1890s, however, he was keen to align himself with what he perceived to be the most promising cultural figures of his generation, including Sibelius, Busoni, and Strindberg. A series of books in the 1890s, loosely modeled on other decadent texts such as Strindberg's satirical 1879 novel *Röda Rummet (The Red Room)*, chronicled the half-imagined exploits of the Schwarzen Ferkel circle, and elaborated their wide-ranging discussions on contemporary art, literature, and the monotony of everyday life. In *En Bok om en Människa* the narrator Hans is Paul, wishfully placing himself at the heart of the group's debates. Other characters include the aristocractic, aloof Trondberg (Strindberg), and the artist Munk (Norwegian painter Edvard Munch). Yet the center of the book is the composer Sillén (Sibelius), a figure who, as Glenda Dawn Goss observes, is partially based on the impoverished artist Sellén in *The Red Room*, and who may also have been inspired by the hero in Knut Hamsun's nearly contemporaneous novel *Sult (Hunger,* 1890), one of the key texts in the emergence of literary modernism in the North.[3]

When *En bok om en Människa* was first published, its scandalous account of the group's alcoholism, extravagant dining habits, and womanizing created an immediate uproar.[4] Though Paul's later work included a historical play about King Christian II of Denmark, for which Sibelius wrote his atmospheric incidental music in 1898, he never attained mainstream status—an accurate reflection, as many commentators have noted, of his restricted literary talents and achievement. For all its sensationalist tone and self-indulgence, Paul's book is valuable for the glimpse it offers into Sibelius's creative process, a portrait whose accuracy is partially corroborated by other accounts as well as the evidence of Sibelius's own sketches and later compositional materials.

Paul depicts Sibelius as the archetypal decadent artist—a naïve genius whose work is possessed by an irrational creative spirit or restless and irresistible inspiration. Yet the focal point of his narrative is the description of Sibelius suddenly leaping up from his chair and beginning a "disjointed fantasia" on the piano. Much of Sibelius's compositional work appears to have been essentially improvisatory in nature, and the free-form structure of the music that unfolds in the background of Paul's novella anticipates Sibelius's later preoccupation with what James Hepokoski has subsequently termed "content-based forms": an idiosyncratic sense of musical architecture determined by the inner demands of basic compositional materials such as themes, chord progressions, and specific textural or registral effects.[5] As Paul vividly describes, such ideas often possessed a synesthesic quality for Sibelius, being associated with particular colors, moods, or times of day. And Sibelius never lost the addictive impulses to alcohol or tobacco that evidently fueled such intensive creative work. The interaction in Paul's account between the fantasia and the characters' dialogue also points toward Sibelius's early preoccupation with melodrama: the combination of spoken text and music became an especially vibrant medium in early twentieth-century Germany and the Nordic countries, but has subsequently faded sharply out of fashion. Works by Sibelius such as *Svartsjukans Nätter* (*Nights of Jealousy*; 1893) to a text by Runeberg, or the chamber version of the tone poem *Skogsrået* (*The Wood Nymph*;1895) to a text by Viktor Rydberg, traverse similar erotically charged territory to that which preoccupies many of the protagonists in *En Bok om en Människa*. Paul's novella cannot be relied upon in any sense as a historically accurate source. Nevertheless, it provides a fleeting glimpse of the intense decadent environment from which Sibelius's creative character first emerged.

From Adolf Paul's *En bok om en människa* (1891)

Chapter XIV

A curious man, this Sillén. Soon it would be two years since they had been friends, and Hans still couldn't quite work him out. The only definitive conclusion he had drawn was that the man was not mad, regardless of a thousand whims and as many contradictions.

Nor were his manners affected. Had they been, he would probably soon have lost his appetite, what with all the sarcasm and merciless taunts his friends offered in carrying out their self-appointed duty to make a man of him.

It followed that he must be a genius. And without further ado Hans discarded Sillén's honest, civil name and christened him the Wunderkind [*Genibarnet*]. It was both easy to use and captured his character.

Because, being the most childish of children, he had innumerable fancies that were far from brilliant, and befitted a spoiled brat more than a grown man.

He was a great gourmet, and loved good cigars more than he loved himself—which is to say, to a considerable extent. For he seldom had a thought for anyone but himself. To him, all human beings were more a necessary evil than fellow travelers through this vale of tears. He was a refined egoist.

Whenever he had a sudden craving—for a two-dollar cigar, perhaps— he suffered terribly from his longing and was the unhappiest man on earth until he held the object of desire in his hand.

But then it became terribly unimportant, and he could throw away the precious cigar without a further thought. Pleasure was to be found not in possession, but only in the satisfaction of such craving.

And his naïveté! He always gave the impression of having suddenly fallen from a distant planet, or having arrived on earth in some other impossible manner.

For his imagination was furnished by everything with the most bizarre characteristics, and nothing could be allowed to happen naturally. His powers of imagination were forever wandering off and finding the most distantly unfathomable causes for every occurrence. And to find connections between the most incompatible objects was for him the simplest and most natural thing in the world.

His "thought factory" was fueled by that most curious of machines, his brain, which did least well in coming up with an idea in the normal, commonsensical way of the decent citizen.

Ideas came to him glittering on a ray of sunshine reflected in the water— falling with a dry leaf—leaping with a bird—or radiating from the perfume of a beautiful woman. Yes, even a simple shower of rain, one of those that falls anywhere in the countryside and drains away into the first available muddy ditch, could make ideas shoot up like mushrooms from the moist earth.

And what ideas they were! As tenuous a relationship as that between mushrooms and the rainfall that forces them out from their dark nothingness existed between his ideas and the external factors that brought them to the light of day.

These external factors were simply the trigger that set off the wondrous machinery in his brain—the instigator, and therefore necessary, but with no further significance for the finished product.

He was a truly natural genius, utterly individual, without the merest relationship to anyone else. Once he told Hans how he composed. The moods that struck him with an impression were identified in his brain with a certain shade or color, and only then, when mood and shade were clear to him, did the actual composition start. Then and only then did the motives, appropriate rhythms, and correct harmonies report for duty.

To run around in search of decent, original motives, then return to one's Chinese-decorated atelier and concoct something that no one else had yet done according to the available rules, without offending any philosophical system—this was a way of composing he could barely grasp, let alone despise.

For him there was a wonderfully mysterious connection between tone and color, between the most secret perceptions of the eye and the ear. Everything he saw brought on a corresponding impression in the auditory organs—every tone impression was transferred and fixed as color on the retina, and from this into memory.

He found all this natural with as good a reason as those who did not possess this quality called him mad or willfully original. And so he told this to Hans in the strictest confidence and under an oath of secrecy. "For otherwise they will make me a laughingstock!" They became good friends.

Chapter XX

The young musicians lived as a family. . . . They were together every day, and always went to the theater and concerts in each other's company.

They also had a more-or-less joint economy, so that when they received a consignment from home, much commerce broke out. Old debts were paid and new ones taken on.

Hans was starting to feel excluded from the group. You see, he did not receive anything from home. After six months, his money was already gone and he was indebted to all his friends. And since he couldn't pay the old debts, instigating new ones was very difficult.

And now the difficult could barely be done at all. To maintain his credit, he had been forced to lie. He had a whole political system of lies, all for borrowing, only borrowing. But it could not continue. The system was exhausted—and they had started to see through it and exercise caution.

Today, for the first time in his life, he was at the pawnbroker's. He had obtained ten marks for his watch. He would pawn everything he owned. And when he no longer owned anything, he would take his life.

Definitely, he would. To die would be nothing. He had the courage to do it—unless something unforeseeable happened.

He felt almost certain that something unforeseeable would happen. This afternoon he was in a good mood. He went up to Trondberg's to meet his friends and chat a while. On the stairs he heard lively voices—a particularly noisy discussion. They were probably all there.

He knocked and entered. Instantly a silence fell and his greeting was returned with some embarrassment. He understood: they had been talking about him and his affairs. Immediately he felt hostile toward them all.

"Yes, that was certainly rather strange." Fredin improvised a continuation to a conversation to try at least to save face. Everyone agreed it was very strange indeed. The Wunderkind went over to the grand piano and started a disjointed fantasia.

It struck Hans, and further confirmed his suspicions, that he had only started to play now, this man who could never leave an open piano alone. Hans struggled to mask his aversion.

The atmosphere remained oppressed. Suddenly Fredin and Munk remembered they ought to go home and practice. They took their hats and left.

"Well," sighed Trondberg, accompanied by the fantasias the Wunderkind was playing.

"Indeed!" Hans said sharply and abruptly. Silence reigned for a little while. "Odd that they were in such a hurry to leave, as soon as I turned up! It sounded so lively in here, I heard it all the way out on the stairs."

No response. Trondberg was cautious, and pretended not to have noticed the outburst. The Wunderkind played on. The bile rose to Hans's head.

Yesterday he had heard Fredin express his astonishment that Hans always wore a frown of displeasure. "You would think it the least I could ask for, no, to be spared the sarcasms," he had said, "even if I don't get my money back." And now they started in with other demands—these, his benefactors!

He was grateful to them for the help they had given him! And they would get the borrowed money back! But their role as moneylenders did not give them the right to make other demands of him. It was too much!

And this coldness—this obvious avoidance.

Trondberg thought he ought to say something. "You're not taking any lessons now, are you?"

"No, I can't afford them! All they're good for is to expose teachers for the frauds they are. All they've taught me is their methods! Nothing but indolence on their part! And those methods: there's a system for each teacher! Show me a teacher whose system is not to have a method and I'll go to him! Otherwise I improve faster without the teaching!"

Trondberg could not understand. To study without a teacher, yet talk about improving!

"Well, for some people lessons are the most important," Hans said in an exaggeratedly vehement and biting tone. "Of course, they're a rod for driving slow oxen down the artistic path."

That hit home. The Wunderkind halted his improvisation. He had happened to overhear what Hans said. And today, by chance, he was inclined to understand what he heard: the fantasia had given his thought permission. He bit into the conversation.

"You're an unpleasant character, Hans! Suspicious and bitter, without the slightest reason. You're more than difficult to be with."

Finally! This is what Hans had been waiting for! Now at last he could say what he really thought about them all, these hypocrites.

And he did. And much more, too. So much that they sat there in astonishment. He didn't let them breathe a single syllable, but subjected the Wunderkind to a thorough, detailed, criticism.

"You—the worst egoist in the world! Always pretending to be such a genius and so absent-minded! Always deep in brilliant thought. So deep you'd rather club your closest relative to death than answer one of his mundane questions!

"And for those to whom you're not close enough to justify being rude you have only empty phrases, a whole supply of readymade responses, all in the prettiest order! Submit the question and out comes the answer, prepared, wrapped, and labeled. No need to interrupt your thoughts! The world should come to an end rather than one of your thoughts perish!— And how touching your friendliness toward me!— I come to you, in anguish, looking for sympathy. You send me away with a memorized phrase, the point of which is to prove that it's all my own fault. And then you say, with great regret, that you didn't mean what you said. Only to repeat the tactic again at the first opportunity.— You're the one it's hard to be with!"

He became more and more agitated, everything spun around and swirled past his eyes like a bloodied sky. He was utterly unable to restrain himself.

Trondberg dragged the Wunderkind outside to prevent a fight and left Hans standing there talking to himself. Eventually he calmed down and followed them out.

The two had stopped at the nearest street corner. They had already forgotten the entire quarrel and were in the process of debating the important question of whether Miss Rosensten was entirely real or partly stuffed.

But their only conclusion was that Trondberg did not want her. Working up a great deal of enthusiasm, the Wunderkind assured him that, upon the sanctity of his soul, neither did he. With his most devoted expression, he put his hand on his heart and declared ecstatically to Trondberg: "Oh how exquisite, how beautiful you are!" And threw his arms around him and kissed him, oblivious of the scorn of passers-by.

Hans shivered and looked positively embarrassed. He had stopped to join them. But they walked on without noticing him. Singing and yodeling, they disappeared into the crowd, arm in arm.

"No one wants to walk with me! No one wants my company! Always alone and without friends!"

Did he not fit in?— What could be the reason for their inability to agree with one another nowadays?

The Wunderkind said Hans was difficult to be with—and so it was all his fault! And yet the Wunderkind knew Hans's past so well, with all his financial difficulties!

It was just as much their fault! Their lack of compassion, their refusal to see that he was ill, that his mind suffered from constant disappointments, that he was slowly and surely sliding toward an abyss where the irrational ghost of suicide was waiting for him. They did not see that he, more than most, needed their forbearance. And instead of giving him the longed-for friendship, without which he was pining away, they fueled his bitter thoughts, forcing him to explode in angry words.

Oh! His hatred for them knew no limits!

NOTES

1. Erik Tawaststjerna, *Sibelius,* vol. 1, *1865–1905*, trans. Robert Layton (London: Faber and Faber, 1976), 54–68.

2. See George C. Schoolfield, *A History of Finnish Literature* (Lincoln: University of Nebraska Press, 1998), 378–79.

3. Glenda Dawn Goss, *Sibelius: A Composer's Life and the Awakening of Finland* (Chicago: University of Chicago Press, 2009), 86–87.

4. Adolf Paul, *En bok om en Människa* (Stockholm: Albert Bonniers, 1891).

5. James Hepokoski, *Sibelius: Symphony No. 5* (Cambridge: Cambridge University Press, 1993), 7.

Some Viewpoints Concerning Folk Music

and Its Influence on the Musical Arts

JEAN SIBELIUS
TRANSLATED FROM THE SWEDISH BY
MARGARETA MARTIN
INTRODUCED BY DANIEL M. GRIMLEY

Sibelius was, by conventional academic standards, little more than a mid-dling student at Martin Wegelius's Music Institute, having aborted his legal studies at Helsinki University. Evidently he felt ill at ease throughout his life in formal academic institutional surroundings. Sibelius's strengths rather lay in an idea of music as an essentially private creative practice, an ability to synthesize a rich range of musical styles and compositional mod-els, and above all in the acute sensitivity of his aural imagination. As Tomi Mäkelä explains in his essay for this volume, Sibelius never sought to cre-ate a formal school of composition, and his own teaching practice appears to have been a largely improvised or anecdotal affair, far removed from the kind of strong didacticism advocated by figures such as Schoenberg or Max Reger. Nor did Sibelius leave any writings of the kind that attempted to construct a formal compositional method or technique, either prospectively or retrospectively. Indeed, his later comments both in public and semi-pri-vate (through diaries and correspondence) frequently sought to deflect analytical attention from his work, stressing the fluid, more contingent nature of his musical inspiration. In this sense, Sibelius strove to maintain an image of himself as an archetypal decadent artist, as a medium entirely in thrall to the shifting patterns of his creative imagination—an image friends such as Adolf Paul were equally keen to promote (see the extract from Paul's *Book About a Human Being* in this section).

One important exception to this pattern of self-obfuscation and deflection can be found in the text of a lecture that Sibelius read at the University of Helsinki on 25 November 1896. The lecture, part of the appointment process for Finland's first tenured full-time Professor of Music at the University of Helsinki, was an exceptional event. The leading candidates for the post were Sibelius's senior colleague, the conductor-composer Robert Kajanus, the future ethnomusicologist Ilmari Krohn, and Sibelius himself. As Erik Tawaststjerna has recounted, the post was initially awarded to Sibelius, presumably in recognition of his political importance as one of the leading cultural figures in the nascent Finnish nationalist movement rather than because of his academic pedagogical credentials.[1] But the position eventually fell to Kajanus, who lodged an energetic appeal following the first round of the competition. Sibelius was instead awarded a state pension intended to support his independent creative work.

Sibelius's lecture notes betray their occasional nature.[2] The surviving draft contains numerous amendments, corrections, and alternative wordings, and it is not hard to suspect that Sibelius, who perennially suffered from stage fright, may not have been the most compelling speaker on this occasion (as Glenda Dawn Goss notes, Krohn was widely acknowledged to have given the best lecture on that day).[3] But Sibelius's text is carefully calibrated to the expectations of its audience: the framework is essentially an outline of the history of folk music and its influence on contemporary art music. Yet underpinning this familiar narrative account (of the evolutionary shift from pentatonic scales through the church modes to diatonicism and beyond) lies a stronger claim for the true character of Finnish folk music, the importance of runic singing and its associated performance practice, and the likely influence of such folk traditions on the development of future Finnish art music. For a nation still searching for creative and political independence, these ideas assumed a more than academic significance.

Veijo Murtomäki has traced Sibelius's relationship with Finnish folk traditions and its influence on the development of his musical style.[4] In an illuminating account, Murtomäki briefly summarizes the history of folksong collecting in Finland, including the work of one of Sibelius's school teachers in Hämeenlinna, Arvid Genetz. He also recounts Sibelius's first encounters with Finnish folk music in the field through meetings with the Karelian runic singers Larin Paraske (1833–1904) and Petri Shemeikka (1825–1915). As Murtomäki and others have noted, it is easy to trace the influence of folk music in Sibelius's early work, from the melodic profile of songs such as "Drömmen," op. 13, no. 5 (1891), to the repetitive rhythmic figuration of the second and third movements of the *Kullervo* Symphony (1892). More intriguing, though, is its lasting legacy on Sibelius's later musical work. Sibelius himself draws attention to the Russian composer Mikhail Glinka as a suitable model who, "permeated with his homeland's folk music, . . . instinctively found its correct basic harmonies." He then proceeds to discuss the harmonic basis of Finnish folk music in terms of an extended Dorian-Aeolian modal collection (a minor scale with variable sixth and seventh scale degrees): a pattern, he suggests, that is supported by the five-note tuning of the *kantele*.[5] As Sibelius notes in his lecture, current performance trends by contemporary folk singers had already begun to raise these scale degrees chromatically, "probably because people are already to some extent influenced by our new tonal system." But most interesting here is the way in which Sibelius himself embraced such modal variation as a structural principle in many of his larger-scale works: the paradigmatic example being the Sixth Symphony (1923). This work can be heard as an extended exercise in the Dorian mode, but with much of its tonal drama derived from the tension between pitch classes B♭ and B♮, and the early incursion (in the bass) of a disruptive C♯, which triggers the opening of the first principal Allegro section. From such chromatic pitch elements, larger-scale modal and diatonic collections emerge (including octatonic and whole-tone patterns, as well as the more familiar major/minor modes of the diatonic system). The climax of the work is the point of complete chromatic saturation at the apex of the finale: the dramatic composing-out, perhaps, of a complete tonal-harmonic universe in crisis.

In his lecture Sibelius is nevertheless keen, at all times, to maintain a sense of pragmatic distance, and he stresses again his reluctance to draw hard-and-fast musical rules from any of his observations: Glinka, he notes, had similarly failed to standardize his approach to folksong harmonization. So Sibelius's 1896 lecture cannot provide a prescriptive model for analyzing his own music. Nor should it be read as an objective ethnographic account of Finnish folk traditions at a crucial moment in the country's modernization—Krohn's work, and the photography of Sibelius's great contemporary I. K. Inha, arguably provide more promising material in this respect. But the lecture is nevertheless insightful as the trace of Sibelius's creative imagination in a formative stage of development. And as a rare glimpse of Sibelius's public voice in formal institutional surroundings, it has particular value.

Some Viewpoints Concerning Folk Music and Its Influence on the Musical Arts

Translator's/Editor's note: Sibelius's draft contains many additional thoughts or alternative expressions or words in brackets and other deletions and signs of correction or revision. We have retained the bracketed comments except where including them would merely confuse the reader. (Editorial explanations or interpolations are not bracketed, but given as endnotes.) Sibelius also likes to use dashes where commas would serve, and though we have usually retained these, we have substituted commas in some cases, in the interest of clarity.

In the following lecture I intend to present some opinions concerning folk music and its influence on the art of music.

If one follows the development of Christian music one finds, on the one hand, that a huge amount of work has been devoted to mastering its material artistically, and on the other that this material has found its principal nourishment in folk music. The origin of folksong has been the topic of numerous interpretations. It is not unlikely that to a large extent it originated in improvisation, especially prompted by a strong inspiration. Later this improvised succession of tones, having gone through innumerable repetitions and consequent changes, assumed a generally applicable form. Often enough a whole people has surely been part of this reworking. This must therefore be the reason why these folk melodies often express, in such an oddly touching way, the basic traits of a people's character and emotional life.

When comparing folk melodies from different countries, as seen in published collections, many noteworthy conclusions can be drawn.

For one, the various folk melodies are based upon different tone systems, especially depending on when they arose; for another, their melody is more developed in countries with an older culture.

Still today in India and China they sing folksongs in what we call a three-part lied form—admittedly a pretty well-developed form of music. These last mentioned melodies are based on a tone system of five tones within an octave[6]—in other words, a tone system that does not recognize any half-tone steps. Researchers in this field consider the 5-tone system the oldest. Folksongs that use this tone system are sung in Europe nowadays only in Scotland and Norway. A much later period saw the origin of the 7-tone system, i.e., seven tones within an octave, a diatonic system. This was much used—as in the [oldest] older Greek music and in church modes. According to researchers, these seven tones also form the basic scale of later Indian and Chinese music.

The Greeks later divided the octave into 21 parts, with the result that no harmony as we know it could be produced. Already, this tonal system carried the seed of its own destruction. Since most Christian folk melodies at the beginning of our chronology were based on this oddly chromatic Greek tonal system, no polyphony could arise, and they were always singing in unison or in octaves. As for rhythm, originally they followed the Greek laws—i.e., meter determined the length of the tones.

Later, when mensural notation was adopted, all tones were made of equal length. In this form these church melodies had a big influence on all folk tunes of then Christian nations. Having originated in folksong, they easily spread everywhere.

I mentioned the moment when mensural notation was adopted. Long before then, the antique Greek keys had to go, to be replaced by another tonal system. The so-called church modes were based upon this new tone system. According to the latest research, the change took place so that all chromatics and enharmonicism was abandoned and a new diatonic system was formed according to the initial tones of the principal scales.

All the tonal systems mentioned up to now lacked [the concept of] tonics and dominants upon which our present tonal system rests, as we know. However, this tonal concept was already dormant in the old-German folksongs.

Here I see the reason why Germans have played such a great part in the realm of music, particularly during the last two centuries, when all created music has been based on this national tonal system.

To prove this I want to point to a few things in the history of music that also clearly show the enormous influence of folk music upon the art of music.

The first independent purely musical forms to develop that were not dependent on the text—the so-called sequences—had their origin in folksong. Actually, they form a bridge between folksong and the Roman church melodies. To mention an example, compare the Gregorian melody *Et in terra pax* with our chorale *Allena Gud* (God alone) whose origin, as you know, is a sequence by Notker Balbulus.[7]— The popular element in the sequences became more and more prevalent, though the church tonal system was retained, and thus the melody arose. Due to its popularity the song pushed aside more and more of the old-German folksongs. Their tonal system, if one may call it that, was scorned by music scholars and lived its life in the so-called *modus lascivus*—the banal, popular[8] key. That it did not totally disappear, we have only to thank the wandering folk musicians.

Despite their confidence, the learned contrapuntalists did suffer from a bad conscience. They noticed where freshness and originality dwelled. They silenced their bad conscience by taking these despised folk melodies as *cantus firmus*, i.e. the leading voice, in their works. Yet they nevertheless reworked them beforehand in accordance with the principles of church music and the rules of counterpoint. Here especially the original rhythm of the folksongs suffered. This method was retained during the entire Netherlandish period—[and] indeed a lot later.

Besides a bad conscience, the learned gentlemen were also bothered by many other signs of the times. In Italy a few naïve artistic souls, though good at counterpoint, had tossed all unnecessary ballast overboard and simply sang ardent popular tunes from the bottom of their heart. The *villanelle* was born—a musical piece that most resembles what we imagine as a rather homophonic piece of music. [Scholars hastened to adopt this new element.] For the learned, its popularity [was] increased in an alarming way. They hastened to adapt this new element that had shown itself to be so vigorous—handled the *villanelle* more artistically—and called it the *madrigal*. However, a few composers—like Petrucci—took the middle road, and in the resulting *frottola* the purely artistic achieves, in company with the naïvely popular, a great triumph.

As we know, the first operas were born in Italy. Nobody can reasonably deny that they are national—sprung forth from the popular temperament,[9] from folk tunes.

English music was, during its glory days, much influenced by British folk music. Even the first operas had their origins there.

Throughout the Middle Ages, the Germans were downhearted. In their rooms they wrote counterpoint respectably and good-naturedly, but secretly, during free moments, out of doors, they thoroughly enjoyed folk music.

A few honest German composers were too simple-minded to reject the thought that their music was false. Especially as, with the development of harmony, the concepts of tonic and dominant—those secretly dear friends of the German composer—raised their heads more and more.— In Germany a fight also began over the old church keys. This battle raged for two hundred years until Johann Sebastian Bach, with his iron hand, rendered tonality victorious. Bach, the greatest composer who ever lived, surely knew that when he had won this great battle the victory was not his but, essentially, a victory for German folk music.

Among the consequences of the German folk tune's slavery under a foreign power one may mention that a few of what one may call folk tunes —those not created by artistic means[—]originated in rhythms (in the sense that the Romance and Slavic peoples have them) that do not exist among the Germans.[10] This is already proven *inter alia* by the fact that Germany has mostly borrowed its dance rhythms and dance forms so that, to mention one example, most dance rhythms in the antique suite as cultivated by Bach, such as the *Bourrée, Courante, Siciliana, Sarabande, Passacaglia, etc.*, are borrowed.

In passing I want to mention that Slavic music is gaining more and more ground in Germany, which over the last few decades has looked down in a rather superior fashion at all that is *fremdartiges*—of foreign origin. The reason for this must surely be that the Slavic peoples have a sense of rhythm that the Germans [for the above-mentioned reasons lack], in my opinion.

If we cast a look back at the musical masters after Bach, we have first and foremost Gluck, who would surely never have had this streak of truth that we admire in his music, unless in his youth—which he spent in Bohemia—he had been thoroughly saturated by folk music. Then we have Haydn, whose entire originality lies in his love of popular music. In Schubert, gypsy music has exerted a great influence. Also Liszt. There has hardly been a more national composer than Weber. Then there's Wagner, whose life's work reminds us so much of Gluck; Chopin, Glinka, and many others—important ones—all more or less influenced by their country's folk tunes.

I mentioned Wagner and Liszt. Their music has given rise to, among other things, a new understanding of tonality. Most of the so-called New German composers have trodden the same path. As indicative of this new concept of a key, I might mention for instance that the tonic in C major tends predominantly to both A-flat major and E major. The seed of this exists already in Beethoven. French folk music is much influenced by the old Latin hymns, which for example held a [totally] tight grip on the troubadour songs. They say that the national trait in French folk music has disappeared. Whatever the case, it is certainly not a coincidence that among the most brilliant and surely most original composers of the French—Bizet—has composed his best works—figuratively speaking—in Spanish.

If I am asked how folksongs may have influenced a composer—especially in a time when art music and folk music did not have much in common, I would answer as follows:

The reason lies in the style of the folksong.— If one calls a piece of music stylish when it says all that it wants to convey—which is a creative original idea above all but also a unified harmonic development of it— then the folksong in all its simplicity and modesty has a style so pure that one seldom finds it in art music.

One speaks of a personal style and a national style in music. The personal style would then be—to express myself briefly—the stamp a composer puts on his work; and the national style would consist of the stamp a people puts on its composers. The important role folk music plays in this latter case teaches us a striking lesson in music history. We thus see what a wide personality-molding influence folk music exerts.

The above statement [clearly] demonstrates, on the one hand, how important folk music's tonal system is when it concerns a nation's contribution to musical development and, on the other, what a precious legacy a people has in its folksongs.

The Finnish folk tune is often characterized as being of a melancholy—somber—character, monotonous, and lacking freshness. If we ponder the matter more closely, we find that the reason for the monotony lies not in the folk tonality but rather that its harmony is understood in a one-sided way—that is, always according to the same pattern.

As we know, harmonization is the method by which you give a melody the harmonious basis that [consciously or unconsciously] has been its foundation since it emerged. Anyone who has occupied himself with composing at least a bit knows that melody and harmony arise simultaneously. Hence, actual harmonization can happen only when a composer handles melodies he has not created himself. If these melodies originated in a far distant time—a time when perhaps no conception of harmony existed—harmonization assumes a quite different character. In that case the composer must clarify for himself the basic mood of the folksong and then allow harmonies to pour out accordingly—to create, so to speak, the milieu in which one imagines the [melody] folksong to have arisen. Only one who has fully immersed himself in the folk tune can instinctively hit upon the right thing. An odd example is Glinka. Permeated with his homeland's folk music, he instinctively found its correct basic harmonies. For the entire latter half of his life he tried to set down rules for his harmonizing—but without success.

Our oldest type of Finnish folksong presents a tonal system that lacks both *tonic* and *dominant*, as we understand them, as well as a final tone as in the old Greek keys, but contains just five notes—D E F G A—joined by two further tones, B♭ and C, when the melody assumes an intensified character. The tuning method for our five-string *kantele* supports this view.

Of course, learned theoreticians might—in many cases though not always—express this tone sequence D E F G A [B♭] as an upper pentachord resting on a similar lower one, with G as its point of departure. Hence we are dealing with a non-chordal series[11] as the harmonic basis for melodies of this type. This tone sequence—D E F G A B C—has been harmonized in such a way that it has been explained as D minor with a modulation to the dominant's minor key. Melodies harmonized in this way assume a somber choral-like coloring. Now it appears that they are actually mostly wedding songs—especially in Karelia, where they exist in quintuple rhythms; elsewhere in Finland folksongs of this type mostly have a quadruple rhythm and often a text of the most boisterous kind. (They are called sleigh-ride songs.)[12] Vocal quartets and folk-like songs were later based on this type—given a text that corresponded to the harmony, so that the original bright, fresh and varied Finnish folk tune became sluggish and dull. I [nevertheless] want to say that I may not have the right view. On the contrary, I gladly admit that in many cases it is not true. One thing is certain: these typical Finnish tunes *can* be explained in a more varied way and, moreover, we have allowed ourselves to alter many a tune without sufficiently noting their peculiarities—or many a characteristic interval—when the so-called harmonization required.

As for our rune melodies, a totally wrong understanding has prevailed in my opinion. It has been assumed that these rune melodies are short verses of one or two strophes. In actuality they are comparable to what we call a theme with variations. The original strophe is hardly ever repeated in unaltered form. Anyone who has heard a rune singer has surely noticed that as the text becomes intensified, its changes become livelier. This is why it is so difficult to write down rune melodies correctly.

A rune singer always puts his own personal stamp on these variations (if I may).

When we compare Finnish folksongs to those of other countries—especially those of the Nordic countries that can be assumed to have influenced our folk music—we find that in recent times we have many in common with Sweden. Thus the ballad *Velisurmaaja* (The fratricide), which contains the melodies to several folk dances—such as the familiar lullaby "Little Carl Slept," which actually originated in northern France—can be found throughout the North. Yet we find that our rune melodies and older folksongs may present great differences in [rhythm,] tonality, and form.

If one can believe researchers [in this field] who have studied Scandinavian, northern German, and Scottish folksongs during this century, the tonal system in all these countries' folk music is rather similar. As mentioned earlier, the pentatonic system can be found in some Scottish and Norwegian folksongs—obviously the oldest ones; otherwise our major and minor prevails. Yet many folksongs follow church modes, especially in Sweden. There has been much talk about a Nordic scale similar to the old Aeolian one, i.e. transposed, notes D E F G A B♭ C. The two last notes, however, are usually sung higher—probably because people are already to some extent influenced by our new tonal system.

It is odd that in northern Germany almost all folksongs are in a major key, while in the Scandinavian countries—above all in Sweden—most are in a minor key.

In none of these countries can be found a folk-tone system that displays the traits that characterize our rune melodies and [oldest] older folksongs' tonal system. This Finnish folk tune system is unique—some future research will probably locate its roots.

Yet another pertinent peculiarity must be mentioned. As I noted above, the Finnish tonal system lacks the final note in the same sense as the church modes. Rune melodies end either on one tone or the other—a clear sign that there is no basic tone [tonality]. As for rhythm, Finnish folk music presents a multitude of the oddest, most compound rhythms—rhythms counted not only in two and three, but also in five, seven, thirteen, fifteen, etc. Few countries [in the world] present such a multitude of original rhythms as ours.

[On this topic] time does not permit a detailed discussion of this topic. [Therefore I will be brief.] I have only wished to point out a few of the peculiarities of Finnish folk tunes, because of their great importance for our future music.

Folk tunes as such do not have any direct importance for art music. Their great significance lies in their educational qualities. A composer immersed in his home country's folk music must naturally get a different view of things, stress entirely new things, seek his gratification in art in quite different ways than others. Therein lies to a large extent his originality. In his works he must liberate himself from the local as much as possible—especially as far as the means of expression are concerned.

He will succeed in this to the extent that he has a distinguished personality.

A remarkable similarity exists between our age and the century before Bach. Then the church keys were in a state of dissolution. [We see clearly now that our modern tonality is shaky.]

[The church keys] 2 could not be retained because they were constructed, and hence lacked a firm foundation. They had to yield to a tonality based on an ancient folksong. 2 [Hence we see history testify . . .] We see clearly now that our modern tonality is shaky.[13]

But we must not tear down the old without being able to replace it with something new. It cannot be done by building [constructing] a [new] tonal system—it must be found living within the folk tune.

I go so far as to contend that all these so-called interesting turns, modulations, etc. [are built on shaky ground] are only of passing value except when their seed is found within the folk music.

NOTES

1. Erik Tawaststjerna, *Sibelius*, vol. 1, *1865–1905*, trans. Robert Layton (London: Faber and Faber, 1976), 1:190–91.

2. The original Swedish text was published, with parallel Finnish translation, in the Finnish journal *Musiikki* 10/2 (1980): 86–105, together with a discussion by Ilkka Oramo, "Kansanmusiikin vaikutuksesta taidemusiikkiin: Sibeliuksen akateeminen koeluento vuodelta 1896" (Folk music's influence on art music: Sibelius's academic lecture, 1896), 106–22. It is this version that forms the basis for the current translation.

3. Glenda Dawn Goss, *Sibelius: A Composer's Life and the Awakening of Finland* (Chicago: Chicago University Press, 2009), 227–29.

4. Veijo Murtomäki, "Sibelius and Finnish-Karelian Folk Music," *Finnish Musical Quarterly* 21/3 (2005): 32–36.

5. A traditional string instrument native to Finland, Estonia, and Karelia. As Murtomäki notes, Sibelius himself had appeared dressed as a *kantele* player at a Helsinki University masquerade in 1889. The instrument was widely promoted as the symbol for an idiosyncratic Finnish cultural identity in the latter half of the nineteenth century.

6. The pentatonic scale.

7. Notker (ca. 840–912) was a Benedictine monk at St. Gall in Switzerland, and an important musician and poet.

8. In Swedish: *folkliga*.

9. In Swedish: *folklynnet*.

10. Sibelius's meaning is unclear in this sentence, but his contention appears to be that German folk music includes a number of tunes based on dance rhythms that originated outside German-speaking lands.

11. In Swedish: *non Akord*.

12. Sibelius uses the Finnish term *rekiviisuja*.

13. In the original draft, Sibelius repeats here word for word the same sentence with which he ended the preceding paragraph. The Arabic numeral 2 possibly refers to a music example (now lost); there is no number 1 indicated in the text.

Selection from Erik Furuhjelm's
Jean Sibelius: A Survey of his Life and Music

TRANSLATED BY MARGARETA MARTIN
INTRODUCED BY DANIEL M. GRIMLEY

Erik Furuhjelm's biography of Sibelius (Stockholm: Albert Bonniers Förlag, 1917) is a landmark volume in the composer's reception and one of earliest substantial monographs on the composer's life and work to be published in the North. A composer and teacher as well as a music critic, Furuhjelm (1883–1964) worked at the Helsinki Music Conservatory (later the Sibelius Academy) between 1907 and 1935, and, alongside musicologist and folklorist Otto Andersson, was one of the leading musical authorities in the Swedish-Finnish cultural movement in the first half of the twentieth century.

Furuhjelm's book, as he explained in his preface, was initially intended to form part of the celebrations associated with Sibelius's fiftieth birthday in 1915—an occasion the composer himself marked with the first version of his Fifth Symphony.[1] Yet a series of delays meant the volume appeared two years later—on the verge of a critical moment in Finland's emergence as an independent nation free from Russian political control. Finland provisionally declared independence in late 1917, following the Russian Revolution. Yet internal political splits between social democrats and Bolshevik factions within the new country, and also between Svecoman (Swedish-Finnish) and Fennoman (Finnish-Finnish) parties, swiftly led to conflict and a brief but brutal civil war in 1918. Sibelius's sympathies throughout were with the eventually victorious "White" side—the group aligned broadly with the Swedish-speaking minority. Furuhjelm's book can be read retrospectively as an attempt, in this rapidly darkening political climate, to anticipate and assuage such cultural-political divisions and use Sibelius as a tool for cultural and political unity rather than conflict. Hence Furuhjelm's text, written in Swedish, gains an urgent political thrust, motivated both by the desire to celebrate Finland's growing sense of cultural emancipation, and to establish Sibelius's higher artistic significance. It seeks to appeal to an international audience, as well as to the opposed groups or constituencies within Finland, by praising the supposedly universal appeal of Sibelius's music.

Furuhjelm's book is also significant as one of the earliest attempts to document Sibelius's life and works in a single span: the terms of Furuhjelm's discussion were influential for later writers including Simon Parmet, Erik Tawaststjerna, and Robert Layton. The extract translated below is taken from the opening passage of Furuhjelm's study. Furuhjelm cites the famous *bon mot* about Sibelius offering pure spring water as opposed to the colorful cocktails of his continental contemporaries—a remark sometimes thought to apply to the Sixth Symphony (1923), though it clearly predates that work. Sibelius is presented by Furuhjelm as the equal of Richard Strauss—the highest-profile European composer of his generation at that point, and a composer whose career, as Leon Botstein explains in his essay for this volume, offers some provocative parallels with Sibelius's own. Yet Sibelius can equally be perceived as a pure Nordic counterpole to Strauss's opulent post-Wagnerian decadence, as Furuhjelm is keen to suggest. Sibelius's work, Furuhjelm argues, is characterized by a sense of "the naturally inspired, the genuine, and the elementary," terms which in the 1930s would carry much greater ideological weight. Sibelius's association with ideas of nature and landscape is also a prominent feature of Furuhjelm's introduction. Sibelius, for Furuhjelm, becomes the "sublimely realistic portrayer of nature," an accolade that places him in the same category as illustrious Nordic predecessors such as Edvard Grieg or, closer to home, the Finnish "national poet" Johan Ludvig Runeberg. Metaphors of nature and landscape evidently perform a nationalist function here, grounding Sibelius's music in the soil of his homeland. Yet they also offer a seemingly more neutral site of gathering and community than language (Finnish or Swedish), which, in late 1916, must have seemed an increasingly fragile medium for celebrating notions of national unity and togetherness.

From Erik Furuhjelm's
Jean Sibelius: hans Tondiktning och drag ur hans Liv (1917)
Pages 9–13

"Abroad you mix cocktails of various colors, and now I offer pure spring water": thus Sibelius is supposed to have spoken when he announced his arrival at the house of a German music publisher. We can assume that he uttered these well-chosen words in his characteristically half ironic, half

modest tone of voice. In any case, I don't start with this appeal to the publisher in order to add to our master's personal characteristics. For I have
a weightier ambition—there is an obvious truth in the cited words; they
actually elucidate, in their own way, Sibelius's position in regard to contemporary music in general and Continental music in particular. Not as if
today's musical arts, especially those of central Europe, were utterly devoid of freshness and clarity, spring water's most obvious qualities. It is not
my intention, nor has it ever been Sibelius's, to hurl insults at those highly
admired representatives of certain modern trends in music in the great
civilized nations—not even the ones on the 60th parallel. But it cannot
be denied that contemporary music reveals many of the qualities of that
alcoholic mixed drink, the cocktail—intoxicating, heterogeneous, artificial—whereas Sibelius's production carries, to a predominant degree, the
stamp of the naturally inspired, the genuine, and the elementary.

To present just a few arguments: Germany—for long the leading
nation—is now living through a period of experimentation, of searching
for absolutely new ways of expression, for harmonic, melodic, and rhythmic musical innovations. The music now cultivated in this country, with
its colossal musical traditions, is part intellectual, part naturalistic, part
even highly romantic—and not infrequently quibbling—art. A significant
diversity characterizes both individual works and the music in general.
The most typical and from a human standpoint the most brilliant representative is Richard Strauss, who in a remarkable way has been able to
combine the individual trends, yet who is so un-doctrinaire that he has
been able to create both *Till Eulenspiegel* and *Salome*. He is, in many of his
pieces, certainly an exception. Reflection often makes room in him for brilliant intuition, exultation for the standard ecstasy. To return to my
introduction: one cannot really deny this brilliant artist his exuberant
freshness and mirror-like clarity. But putting Sibelius and Strauss side by
side, we can equally perceive the contrast indicated by our introductory
quotation. Even during excursions into the most unreal domains, Strauss
is able to retain above all a healthy mind, a clear intellectual sharp-
sightedness. With Sibelius's music our comparison gains a more concrete
meaning, for here there is something more—not just health and transparency, but also the spring's quality of a natural mirror; in its shifting
forms it is itself a realistic reflection of the milieu against which the events
and situations in his works are outlined. Not only does Sibelius privilege
naturalness and the demands of the style as opposed to the pretentious
and eclectic, he points just as convincingly to the possibilities of natural
surroundings as the object for a composer's creative activity.

Sibelius is the sublimely realistic portrayer of nature. No matter how
"romantic" he often seems in his choice of motive, of invention or plot de-

velopment, he seldom gives his descriptions of nature or environment any peculiar or unrealistic traits. In this he is the absolute contrast to Wagner and to the entire Wagnerian School. In Scandinavia Sibelius certainly has his equals in this respect—Grieg, the great realist, was a pioneer; and here and there also in other countries—I think, for example, of the American MacDowell and his beautiful and characteristic [*karaktärsfulla*] nature images. Furthermore we have French realism, which seems almost to over-turn our claim that Sibelius is a rather isolated phenomenon in our modern musical life. But this French art has a strongly exotic strain, and this element has a romantic tendency and a reflective [*reflekterad*] trait that marks an important difference from Sibelius's music.

Sibelius is currently ahead of others as the great representative for the totally unreflective, spontaneous depiction of nature. This depiction of nature constitutes the obvious background for the majority of his composi-tions. It is never the goal, never merely an excuse for the introduction of orchestral or harmonic effects. But it is almost always there, generally not as naturalism, but rather as a soulful realism. Indeed, it would not be an exag-geration to say that whatever events Sibelius attempts to describe always take place in a fair or magnificent natural environment, seen and enjoyed and understood with a unique sense of reality and beauty. As I said, one can in many senses call Sibelius a romantic, but one cannot help but observe that his representations almost always maintain contact with the seen reality. The foundation of his music is seldom fantastic, and just as seldom fashionable or neutral. This combination of romantic topic and realism is one of the fac-tors that gives Sibelius a special place in today's music. And this is a factor I wished to stress from the start, not because it is the most important, but because it is the most visible and most characteristic.

To mention those compositions that lack elements of idyllic or somber rusticity would actually require little space; attempting to mention all those where the natural environment as background or decoration plays a greater or lesser role, however, demands acquaintance with most of Sibelius's works. We find nature description, or at least attempts at such description, in compositions from his school years. We see how it becomes a life-giving component in several of the chamber music compositions from his study years at home—chamber music is, after all, the domain of subjectivity. In works from his study trips abroad it gains a lesser importance—for natu-ral reasons—but in *Vårsang (Spring Song)* and in *Kullervo* and *En saga* and the other mythological and romanticizing poems, it appears in the form of a pastoral or as mostly realistic wilderness description. And after that we meet it almost everywhere—in the great works, the symphonies and the freer so-called symphonic poems, in the lyrical suites—but as exoti-cism in *Belshazzar's Feast*—in songs and piano pieces, etc.

The love of nature seems to be the primary, the basic characteristic [*urkaraktaristiska*] of Sibelius, and surely we do no injustice to our master's other inclinations by pointing this out or by taking this phenomenon as the starting point for our contemplation. For out of the child's and young man's ecstatic admiration of nature and his vivid sense of reality, the tone-smith's entire oeuvre seems to have grown, and whatever Sibelius has become, we see at all turns, during all periods, the fascinating nature-teller as a continually active, but never dominating, part of the artist's personality.

NOTE

1. The preface is dated "Helsinki 1916." Part of the reason for the delay, Furuhjelm explained, was the opportunity to include pages of the manuscript from the early *Kullervo* Symphony, which Sibelius had allowed to be performed in 1915 for the first time since its premiere in 1892. *Kullervo* is discussed on pp. 124–29 of Furuhjelm's study.

Figure 1. Photograph of Sibelius as it appears on page 225 of Furuhjelm's biography.

Adorno on Sibelius

TRANSLATED BY SUSAN H. GILLESPIE
INTRODUCED BY DANIEL M. GRIMLEY

Theodor W. Adorno's short, trenchant critique, "Glosse über Sibelius," has gained significance in Sibelius criticism out of all proportion to its length. First published in the *Zeitschrift für Sozialforschung* in 1938, and reprinted in *Impromptus* thirty years later, it was written at a pivotal point in Adorno's life: the year he emigrated to the United States, after having been resident at Oxford's Merton College since 1934, when he was forced to flee Germany because of the rise of the Nazi regime. The critique is closely contemporary with other of his key articles on musical aesthetics, including "On the Fetish-Character of Music and the Regression of Listening" and his "Social Critique of Radio Music," similarly concerned with what Adorno believed was the parlous state of art music composition and the decline of popular musical taste. Adorno's attack was prompted by the 1937 publication of Bengt de Törne's eulogistic biography, *Sibelius: A Close-Up*. But it must also have been motivated by the impact in the UK of other recent writing, such as Constant Lambert's *Music Ho! A Study of Music in Decline* (1934) in which Sibelius's work was paraded as the paradigm for modern composition.

The focus of Adorno's criticism, as Max Paddison explains in his essay in this volume, is the ideology of the nature imagery with which many of Sibelius's supporters associated his work. The claim for the "natural order" of Sibelius's work, and its associations of profundity, seriousness, and aesthetic autonomy, applauded by writers such as Lambert, Cecil Gray, and Ernest Newman, was deeply problematic for Adorno. Sibelius's apparent reliance on such naïve pictorial imagery constitutes an attempt to conceal what Adorno perceives as the technical inadequacy of his musical language and its failure to engage critically with the social context in which it was created and consumed. For Adorno, this signals a fundamental failure of artistic responsibility.

Adorno's essay also raises the issue of Sibelius's reception in Germany during the Third Reich—not least given the prevalence for essentialist metaphors of blood and soil that fueled the regime's extreme racist ideology. This in turn prompts the question of the degree to which Sibelius was himself aware of such political appropriation, and may even have been party to such thinking. Sibelius does not appear to have openly expressed sympathy for far right-wing political movements in the way that Knut Hamsun did during the 1940s, and though he accepted the Goethe Medal in 1935 on the occasion of his seventieth birthday, he did not travel to Germany to collect the award in person. Sibelius's position throughout the Second World War (during which Finland fought both the Red Army, and later the retreating German forces) was at times ambivalent or unclear, but no documentary evidence survives that definitively links him with Fascist tendencies.[1] Sibelius's pithy diary entries of 9 August and 6 September 1943, written during the darkest days of the war—"The question of Origin does not interest me. . . . These primitive modes of thought, anti-Semitism, etc., I can no longer accept at my age"— are deeply inconclusive, as Tomi Mäkelä observes.[2] Sibelius's most culpable offense during the conflict, it seems reasonable to assume from the surviving evidence, is that whenever possible he attempted to maintain an aloof distance from political events. For some scholars, this remains an open question.[3]

For Adorno, however, the musical materials themselves are already deeply politicized, and the central thrust of his essay becomes the extent to which Sibelius's music perpetuates a regressively conservative worldview under the guise of a formless elementalism. Adorno's aim is therefore wider than the simple critique of Sibelius's music implied by his essay's title: "Glosse über Sibelius" becomes part of a broader analysis of contemporary musical culture, one as much concerned with patterns of listening and reception as with the supposed technical shortcomings of Sibelius's work. It is a defense of the New Music—especially of Schoenberg and the Second Viennese School, whose work was under particular attack in Germany in the late 1930s—but it is simultaneously a challenge to unmediated notions of creativity and being-in-place. In its insight and philosophical ambition, Adorno's "Glosse" and his note on Sibelius and Hamsun, translated below, remain continually provocative.

Gloss on Sibelius

THEODOR W. ADORNO

To anyone who has grown up in the Austro-German musical sphere, the name of Sibelius does not say much. If Sibelius is not conflated geographically with [Christian] Sinding, or phonetically with Delius, then he is familiar as the composer of *Valse triste*, a harmless bit of salon music, or of filler pieces that can be encountered in concerts, such as *The Oceanides* or *The Swan of Tuonela*—shorter pieces of program music with a rather vague physiognomy that is difficult to recall.

But come to England, or even America, and the name begins to become boundlessly inflated. It is dropped as frequently as the brand name of an automobile. Radio and concerts resound with the tones of Finland. Toscanini's programs are open to Sibelius. Long essays appear, larded with musical examples, in which he is praised as the most significant composer of the present day, a true symphonist, a timeless non-modern and positively a kind of Beethoven. There is a Sibelius Society that is devoted to his fame and busies itself bringing gramophone records of his oeuvre to market.

You become curious and listen to a few of the major works, for example the Fourth and Fifth symphonies. First you study the scores. They look skimpy and Boeotian, and you imagine that the secret can only be revealed through actual hearing. But the sound does nothing to change the picture.

It looks like this: a few "themes" are set out, some utterly unshapely and trivial sequences of tones, usually not even harmonically worked out; instead, they are *unisono*, with organ pedal points, flat harmonies, and whatever else the five lines of the musical staff have to offer as a means of avoiding logical chord progressions. These sequences of notes are soon befallen by misfortune, rather like a newborn baby who falls off the table and injures its back. They cannot walk properly. They get bogged down. At some unpredictable moment the rhythmic movement ceases: forward movement becomes incomprehensible. Then the simple sequences of notes return; all twisted and bent, but without moving from the spot. The apologists consider these parts to be Beethovenian: out of insignificance—the void—a whole world is created. But they are worthy of the world in which we live; at once crude and mysterious, tawdry and contradictory, all-familiar and impenetrable. Again, the apologists say that precisely this testifies to the incommensurability of a master of creative form who will accept no conventional models. But it is impossible to have faith in the incommensurable forms of someone who obviously hasn't mastered four-part harmony; it is impossible to think of someone as far above the school who uses material that is appropriate for a schoolboy but simply does not know how to follow the rules. It is the originality of helplessness: in the category of those amateurs who are afraid to take composition lessons for fear of losing their originality, which itself is nothing but the disorganized remains of what preceded them.

On Sibelius as composer one should waste as few words as on such amateurs. He may have made a considerable contribution when it comes to the colonization of his fatherland. We may easily imagine that he returned home following his German composition studies with justified feelings of inferiority, quite conscious that he was destined neither to compose a chorale nor to write proper counterpoint; that he buried himself in the land of a thousand lakes in order to hide from the critical eye of his schoolmasters. There was probably no one more astonished than he to discover that his failure was being interpreted as success, his lack of technical ability as necessity. In the end he probably believed it himself and has now been brooding for years over his eighth symphony as if it were the Ninth.

What is interesting is the effect. How is it possible that an author achieves world fame and a kind of classicism—albeit manipulated—who has not merely lagged completely behind the technical standard of the times—for precisely this is what is considered good about him—but who fails to live up to his own standards and makes uncertain, even amateurish use of the traditional means, from the building materials to the large constructions themselves? Sibelius's success is a symptom of the disturbance of musical consciousness. The earthquake that found its expression in the dissonances of the great New Music has not spared the old-fashioned, lesser kind. It became ravaged and crooked. But as people flee from the dissonances, they have sought shelter in false triads. The false triads: Stravinsky composed them out.[4] By adding false notes he demonstrated how false the right ones have become. In Sibelius, the pure ones already sound false. He is a Stravinsky *malgré lui*. Except that he has less talent.

His followers want to hear nothing of all this. Their song echoes the refrain: "It's all nature; it's all nature." The great Pan, and as needed Blood and Soil too, appears promptly on the scene. The trivial is validated as the origin of things, the unarticulated as the sound of unconscious creation.

Categories of this kind evade critique. The dominant conviction is that nature's mood is bound up with awestruck silence. But if the concept of "nature's mood"[5] should not remain unquestioned even in the real world, then surely not in works of art. Symphonies are not a thousand lakes, even when riddled with a thousand holes.

Music has constructed a technical canon for the representation of nature: Impressionism. In the wake of nineteenth-century French painting, Debussy developed methods for expressing the expressionless, for capturing light and shadow, the color and the half-light of the visual world in sounds that go deeper than the poetic word. These methods are foreign to Sibelius. *Car nous voulons la nuance encore*[6]—this sounds like a mockery of his muted, stiff, and accidental orchestral color. This is no music *en plein air*. It plays in a messy schoolroom, where during recess the adolescents give evidence of their genius by overturning the inkwells. No palette: nothing but ink.

Even this is reckoned as an achievement. On the one hand Nordic profundity is supposed to become intimate with unconscious nature—without, on the other, taking frivolous pleasure in her charms. It is a cramped promiscuity in the dark. The asceticism of impotence is celebrated as self-discipline of the creator. If he has a relationship with nature, then it is only inwardly. His realm is not of this world. It is the realm of the emotions. Once arrived there, you are released from all reckoning. If the emotional content is as indeterminate as its foundation in the musical events themselves, this is seen as the index of their profundity.

It is not. The emotions are determinable. Not, it is true, as they might prefer, in terms of their metaphysical and existential content. They have as little of this as Sibelius's scores. But in terms of what is unleashed in the scores. It is the configuration of the banal and the absurd. Each individual thing sounds quotidian and familiar. The motives are fragments from the current material of tonality. We have already heard them so often we think we understand them. But they are placed in a meaningless context: as if one were to combine indiscriminately the words *gas station, lunch,*[7] *death, Greta, and plowshare* with verbs and particles. An incomprehensible whole made up of the most trivial details produces the false image of profundity. We feel good that we can follow from one thing to the next, and are pleased, in good conscience, while realizing that in actuality we don't understand a thing. Or: complete non-understanding, which constitutes the signature of contemporary musical consciousness, has its ideology in the appearance of comprehensibility produced by Sibelius's vocabulary.

In the resistance to advanced New Music, in the mean-spirited hatred with which it is defamed, we hear not just the traditional and general aversion to the new, but the specific intuition that the old means no longer suffice. Not that they are "exhausted," for mathematically the tonal chords certainly still permit an unlimited number of new combinations. But they have become mere semblance, un-genuine: they serve the transfiguration of a world that has nothing left to transfigure, and no music can lay claim to being written, any more, that does not present a critical attack on what exists, down to the innermost cells of its technical methodology. This intuition is what people hope to escape by means of Sibelius. This is the secret of his success. The absurdity that the truly depraved means of traditional post-Romantic music take on in his works, as a result of their inadequate treatment, seems to lift them up out of their demise. That it is possible to compose in a way that is fundamentally old-fashioned, yet completely new: this is the triumph that conformism, looking to Sibelius, begins to celebrate. His success is equivalent to longing for the world to be healed of its sufferings and contradictions, for a "renewal" that lets us keep what we possess. What is at stake in this kind of wishing for renewal, what is equally at stake in this "Sibelian" originality is revealed by its meaninglessness. This lack of meaning is not merely "technical," any more than a sentence without sense is merely "technically" devoid of meaning. It sounds absurd because the attempt to express something new using the old, decayed means is itself absurd. What is expressed is nothing at all.

It is as if for the autochthonous Finn all the objections ginned up in reaction to cultural Bolshevism were coming into their own. If reactionaries imagine that the New Music owes its existence to a lack of control over the material of the old music, this applies to none other than Sibelius, who holds fast to the old. His music is in a certain sense the only "corrosive" one to emerge from our times. Not in the sense of the destruction of the bad existing, but of a Caliban-like destruction of all the musical results of mastery over nature that were sufficiently hard-won by humanity in its handling of the tempered scale. If Sibelius is good, then the criteria of musical quality that have endured from Bach to Schoenberg—a wealth of relations, articulation, unity in diversity—are done in once and for all. All that Sibelius betrays in favor of a nature that is nothing but a tattered photograph of the familiar apartment. For his part he contributes, in art music, to the great degradation at which industrialized music easily outdoes him. But such destruction masks itself in his symphonies as creation. Its effect is dangerous.

Footnote on Sibelius and Hamsun

THEODOR W. ADORNO

Translator's note: Adorno wrote this brief text in connection with Leo Lowenthal's 1937 essay "Knut Hamsun: On the Prehistory of Authoritarian Ideology" (Zeitschrift für Sozialforschung 6). It was printed as a note to the following sentence by Lowenthal: "If the poverty of the cultural inventory and the shadowy quality of the people in his works are interpreted by readers and critics as a sign of particular modesty, mature austerity, reverential reserve toward nature, and 'epic grandeur,' then what is expressed in this kind of encomium of the writer is a tired resignation, a social defeatism" (338).

The same tendency can be observed in a strictly technical sense in the symphonies of Jan Sibelius, which are of Hamsun's ilk in their material construction as well as their effect. Here one should think not only of the vague and at the same time coloristically undeveloped "Pan-like" nature mood, but of the compositional methods themselves. This type of symphonic style knows no musical development. It is a layering of arbitrary and chance repetitions of motives whose material, in itself, is trivial. The resulting appearance of originality is ascribable only to the senselessness with which the motives are put together, without anything to guarantee their meaningful context other than the abstract passage of time. The obscurity, a product of technical awkwardness, feigns a profundity that does not exist. The constructed opaque repetitions lay claim to an eternal rhythm of nature, which is also expressed by a lack of symphonic consciousness of time; the nullity of the melodic monads, which is carried over into an unarticulated sounding, corresponds to the contempt for humanity to which an all-embracing nature subjects the Hamsunian individual. Sibelius, like Hamsun, is to be distinguished from Impressionist tendencies by the fact that the all-embracing nature is prepared from the dessicated remains of traditional bourgeois art, rather than being the primal vision of a protesting subjectivity.

NOTES

1. For a summary, see D. G. Kirby, *Finland in the Twentieth Century: A History and an Interpretation* (Minneapolis: University of Minnesota Press, 1979), 106–47.

2. Tomi Mäkelä, *"Poesie in der Luft": Jean Sibelius, Studien zu Leben und Werk* (Wiesbaden: Breitkopf & Härtel, 2007), 43.

3. The issue is examined exhaustively in Ruth-Maria Gleissner, *Der unpolitische Komponist als Politikum: Die Rezeption von Jean Sibelius im NS-Staat* (Frankfurt: Peter Lang, 2002); as well as in Mäkelä, *"Poesie in der Luft."* More recently Timothy L. Jackson has reopened the question of Sibelius's sympathies during the war in his chapter in *Sibelius in the Old and New World: Aspects of His Music, Its Interpretation and Reception*, ed. Timothy L. Jackson, Veijo Murtomäki, Colin Davis, and Timo Virtanen (Frankfurt: Peter Lang, 2009).

4. In German: *auskomponiert*.

5. In German: *Naturstimmung*.

6. French in the original. The quotation, which concludes "Pas la couleur, rien que la nuance" ('Because all we want is greater nuance/Not color, but rather nuance'), is from the fourth verse of Paul Verlaine's symbolist poem "Art Poètique" (from *Jadis et naguère*, 1884), beginning "De la musique avant tout chose!"

7. English in the original.

Monumentalizing Sibelius:
Eila Hiltunen and the Sibelius
Memorial Controversy

INTRODUCED AND TRANSLATED
BY DANIEL M. GRIMLEY

On the western outskirts of central Helsinki, on the edge of a leafy sub-
urb en route to Seurasaari, the open-air island museum that is the summer
haunt of tourists, tour buses, and picnicking locals, stands Eila Hiltunen's
Sibelius monument, *Passio Musicæ*. Though it has now become one of the
city's principal sights, reproduced on countless "Greetings from Helsinki"
postcards, the monument was highly controversial when it was first unveiled by Finnish president Urho Kekkonen on 7 September 1967, following
a two-stage competition in 1961–62.[1] Strenuous objections were made in the
local press to the abstract non-representational design, which consists of
a series of bright silver metallic tubes with sculpted textural effects, arranged
in a gently curving arc across a rough pink granite outcrop, typical of the
series of rocky strata that erupt through the soil everywhere in the Finnish
capital and seem to shape the city's built environment. Hiltunen's design,
originally called *Credo*, might suggest a set of organ pipes (though, unfortunately, Sibelius wrote very little organ music) or the movement of the aurora
borealis across the northern winter sky. Or it might also evoke the edge of
a vast glacier or ice sheet of the kind that moved across and scoured the
Finnish landscape in ancient geological time: a powerful representation
of the morphological forces that shaped the characteristic Finnish landscape of lakes, boulders, and dense boreal forest. In an attempt to assuage
criticism, Hiltunen later added a bust of the composer, depicted in his
brooding middle age ca. 1911, at the time of the composition of the Fourth
Symphony. The bust stands rather awkwardly to one side of the monument. Even without it, however, the monument is remarkable for the way
in which it captures the dual sense of stillness and momentum that char-

acterizes much of Sibelius's music, the feeling of two or more things happening at once in different temporal domains, as well as his preoccupation with the elemental, animating forces of the Finnish landscape. And the memorial literally sets in stone Sibelius's perceived associations with Finnish nature, reinforcing the impression, promoted by numerous representations in the media (CD covers, books, radio and television programs, pre-concert talks) that his work is somehow an expression of the Finnish natural world.

The documents translated below offer a snapshot of the controversy that took place over Hiltunen's design at the time of the competition—before the monument was actually constructed. The protagonists are two key figures in the debate: Simon Parmet (1897–1969), composer and conductor of the Finnish Radio Orchestra between 1948 and 1953 and a vital interpreter of Sibelius's music, and Erik Kruskopf (b. 1930), art critic, author, and editor at the Swedish-language newspaper *Hufvudstadsbladet* (1956–65). Besides his activities as a conductor, Parmet's contribution to Sibelius's critical reception included a highly influential monograph on the symphonies, in which he expounded the principle of thematic development in Sibelius's work, deriving large-scale structures from a single thematic germ or *kärnmotiv* (see Byron Adams's essay in this volume for the Anglo-American context).[2] Kruskopf was an early supporter of Hiltunen's work, and later published, with the sculptor, an important monograph on her oeuvre.[3] The debate, which took place in Swedish in the pages of *Hufvudstadsbladet*, revolves partly around the question of realism versus abstraction as the most appropriate mode of expression for a memorial sculpture. But at a more fundamental level it involves a generational shift in Finnish culture, in particular the movement from an essentially conservative but nevertheless modern civic nationalism (in Parmet's case) to a more internationally oriented avant-garde modernism (in Kruskopf's). It therefore parallels a crucial stage in the evolution of Finland's own political identity, the transformation from a newly independent but ostensibly peripheralized member of the Nordic region in the first half of the century to a crucial buffer zone between Eastern and Western blocs, on the fragile frontline of a new political order after the end of the Second World War.

The debate also involves competing claims over Sibelius's creative legacy. For Parmet, who had been closely acquainted with the composer himself, Sibelius's music combines a deep personal resonance with a strong sense of patriotism and national duty: the true value of art, for Parmet, lies in its capacity to serve a wider community. In contrast, for Kruskopf, whose relationship with Sibelius was necessarily more distant, art is more properly concerned with an authenticity of expression, a sense of intellectual and artistic rigor that transcends more localized questions of abstraction or representation. Though the details of the exchange largely center around the details of Hiltunen's design and other monumental sculpture in Helsinki and beyond, it might also be understood in the context of the shifting patterns in Sibelius's own critical reception, in particular the tension between the idea of the national romantic cultural figurehead and an international modernist artist. Yet, as Tomi Mäkelä, Glenda Dawn Goss, and others have observed, in the last thirty years of his life Sibelius had already become in some sense a monument: a figure who had already outlasted his time and whose longevity and apparent creative silence had become symbolic of a lost age and distant past. Even before his death in 1957, in other words, Sibelius had begun to seem petrified, or set in stone.[4] Hiltunen's sculpture might therefore be understood as the tribute to a man who had already, in this sense, become his own memorial. The desire for a figurative portrait, as Kruskopf perhaps sensed, was therefore potentially reductive and redundant. The essence of Hiltunen's design lay not in its ability to capture Sibelius's human character or physiognomy, already deeply ingrained in the Finnish popular consciousness, but rather in its response to the idea of Sibelius's music as an imaginative force. This fine-grained feeling for line, shape, and shifting color, framed by the trees, rocks, and water of its park setting (originally designed by landscape artist Juhani Kivikoski), is the key element of Hiltunen's vision.

Figure 1. Sibelius Monument

A Decent Monument—Or Nothing Else

Erik Kruskopf

Hufvudstadbladet, 18 September 1962

When the first round of the Sibelius monument competition took place a year ago, it was clear that only a single entry had the potential to form the basis for the development of a suitably dignified, sculptural, and artistically satisfying monument to the composer.[5] Eila Hiltunen's proposal was so poorly judged by both competition organizers and jury, however, that after a lengthy delay following official publication of the result it was ranked only sixth among the prizewinning entries. First place was awarded to a highly unpleasant and amateurish proposal.

Now that the second round has taken place, the distance between the other participants and Eila Hiltunen has widened even further. Eila Hiltunen has substantially, though not yet sufficiently, improved the earlier version of her design, while three of the other contestants, Ben Renvall, Toivo Jaatinen, and Kauko Räsänen, have entirely abandoned their preliminary versions and produced new designs. Jaatinen's is, if possible, even more immature than his first. Räsänen is a proficient sculptor, yet he has not succeeded in the task of creating on a monumental scale a sufficiently interesting sculpture upon an abstract theme. Ben Renvall has in this sense sunk himself: he is an intimate artist, which is fine in the smaller format, but his work is ultimately not adaptable to larger proportions.

Martti Peitso, who is now in second place, has done a splendid piece of work. To my eyes, however, it looks almost like a caricatured and distorted stereotype, mannered and hence rather tasteless. Harry Kivijärvi, whose idea offered the richest possibilities for development after Eila Hiltunen's a year ago, has unfortunately not succeeded in progressing very far forward. All of the errors that marred the proposal, then, namely its monotony, the compact heaviness, and lack of rhythm, persist. The young artist has not found a solution that can yet do his idea justice.

Eila Hiltunen's proposal, whose character owes much to the positive impression made by her husband Otso Pietinen's splendid photographs and architectural collaborator Juhani Kivikoski's drawings, has now gained a richer variety than was previously the case. The construction of the pipes is arranged in a waveform, and their surface is torn asunder so that the material does not have such an obviously cylindrical quality as before. And yet I believe the idea can be developed even further. Above all, it would benefit from gaining a sense of formal shape that distinguishes it from the surrounding environment, yet at the same time possesses such strong rhythmic vitality when seen from any angle that the monument does not lose any of its current power. Finally, the environmental landscaping should take on a more defined form: paths, avenues, and other similar features should be arranged according to the monument.

The Sibelius Society, which organized the competition and supports the monument's realization, is unsatisfied with Eila Hiltunen's proposal. They stress that the design does not pay sufficient respect to Sibelius's figure. But what this is intended to mean is unclear: does it suggest rather an old seated gentlemen? Their objections to the projected cost of the monument, which the artist estimates to be 200 million marks, are easier to understand. This is undeniably a lot of money, and the Society admits that it does not have the appropriate funds at its disposal. These costs should be calculated more precisely before any final decision is taken. And finally, one might then ask: if the money for a decent monument is not available, should one be satisfied with a poor one? Is it not better to do without any monument at all, which, in these monument-crazed times, might ultimately be the best solution? Either we need an artwork that meets the very highest standards and pays no sidelong glances to nationalism and its level of public accessibility, much less to such trivialities as those raised by Sibelius's figure—or we need no monument at all. Surely the money could be used for many other equally valuable purposes: perhaps an annual international composition competition—or a generously supported fund for Finnish composers? The possibilities are endless, and perhaps a way forward can be found that bestows greater permanence to a composer—since that is what he is, after all—than a monument somewhere in a park.

Organ Pipes or a Bronze Statue
Simon Parmet
Hufvudstadbladet, 16 October 1962

Translator's note: This article follows a second round of the competition, when Hiltunen's revised entry had been placed first in the new rankings. As Parmet's contribution and subsequent exchange with Kruskopf reveals, the decision was by no means an uncontroversial one, and it was five years before the monument was finally unveiled.

To judge by the memorial statues that have risen one by one across our fair city, we have of late become utterly "monument-minded."[6] Yet the commendable desire both to immortalize the memory of the country's leading man and to furnish the capital city with a beautiful new monument has failed to live up to its well-intended result as far as the second is concerned. Now, unfortunately, it seems as though we are also about to place yet another obstacle in the path of the first desire. It stands to reason that opinion has been widely exercised, sounding a warning note before misfortune can occur. For the question is now of none other than Jean Sibelius, one of our greatest minds, a greater object of our nation's affection and admiration than any other figure this century. The cause of this unanimous and often unreflectively widespread feeling of affectionate reverence for the great Finnish composer lies buried deep within the popular consciousness and has less to do with music and art than with the profound spiritual bond that ties Sibelius to the most insignificant and musically least-trained members of his world.

It is therefore unsurprising that the idea of a Sibelius monument was met with such enthusiasm when it was first proposed. This was evident from the large sums of money raised among the master's admirers across the country, and likewise by the pains the authorities took to achieve a monument worthy of its great subject. Unfortunately, as the voluminous correspondence and discussion in the newspaper columns suggests, enthusiasm no doubt cooled significantly or was transformed into opposition once the result of the monument competition became known. The general dismay, not to say ill will toward the prizewinning proposal, which in its final modified form appears to be precariously close to approval and realization, glaringly reveals the gulf that separates the parties over the divisive issue of what is art and what is not.

Those who believe that all art must to a certain extent preserve its connection with time-honored forms of expression and the elementary realism that constitutes our life refuse to accept the recommended proposal partly on fundamental aesthetic and philosophical grounds. We can all agree that it presents a spectacle with no connection to either conventional form or simple human realism. To take sides over the fundamental question of whether the controversial project is art or not is in this case entirely unimportant. What is of the greatest importance—and cannot be emphasized enough—is that in most people's eyes the project is not art. They will never experience it as art, and no one, not even all the world's experts with their most convincing arguments, could persuade them otherwise. Let ultramodern artists issue their dictates that seek to standardize the idea of art in our time; the often unconscious but no less pressing demand for spiritual integrity in vital artistic questions does not allow our people to abandon themselves in cozy escapism. If an artwork praised for its modernity strikes them as ugly, they say so without fear, at the risk of being called foolish or old-fashioned. So especially now, on the question of erecting a monument to one of the nation's greatest sons, they feel compelled to articulate their opinion: a monument should be seriously conceived and authoritatively justified; it should not become a battle-ground for artistic speculation and experiment.

The artistic aim of the radicals is precisely the emancipation from such overworn convention and human realism. Their ideal has grown out of our time's fertile intellectual soil and is shared by artists across the world: they say that ultramodernism alone produces the true artistic expression of our epoch. Many of the entrants in this competition have pursued this conviction in trying to create a national memorial to an intellectual giant of our time. If we consider the outcome of their efforts, especially in the prizewinning entries, we cannot escape the conclusion that their artistic intentions, over and above the unrealized aim of representing the master's musical inspiration in sculpture, are primarily less concerned with preserving the memory of the great composer and his achievements than with marking how our contemporary generation—above all, the radical artists themselves and their interpreters—have experienced him and his work. Such a conception of the monument project will be an ideal impression of the representative's personality rather than the represented, of the time that succeeded the latter rather than the space he himself occupied.

One should reject this kind of interpretation as a fundamental idea for any monument conceived as the homage to a single individual. Such a monument is principally a gesture of gratitude toward a departed citizen who has won his fellow creatures' love and respect. Its primary purpose is to immortalize the object of these affections, not those who entertain them. Nonetheless, it is not inconsistent with the idea of a monument to a great man to transfer the weight of artistic expression toward the symbolic representation of the feelings he awoke within his contemporaries, or to the manner in which they experienced him. In a literary form both might be possible, but in sculpture it is quite simply impracticable beyond the fixed boundaries of its mode of expression. Such clumsy attempts to poeticize in stone are entirely unnecessary, and in the deepest sense inartistic. Misled by their imagination, these dithering artists have announced nothing more than what was stated by the mere fact that a monument is being raised. That this has happened effectively with the practical support of the whole nation is telling evidence of Jean Sibelius's status among his contemporaries and the intensity with which they experienced him.

In the combination of purely abstract and heavily rendered realism that characterized the prizewinning entry (organ pipes!) let us suppose that the artist, as suggested above, has wished through her choice of form to produce a sculptural-architectonic interpretation of the mysteries of the master's music. An allegorical reference to music is extremely difficult in any circumstance, and doubly so when it concerns that of Sibelius, a full-blooded musician. Music can be expressed in a symbolic manner only awkwardly, and so any ambitious attempt to form, allegorically, a monument to Sibelius's music, is bound to be unsuccessful. Any allegorical representation, it emerges, whether realist, romantic, or non-figurative, can only be marked as the direct opposite or trivialization of everything Sibelius and his art represents. The master himself condemned as an abomination any attempt to interpret music other than through music itself. To recognize this means to regard as a failure any attempt, hopeless or faithful, to describe his music in a sculptural medium, whether stone or metal. Keeping in mind Sibelius's opposition to any translation of music into another artistic medium merely confirms for us how far the current proposal for a Sibelius monument stands from the master's own artistic ideals. All the more disastrous that the prizewinner evidently sees in her monument a sculpturally rendered expression of the spirit of Sibelius's music, celebrating among other things precisely that ideal.

No one can admonish an artist about the right to be as radically modern as anyone else in his private work, especially if he believes that, in the battle of ideas, his convictions will come good when the time is right. But one must question the radical artists' self-assumed right to monopolize the intellectual current of our time. Assuredly, these artists constitute a large and undoubtedly vociferous part of all those who have dedicated their life to art. But nothing aside from their own self-declaration indicates that they are the best suited or form the best part to represent our epoch. In many parts of the world, including our own nation, are groups of artists who rest on more traditionally based cultural-ideological grounds than the radicals and who, without constantly blowing their own trumpets, march with honor at the head of their time, following their own declared path. All talk that justifies the radicals' claim to be the sole adequate expression of our time and its spirit must therefore be resisted. A Sibelius monument in good, traditional style could give posterity an impression of how our time conceived of art and how it understood Sibelius, as well if not better than any enigmatic, non-figurative work. (In the case of the monument to Mannerheim, the idea emerged naturally.)[7] We recognize, as suggested above, that artists may be as radical as they like in their private artistic work, but it does not necessarily follow that the same applies in the case of an official commission. Even the ultramodernism of its day is often helplessly aged and antiquated the next morning—think of Eliel Saarinen's 1905 proposal for a concert hall in Helsinki, a project nowadays terrifying but in its day truly high modernist, which luckily never came to fruition. As far as style is concerned, we should in such cases pursue an artistic moderation, and stick more to the tried and tested than to the experimental. For this reason, in erecting an official monument to one of the country's great men, we need to take into account more than purely artistic opinions. The challenge is to produce nothing less than a genuine work of art, one which does not compromise artistic requirements but, unlike so many discarded radical fashions, has the qualities to ensure a certain degree of universality and chronological independence. Only the artist who, without abandoning artistic standards, takes note of the non-artistically inclined majority's capacity to experience art can expect to create a work that has the necessary qualities to rise to the level of an official, national monument. In the opinion of many, the prizewinning and expertly recommended proposal does not have these necessary qualities.

However we twist and turn this proposal, we find in it no association with the idea of Sibelius. All claims to the contrary must be regarded as wishful thinking. However, the proposal does certainly lead thoughts toward its author and her circle's advanced conception of art, and to much else besides—but not to Sibelius. A sculptural impression of Sibelius can only succeed through Sibelius, through an impression of the man as he lived and worked among us. Plain and simple: a portrait carved in stone or cast in bronze. This is what we who saw him in the flesh and posterity will see: the great composer's powerful figure and noble profile. The monument should be a memorial to Sibelius the man, and nothing else. The master has erected in his own music a monument to his life's work, to his brilliant individuality. It stands there indestructibly aloft, where future generations can read as much as they wish about the breadth and depth of the world created by Sibelius. We do not need to speak of it on their behalf, least of all in indecipherable ways.

The preceding article being inspired by a wish to support those who, in the final hour, attempt to avert the danger of an unfortunate decision in this matter, attention must also be directed toward another blunder that threatens to be committed. This does not concern the monument itself, but rather its placement in the city. For some unexplained reason there seems to be a general assumption that the Sibelius monument should be placed in Sibelius Park. Why this park, other than that it bears the master's name, when the right place for the monument is one of the other streets that emerged in association with the planned monument? Sibelius Park lies a long way outside the city center, in certain respects on the downtown's periphery. It is hard to grasp why the monument to Sibelius, this great central figure in our nation's cultural history, should be banished to one of the city's outer corners. With some good will and a bit of imagination, a worthy place in the city center could surely be found for this purpose. Sibelius belongs to the heart of Helsinki, where Runeberg and Mannerheim also belong. Space should be found for poet, warrior, and composer.

It has been a long time since Europeans, or any other people, have had occasion to celebrate one of music's masters by erecting a monument to his memory. Now that we in Finland find ourselves in the fortunate position to have both the will and desire to do so, we should stay sharply vigilant so that the great opportunity is used correctly, that nothing happens which in the future we wish had never been done. As an exemplary demonstration of the risk of handling things poorly, I will conclude with a story that took place on one of Helsinki's streets many years ago, one that involves Sibelius and a friend of his, an architect by trade. The two gentlemen passed a prominent building of the townscape, built by the architect friend, but totally rejected by him since on artistic grounds.

"You, Janne, can either tear up or burn a poor composition," he complained. "But what in God's name should I do with this unhappy building?"

One can only hope that a similar question will never be asked in connection with the prospective Sibelius monument.

Only the Best Will Suffice
Erik Kruskopf
Hufvudstadsbladet, 17 October 1962

Unfortunately, discussion of the Sibelius monument has to a large extent degenerated into general wrangling, in which complex intrigues and mutually aggressive exchanges have emerged in swift succession.[8] I do not direct myself toward the justifiably important question of the financial implications that it raises, in the cold light of day. But the uncomfortable whiff of a quarrel has served to deter many who would otherwise have had important contributions to make from taking part in the debate. It is therefore pleasing that in a reasonably worded article Simon Parmet has taken up the question sensibly and from a point of view that is undeniably important: what is the fundamental purpose of this monument, what function should it fulfill? In such matters he is undoubtedly right: the question is not one of art and artistic qualities alone.

So far as I can tell, Simon Parmet represents a consensus of opinion among the more conservative of the artistically inclined as well as a wider public largely unfamiliar with artistic questions. But I am surprised when Parmet, while considering it unimportant "to take sides in the fundamental question of whether the controversial project is art or not," nevertheless maintains that in most people's eyes the current proposal is not art. Such discussion is often extremely misleading. Without venturing the use of a single known opinion poll, it amounts to advance betting on the outcome of a fight. That many in Parmet's circle happen to speak against the proposal does not mean that "most people" are therefore against it. No more than the many people I have been in contact with who are for the proposal means that, without further ado, the opposite can be assumed. Nothing less than an inventory of the correspondents' views can give any objective impression of the division of opinion. My impression in this case is rather the opposite from Parmet's: a surprising number of people have supported the project, many of whom clearly stand far outside the circle of "radicals," as Parmet describes them in his article.

There must be a way of gaining clarity on this issue, and it could take the form of a public vote. Perhaps it would then emerge that Parmet was right. But is this really the way a monument should happen? Examples can be found of monuments that have been realized after the public voted between two or more different proposals. I know of no case, however, in which the public has not been sorry afterward. One of the most recent examples can be found in Kajana, where the public voted between two proposals for a Per Brahe statue—and of course chose the wrong one. Today many are readily prepared to recognize this. Still, today the wrong sculpture stands there—and it is too late to take it away, just as it was too late for Sibelius's architect friend to undo his work. I absolutely do not believe that what one calls popular taste should be decisive when it comes to erecting a monument. We all know from our own experience that some things that initially seem beautiful and attractive can quickly lose their charm and become sad, tired, or perhaps cloyingly sweet or superficial. Both so-called experts and others fall into the trap of such effects and sensations—the only difference is that the so-called expert knows, through experience, the types of things that function this way and swiftly becomes tired of them. He also knows that some other things do not immediately reveal all their individual qualities, disclosing themselves only after long contemplation. This applies equally to music and to visual art, as far as I understand. All forms of art demand of their recipients a certain kind of activity, a truth as relevant to the older arts as to those Parmet describes as modernist or radical.

Surely we should not set up a Sibelius statue only to become sick to death of it after a few weeks?

In his article, Parmet maintains, additionally, that the monument's artistic qualities would not suffer if it were to assume a more traditional form. Accordingly, he points to the Mannerheim statue, which he finds successful.

I on the contrary would point to the statues of Eino Leino, Ståhlberg, Svinhufvud, Larin Paraske, Juhani Aho (done by the same sculptor as the riding Mannerheim), Arvid Mörne, and Albert Edelfelt, which I do not find successful. I believe that neither Sibelius nor anyone else is well served by a monument modeled like those of the aforementioned cultural figures and statesmen. Other figurative statues in the city have perhaps a greater retail value because they have been in place longer and therefore have a certain position in residents' consciousness. But I wonder who, standing at the base of the statue of Alexander II or Runeberg, could say how these people really appeared? Nevertheless, Alexander is quite formally dressed, and even Runeberg is attired in a costume that is more appropriate to sculptural representation than the jackets and sweeping trousers of Sibelius's time and ours.

Almost without exception, a portrait in either stone or bronze is ridiculous—if not immediately after its unveiling, then at any rate after a certain amount of time.

Exceptions such as Mannerheim, Paavo Nurmi, and Aleksis Kivi (where opinions are also divided) do not help the issue. Paavo Nurmi runs naked—something we cannot allow Sibelius to do; he would hardly be particularly elegant that way—and Mannerheim has a fine horse on which to ride. Besides, the horse is the best part of the monument. Aleksis Kivi's monument is controversial, as suggested above, but in any circumstance there is no artist currently among us capable of executing such a figurative creation as this gigantic work.

In any case, I struggle to see why the debate should be between the figurative and the non-figurative. I can well imagine how the monument could be figurative—to the extent that it could even directly represent the composer himself, as reconstructed on the basis of photographs and other documents during his active, creative period. But the presumption must be that it be good. A competition was arranged for precisely this purpose. A mass of proposals was received. Has Simon Parmet seen them? Did he find any among them that he could happily recommend for realization?

This is precisely what we are about: choosing the best proposal. One that satisfies not only the wider public but the experts as well—in other words, those who have some experience in artistic judgment. This is exactly what has happened. There has been a large jury, with experts and laymen, and no less than two competitions. No one can maintain that either the jury or anyone else from within the organizer's circle has done anything whatsoever to impose a non-figurative solution for the monument. On the contrary, my understanding is that everything was done to comply with the wishes of the wider public—namely, that in principle the monument should be undertaken by a portrait sculptor.

That leaves Eila Hiltunen's proposal, which received such a satisfactory write-up from the experts that there can be no doubt that it is both artistically satisfying and of a level worthy of its subject, Sibelius. That this has been contested reveals that expert opinion is not regarded especially highly. This is, in a sense, a sound principle: art is not just for the experts. On the other hand, one should be confident that, in spite of everything, the experts have the greatest chance of looking into the future, as difficult as that is. It appears to be a rule that art appreciated initially by only the minority with the chance to become closely acquainted with it will gradually gain a wider response before being generally accepted by the public. Trivial—but a fact nonetheless.

The question is not whether the "radical" artists in any sense monopolize or try to monopolize "the representation of the intellectual current of our time," as Parmet writes. On the contrary, the conventional can just as easily attempt such monopolization, as when Parmet maintains that wider popular opinion, not artistic qualities, should be decisive when selecting the form of a monument.

This freedom from all attempts at monopolization is a characteristic trend in the modern understanding of art. While countless artistic movements, up to and including Cubism and perhaps one or two others afterward, talked about "the only salvation," the wheel has now turned full circle, and modern aesthetics recognizes old art as well as new, figurativism as well as informalism. The question is ultimately one of a certain degree of authenticity of expression. If a sculptor can be found to produce a portrait sculpture that genuinely functions in the way this one is intended to function, he is welcome to realize whichever monument he likes. It is not unthinkable that one day such a creative artist may show up. But we must remember that our way of looking in a contemporary, strongly visualized environment is constantly shifting, and strongly. Our viewing customs are not the same today as they were thirty years ago. In erecting a monument, our intention is not merely that it satisfy the few who are there when it is unveiled. It should also interest and fascinate in the future. Only if it can do that does it function properly. Only then will it fulfill its task—to commemorate some person or event from a previous era. It does not necessarily have to have a symbolic character, since symbols can often be misinterpreted, and there are many things that cannot be represented symbolically, as Parmet very rightly points out.

In her monument proposal Eila Hiltunen has chosen to place the emphasis not on the plastic-figurative, but on purely architectonic means (the organ pipes are virtually the only thing that remains from the very first proposal; when the monument is realized no one in their wildest dreams will be able to find anything similar). This reveals without a doubt that she has realized that architecture is the only art form with whose help one can achieve the greatest effect upon the untrained observer. No other form of artistic experience is as powerful as that of experiencing an architectural space from inside. Whether this experience is associated with music, mathematics, or something else depends upon the observer. But if this immense experience can be associated with the celebrated person's name, it has functioned as it should. It is then a proper monument.

It is not inconceivable that the artist who realizes the monument also reveals himself. This is often the case with a great monument. Where would Colleoni be today without Verrocchio? And dare one ask: Where would Moses be without Michelangelo?

Parmet-Kruskopf Exchange
Hufvudstadsbladet, 18 October 1962

Parmet: Since Erik Kruskopf has asked me a question directly, I would like to reply, as well as comment on the monument debate.

Yes, I saw the proposals that were shown during the official exhibition of prizewinning entries. And I fully agree that none of the proposals, neither the figurative nor the non-figurative, have the slightest qualification to serve as a Sibelius monument. Regarding Eila Hiltunen's award-winning design, I recognize that, in spite of my essentially negative initial response, I found the proposal beautiful, though unsuitable for the purpose for which it is intended. Furthermore, I believe that it cannot justifiably deserve to be called art. Not everything that is beautiful can be art, even if all art must be beautiful.

I must also wholeheartedly share the opinion of the dubious artistic merit of the memorials that Kruskopf, as he so moderately expresses it, does "not find successful." The fact that the memorials mentioned turned out so poorly was not, I believe, up for debate in the previous discussion. Nevertheless, we should not cast out the baby with the bathwater simply because some artists failed so grievously. We should not blame the very style that individual presentations lack. We can easily demonstrate that the style at issue here has produced outstanding sculptural memorials—especially in ancient Greece—and throughout the greater cultural nations, as is evident from the Balzac and Beethoven statues I reproduce in my article. The notion that these or other equivalent portrait statues should ever be ridiculous—"a portrait statue . . . is always almost without exception ridiculous," says Kruskopf—is too grotesque to be taken seriously. That some statues exist that only provoke ridicule does not imply a similar assessment of those that are sublime.

The belief that "the experts are, in spite of everything, those who stand the best chance of seeing into the future" is contradicted, at least in the case of music history—I cannot comment on the other arts in this respect—by the countless remarkable cases where experts, utterly dependent in their capacity to act as a Vox Dei, have carved their judgment in stone only to revise it on the grounds of the wider public's reaction. Many of the masterworks we rank today among our culture's priceless treasures were initially disapproved of by the experts, while the public hailed them immediately as the masterpieces they were and always will be.

To Kruskopf's little bon mot, "where would Moses be without Michelangelo?" I would just say that Moses was Moses for more than 2,500 years before Michelangelo appeared upon the stage, just as Sibelius will be Sibelius whether we erect a monument to his memory or not and independent of who does it—or does not. What Michelangelo did was fill a void in our knowledge of the mortal element of Moses' character, thereby creating an aid for our remembrance. This is precisely where I perceive the deepest meaning in any memorial to a great man: to preserve the mortal aspect of those who have created the immortal.

Kruskopf Response: I would simply reiterate: I have nothing in principle against any artistic style. But we do not have a Rodin. Can Simon Parmet point to any conceivable alternative to Eila Hiltunen's proposal? Rodin's portraits are not ridiculous, merely those of his disciples.

So far as I can judge, Eila Hiltunen's sculpture will become a very strong work if it is realized. And this is precisely how a monument should function, isn't it?

Concerning Moses and Michelangelo, I referred, of course, to the former's appearance. Michelangelo created a new impression of it, one that demanded a portrait statue. Sibelius's appearance is well documented in photos and countless other portraits. He therefore does not need any portrait statue.

NOTES

1. The successive versions of Hiltunen's design, and the story of the competition, are summarized in Tuula Karjalainen et al., *Eila Hiltunen: Sibelius Monumentti, "Passio Musicae"* (Helsinki: Helsingin kaupungin taidemuseo, 1998).

2. Simon Parmet, *Sibelius symfonier: En studie i musikförståelse* (Helsinki: Söderström, 1955); English version, *The Symphonies of Sibelius: A Study in Musical Appreciation,* trans. Kingsley A. Hart (London: Cassell, 1959).

3. Erik Kruskopf and Eila Hiltunen, *Eila Hiltunen* (Helsinki: Otava, 1976).

4. For a comparable example of self-monumentalization, see Mark Everist's discussion of Rossini's long creative silence and the French aesthetics of *la belle morte*, "'Il n'y a qu'un Paris au monde, et j'y reviendrai planter mon drapeau!': Rossini's Second Grand Opéra," *Music & Letters* 90/4 (November 2009): 636–72.

5. The Swedish title of this first Kruskopf article is "Ett bra monument—eller inget alls."

6. The Swedish title of Parmet's article is "Orgelpipor eller Bronsstod."

7. Aimo Tukiainen's equestrian statue of General Carl Gustaf Emil Mannerheim (1867–1951), a leading figure on the "White" side in the Finnish civil war and later commander of Finnish military during the Winter War (1939) and briefly the country's president, stands opposite the Museum of Modern Art in Helsinki and was unveiled in 1960, seven years before Hiltunen's statue of Sibelius. Tukiainen's design is essentially realist, in sharp contrast to the more abstract quality of Hiltunen's monument.

8. Kruskopf's second article carries this title in Swedish: "Endast det bästa duger."

Index

Page numbers followed by n indicate notes; italicized page numbers indicate material in tables, figures, or musical examples.

Index to Sibelius's Works

Name and Subject Index

Index

Notes on the Contributors

Byron Adams, professor of composition and musicology at the University of California, Riverside, has been published widely on English music, and has broadcast over the BBC. He is co-editor of *Vaughan Williams Essays*, and contributed entries on William Walton and Sylvia Townsend Warner to the second edition of the revised *New Grove Dictionary of Music and Musicians*. His articles, reviews, and essays have appeared in journals such as *19th-Century Music, Music and Letters*, and the *John Donne Journal*, and have been included in volumes such as *Queer Episodes in Music and Modern Identity* (University of Illinois Press, 2002), *The Cambridge Companion to Elgar* (2004), and *Walt Whitman and Modern Music* (Garland, 2000). In 2000, he was presented with the Philip Brett Award by the American Musicological Society.

Leon Botstein is president and Leon Levy Professor in the Arts of Bard College. He is the author of *Judentum und Modernität* (1991) and *Jefferson's Children: Education and the Promise of American Culture* (1997). He is the editor of *The Compleat Brahms* (1999) and *The Musical Quarterly*, as well as the co-editor, with Werner Hanak, of *Vienna: Jews and the City of Music, 1870–1938* (2004). The music director of the American Symphony Orchestra and conductor laureate of the Jerusalem Symphony Orchestra, he has recorded works by, among others, Szymanowski, Hartmann, Bruch, Dukas, Foulds, Toch, Dohnányi, Bruckner, Chausson, Richard Strauss, Mendelssohn, Popov, Shostakovich, and Liszt for Telarc, CRI, Koch, Arabesque, and New World Records. For his contributions to music he has received the Austrian Cross of Honor for Science and Art and the Award for Distinguished Service to the Arts from the American Academy of Arts and Letters.

Philip Ross Bullock is university lecturer in Russian at the University of Oxford and tutor and fellow at Wadham College, Oxford. He is the author of *The Feminine in the Prose of Andrey Platonov* (2005), *Rosa Newmarch and Russian Music in Late Nineteenth and Early Twentieth-Century England* (2009), and *The Correspondence of Jean Sibelius and Rosa Newmarch, 1906-1939* (forthcoming 2011), as well as numerous articles on aspects of nineteenth- and twentieth-century Russian literature, music, and culture. He is the recipient of a number of awards and fellowships, including a British Academy Postdoctoral Fellowship (2001), the Edward T. Cone Membership in Music Studies at the Institute for Advanced Study, Princeton (2007), the Philip Brett Award of the American Musicological Society (2009), and a Philip Leverhulme Prize (2009).

Susan H. Gillespie is vice president for Special Global Initiatives at Bard College and founding director of Bard's Institute for International Liberal Education. Her published translations of novels, nonfiction works, poems, and works on musicology and philosophy include *Music in German Philosophy* (University of Chicago Press, 2011) and *The Correspondence of Paul Celan & Ilana Shmueli* (Sheep Meadow Press, 2011).

Glenda Dawn Goss is the author and editor of various books on Renaissance and American music as well as on Jean Sibelius. Her most recent volume, *Sibelius: A Composer's Life and the Awakening of Finland*, received the ASCAP-Deems Taylor Award in 2010. Along with an award-winning *Guide to Research* and two Sibelius letter editions, she has also produced a critical edition of *Kullervo* (2005). Former editor-in-chief of the Sibelius works, she currently teaches at the Sibelius Academy, Helsinki.

Daniel M. Grimley is a university lecturer in music at Oxford and is the tutorial fellow in Music at Merton College, having taught previously at the universities of Surrey and Nottingham. He has published widely on Scandinavian music, Finnish music, the work of Edward Elgar and Ralph Vaughan Williams, and music and landscape. His books include *Grieg: Music, Landscape, and Norwegian Identity* (Boydell & Brewer, 2006) and *Carl Nielsen and the Idea of Modernism* (Boydell, 2010), and he edited the *Cambridge Companion to Sibelius* (2004). Future projects include a study of music and landscape in Nordic music, 1890–1930.

Jeffrey Kallberg is professor of music history and associate dean for arts and letters at the University of Pennsylvania. In the Nordic realm, he writes on concepts of modernism in Scandinavian music, and has plans for a broader study of song in the early twentieth century. He also publishes widely on Chopin's music and its cultural contexts.

Annika Lindskog is a lecturer in Swedish at University College London, and has published on collective identity and cultural practice, with particular interests in landscape and cultural history. She gained her first degrees from Sweden and Germany, before undertaking a master's degree in music, culture, and politics at Cardiff. She has taught at universities in Wales, Ireland, and Belgrade before moving to London, where she is also a keen amateur choral singer.

Tomi Mäkelä is the author of several books and essays on Finnish music from Fredrik Pacius to Kaija Saariaho and on German modernism from Max Reger to Otto Preminger, as well as on aspects of virtuosity and music education. He studied music and musicology in Lahti, Vienna, Helsinki, and Berlin, wrote his doctoral dissertation in West Berlin under the guidance of Carl Dahlhaus, and has worked in a variety of academic environments in Finland and Germany (including a research project on exiled musicians in California) as well as writing for press and radio. From 1996 to 2008 he was professor of musicology at Magdeburg, and since 2009 he has taught at the Martin Luther University of Halle-Wittenberg. An English translation of his monograph *Jean Sibelius: Poesie in der Luft* (Breitkopf & Härtel, 2007) is forthcoming from Boydell & Brewer.

(Irma) Margareta Martin is a freelance translator of Finnish and Swedish texts into English. Her published translations include *Voices at the Late Hour* by two-time Finlandia Prize winner Bo Carpelan, and *Rich and Respectable* by popular novelist Eeva Joenpelto. She was the longtime editor of the newsletters of the Scandinavian American Foundation of Georgia and the Atlanta Suomi Finland Society (of which she is currently writing a history). Her articles on cultural topics have also appeared in *Hufvudstadsbladet* (Helsinki) and *New World Finn* (Duluth MN).

Sarah Menin is an architectural academic. Her research concerns the work of Alvar Aalto and its parallels with the music of Sibelius, addressing the place of the psyche in the sphere of architecture and the creative imagination. She has published widely, and her books include *Nature and Space*, with Flora Samuel; *An Architecture of Invitation*, with Stephen Kite; and *Constructing Place: Mind and Matter*. Dr. Menin is visiting fellow at Newcastle University, and continues to practice architecture.

Max Paddison is professor of music aesthetics at the University of Durham. He has published extensively on Adorno, aesthetics, and critical theory, and also on contemporary music, the avant-garde, and the concept of modernism. He is author of *Adorno's Aesthetics of Music* (Cambridge University Press, 1993); *Adorno, Modernism and Mass Culture* (Kahn & Averill, 1996); and joint editor (with Irène Deliège) of *Contemporary Music: Theoretical and Philosophical Perspectives* (Ashgate, 2010).

Timo Virtanen completed his doctoral studies in 2005 at the Sibelius Academy in Helsinki with a dissertation on Jean Sibelius's Third Symphony. He joined the editorial staff of the complete critical edition *Jean Sibelius Works* (JSW) in 1997, and since 2006 has worked as editor-in-chief of the project. Virtanen has also been appointed as docent of music philology at the Sibelius Academy. His editions of Sibelius's Symphonies nos. 1 and 3 (JSW I/2 and I/4) were published in 2008 and 2009, and a volume containing the two versions of *Cassazione*, op. 6, will appear in 2011.

Franz Liszt and His World
edited by Christopher H. Gibbs and Dana Gooley (2006)

Edward Elgar and His World
edited by Byron Adams (2007)

Prokofiev and His World
edited by Simon Morrison (2008)

Brahms and His World (revised edition)
edited by Walter Frisch and Kevin C. Karnes (2009)

Richard Wagner and His World
edited by Thomas S. Grey (2009)

Alban Berg and His World
edited by Christopher Hailey (2010)